"I welcome Pastor Andy Davis's contribution to the Christ-Cent.. Exposition Series. His love of the Scriptures and his love of the Savior are equally well represented in his exposition of Isaiah. Davis applies his wealth of pastoral experience with remarkable contemporary references to make this commentary insightful, accessible, and useful for congregations as well as pastors."

Bryan Chapell, pastor, Grace Presbyterian Church, Peoria, Illinois; founder and chairman of Unlimited Grace, a radio and online Bible-teaching ministry; and President Emeritus of Covenant Theological Seminary

"As a part of the Christ-Centered Exposition series, Andy Davis's pastor's commentary on Isaiah fits well. I have known Dr. Davis for many years, and he is one of the most careful, thoughtful, biblically centered theologians I know. Davis well affirms Christ in Isaiah and ties in the unified story of redemptive history of which Jesus Christ is preeminent. The book contains easy-to-read, rich, practical, sermonic presentations of each chapter of Isaiah that will be a great resource for any pastor or teacher working through his prophecy."

Eric A. Mitchell, associate professor of Old Testament & Archaeology, Southwestern Baptist Theological Seminary

"Without a doubt Isaiah is one of the most important books in the Old Testament, and the New Testament use of Isaiah gives it a particular significance. Andy Davis's commentary is a helpful addition to studies on Isaiah at several levels. He takes seriously the historical message of Isaiah so that he doesn't simply leap to the New Testament and avoid the Old Testament context. At the same time, the fulfillment of Isaiah in the New Testament receives careful and wise attention. Finally, Davis applies the message of Isaiah to today's world. I recommend this work enthusiastically."

Thomas R. Schreiner, James Buchanan Harrison Professor of New Testament Interpretation at the Southern Baptist Theological Seminary

"This wonderful commentary by Andy Davis is theological through and through, with a focus on the glory of God and the salvation he offers in Jesus the Messiah. Davis helps us see the urgency of Isaiah for today and apply the book to the church in practical terms. I warmly commend this commentary for pastors and theologians alike."

Heath A. Thomas, dean and professor of Old Testament, Herschel H. Hobbs College of Theology and Ministry, Oklahoma Baptist University

"Andy Davis is a faithful, seasoned expositor with theological depth and pastoral care, and in this volume he provides steady guidance for anyone endeavoring to preach the prophecy of Isaiah. With clear, detailed outlines and concise explanations, Davis explains the text, making theological and practical points of application. This volume will be a blessing to preachers."

Ray Van Neste, associate professor of Christian Studies and director of the R. C. Ryan Center for Biblical Studies at Union University

CHRIST-CENTERED

Exposition

AUTHOR **Andrew M. Davis**

SERIES EDITORS **David Platt, Daniel L. Akin, and Tony Merida**

CHRIST-CENTERED
Exposition

EXALTING JESUS IN

ISAIAH

HOLMAN®
REFERENCE
NASHVILLE, TENNESSEE

Dewey Decimal Classification: 220.7
Subject Heading: BIBLE. O.T. ISAIAH—
COMMENTARIES\JESUS CHRIST

Printed in the United States of America
2 3 4 5 6 7 8 9 10 • 22 21 20 19 18
BTH

SERIES DEDICATION

Dedicated to Adrian Rogers and John Piper. They have taught us to love the gospel of Jesus Christ, to preach the Bible as the inerrant Word of God, to pastor the church for which our Savior died, and to have a passion to see all nations gladly worship the Lamb.

—David Platt, Tony Merida, and Danny Akin
March 2013

TABLE OF CONTENTS

ACKNOWLEDGMENTS

I am deeply grateful to the elders and members of First Baptist Church for giving me the time to write this commentary during a sabbatical several years ago, and for listening with delight and faith to the sermons that flowed from my study of this majestic book of prophecy. No pastor could ask for more than the godly and fruitful congregation FBC has become! I am truly honored to serve you with a team of godly elders as we all seek to be humble and contrite in spirit and tremble at the Word of God (Isa 66:2), and to spread the gospel of Christ among those who have never heard of his fame or seen his glory (Isa 66:19).

SERIES INTRODUCTION

Augustine said, "Where Scripture speaks, God speaks." The editors of the Christ-Centered Exposition Commentary series believe that where God speaks, the pastor must speak. God speaks through His written Word. We must speak from that Word. We believe the Bible is God breathed, authoritative, inerrant, sufficient, understandable, necessary, and timeless. We also affirm that the Bible is a Christ-centered book; that is, it contains a unified story of redemptive history of which Jesus is the hero. Because of this Christ-centered trajectory that runs from Genesis 1 through Revelation 22, we believe the Bible has a corresponding global-missions thrust. From beginning to end, we see God's mission as one of making worshipers of Christ from every tribe and tongue worked out through this redemptive drama in Scripture. To that end we must preach the Word.

In addition to these distinct convictions, the Christ-Centered Exposition Commentary series has some distinguishing characteristics. First, this series seeks to display exegetical accuracy. What the Bible says is what we want to say. While not every volume in the series will be a verse-by-verse commentary, we nevertheless desire to handle the text carefully and explain it rightly. Those who teach and preach bear the heavy responsibility of saying what God has said in His Word and declaring what God has done in Christ. We desire to handle God's Word faithfully, knowing that we must give an account for how we have fulfilled this holy calling (Jas 3:1).

Second, the Christ-Centered Exposition Commentary series has pastors in view. While we hope others will read this series, such as parents, teachers, small-group leaders, and student ministers, we desire to provide a commentary busy pastors will use for weekly preparation of biblically faithful and gospel-saturated sermons. This series is not academic in nature. Our aim is to present a readable and pastoral style of commentaries. We believe this aim will serve the church of the Lord Jesus Christ.

Third, we want the Christ-Centered Exposition Commentary series to be known for the inclusion of helpful illustrations and theologically driven applications. Many commentaries offer no help in illustrations, and few offer any kind of help in application. Often those that do offer illustrative material and application unfortunately give little serious attention to the text. While giving ourselves primarily to explanation, we also hope to serve readers by providing inspiring and illuminating illustrations coupled with timely and timeless application.

Finally, as the name suggests, the editors seek to exalt Jesus from every book of the Bible. In saying this, we are not commending wild allegory or fanciful typology. We certainly believe we must be constrained to the meaning intended by the divine Author Himself, the Holy Spirit of God. However, we also believe the Bible has a messianic focus, and our hope is that the individual authors will exalt Christ from particular texts. Luke 24:25-27,44-47 and John 5:39,46 inform both our hermeneutics and our homiletics. Not every author will do this the same way or have the same degree of Christ-centered emphasis. That is fine with us. We believe faithful exposition that is Christ centered is not monolithic. We do believe, however, that we must read the whole Bible as Christian Scripture. Therefore, our aim is both to honor the historical particularity of each biblical passage and to highlight its intrinsic connection to the Redeemer.

The editors are indebted to the contributors of each volume. The reader will detect a unique style from each writer, and we celebrate these unique gifts and traits. While distinctive in their approaches, the authors share a common characteristic in that they are pastoral theologians. They love the church, and they regularly preach and teach God's Word to God's people. Further, many of these contributors are younger voices. We think these new, fresh voices can serve the church well, especially among a rising generation that has the task of proclaiming the Word of Christ and the Christ of the Word to the lost world.

We hope and pray this series will serve the body of Christ well in these ways until our Savior returns in glory. If it does, we will have succeeded in our assignment.

David Platt
Daniel L. Akin
Tony Merida
Series Editors
February 2013

Isaiah

Introduction

Jesus Christ stands today in the marketplace of ideas, philosophies, and religions, calling to people that he himself crafted to repent of their sins and find salvation in him as their Savior. Billions of people around the world are bustling through their lives, imprisoned in an invisible dungeon of deception that Satan, the god of this age, has crafted for their eternal destruction. The church in the West faces the challenge of proclaiming Christ as the only hope to an increasingly hostile audience, a postmodern and pluralistic people who challenge all claims of exclusive truth. How do we Christians know that our faith is the only true faith and that our Savior is the only hope for every nation on earth? What is unique about Christianity that makes it stand alone above the marketplace of ideas?

The strongest answer to that vital question is this: the supernatural nature of the Bible in its clear testimony to Jesus Christ. The Bible is most clearly supernatural in its eternality, its ability to rise above time and predict the future. The prophets, empowered by the Spirit of God, stood outside of time and clearly saw vital aspects of human history, past, present, and future. We humans are locked in time, following a linear progression: "There was an evening, and there was a morning: one day . . . the second day . . . the third day" (Gen 1:5,8,13). There is a beginning, and there is an end. James says we do not even know what will happen tomorrow (Jas 4:14). How could we possibly predict events that will take place centuries from now? Yet this is exactly what the prophet Isaiah did. He stood as if he were on a mountaintop and looked ahead over misty mountain ranges, peak upon peak of future events. And as one looks out over such peaks, they appear as if they were layered right on top of each other, though they are separated by dozens of miles. So also Isaiah could see distant future events on top of each other, as if they were side by side, though they were separated by many years: both Judah's victory over Assyria and their future exile to Babylon, both the rise of Babylon and its fall, both the destruction of Jerusalem and its rebuilding. The eternal God knows the end of history from the beginning and has revealed the future to his servants, the prophets. Only Christianity has this gift of predictive prophecy so clearly fulfilled in the pages of history. There are no such Hindu prophecies, or Buddhist or Muslim. None of those competitors in the marketplace of ideas can point to verifiable prophecies that have been fulfilled in space and time. But Isaiah the prophet, empowered by the Holy Spirit, made hundreds of such predictions, telling things before they happened, "so that when it does happen you may believe" (John 14:29). Isaiah stood over the nations of his time and spoke their future, and his words came to pass.

Still, the clearest and most powerful visions Isaiah had were of Christ. Moses courageously left a comfortable life of sin in Egypt's palaces to suffer with God's people because he "saw [Christ] who is invisible" (Heb 11:27). Isaiah saw him too, only with much more vivid detail. The Spirit enabled ungodly Balaam to say of Christ, "I see him, but not now; I perceive him, but not near" (Num 24:17). How much more clearly did the godly prophet Isaiah see Christ, enthroned and glorious (Isa 6:1) before he was incarnated (John 12:41)? This commentary is an attempt to capture through Christ-centered exposition of Isaiah the message and the mission of the gospel of Jesus Christ.

I believe in the Holy Spirit's inspiration of every word of Isaiah (2 Tim 3:16; 2 Pet 1:21). In the text of Isaiah, God openly claims to be the only one who can decree, declare, and determine the future by his sovereign power (41:21-29; 46:10), the only one who makes a plan that cannot be thwarted and has a hand that stretches out over all nations (14:26). Therefore, I reject the antisupernatural bias of scholars who must have a "Second Isaiah" (or even a "Third Isaiah") because they cannot accept how any human could name Cyrus as Israel's deliverer more than a century before his parents named him (44:28; 45:1,13). Bible-believing Christians have no such problem. We know that God has spoken through the prophets.

The Message of the Gospel

At our church we teach people to share the gospel in a four-part outline: (1) God, (2) Man, (3) Christ, (4) Response. No Old Testament prophet so vividly saw and so richly proclaimed these themes as did Isaiah. After his resurrection from the dead, Jesus Christ taught his disciples the prophetic foundation of his work of salvation:

> *This is what is written: The Messiah would suffer and rise from the dead the third day, and repentance for forgiveness of sins would be*

proclaimed in his name to all the nations, beginning at Jerusalem. You are witnesses of these things. (Luke 24:46-48)

Isaiah was the foremost of those by whom this salvation plan and its spread was predicted in writing.

God

Isaiah proclaims an awesome God, dwelling in a high and holy place (57:15), enthroned in heaven and the earth is his footstool (66:1), enthroned above the circle of the earth and all its people are like grasshoppers (40:22). All the nations are as dust on the scales and like a drop from a bucket (40:15). He created the universe alone (44:24) and rules completely alone; he will not share his glory with any created being (42:8). He has made a plan for the whole world, and he has the sovereign power to execute his plan to the smallest detail with his mighty, outstretched hand (14:26). He created the human race for his own glory (43:7), forms each person in his or her mother's womb (44:2), and has spoken laws by which we are to be governed and judged (33:22). With justice he will judge every nation and all individuals on earth (59:15-16). He displays his love in his gracious care for all his creatures (34:14-15), and he displays his fierce wrath against all transgressors of his laws (13:9). It is this God who sent his only begotten Son into the world to bring salvation to the ends of the earth (49:6).

Man

Human beings were created in the image of God, formed for his glory and pleasure (43:7). We joined Satan in his arrogant rebellion against God's sovereign rule (14:13-14) and fell into total depravity through our sin. The sins of religious Israel, despite its endless machinery of old-covenant religion, are repugnant in God's sight (1:11; 66:3); these people honored God with their lips, but their hearts were far from him (29:13). The sins of the pagan nations, who follow idols and carry their burdensome and lifeless gods, will sink them into the grave (45:20; 46:1). No one is righteous in God's sight; all our best actions are like filthy rags (64:6). Even the godly prophet Isaiah proclaimed, "Woe is me for I am ruined" when he stood in the presence of the holy Judge (6:5). Our endless sacrifices and fasts are worthless because of our heartless oppression of the poor and our callous indifference to the glory of God

(58:3-4). We are in danger of eternity in endless burning under the just wrath of God (33:14; 66:24).

Christ

Isaiah had the clearest vision of the preincarnate Christ of any Old Testament prophet. He saw him seated on a throne, high and exalted, whose holiness is the endless wonder of the godliest angels (6:1-3). Christ would be born of a virgin and be Immanuel, "God with us" (7:14). He would be born a child, a son of David, to be our Wonderful Counselor, Mighty God, Eternal Father, Prince of Peace, and the government of the world would be on his shoulders (9:6). He would spring up like a shoot from Jesse's stump and be anointed with the Spirit of God so that he can rule the nations justly (11:1-5; 61:1). He would live a sinless life (53:9) and do great signs and wonders of healing (35:5). As the "Suffering Servant" (49; 50; 53), he would die an atoning death: "We all went astray like sheep; we all have turned to our own way; and the LORD has punished him for the iniquity of us all" (53:6). No chapter in the entire Bible so clearly expounds the principle of substitutionary atonement by which Jesus Christ saves sinners as does Isaiah 53. And Isaiah also makes it plain that Christ would rise from the dead (53:11), destroying death forever (25:7). And by his gentle care of "bruised reeds" (broken-hearted sinners) and his proclamation of peace, he would gradually build a kingdom (42:1-4). By his relentless zeal for the holiness of his bride, he will continue to speak to her until she is perfectly glorious (62:1). But his terrifying wrath will consume all the wicked rebels who oppose his kingdom, bringing just vengeance on them all (63:1-4).

Response

No book in the Bible so clearly exposes the falsehood of salvation by religious works (1:11) as does Isaiah. It is by repentance and faith alone (30:15) that sinners are justified in the sight of such a holy Judge. This faith is a gift of God's revelation to the elect (53:1). Good works cannot save us (64:6); faith in Christ alone can. God dwells in a holy place but also with broken-hearted, humble sinners who reject their own righteousness and trust in Christ alone (57:15). After we are justified (53:11) and transformed by grace, God then calls us to a lifetime of good works in the pattern of his holy law (1:17).

The Mission of the Gospel

Isaiah also clearly predicted the spread of the gospel from Jerusalem to the ends of the earth. Through him we hear God the Father say to his eternal Son,

> *It is not enough for you to be my servant raising up the tribes of Jacob and restoring the protected ones of Israel. I will also make you a light for the nations, to be my salvation to the ends of the earth.* (49:6)

The worldwide spread of the gospel of Jesus Christ would begin in Jerusalem, for the law would go out from Zion. And many peoples would "come to Zion" (the city where God dwells with his redeemed people) spiritually by their faith in Christ, and would also say, "Come," to their surrounding lost neighbors (2:3). So this message of Christ would spread to the distant coastlands and the furthest islands (66:19). The vast wealth of the nations will flow into "Zion" (the heavenly Jerusalem) by the conversion of the elect from all over the earth (60:5-7). The final triumph of the gospel will be a multitude of the redeemed from every nation on earth in the new heavens and new earth, who will eternally worship God. The terror of eternal hell will be visible to them, feeding forever their sense of God's lavish grace to them in Christ (66:22-24).

An Anguished Father Deals with Rebellious Children

ISAIAH 1

Though your sins are scarlet, they will be as white as snow; though they are crimson red, they will be like wool. If you are willing and obedient, you will eat the good things of the land. But if you refuse and rebel, you will be devoured by the sword. (Isa 1:18-20)

Main Idea: God summons to court the people of the religious-yet-wicked Jewish nation for their many sins and pleads with them to repent so he can save them.

I. **A God Who Speaks (1:1-2)**
   A. A river of words but a seemingly silent God
   B. God's apparent silence misleading
   C. A heavenly court trial

II. **A God Who Judges His People (1:2-9)**
   A. The heartbreak of rebellion
   B. God's active judgment against his people
   C. Yet in wrath, a God who remembers mercy

III. **A God Who Despises Religious Hypocrisy (1:10-15)**
   A. A parade in hypocritical religion
   B. God's utter revulsion at formalism and hypocrisy

IV. **A God Who Pleads with Sinners (1:16-20)**
   A. A call to come, a call to reason, a call to repent
   B. A promise of total forgiveness
   C. A warning of total destruction

V. **A God Who Works Salvation and Threatens Judgment (1:21-31)**
   A. Total purification offered, but how?
   B. Complete righteousness predicted, but how?
   C. Isaiah's answer: in Christ alone!

A God Who Speaks

ISAIAH 1:1-2

We live in a world flooded by an overwhelming river of words. Research indicates that on average a human being speaks approximately seven thousand words per day (Liberman, "Sex-Linked Lexical Budgets"). With the world's population having climbed to more than seven billion, that means the human race speaks as many as fifty trillion words every day! With the explosion of multimedia, Wi-Fi, Internet, cable TV, podcasts, etc., we are drowning in words on a daily basis. But we never hear the voice of God—not with our ears anyway. God does not air a daily podcast, appear on the nightly news, or speak to us audibly from the mountaintop or from a bright cloud in the sky; he seems to be silent.

But the Bible is filled with God's speech. And the book of Isaiah begins with a call for heaven and earth to listen to God's words (v. 2). In 1972 Francis Schaeffer published a book with the unforgettable title, *He Is There, and He Is Not Silent*. He argued that the primary philosophical question facing the human race is, Why is there something rather than nothing? Schaeffer concluded that the only possible final answer to this question is a triune God who speaks and thereby reveals himself to us. Given that we live in a vast, terrifyingly huge universe, it is easy to wonder if we are completely alone. Schaeffer's title implies the apparent silence of God; it accepts as a premise that God does not *seem* to be there, and he does not *seem* to speak.

But he is, and he does. God speaks every single day to those who have faith to hear him. He speaks powerfully by creation, which pours out speech day by day (Ps 19:1-2), proclaiming the invisible attributes and divine nature of God (Rom 1:20). And God has most clearly spoken by the Holy Spirit through the prophets (Heb 1:1). This is the very thing the Jewish nation requested of God at Mount Sinai when God's awesome voice was terrifying them (Deut 18:16-18). That was the origin of the office of the prophet, the one who was gifted to hear God speak words directly to him by the Spirit and relate them in speech and writing to the people of God. And through the writings of the prophets, God continues to speak to the human race every single day. This is the significance of the verb tenses: "Listen [**now**], heavens, pay attention [**now**], earth, for the LORD has spoken [in the **past**]." God is still speaking to the universe by the words of Isaiah the prophet, but only those with faith in Christ can hear all that he's saying.

In Isaiah 1 God is summoning his sinful people, Israel, to a court trial. When God gave Israel its law under Moses, he promised them blessings for obedience and curses for disobedience. In the book of Deuteronomy, four times he calls heaven and earth as witnesses concerning the covenant he was making with the nation at that time: "I call heaven and earth as witnesses against you today that I have set before you life and death, blessing and curse" (Deut 30:19; see also 4:26; 31:28; and 32:1). By Isaiah's day Israel had repeatedly broken the covenant, and God was about to exile ten tribes to Assyria; he would soon exile Judah to Babylon. Before doing that, he was assembling the court of the universe so that he could press his case against his own people. Heaven and earth were ready to take the witness stand against Israel. The rest of Isaiah 1 lays out the devastating case God was prosecuting against his own sinful people.

A God Who Judges His People
ISAIAH 1:2-9

God begins his case in verse 2, but the "courtroom" (heaven and earth) is shocked to find out he is prosecuting his own children! Any godly parent of a wayward child can easily hear the heartbreak in God's accusation: "I have raised children and brought them up, but they have rebelled against me." When children rebel, mortal parents will rightly admit, "I was not a perfect father" or "I was not a perfect mother." There has been only one perfect Father in history: God. And yet, all but one of his children rebelled anyway.

But God is not only a loving Father; he is also a righteous and holy Judge. And his zeal for his law and his holy reputation drives him on to prosecute the case against this rebellious nation. Step by step in this chapter Isaiah exposes Israel's sin: rebellion against God (v. 2); beastlike ignorance of him who has provided everything for them (v. 3); sinfulness so weighty it threatens to sink them down (v. 4); a "brood of evildoers" (v. 4); depravity (v. 4); contempt for and abandonment of the Lord (v. 4); a nation who have turned their backs on God (v. 4); persistence in rebellion despite many warnings (v. 5); violence (v. 15); murder (v. 21); sexual immorality (v. 21); robbery (v. 23); injustice and oppression of the poor and needy, especially on the part of the rulers and judges of the people (v. 23); and idolatrous worship (v. 29). To make matters much worse, over this seething pot of wickedness is draped a flimsy coat of religiosity: their claimed continual observance of the law of Moses with no sense whatsoever of their hypocrisy. God had not been passively waiting for his people to repent. In verses 5-7 God speaks of the devastated state of his people, likening them to a body that has been beaten almost beyond recognition: "From the sole of the foot even to the head, no spot is uninjured" (v. 6). This implies the aching desire God has to be a loving Father to heal the wounds he himself has inflicted, just as he said in the Song of Moses: "I bring death and I give life; I wound and I heal" (Deut 32:39). In Isaiah 1:7 he makes it plain he is speaking about the destruction of the countryside by a foreign army, the very thing he warned about before Israel ever entered the land (Deut 28:49-52; 32:21,30).

Given Isaiah's context, verses 5-9 probably speak of Assyria's final invasion of Judah during which the only part of the promised land not conquered was Jerusalem. Isaiah says that "the Daughter of Zion" (Jerusalem) is left "like a shack in a cucumber field, like a besieged city," and it is clear the beating given to the nation of Israel is directly from God for all these sins. So it is for Christians today—God "disciplines the one he loves and punishes every son he receives" (Heb 12:6). Sometimes when his children go after idols or become stubborn in sin, God brings severe repercussions—health issues, financial woes, natural disasters, etc. These are to train us to hate our sin as much as he does.

In verse 9 God speaks of the "survivors" left under this onslaught of judgment. This is evidence of how God in wrath remembers mercy (Hab 3:2). Isaiah concedes that his people are no better than Sodom and Gomorrah (vv. 9-10), but by his amazing grace God chooses a remnant for salvation. The apostle Paul picks up on this verse as part of his powerful teaching on God's sovereign election for salvation, the remnant chosen by grace in Romans 9:29. In our sins we are no better than the worst people who ever lived—the residents of Sodom and Gomorrah. Yet for his own glory God chose us to be part of his remnant, a remnant chosen not because God found anything of value in us but rather for his own purpose in grace.

A God Who Despises Religious Hypocrisy
ISAIAH 1:10-15

In verses 10-15 God cries out against the religious machinery that was constantly running in this wicked nation. They were absolute hypocrites, trampling his temple courts with a seemingly endless parade of animal sacrifices. Year after year this mindless machine of meaningless religious exercises continued. But all this religion was being done by people who were living the wicked lives described in Isaiah 1. This chapter stuns us by telling us that God *hated* their religion.

In these verses God reveals his heart about religious formalism and hypocrisy. He detested their incense (v. 13) and hated their festivals (v. 14). Their constant sacrifices, however costly and of high quality, he called "useless" (v. 13). Even their prayers were offensive to God; he considered them a burden he was weary of bearing, and he vowed to refuse even to look at them when they prayed. What's amazing about all this is that God had *commanded* all these things to be done. But God cares about the heart attitude behind all of these actions. Later in Isaiah, God will say of them, "These people approach me with their speeches to honor me with lip-service—yet their hearts are far from me" (29:13).

This insight is vital for us in the twenty-first century as well. It is so easy to get into a pattern of religious observance and have our hearts grow increasingly hard toward God because of our sinfulness throughout the week. Many people go to church every Sunday and then live like complete unbelievers the rest of the week. God despises religion that is a mere external machine, that never draws the worshipers into a clear understanding of the holiness of God and their own need for Jesus Christ as Savior.

A God Who Pleads with Sinners
ISAIAH 1:16-20

Even more amazing than God's utter disdain for mindless religion is his willingness to save sinners from the judgment they so richly deserve. In verses 16-20 is one of the most famous calls to repentance and salvation found anywhere in Scripture. Here the holy God is calling on filthy, corrupted sinners to come to him. In verse 18 is the command to "Come," to draw near to God. Their sins have made them distant from him, but now God beckons them to come close to him. Along with this is a call to "settle" the issue. The Hebrew word is rich, as though God were opening up a line of communication, urging them to use the reasoning powers with which he endowed them at creation. At its essential nature, sin is unreasonable, irrational, insane. It produces corruption and misery; it results in estrangement from God and enslavement to ever-increasing wickedness; it stores up an ever-increasing wrath on judgment day. Sin is the ultimate tyrant, seeking to destroy our very lives. Conversely, God is the most delightful being in the universe; in his presence is the fullness of joy (Ps 16:11). "Come, let us settle this" means, "Let us talk about all this, let me reason with you to forsake your sins, come to your senses, and come home to the God who loves you."

At the core of this is a call to repentance. It is not a call to more religious activities, sacrifices, and empty prayers. Rather, it is a call to wash the filth of sin from your hands, to put away sins from God's sight, to stop violating God's laws. It is a call to live a righteous, morally pure life, one that is filled with compassion for the poor, the needy, the oppressed, and the widow. Genuine repentance will result in a sacrificial life of concern for others, even a costly concern that spends oneself for the most destitute in society. This is a call to complete and radical transformation. The question is, Is it possible for a sinner to do this?

Verses 18-19 contain some of the richest promises of cleansing and total forgiveness in the Bible. Sin had left the deepest stain, indelible in the sight of a holy God who sees all and forgets nothing. God is able to wash away the scarlet stain and make sinners white as snow. At the core of this forgiveness is a transformation of the hearts of sinners; formerly rebellious and unyielding, they are now made "willing and obedient." And having been so transformed, they will eat all the good things of the promised land, as if they had never sinned at all. But once again the question stands before us: Can we make our own hearts willing and obedient?

On the other side of this lavish promise of forgiveness and rich restoration is a terrifying warning of total destruction (v. 20). This is nothing different from the original blessings-and-curses aspect of the Mosaic covenant by which the people of Israel had inherited the promised land to begin with. This same dual outcome is repeated in verses 27-28: The repentant sinners will be redeemed, but rebels who abandon God will perish. God clearly threatens the destruction of all sinners who refuse his offer of forgiveness and restoration. In Isaiah's day this most likely would come by being devoured by the sword of some invading army.

A God Who Works Salvation and Threatens Judgment
ISAIAH 1:21-31

The people are pictured as completely sinful and completely defiled, dripping with blood. They are told to wash and cleanse themselves (v. 16). They are told to become as pure as snow and clean wool (v. 18). But how can this be done? Jeremiah asked rightly, "Can the Cushite change his skin, or a leopard his spots? If so, you might be able to do what is good, you who are instructed in evil" (Jer 13:23). It seems like an impossible command for sinners like us to obey. These verses speak of a terrifying judgment that God will bring on all who do not repent: rebels and sinners (Isa 1:28) will perish in the flames (v. 31).

In verses 26-27 Isaiah predicts the day when "Zion" (the city where God and humanity dwell together, pictured by Jerusalem) will be restored to perfect righteousness. But how can sinners like these ever be "redeemed by justice"? Justice stands against such sinners, accusing them and condemning them to destruction. But still, the prediction stands that Zion will someday be righteous in God's sight. The issues of Isaiah 1 couldn't be more poignant, and the desperate question stands again and again: How can sinners like us be redeemed with justice and be seen as perfectly righteous in God's sight?

The answer of the entire book of Isaiah, indeed of the whole Bible, is clear: in Christ alone can sinners be washed, be transformed, be redeemed with justice, and stand righteous in God's sight. Christ is the perfect sacrifice whose blood actually can cleanse the guilty, defiled conscience and make it whole again. Isaiah 53 will clearly predict the sacrifice of Jesus in the place of sinners, the one who was "pierced because of our rebellion, crushed because of our iniquities; punishment for our peace was on him, and we are healed by his wounds" (v. 5). By this "righteous servant" many wicked people will be justified (v. 11), which means "redeemed by justice [and] righteousness" (1:27). In the cleansing fountain of Christ's redeeming blood alone, our filth and sinful wickedness can be cleansed. In Christ alone we can stop doing wrong and learn to do right. In Christ alone we can stop bringing meaningless sacrifices. In Christ alone we can learn genuine concern for the poor, the widow, the orphan. In Christ alone even though our sins are like scarlet they will be as white as snow and as pure as wool. In Christ alone can God make wicked sinners like us righteous in his sight; and through his death on the cross the penitent ones will be redeemed with justice. Written seven centuries before Christ, this entire chapter yearns for Jesus to come and make it a reality.

Applications

Though this chapter was written to Israel more than twenty-seven centuries ago, by it God still is speaking to us today. We are every bit as sinful as that nation ever was. We still struggle with violence, sexual immorality, and injustice on the part of our leaders, flowing from deeply rooted idolatry. We are just as apt to make machinery out of religion—to go to church Sunday after Sunday while living corrupted lives during the week. God has never changed: He still searches hearts and hates hypocrisy. He still brings severe judgments on his people for sins. He still threatens the unrepentant with destruction in the eternal fires of his judgment. He still summons senseless rebels to settle the issue of their sins. And he still offers one Savior—Jesus Christ—by whom alone can all the sweet promises of Isaiah 1 come true. It is for us to acknowledge our sins, to reject any hope of moral reformation apart from God's grace in Christ, and to flee to Jesus, so we can eat the best of the land eternally. And having come to Christ, it is our responsibility to stand as though God were making his appeal to us and to call on sinners from every nation to repent and trust in Christ alone for the cleansing only his blood can give and the transformation of heart only his Spirit can work.

Reflect and Discuss

1. How might the fact that God, the only perfect Father, has raised rebels as his children be a comfort to believing parents of rebellious children?
2. What sin patterns do you see in Isaiah 1 that are still evident in our day?
3. How do you see empty religious machinery running year after year in our Christian context?
4. Why do you think God hates religious formalism (just going through the motions) and hypocrisy so much?
5. What is the significance of God's comparing Israel to Sodom and Gomorrah? How should that humble them?
6. What is the significance of God's sovereign grace in saving a remnant from such a corrupt nation (Rom 9:27; 11:5-6)?

7. How does the invitation of verses 16-20 point to Jesus Christ? Is it possible for sinners to obey this call apart from the work of the Holy Spirit in their hearts? If not, how does this call humble us while it saves us?
8. How does true salvation result in concern for the poor and needy, as in verse 17?
9. God says, "Come, let us settle this." How is sin utterly insane? How is repentance a step toward true sanity?
10. How do you see the blessings and curses aspect of God's promises/warnings in this chapter?

Competing High Places: God versus Man

ISAIAH 2

In the last days the mountain of the LORD's house will be established at the top of the mountains and will be raised above the hills. All nations will stream to it. (Isa 2:2)

Main Idea: God levels all human idols, establishing and exalting his temple, causing the nations to stream to him.

I. **Peace: The Mountain of the Lord's Temple Exalted (2:1-5)**
   A. The exaltation of the mountain of the Lord
   B. The amazing streaming of the nations—uphill!
   C. Missions: come, and say, "Come!"
II. **Shame: Full of Things, Empty of God (2:6-9)**
   A. Full of superstitions, not of true religion
   B. Full of silver and gold, not of true wealth
   C. Full of horses and chariots, not of true power
   D. Full of idols, not of the Lord
III. **Terror: Lofty Things Humbled (2:10-21)**
   A. The day of the Lord proclaimed
   B. The day of the Lord described: the lofty humbled, the Lord exalted
   C. The result: fleeing in sheer terror
IV. **Invitation: Stop and Come (2:22,5)**
   A. Stop trusting in man.
   B. Come, let us walk in the light of the Lord.
   C. Come, and say, "Come!"

Since the beginning of the church Christians have speculated about the end of the world. Perhaps no more poignant moment in history for this speculation occurred on August 24, 410, the day Rome fell to the Visigoths. Many thought the end of the world was imminent. Augustine, the great bishop of Hippo in North Africa, took quite a different view. In his masterpiece, *The City of God*, Augustine saw in history two different cities battling each other on infinitely unequal terms: the

City of Man, represented by Rome; and the City of God, represented by the true Christian church. At the core of the City of Man is one driving spirit: love of self, resulting in contempt of God. At the core of the City of God is an opposite driving spirit: love of God, resulting in contempt of self. The story of history is this: two cities battling for glory—the City of God and the City of Man; love of God vs. love of self. The outcome of that struggle is the topic of Isaiah 2.

Peace: The Mountain of the Lord's Temple Exalted
ISAIAH 2:1-5

This magnificent chapter is a vision seen by Isaiah concerning "the last days." The Bible reveals plainly that we are now in the last days, and we have been ever since Jesus Christ came to earth (Heb 1:2; 1 John 2:18). We are now in the final phase of the magnificent redemptive plan God conceived before the foundation of the earth. The essence of that plan is his glory in the salvation of sinners from every tribe, language, people, and nation on earth. Isaiah sees it as a miraculous streaming of the nations to the mountain of the Lord's house (v. 2). As it is exalted above all mountains and hills (i.e., idols), all nations will stream to it.

The idea of the "mountain of the LORD's house" has its origin in the temple of the Lord that Solomon built in Jerusalem. But now Christians have been instructed in the New Testament to understand both the mountain and the temple of the Lord differently. In Hebrews 12:18-22 the author says, "You have not come to what could be touched. . . . Instead, you have come to Mount Zion, to the city of the living God." In John 2:19 Jesus called his body the temple. Hebrews asserts that, with the death of Christ, animal sacrifices would never again be needed or accepted by God. So what is this "LORD's house" that attracts all nations in the last days? Some Christian interpreters think it refers to a rebuilt temple at the end of history or to a temple established during the millennial reign of Christ in Jerusalem.[1] But another way to understand this "house" is the streaming of the nations to faith in Jesus that results from the preaching of the gospel of Christ to all nations. As the clear proclamation of his life, death, and resurrection exalts Christ, people from every nation on earth will be moved

---

[1] More on the millennium later; see this commentary on Isaiah 65:17-25.

to follow him. They then become part of the "LORD's house" spiritually (Eph 2:19-22; 1 Pet 2:4-9).

The vision that Isaiah had was of an amazing river of all nations streaming to the exalted mountain of the Lord. As a river physically flowing up a steep mountain would be clearly supernatural, contrary to all laws of physics, so all nations spiritually streaming to worship the Jewish God is supernatural, contrary to all expectations. The movement of these peoples is spiritual, not physical; Christianity requires no actual pilgrimages to Jerusalem as the Jews in the old covenant did three times a year and as Muslims are to do to Mecca once in their lifetime. The streaming to the Lord's house is the lifelong following of Christ that his disciples make, a journey that ends in the new Jerusalem at the end of the age. As Jesus says, "I am the *way*, the truth, and the life. No one *comes to* the Father except through me" (John 14:6; emphasis added). The Christian pilgrimage begins when sinners hear the gospel clearly and by faith see the exaltation of Christ, the infinite superiority of Jesus to all idols. They begin to pursue Jesus, resulting in an eternal place in God's house as "living stones" in an eternal "spiritual house" (1 Pet 2:5). This is the amazing streaming of the nations that Isaiah foresaw.

Isaiah 2:3 gives an additional insight that is vital for us concerning missions. The very same people who are already on the pilgrimage are inviting others to join them. While we travel to our heavenly destination, we are to persuade others to join us. We are both to "come" and to "say, 'Come!'" As it says in Revelation 22:17, "Both the Spirit and the bride [the church] say, 'Come!' Let anyone who hears, say, 'Come!' Let the one who is thirsty come. Let the one who desires take the water of life as a gift."

And at the mountain of the Lord's house we will find the King, Jesus, who dispenses laws by which we will walk as we journey to heaven. The Great Commission says that disciples are to be taught to obey everything Christ has commanded (Matt 28:19). So in Isaiah 2:3 King Jesus will teach us his ways so that we may walk in his paths. His word will transform every aspect of our daily lives. And only those people whose lives are being so transformed by the law of the King are truly on that pilgrimage to the heavenly house of the Lord.

The ultimate result of the King's laws is the destruction of all sin between people. As formerly warring peoples come to faith in Christ, they become one in the Spirit and change their entire way of relating together. The imagery is beautiful: beating swords into plows and spears into pruning knives. Hatred between people is wasteful and destructive. As Christ's gospel takes hold of human hearts, people no longer war with one another, but they devote themselves to producing a rich harvest. The end of all wars is promised in this passage, but it will not occur until the second coming of Christ, no matter what diplomacy occurs at the United Nations.

Shame: Full of Things, Empty of God
ISAIAH 2:6-9

Verses 6-9 make it plain that the house of Jacob is spiritually corrupted. They have imbibed the superstitions of the East and the occult practices of the Philistines, turning their backs on the true religion given them by God. They are rich with silver and gold (v. 7), not of the true wealth only God can give. There is no limit to their chariots (v. 7), but they know nothing of the true power that comes from the Lord. Ultimately, they are idolaters, bowing down to created things rather than the Creator (Rom 1:25). This brings the human race very low, into a degraded state (Isa 2:9). This is the shame of the house of Jacob, and because of it, God abandoned his people (v. 6).

Terror: Lofty Things Humbled
ISAIAH 2:10-21

For the rest of the chapter, Isaiah describes the terror that is coming on the earth because of humanity's idolatries. He warns of a "day belonging to the Lord" that is coming, a day in which God's holiness will be vindicated and man's sins punished severely. Isaiah says it plainly in verse 12: "For a day belonging to the LORD of Armies is coming." This is the power of the Word of God, to warn us of the coming wrath and urge us to flee to the refuge that he alone can provide.

The word "*Armies*" (Hb *tsebaoth*, traditionally "Hosts") here probably refers to the legions of angels who surround Yahweh's throne and do his bidding (1 Kgs 22:19). It can refer to the stars—the "heavenly host"—that God created and that glorify him (Neh 9:6). In the prophets in general it is also a reminder that Yahweh is sovereign over the human armies of Israel as well as those of all the nations, so he directs them to march out and determines which of them succeed.

On the day belonging to the Lord, he will reveal his "majestic splendor" (v. 10) and will alone be exalted (v. 11). "Lofty" things are in direct competition with God's glory; they are idols. Isaiah describes all the competing high places and lofty things that exalt themselves against the glory of God: naturally lofty things—cedars of Lebanon, oaks of Bashan, towering mountains, high hills; man-made lofty things— every lofty tower and every fortified wall (military pride), trading ships (commerce), stately vessels (pleasure vehicles). The most direct competitor to the glory of God is human pride (v. 11). Just as Satan's pride led to his attempt to take God's throne in heaven, resulting in his downfall (Isa 14), so human pride soars like the tower of Babylon, seeking to exalt self and belittle God. God is determined to pull all the soaring ambitions of humanity down so he alone will be exalted in that day. He is jealous for his glory and will brook no rivals.

A powerful picture of this occurred during the Communist era in Eastern Europe. In downtown Budapest the Hungarian Communist party erected the Stalin monument, completed in December 1951 as a gift for Josef Stalin. It was torn down on October 23, 1956, during Hungary's October Revolution. The statue was more than seventy-five feet high! The people pulled it down by placing a thick steel rope around its neck and using acetylene torches to cut the feet. After an hour, it toppled (Sebestyen, *Twelve Days*, 118–19). Similarly, God will come with a fiery indignation and a passion for his glory and will topple all the monuments to human pride that sinners have erected to challenge his supremacy.

On that day sinners will be fleeing into the rocks and hiding in caves from the terror of the Lord as he reveals his glory. The fear of the Lord at that time will not be by faith but by sight. All the nations of the earth will see his glory as he comes with the holy angels to judge the whole earth, and they will run from terror of the Lord and dread of his splendor. They will throw away to the moles and bats their idols, and they will seek some place of refuge when God rises to shake the earth (vv. 10,19-22). They will realize at that time the wickedness of their idolatry, and they will reject their idols, but it will be too late—the era of faith and the open door of the gospel will have closed with the coming of that dreadful day.

Invitation: Stop and Come
ISAIAH 2:22,5

This chapter levels everything that the human race can trust in and exalts the true and living God. The clear application of this doctrine is given in verse 22: "Put no more trust in a mere human, who has only the breath in his nostrils. What is he really worth?" Stop trusting in your own righteousness, your religious works and efforts, to save you from sin. Stop trusting in your own efforts to keep yourself healthy and safe, whether individually—by healthy living, exercise, medicine—or nationally, by lavish military expenditures. Stop trusting in human wealth: gold, silver, money, possessions, investments. Stop trusting in human pleasures: entertainment, food, clothing, music, movies, amusement parks, material pleasures. Turn your back on every idol that clamors for the highest place in your heart. Repent from these false gods!

And stop being enamored with human glory. Seeing what Jesus has accomplished at the cross and the empty tomb, how can any human achievement compare? So it's time to level the lofty or high places erected by human pride. Level all the Olympic gold medals, the Nobel prizes, the Fortune 500 list, the World Series and Super Bowl championships, the mighty emperors, the ridiculous Oscar and Emmy winners. Level them all! The Lord Jesus alone will be exalted someday. Therefore, why not exalt him now? Why not live by his Word now?

And as we are making our pilgrimage to the heavenly Zion, we are commanded to be witnesses to others who have not yet begun the journey. We are to both "come" and to "say, 'Come!'" We are to make progress in holiness day by day in submission to Christ's law, and we are to share the gospel to the ends of the earth.

Reflect and Discuss

1. Why do you think people are so fascinated in the question, Are we in the last days?

2. How do you understand the exaltation of the "mountain of the LORD's house"? Do you think it refers to a literal temple to which the nations will stream during the millennium or to the spiritual streaming of the nations through the advance of the gospel around the world? How does 1 Peter 2:4-5 give us insight into a possible spiritual understanding of "the LORD's house"? See also Ephesians 2:21-22.

3. How does this chapter show the zeal God has for his own glory above all other competing high places? Why is it vital for missions that the church exalt the glory of God now and level competing high places by clear preaching and teaching?

4. What is the significance of the twin command, "Come" and "Say, 'Come!'"? How does it point to both sanctification (growth in holiness) and missions/evangelism? How are both vital for Christians?

5. How does Revelation 22:17 harmonize with "Come" and "Say, 'Come!'"?

6. How does this text speak to your heart about the need to be involved in missions? What specific resolutions would you like to make about that?

7. How do verses 6-9 convict us about various forms of idolatry? How does Romans 1:25 teach us what idolatry is? How do you see people today struggling with the same forms of idolatry listed in verses 6-9?

8. What do verses 10-21 teach us about the coming day of the Lord?

9. How is the desire to run and hide *from* the coming terror depicted so clearly in Isaiah 2 really an excellent theme evangelists and missionaries should use now to preach the gospel and call people to flee *to* Christ?

10. How are verses 22 and 5 excellent applications for Isaiah 2?

Clearing the Site: From Vainglory to True Glory

ISAIAH 3–4

*On that day the Branch of the LORD will be beautiful and glorious,
and the fruit of the land will be the pride and glory of Israel's
survivors.* (Isa 4:2)

Main Idea: God clears the wreckage of his people's sins so that he can
build a perfect Zion in its place.

I. **Bookends of Grace Surround Severe Judgment.**
   A. The mountain of the Lord (Isa 2) and the Branch of the Lord
      (Isa 4)
   B. Clearing the building site (Isa 2–3)
II. **Loss of Stability (3:1-15)**
   A. The "pillars of society" are gifts of God.
   B. God removes these pillars, resulting in anarchy.
III. **Loss of Unstable, Luxurious Vainglory (3:16–4:1)**
   A. Luxurious daughters of Zion
   B. Luxury stripped away
   C. The fall of the men
IV. **Gain of Stable, Luxurious Glory (4:2-6)**
   A. The Branch of the Lord is Jesus Christ.
   B. The remnant will bask in his glory.
   C. The dwelling of God is with men at last.

In the aftermath of the terrorist attack on the World Trade Center in New
York on September 11, 2001, a huge pile of debris was left on Ground
Zero; twisted steel girders, rubble, and other wreckage continued to smol-
der for five months after the attack. On May 30, 2002, there was a signifi-
cant ceremony: the last piece of steel from the World Trade Center was
removed from the site to be recycled as the bow of a new assault ship, the
USS *New York*. Without the clearing of the pile of debris, the new Freedom
Tower, 1,776 feet high, could never have been built (Okwu, "Ceremony").

By spiritual analogy, God's ultimate building site is both the hearts
of his people and an eternal city—the new Jerusalem, a combination

of spiritual dwelling place and literal city. The rubble is the residue of human arrogance and sin that must be cleared or the eternal structure cannot be built. The history of the actual city of Jerusalem is a spiritual picture of God's spiritual building project in his people. So in our passage in Isaiah 3–4 we see the destruction of Jerusalem for sin; but it is destruction with a redemptive purpose so the new Jerusalem can be built. This is a passage that speaks a word of warning to our own time, a word of repentance and prayer, not presumption, to present-day Christians.

Bookends of Grace Surround Severe Judgment

Isaiah chapters 2 and 4 contain two of the sweetest and clearest prophecies of the future glory of Christ's kingdom. They stand like bookends around the smoldering words of chapter 3. Bookend 1 is Isaiah 2:1-4: the mountain of the Lord's temple exalted and the streaming of the nations. Bookend 2 is Isaiah 4: the Branch of the Lord fruitful and Mount Zion cleansed and protected by a canopy of glory. But between the glorious bookends, Isaiah 2:10-21 and Isaiah 3 are smoldering with descriptions of the terrible judgment on Judah and Jerusalem. It is as though the building site is being scraped clean for a future and glorious building.

Loss of Stability

ISAIAH 3:1-15

As with any building, society itself depends on structural pillars to hold it up. Architects and builders know how significant a load-bearing pillar or beam is; if it cracks, the building crumbles. In a similar way, all of human society is built on some key social pillars: supplies of basic commodities and key individuals whose skills are vital to the smooth functioning of the community. These "pillars of society" are gifts of God, and in this chapter he is threatening the removal of all the structural supports of Jerusalem and Judah, causing a total collapse. God threatens the supplies of food and water to the city, ultimately by the invading Gentile armies (Assyrian and Babylonian) whose conquests would put an end to farming and the flow of water. God also threatens to remove the key men whose leadership is vital to the smooth function of society.

Start with good political leaders: godly kings and ministers whose wise rule provides stability for the nation. Proverbs 29:14 says, "A king who judges the poor with fairness—his throne will be established forever." But Isaiah 3 depicts the total vacuum of leadership, the scourge of anarchy and instability. Furthermore, military heroes are gone, those warriors who rally the troops to make heroic stands against the enemy. The courageous men will all be dead; the men who are left are stripped of courage and flee for their lives.

Beyond these, the removal of the "pillars of society" goes to every level: judges, prophets, elders, lower-level commanders, counselors, skilled craftsmen; even cunning magicians and fortune-tellers are gone. All of the old order has been removed, and the remaining flimsy structure is tottering and ready to collapse. The resulting vacuum of leadership is devastating, and the anarchy is a direct judgment from God. His ordinary pattern of leadership is qualified men. He raises them up, seasons and trains them, preparing them to bear the burden of leadership. From the moment God created Adam alone for a time without a wife, God was establishing men to lead in the home and in society. In the whole Bible, Deborah is the only example of a godly woman established as a leader over men (in the book of Judges). And that era was a strange one in redemptive history, in which Israel had no king and everyone did what was right in his own eyes. But in Isaiah's prophecy concerning Judah and Jerusalem, the qualified men are dead or removed; all that are left are women and children and weak, unqualified men. In verse 4 unseasoned boys become rulers. In verses 6-7 we have a shameful vignette in which one of the few remaining men is forced into leadership simply because he still owns a cloak. But this weak man refuses to take the role of ruler of "this heap of rubble"; he has no remedy for the ravaging disease of his people. In verse 12 the fact of women ruling over men is clearly displayed as shameful, a judgment from God.

The root cause of this judgment from God is the sweeping wickedness of the people. Verses 8-11 make it plain that the evil of their hearts is pouring out into open patterns of wickedness similar to that in Sodom. Amazingly, verse 9 implies that openly parading and flaunting sin is a final stage of rebellion. When people no longer feel the need to hide their sin, but are actually proud of it and boast over it, society has reached its nadir. Verses 14-15 single out the corruption of the leaders that led to their judgment: they have used their positions of power to plunder the poor and grind their faces into dust.

For all of this, God is bringing severe judgment on his people. But in the middle of this dire warning, God speaks a message of consolation to the righteous in verse 10. God will judge everyone according to their deeds (Rom 2:6-8), and he makes no mistakes.

Loss of Unstable, Luxurious Vainglory
ISAIAH 3:16–4:1

Isaiah gets very specific in 3:16-24 about the arrogance and selfish luxury of the "daughters of Zion." In a chapter in which the plundering of the poor is exposed and judged, we have a long list of luxury items with which the women of Judah made themselves beautiful. First Peter 3:3-5 makes it plain that a godly woman's beauty does not come from outward adornments but from the godliness and submissiveness of her heart. But these women are like the proverbial pigs wearing gold rings in their snouts (Prov 11:22); the only beauty they possess is a lie, an outward disguise of their inner corruption. When the judgment falls, all their outward luxuries will be snatched away by their conquerors. Then, instead of soft garments and luxurious accessories, they will wear sackcloth bound with a rope; and instead of smelling lovely, they will stink (Isa 3:24). In the end their physical condition will match the ugliness of their souls.

The women of Zion will have lost their men in battle and now they stand exposed, with no shelter (3:25-26). Their shame is completed by seven of them pleading with one of the few men left for the mere honor of a marriage in name only; he wouldn't even have to provide food or clothing for them (4:1). How the mighty have fallen!

Gain of Stable, Luxurious Glory
ISAIAH 4:2-6

In the midst of the darkest night of Zion's history, the glory of the Lord shines the brightest. God will not finally exterminate the seed of Abraham; his promises to David will be fulfilled. God will protect a remnant by his sovereign power (4:3); and in the smoldering ruin of Jerusalem the Branch of the Lord will flourish. The branch of the Lord in Isaiah 11:1 is clearly Jesus, growing from the stump of Jesse. Christ is called "Branch" in other prophetic passages (Jer 23:5; Zech 3:8). In Isaiah 4:2 the word "Branch" could be seen to refer first to the remnant of Jews that the sovereign Lord allows to survive and then ultimately to Jesus, whose human ancestry would come from those survivors (Rom 1:3).

The Branch here is described as "beautiful and glorious," a radiant display of the attributes of God. So Jesus was seen to be the "radiance of God's glory" (Heb 1:3). By contrast with the darkness and wickedness of the circumstances in Jerusalem leading to the judgment of God, Christ will stand forth as the perfect man, the perfect ruler.

In the immediate horizon, Isaiah predicts that God will restore the remnant to a peaceful and fruitful dwelling in the promised land. The people will delight in the fruit of the land and take pride in it as evidence of God's restorative favor. But the ultimate glory of the people will be in the Branch, Jesus Christ. Not only will Christ be our perfect ruler, but the fruit of his perfect righteousness will be the pride and glory of the remnant whom God will save by his grace. According to 4:3, this remnant was elected by God's grace, for the Hebrew says they were "recorded for life." For eternity this remnant will boast in the Lord, and his achievements at the cross will be their righteousness, their glory. The remnant will be called holy, and all their filth will be washed and burned away by the spirit of God's judgments (4:3).

The final image of this chapter is one of a lasting dwelling place between God and his remnant. God will create a cloud of smoke by day and the brightness of a flaming fire by night. The smoke and fire refer immediately back to the "spirit of burning" of verse 4 by which God purged Jerusalem. So our God who is a "consuming fire" will actively guarantee the ongoing purity of his holy city. But beyond that, the cloud and fire evoke memories of God's leadership of Israel during the days of the exodus. Just as the pillar of cloud and fire led Israel every step of the way (Exod 13:21), so God now promises to guide his settled city of Jerusalem. And just as God's pillar stood between Israel and Egypt as a wall of protection (Exod 14:20), so God will now be a shelter of protection from the heat, storm, and rain. This image is one of total safety for the people of God against all their enemies, a safety ultimately fulfilled in Christ. The atoning work of Christ on the cross is our final protection from all our enemies. These rich images point ahead to the day when, at last, the dwelling of God will be with his people, and he will live with them (Rev 21:3).

Applications

We should realize the gift of God that all skilled laborers and leaders are to society, and we should thank God for them when they do their work well. Anarchy is a great judgment on a society, and so we should pray for our leaders, that they would do their leading for the glory of God. We should yearn for God to raise up competent and skilled men to be our leaders, and we should pray that they would not use their positions to crush the poor and needy but rather to care for them. Any man should read Isaiah 3 and yearn to be a strong leader of his home and in society as God raises him up to lead. Any woman should read Isaiah 3 and yearn not to be characterized by the vapid, arrogant, and deceptive beauty of outward adornment. First Peter 3:3-5 is an excellent remedy to the kind of selfish "beauty" that Isaiah 3 describes. The accumulation of a wardrobe or the latest fashion accessories is shameful if not accompanied by "a gentle and quiet spirit." The overall wickedness and corruption of the people in Isaiah 3 should make us yearn for God to search us and cleanse us from all unrighteousness. It should make us confess our sins in detail and have the fire of his Spirit and Word purify us. Finally, Isaiah 4 points to a day when Christ's saving work will be completed and God and redeemed humanity will dwell together forever in the new Jerusalem. We should look forward to this day and speed its coming.

Reflect and Discuss

1. How does this chapter show the "common grace" blessings of various skilled laborers and leaders in society? In other words, how is a skillful plumber or an honorable senator a gift of God to a nation?

2. How is the removal of such "pillars of society" a great judgment from God? How is anarchy a severe trial, worse than dictatorship or other bad forms of government?

3. In what way is the luxury of the women of Zion reflected in our culture? How is this chapter a clear commentary on the emptiness of an external beauty that is purchased at the mall and not wrought in a woman by the Spirit and the Word?

4. Why is it far worse for someone to parade their sin like Sodom than for them to hide it? How do you see this kind of bold pride in sin in our culture today?

5. What encouragement does 3:10 give to the godly in a society that is suffering the general surrounding wickedness? How does verse 10 relate to Romans 2:6-9?

6. Do you think verse 12 implies that female leadership of the nation was a judgment from God? Do you think the modern world has outgrown such thoughts, or is it still the biblical norm for men to lead in the home and in society?

7. What rich imagery do you see Isaiah use in 4:2-6 for the future restoration of Jerusalem? How do these images point both back to the exodus and ahead to the Christ?

8. How does Isaiah 4 give you a picture of God's constant protection of believers now through the work of Christ on the cross?

9. How can we grow in our yearning for the final fulfillment of Revelation 21:3, which Isaiah 4 also predicts?

10. Why is it important for us to live our lives here as aliens and strangers, as though we still lived in tents?

God's Lavished Grace Tragically Rendered Fruitless

ISAIAH 5

What more could I have done for my vineyard than I did? Why, when I expected a yield of good grapes, did it yield worthless grapes?
(Isa 5:4)

Main Idea: God exposes the many sins of his richly blessed people in a parable of a failed vineyard, and he predicts the coming judgment on these sins by his righteous wrath.

I. **God's Lavished Grace: What More Could He Have Done (5:1-7)?**
II. **Six Clusters of Bad Grapes (5:8-23)**
    A. Woe 1: Aggressive greed (5:8-10)
    B. Woe 2: Sinful excess (5:11-12)
    C. Woe 3: Self-deceived enslavement and mocking of God (5:18-19)
    D. Woe 4: Redefining of truth (5:20)
    E. Woe 5: Arrogant false wisdom (5:21)
    F. Woe 6: Drunken, corrupt justice system (5:22-23)
III. **"Therefore" Judgment Comes (5:13-17,24-30).**
    A. "Therefore" is the reasonable justice of God.
    B. The basic sin is rejecting God's Word.
    C. Resultant judgments
IV. **The Sweet Fruits of God's Terrible Judgments (5:15-17)**
    A. The Lord Almighty exalted and displayed
    B. Sheep peacefully grazing
V. **The Gospel of Christ: Consummation of These Themes**
    A. "What more could I have done?"—Sovereign grace produces its own harvest.
    B. Judgment of all sins at the cross
    C. An eternity of peace in the presence of God

God's Lavished Grace: What More Could He Have Done?

ISAIAH 5:1-7

In 2 Corinthians 6:1 the apostle Paul made a powerful appeal to the talented but troubled Corinthian church: "We also appeal to you: 'Don't receive the grace of God in vain.'" What does it mean to "receive the grace of God in vain"? This is a troubling and often misunderstood concept. In order to answer the question we have to understand the doctrine of God's grace, which is his determination to do good to people who deserve his wrath. Common grace is lavished on the world in a variety of ways: sunshine, rain, food, clothing, shelter, families, friends, health, scenic vistas, education, the written Word of God, and many others. But all of these forms of grace can be received "in vain": if we fail to make the most of our opportunities, if we rebel and follow a lifestyle of sin, we have received God's grace in vain.

This is exactly what happened to the Israelites of Isaiah's day. Having been lavished with an astonishing array of blessings from God historically—the promises to Abraham, the exodus under Moses, the manna in the desert, the conquest of the promised land under Joshua, the joy of eating harvests they did not plant and living in houses they did not build, the patience of God through the rebellions in the time of the Judges, the gift of leadership by David, the repeated warnings and encouragements from many prophets—Israel responded with a shameful array of sins for generations. They had "received the grace of God in vain." Isaiah 5 unfolds the anguish of that reality in powerful terms.

Isaiah begins in verses 1-7 with a parable about a vineyard. It is couched in the terms of a love song that the prophet sings for the one he loves (the Lord; v. 1). Intense heartbreak is in the prophet's words, but that only dimly reflects the anguish the Lord feels at the failure of Israel's harvest. Isaiah unfolds the lavish grace of the Lord on Israel: a well-chosen site, hard labor invested, skillful gardening, diligent protection. All this is done with a clear expectation of a rich harvest, for the Gardener has hewed out a winepress. He expected it to yield good grapes, but instead it yielded worthless grapes.

Having granted these rich blessings with such wretched results, the owner is angry and brings his vineyard to court, calling on the residents of Jerusalem and men of Judah to render the same verdict he will render. This is the second time this courtroom image is used in Isaiah (see 1:2). God wants to bring these people to see the justice of his judgments concerning the scandal of such lavish grace resulting in such a tragically disappointing harvest. The haunting question hangs over Israel's entire history: "What more could I have done for my vineyard than I did?" And the secondary question: "Why?!" It is the unanswerable question in all of history: Why do we choose sin instead of God?

God has already rendered his own verdict (vv. 5-6): He is going to destroy it completely. He will personally remove its hedge of protection, and it will be consumed. He will make sure the clouds do not rain on it. He will turn it into a wasteland, not pruned or weeded, and thorns (the symbol of God's curse on the earth in Eden) will grow up. God will remove his grace from this fruitless people.

In verse 7 he makes it plain who he is talking about: "the house of Israel and the men of Judah." He declares plainly what he sees: "He expected justice but saw injustice; he expected righteousness, but heard cries of despair." And God was enraged over it.

Six Clusters of Bad Grapes
ISAIAH 5:8-23

Through Isaiah, God gets quite specific about the "worthless grapes" he saw in Israel and Judah. We can trace out these clusters of bad grapes by seeking the word *woe* in verses 8-23. *Woe* is a word of prophetic judgment used again and again in the Scriptures. It means, "Beware of the judgment about to come on you for your sins!" Isaiah uses the word six times in this chapter, and these six woes speak plainly of the corruption of the Israelite nation in the promised land:

Woe 1: Aggressive Greed (vv. 8-10)

These are economic empire builders, ruthlessly taking over the property of the poor and needy, like evil King Ahab, who had Naboth murdered and took over his vineyard.

Woe 2: Sinful Excess (vv. 11-12)

These people live for sensual pleasures rather than God: zealously dedicated to pursuing excess, waking up early just to run after drinks, lingering at it throughout the day; calling for the next new tune on the harp.

Woe 3: Self-Deceived Enslavement and Mocking of God (vv. 18-19)

They have deceived themselves, but they are enslaved to sin, as though they are beasts of burden serving sin and they cannot escape it. Yet they mock God, question God, challenge God, defy God. They arrogantly demand that God carry out his plan on their timetable.

Woe 4: Redefining of Truth (v. 20)

Long before the postmodern assertion that everything is relative, people have questioned truth and sought to redefine it. God alone is the absolute standard of good and evil, and the ultimate evil is to deny him his glory, to fail to love him with all our hearts. Lesser evils come when people call actions "good" that God has called "evil" and call actions "evil" that God has called "good." This is the evidence of a depraved and arrogant mind.

Woe 5: Arrogant False Wisdom (v. 21)

In the garden of Eden, Eve perceived that the fruit was good for making her wise and she ate it. This kind of wisdom is rooted in self-worship, the ultimate form of idolatry. In the same way, the Israelites of Isaiah's day were truly impressed with themselves. Technology, achievement, and affluence tend to make us wise in our own eyes, forgetting the immeasurable wisdom that God displayed in creating the universe to begin with.

Woe 6: Drunken, Corrupt Justice System (vv. 22-23)

One of the fundamental functions of government is to assure justice for all its citizens, that neither the rich nor the poor will get any preferential treatment but that everyone will be judged fairly. The symbol of this for the United States Supreme Court is Lady Justice personified, a blindfolded woman carrying scales and a sword, representing fair trial and justice meted out with authority, irrespective of persons. In Isaiah's day judges loved the lush life, were champion wine drinkers, and sold their services to the highest bidder.

So there we have a sixfold woe, six clusters of bad grapes—a detailed and comprehensive description of the harvest of sins that breaks the heart of God.

"Therefore" Judgment Comes
ISAIAH 5:13-17,24-30

Each of the woes describes a horrendous sin pattern on the part of God's people, and each of them results in a "therefore"—a corresponding judgment from our reasonable and righteous God. In verses 9-10 God swears that luxurious homes of the economic empire builders will become desolate and their vineyards will experience massive crop failure. In verses 13-15 God makes it plain that the pleasure-loving drunkards will either die or go into exile to starve. In verses 24-25 God describes the fiery indignation of his wrath consuming the people who have despised and rejected his holy Word, and it is terrifying: the ground shaking and corpses filling the streets. It is very clear from verses 26-30 that the primary means of judging this people will be an invasion by a highly skilled and magnificently equipped army from distant Gentile nations (the Assyrians and the Babylonians, and then a series of Gentile invaders after them).

The Sweet Fruits of God's Terrible Judgments
ISAIAH 5:15-17

God does not delight in bringing these judgments on his people, but he does delight in the outcome described in verses 15-17: arrogant humanity is humbled, God alone is exalted by his justice and righteousness, and sheep may graze peacefully in the ruins of the rich. God's judgments are designed to bring about final salvation for his elect, and the focus of their eternal joy will be the radiant attributes of God so plainly put on display throughout redemptive history.

The Gospel of Christ: Consummation of These Themes

Let us return to the question of this chapter: What more could he have done? God's grace lavished on Israel is astonishing, and the advantages they enjoyed as God's people were vast. One thing, however, was lacking: the internal transformation of their hearts by the sovereign grace of God. Without that transformation, all those external blessings would only corrupt them and harden their hearts. Their hearts of stone needed to be removed and hearts of flesh given instead; God's Spirit could have been poured out on them from on high, moving them (indeed, compelling them by his sovereign power) to follow his statutes and ordinances (Ezek 36:26-27). The experience of Israel in history puts plainly on display two types of grace: that which can be resisted and turned to judgment and that which cannot. The second type of grace is sometimes called "irresistible," but it is better to call it "effectual." It is a grace that cannot be "received in vain":

- It was by grace that Lazarus was raised from the dead. He could not receive that in vain; he would most certainly breathe again.
- It was by grace that the man born blind received his sight. He could not receive that grace in vain; he would most certainly see light.
- It was by grace that God revealed to Peter that Jesus was the Christ, the Son of the living God. He could not receive that grace in vain; he would most certainly understand who Jesus is and trust in him (Matt 16:16-17).
- And it is by grace that all genuine Christians in history have been born again by the Holy Spirit of God; that their hearts of stone were removed and the hearts of flesh put in; that each one saw the light of the knowledge of the glory of God in the face of Christ. Not one of them could receive that grace in vain, but God's grace would produce salvation in their hearts.

Application

Isaiah 5 and the whole experience of Israel in the old covenant stands as a warning to the church in the new covenant. We have been given far greater privileges through the death and resurrection of Jesus Christ than Israel experienced under the law of Moses. And this chapter stands as a warning to all nations in which the gospel has long flourished, not to take lightly the many blessings of the Christian faith that have surrounded them for centuries. Isaiah 5 speaks a word of warning to the American evangelical church, for no church in history has had as many spiritual advantages as Christians in America: Bibles in a variety of translations; good seminaries teaching the truths of the Word of God; publishers, book distributors, Internet resources; good preaching in tapes, CDs, digital downloads, and streaming; godly role models, men and women openly living for Christ; opportunities to serve the Lord in short- and long-term missions; good, Bible-believing churches.

And yet, for all the avalanche of God's grace, it is amazing to many observers how little fruit is being produced here. We must be warned not to receive these graces from God in vain but live to display his holiness in an increasingly corrupt age and to spread the name of Jesus from shore to shore. "From everyone who has been given much, much will be required" (Luke 12:48).

We should learn to love God as passionately as Isaiah did (v. 1) and to grieve over what breaks God's heart. We should look at the sins listed in Isaiah 5 and see roots of those same sins in our own hearts. We should look to the cross of Christ as our only righteousness and to the empty tomb of Christ as the only power for new life by the Spirit. We should proclaim the coming wrath of God, for the exact same sins that plagued Isaiah's society plague our own. We should expose the moral relativism of postmodernism by the light of verse 20 and courageously call what is evil to be evil and what is good to be good. Finally, we should long for the societal righteousness that Isaiah yearned for, in which the poor and needy are not deprived of justice.

Reflect and Discuss

1. How does Isaiah's obvious love for God and compassion with God in his grief over Israel's failure to produce good fruit set an example for us as Christians (v. 1)?
2. How is the parable of the failed vineyard a powerful tool for exposing the Israel's sins and God's disappointment over the failed harvest?
3. How did Jesus use this parable of the vineyard in Matthew 21:33-41? What are the similarities and differences between Isaiah's parable and Jesus's?
4. What is the answer to the question, "What more could I have done for my vineyard than I did?" How do you understand various types of grace from God? What is the difference between "resistible" and "effectual" grace? What are some examples of each?
5. How many of the sins exposed by the six woes are still obvious in our culture today? How should this make us fear for the future?
6. How is verse 20 especially vital for us in the postmodern, relativistic world today? What are some examples of the ways that people call evil good and good evil today?
7. How are the materialism of verse 8 and the love of pleasure of verse 22 obvious today?
8. Why does God want the residents of Jerusalem and men of Judah to understand God's justice in bringing these severe judgments on the nation (v. 3)? How is it vital for us to see how reasonable God is for bringing these judgments?
9. How does the gospel of Jesus Christ draw out many of these same themes and give us the only hope for salvation from God's coming wrath?
10. What aspects of the "Application" section spoke most powerfully to you?

The Lord of Glory Calls His Messenger

ISAIAH 6

*And one called to another: Holy, holy, holy is the L*ORD *of Armies; his glory fills the whole earth.* (Isa 6:3)

Main Idea: God reveals Christ to Isaiah, convicts him of sin, purifies him, and calls him to preach.

I. **The Lord's Holiness Exalted (6:1-4)**
   A. The central reality of the universe: a King on a throne
   B. A glimpse into heavenly worship
II. **The Lord's Messenger Purified (6:5-7)**
   A. The Lord's "ruined" messenger must be holy.
   B. The Lord's messenger purified
III. **The Lord's Messenger Recruited (6:8)**
   A. A general invitation: "Who should I send?"
   B. A specific response: "Here I am. Send me."
IV. **The Lord's Message Entrusted (6:9-10)**
   A. A shocking message of hardness
   B. The answer to the question, Why did Israel reject Christ?
V. **The Lord's People Humbled, Then Exalted (6:11-13)**
   A. Israel hardened and judged
   B. The remnant: the stump in the land
VI. **The Lord's Identity Revealed (John 12:41)**
   A. Israel's rejection of Christ was predicted, effected, and removed.
   B. Isaiah saw Jesus's glory.

The Lord's Holiness Exalted

ISAIAH 6:1-4

In Revelation 4:1-2 the apostle John had an extraordinary invitation from almighty God to ascend from earth through a doorway into the heavenly realms, to see things that are invisible and overwhelming. As John passed through that doorway, the first thing he saw was someone seated on it. That throne and the One seated on it are the central reality of the universe, for God created the universe, owns it, and actively rules over it. That throne is the very thing that sinners rebelled against, and it is in reconciliation with that throne that we find our salvation. Isaiah had a similar vision at the beginning of his service as a prophet. This vision shaped everything else Isaiah ever wrote. It came in the year of the death of King Uzziah (740 BC), a (mostly) godly king whose long and prosperous reign of fifty-two years was a gift of God's grace to the people of Judah. Now he was dead, and questions of possible instability and anxieties about the future would naturally crowd into the hearts of the people. Isaiah had a vision of a throne that can never end, with someone seated on it whose glory will someday fill the new heaven and new earth.

Isaiah saw the Lord on a "high and lofty throne," its elevation conveying its authority and superiority. The mere hem of the Lord's robe majestically filled the temple. Surrounding the throne were seraphim (mentioned in the Bible only here, meaning "burning ones"). Each of these seraphim had six wings, and four of their six wings were devoted to covering themselves because of the unapproachable glory of the one they were flying to serve. They were continually crying to one another, "Holy, holy, holy is the Lord of Armies; his glory fills the whole earth." What an awesome picture of heavenly worship this is! They see the Lord of glory, and they cry out *to one another* what they are seeing, as if they were saying, "Proclaim the Lord's greatness with me; let us exalt his name together" (Ps 34:3). The topic of their heavenly worship is the indescribable holiness (separation) of the Lord; they can never stop crying aloud about it. What is amazing is that these beings are themselves holy in the sense of being perfectly pure from evil. But the Lord is holy because he is separate not only from evil but from them and from every other created being. A. W. Tozer captured that infinite gulf between the Lord and all creation:

> We must not think of God as the highest in an ascending
> order of beings, starting with the single cell, and going on
> up from the fish to the bird to the animal to man to angel to
> cherub to God. God is as high above an archangel as above a
> caterpillar, for the gulf that separates the archangel from the
> caterpillar is but finite, while the gulf between God and the
> archangel is infinite. (*Knowledge of the Holy*, 70)

The seraphim say, "holy, holy, holy" to emphasize how overwhelming this attribute is. It is the attribute of God that we sinners most need to understand and be transformed by.

The seraphim also cry aloud that the whole earth is filled with God's glory (Isa 6:3). This is a vital concept. Romans 1:20 makes it plain that the creation reveals the existence and attributes of God, but sadly verse 25 says that people exchanged the truth of God for a lie and worshiped and served created things rather than the Creator. So the world is already filled with the glory of God *right now*, but we have become idolaters. Habakkuk 2:14 predicts that someday the earth will be filled with the knowledge of the glory of the Lord as water covers the sea. When the redeemed walk in resurrection bodies in a perfect universe radiant only with the glory of God through Christ, then this prediction will be fulfilled: we will no longer worship creation but the Creator based on the glory we will see.

The Lord's Messenger Purified
ISAIAH 6:5-7

At the sight of this holy Lord, Isaiah feels most painfully his own sinfulness, and he cries out against himself the same word of prophetic judgment ("Woe") that dominated chapter 5. A true vision of God's holiness always results in conviction of sin on the part of us sinners. Isaiah is rightly afraid that the fire of the Lord will lash out against him and purify that heavenly scene of his own uncleanness. He specifically feels the corruption of his tongue, the very instrument of his prophetic ministry, and he feels the corruption of his people as well.

But the Lord of glory is also the Lord of grace, and instead of killing the sinner as he deserves, he commands that Isaiah be purified. An angel flew to Isaiah with a live coal that he had taken with tongs from the altar. With it he touched Isaiah's lips, cleansing him from his sins. Though God can speak through a donkey (Num 22:28) and even through a hate-filled enemy of Christ (John 11:51), he chooses ordinarily to speak through consecrated and holy messengers whose sins have been atoned for. The symbol of a live coal shows how the Lord maintains his status as a consuming fire while making a way to purify sinners like Isaiah.

The Lord's Messenger Recruited
ISAIAH 6:8

The next act in this heavenly drama changed Isaiah's life forever. He heard the Lord calling, "Who should I send? Who will go for us?" The word *us* clearly has a trinitarian basis, for the dual question parallels "I" ("Who should *I* send?") with "us" ("Who will go for *us*?"). Only the triune God can speak like this. The Lord has a mission, and he deliberates openly in the heavenly council. Daniel 7 pictured God enthroned, served by a hundred million angels (v. 10), any of whom would have been eager to serve the Lord's purposes. But the Lord willed a human messenger to go on this mission to Israel. A compulsion overcame Isaiah, and he boldly presented himself for service: "Here I am. Send me" (6:8). What a beautiful sequence in this narrative: a vision of the enthroned Lord in his glory leads to overpowering heavenly worship, and it also leads to Isaiah's awareness of his sinfulness, which leads to him crying out against himself, which leads to the atoning work for his sin, which leads to hearing the Lord call for a messenger, which leads to Isaiah presenting himself for service. In this sense, Isaiah 6 stands as a lasting paradigm for all who would enter the Lord's service.

The Lord's Message Entrusted
ISAIAH 6:9-10

The message entrusted to Isaiah is shocking both to him and to the generations that followed him. It involves the Lord's surprising work in hardening the hearts of the Israelites to refuse to listen to God's word. The message itself is much like the live coal taken with tongs from the altar of God: it has a divine origin, it burns with searing power, and the messenger has no power to alter it in any way. The prophet must drop this live coal into the hearts of God's people with its heavenly fire unquenched. The prophet may not be silent, for then would God's word burn like a fire within his heart, within his very bones, and he would be unable to hold it in (Jer 20:8-9). God's message through Isaiah is shocking because it seems that God is ordaining that he will harden the hearts of the Israelites against his word, with the outcome that they will refuse to repent and be healed of their sins. This judicial hardening from God confirms their pattern as a "stiff-necked people with uncircumcised hearts and ears" (Acts 7:51). Scripture reveals that Satan blinds human eyes from the work of God (2 Cor 4:4), and many passages (like Acts 7:51) teach that the people harden their own hearts and blind their own eyes. But this passage clearly teaches the role of God in hardening hearts and blinding eyes against his word; the verbs are active and decisive, "do not understand, . . . do not perceive. Make the minds . . . dull; deafen their ears and blind their eyes." These strong commands from God are designed to *prevent* the Israelites from seeing, hearing, understanding, turning, and being healed. It is troubling to people who think God always only acts to open blind eyes, soften hardened hearts, and work salvation in everyone to whom he sends a messenger. But clearly this passage teaches the opposite: sometimes God sends a messenger specifically to harden hearts and confirm the condemnation of people.

In the New Testament this passage is quoted four times to explain why Jesus used parables to teach the people. In effect, Jesus said he used parables so that the people *will not* understand and turn and be healed. It is a powerful weeding-out process. The elect hear Christ's parables and, not understanding, humble themselves and come to Jesus for the explanation; then, by God's sovereign grace through Christ, they are blessed with explanations leading to insight. The "outsiders" get everything in unexplained parables to confirm their hardening (Matt 13:10-17; Mark 4:11). This is the doctrine of sovereign grace—both for mercy and for hardening (Rom 9:18)—worked out in the actual pattern of the message. Isaiah 6:9-10 is also quoted in John 12:39-40 to explain how it could be possible for the Jews to see all of Jesus's miracles and still not believe in him. John's use of Isaiah 6 shows that God actively blinds eyes and hardens hearts resulting in unbelief when it comes to Christ. Salvation is from the Lord, and it only comes when he works to remove the blindness and hardness.

The Lord's People Humbled, Then Exalted
ISAIAH 6:11-13

Like Jesus who wept over Jerusalem and the apostle Paul who had "great sorrow and unceasing anguish" (Rom 9:2) in his heart over unbelieving Jews, so Isaiah cries out, "Until when, Lord?" He is asking, How long will I preach only to harden hearts? And how long will the hardening last? God replies that his ministry must continue until the Lord has carried out the judgments he intends against Israel: the cities will lie in ruins, empty, desolate; the people will be driven into exile. That is the judgment of the holy God against such a sinful people, the very thing he warned he would do before they ever entered the promised land (Deut 28:49-52).

But amazingly, by the grace of God, the Lord will leave a remnant, and like a tree that is felled leaving a healthy root system, so the remnant will become the future of Israel. The "holy seed" is the remnant of survivors, and they will be the stump that will again flourish under God's hand. The apostle Paul speaks of the Jewish nation, which has generally rejected the gospel of Jesus Christ, in similar terms: an olive tree with fruitless branches stripped off but with a holy root system (Rom 11:16). No matter how desolate the land will become, God is not finished with the Jewish nation. Paul means the people will be humbled to the dust then exalted to heaven at the end through faith in Christ (v. 26).

The Lord's Identity Revealed
JOHN 12:41

The final surprise of Isaiah 6 comes when the apostle John unveils the true identity of the enthroned Lord, the glorious ruler of the universe—before whom seraphim veil their faces, whose glory fills the whole earth. After citing Isaiah 6:9-10 to explain why the Jews were rejecting Christ despite his many miracles, in chapter 12 John says these astonishing words: "Isaiah said these things because he saw his glory and spoke about him" (v. 41). In the context of John 12 the "his" and "him" cannot refer to God the Father but only to Jesus. In verse 37 it speaks of the one who performed many miracles before their eyes, but they still wouldn't believe in him. Verse 42 speaks of many who *did* believe in him but were unable to confess him freely so they wouldn't be banned from the synagogue. So verse 41 is speaking of Jesus. The great God of glory, seated on a throne high and exalted, the one whom the seraphim cannot see fully and they veil their faces because of his glory—that one is Jesus! The mystery of the incarnation: Jesus of Nazareth is the God of heaven and earth, the creator of fiery archangels and of lowly caterpillars alike, the one who crafted and shaped the mountains and who spread the stars throughout space. This is the one whose blood provides the only sure purifying remedy for sin. Isaiah cried out, "Woe is me! I am ruined by my sin!" The live coal taken from the altar represents Christ, his purifying ministry. Isaiah saw the glory of the preincarnate Christ and wrote about him. The glory of Jesus is infinite and will radiate throughout the new heaven and new earth forever. And Isaiah wrote about him so that we could see that glory by faith and turn and be healed.

Applications

This magnificent chapter calls us to a heavenly worship of the glorious Christ, to match the seraphim in their awe-filled cries before Jesus of "Holy, holy, holy!" It calls on us now, by faith, to understand that the universe is filled with his glory. It calls on us to understand the holiness of Jesus and how undone we are by the pollution of our sins. It calls on us to understand that the only atonement there can ever be for our sins is that which God works by the shed blood of Jesus Christ. It calls on us to hear Jesus calling out, "Who should I send? Who will go for us to the ends of the earth to proclaim the gospel?" It calls on us to answer by faith with full consecration, "Here I am, Lord; send me!" And it calls on us to understand God's mysterious plan for showing mercy to some and hardening others by the proclamation of the Word.

Reflect and Discuss

1. How does the stability of the reign of King Jesus on his heavenly throne give us confidence, even in times of political instability (like when godly King Uzziah died)?
2. Isaiah says, "I saw the Lord seated on a high and lofty throne." How can we "see" the Lord now by faith in his Word? How would such a spiritual vision of the Lord fuel our worship?
3. What is the significance of the fact that the seraphim are sinless yet they still covered their faces before Jesus?
4. What does *holy* mean? Why do the seraphim say it three times? Why would you say that holiness is the most important attribute of God for us sinners to embrace?
5. What effect did this awesome heavenly scene have on Isaiah? How should a proper contemplation of the holiness of the Lord result in a humble awareness of our own sinfulness? Why is such an ongoing awareness both reasonable and necessary to our full and final salvation from sin?
6. How does the burning coal from the altar represent Christ?

7. In what way is the call of Isaiah unique, and in what way is it a pattern for all Christians to follow?
8. Do you find the message of verses 9-10 difficult to swallow? How can we understand the intentions of God in purposely hardening hearts and blinding eyes against spiritual truth? How does that message relate to Christ's use of parables and the explanation for why the Jews could not believe in Jesus despite his miracles (John 12:39-41)? How does it relate to Romans 9:18?
9. How is the image of a stump as it relates to Israel both humbling and hopeful for them?
10. How do you feel the message of Isaiah 6 speaking into your life right now? As a result, what do you think God wants you to understand or do differently?

Stand Firm in Faith, or You Won't Stand at All

ISAIAH 7

Therefore, the Lord himself will give you a sign: See, the virgin will conceive, have a son, and name him Immanuel. (Isa 7:14)

Main Idea: God uses the crises of life to expose our true faith: if we do not stand firm in our faith in Christ, the virgin-born Savior of the world, we will not stand at all.

I.   **Crisis Reveals True Faith (7:1-2).**
    A.   The crisis: a scary alliance
    B.   Fluttering like a leaf
II. **The Sovereign Lord Intervenes, Promises, and Warns (7:3-9).**
    A.   God's command: Don't be afraid, only believe.
    B.   God's promise: The plans of man will fail.
    C.   God's warning: There is grave danger for unbelief.
III. **The Sovereign Lord Gives a Sign: Immanuel (7:10-17).**
    A.   Stooping to our weakness: the Lord gives a sign.
    B.   Three issues with the sign "Immanuel"
IV. **False Faith Proves Ruinous: Assyria Is Coming (7:17-25)!**
    A.   Both God and Ahaz summon Assyria.
    B.   Faithless Ahaz turns from God to Assyria for help.
V.   **The Immanuel Sign Fulfilled: Christ Is Born.**
    A.   The virgin birth
    B.   "God with us"
    C.   The true deliverance
    D.   The final fulfillment: eternally with God
VI. **Central Lesson: In What Are You Trusting?**

This is one of the biggest questions in life: What are you trusting in? What is your truest source of confidence for the dark future? On most days, this question never really comes up. We live day to day in a comfortable bubble, able to handle whatever comes our way because we've done it many times before. We don't ask, "What am I trusting in?" as we pour milk on cereal, as we answer a ringing cellphone, as we sit on the couch in our living room, or as we lie down to go to sleep at night. All those activities and countless others are so completely ordinary we assume we can do them ourselves, so we feel we don't need anything to trust.

But this is a grave misunderstanding! The fact is, at every single moment of our lives, we are trusting in *something*: if we feel confident we can handle that situation ourselves, we are trusting in *ourselves*. This is the most devastating state we can be in spiritually. People can trust in all kinds of things, depending on the circumstances: high IQ, diligent preparation, skill in martial arts, athletic training, musical talent, a hall-of-fame coach, a balanced retirement portfolio, a nation's military power. What you're trusting in is most clearly revealed during a crisis. To prove this to us, God brings trials and circumstances that will jar us from our comfort zones. And sometimes he will bring extreme suffering to cause us to lose all other sources of trust than God himself. So it is in this chapter; the lesson of Isaiah 7 is, "Stop trusting in yourself, and stop trusting in your shrewd alliances; throw yourself on God alone."

Crisis Reveals True Faith
ISAIAH 7:1-2

In the Old Testament, God often taught vital spiritual lessons to his people through political and military events. The historical context of Isaiah 7 is such a time. After the death of Solomon, Israel had been split into two—the northern kingdom of Israel and the southern kingdom of Judah. At the time of Isaiah 7, Judah was ruled by a wicked king named Ahaz. The two Jewish kingdoms were often at war with each other, and so it was in Ahaz's day. These two tiny kingdoms were among several small nations of the region—like Edom, Aram, Syria, and Philistia—bit players on the stage of geopolitics. They were often dominated by larger empires, such as the Assyrians, who threatened the entire region with their military power. Assyria was the big monster swimming in the small pool of the ancient Near East: its people were violent and ruthless, the Nazis of the ancient world. Their emperor, Tiglath-pileser III, was an expansionist who wanted Egypt, the breadbasket of the world. Palestine stood in the way, composed of all these small nations. This monster, Assyria, was poised to gobble up all these minor nations like a lion devouring scraps of meat.[2]

---

[2] For a good overview of the Assyrian threat, see Pfeiffer, *Old Testament History*, 331–36; also Bright, *A History of Israel*, 269–88.

Beyond that looming threat, sometimes these smaller kingdoms allied together and threatened other small kingdoms with conquest. This is just what King Ahaz and Judah were facing: Israel (under Pekah) and Aram (under Rezin) allied together and sought to conquer Judah, and specifically Jerusalem, its capital city. The news of the alliance between Aram and Israel resulted in the hearts of Ahaz and his people trembling like trees of a forest shaken by a strong wind (v. 2). Their fear was faithless; they never seemed to think of turning to the sovereign Lord for protection. The people were as weak in faithlessness as their leader. God brought this crisis on Ahaz to show him how empty his soul was and how great was his need to trust in the Lord. The plans of the scary alliance of Israel and Aram were plain: to put an end to the Davidic dynasty and install their own puppet king, "Tabeel's son," over Judah (v. 6). Judah's trembling hearts show the weakness of their faith.

The Sovereign Lord Intervenes, Promises, and Warns
ISAIAH 7:3-9

God is not an idler, standing passively by on the sidelines of human history. God is not merely rooting for the proper outcome; he brings it about! He is sovereign in deciding what will occur on the stage of history; he moves his little finger, and the nations convulse. But God's real desire is that his people would trust in him. In order for them to trust, he must speak to them, make promises to them. This he does through Isaiah the prophet. God sends Isaiah to speak to Ahaz and to the nation of Judah: "Calm down and be quiet" (v. 4). This is also what the Lord Jesus said to the menacing waves on the sea of Galilee (Mark 4:39), then he rebuked his terrified disciples for their lack of faith. Isaiah speaks directly to Ahaz about the two allied kings, Pekah and Rezin, telling him not to fear them at all. God knows about the plot those kings have made to conquer Judah for themselves and put an end to David's lineage.

But God speaks a simple and sovereign answer: "It will not happen; it will not occur." And that's the end of that! All the nations are as "a speck of dust on the scales" (Isa 40:15), but God is like a million-pound weight on the scales. Whatever side he lands on, the scale tips absolutely to his will. When God decrees, "It will not happen," then it will not happen. "Many plans are in a person's heart, but the LORD's decree will prevail" (Prov 19:21). God has planned to bring a Savior to the world through the lineage of David, and these two small kings will not stop it.

God goes beyond that and predicts plainly that, within a short sixty-five years (that's nothing to God, for whom "a thousand years [are] like one day"; 2 Pet 3:8), Ephraim (Israel) will be so decimated it will no longer be a nation. These two small nations are led by two small men—Rezin and Pekah—and what are they to God?

But at the end of this assurance of the nation's survival, God speaks a word of warning to the man, Ahaz: "If you do not stand firm in your faith, then you will not stand at all." In other words, my plans are for the whole nation to survive, but your individual survival depends entirely on your faith. This is the clear teaching of the Bible: "The righteous one will live by his faith" (Hab 2:4; Rom 1:17). Faithless Ahaz must repent and believe, or he too, like Pekah and Rezin, will be swept away by God's judgments. The warning has to do with Ahaz's scheme for self-salvation. If he refuses to trust this good news from the Lord through Isaiah, he will act on a scheme of his own: a fatal alliance with Assyria to deliver his small nation from these other two small nations. This is the very thing that would end up destroying him and Judah almost entirely.

The Sovereign Lord Gives a Sign: Immanuel
ISAIAH 7:10-17

In this amazing interchange the holy God stoops to Ahaz's weakness and offers his weak faith the advantage of a sign, anything as deep or high as he could possibly think of. Isn't it amazing how patient God is in dealing with sinners like us? In effect, he was handing Ahaz a blank check, asking him to fill in the amount! Even more striking are the words of the invitation: "Ask for a sign from *the LORD your God*" (emphasis added). Ahaz has not lived out any faith toward the true God, but God is not ashamed to offer to be his God now.

Tragically, Ahaz refuses! He puts on the air of a humble man by saying, "I will not test the LORD" (v. 12). But God had commanded Ahaz to ask for a sign, and Ahaz refused. So Isaiah, exasperated in this man's rebellion, rebuked him for testing the patience of God and man alike. And notice the shift from "your God" in the invitation of verse 11 to the "my God" in the rebuke of verse 13. Then the prophet spoke one of the most famous prophecies in the book of Isaiah: "Therefore, the Lord himself will give you a sign: See, the virgin will conceive, have a son, and name him Immanuel" (v. 14). The sign is given to the whole nation: the word "you" is plural.

This sign of Immanuel carries with it three difficult interpretive issues:

1. Was there an immediate sign in Ahaz's time?

2. Does this verse teach the virgin birth?

3. What is the significance of the word "Immanuel"?

Let's look at each issue.

First, was there an immediate sign in Ahaz's time? Answer: yes. Christian prophecy often has a type and a fulfillment, a shadow and the reality. Something was acted out imperfectly in space and time illustrating some aspect of Christ's future coming. Christ then perfectly fulfills that shadow with the bright light of his life and ministry. In Ahaz's day an actual child was born and given this mysterious name "Immanuel." Immanuel was a normal child, growing up in the normal way. His development was like a timepiece for the total erasure of the military threat to Judah from Ephraim and Aram: he will grow up to the point where he can learn to reject bad and choose good and eat butter and honey. Before all that occurs (perhaps a five- or six-year-old boy would have enough moral training to discern between good and bad), the land of the two kings they were dreading would be abandoned.

Second, does this verse teach the virgin birth? Again, yes. Matthew 1:22-23 directly ascribes this prophecy to Jesus, settling for Christians whether Isaiah 7:14 taught the virgin birth. The challenge with this prophecy is that the virgin conception and birth of Jesus Christ were unique in all of history. So the Hebrew word "virgin" is *almah*, a word that can refer to a virgin but that doesn't emphasize her virginity.[3] The imperfect, shadowy prophetical type of Isaiah's day was that an ordinary young woman would conceive Immanuel in the ordinary way. But the perfect fulfillment was of a true virgin, Mary, who conceived by the power of the Holy Spirit. More in a moment.

Third, what is the significance of the name *Immanuel?* This word means "God with us," and the significance in Ahaz's day was that the

---

[3] Martin Luther offered one hundred gold coins to anyone who could show that *almah* ever referred to a married woman. In characteristic humorous fashion, Luther also added that only the Lord knew where he'd get the one hundred gold pieces if someone could meet his challenge (*Saemmtliche Schriften*, 20:2093)!

true source of Judah's safety was the fact that Almighty God was protecting it. As Isaiah 8:9-10 will make plain, any nation can prepare for war against little Judah, and they can make lavish plans, but all such preparations will fail, for "God is with us." As Paul would later write, "If God is for us, who is against us?" (Rom 8:31).

False Faith Proves Ruinous: Assyria Is Coming!

ISAIAH 7:17-25

Sadly, Ahaz will not listen to any of these marvelous words. He will not stand firm in faith, so he will not stand at all (v. 9). He will trust in his scheme to make an alliance with the evil king of Assyria to deliver him from these two small kings. So in verses 17-25 God makes it plain that Assyria will most certainly come, having been summoned by *both* God and Ahaz, but for very different purposes. The tragic story of Ahaz's faithless alliance with Assyria is told fully in 2 Kings 16:7-12. Turning away from these sweet promises of God through Isaiah, Ahaz invites the monster to save him from these two small kings. He pledges allegiance to Tiglath-pileser III, king of Assyria, saying, "I am your servant and your son! March up and save me!" Ahaz's faithlessness led him directly into idolatrous worship of pagan deities. He eventually shut the doors of the Lord's temple entirely, set up altars at every street corner in Jerusalem, and worshiped false gods after the pagan pattern of Assyria and the other nations. All of this came from the turn in Ahaz's heart: I will *not* ask the Lord; I will save myself!

So the Lord would bring Assyria into Judah—"He will bring the king of Assyria" (Isa 7:17). Isn't it amazing that both a wicked king and a holy God can bring about the same thing for radically different reasons? Ahaz wanted the king of Assyria to come and save him from Israel and Aram; God wanted the king of Assyria to come and judge his faithless people. So the Assyrian troops will swarm into the land like flies and bees, summoned by God's whistling for them (vv. 18-19). The king of Assyria will be like a razor coming to shave the hair from the bodies of this faithless people—a sign of total humiliation (see 2 Sam 10:4). The final result of verses 23-25 is a land totally destroyed by the Assyrian invasion, symbolized by "thorns and briers" mentioned in all three verses. Bottom line: what you trust in other than the Lord will totally destroy you in the end.

The Immanuel Sign Fulfilled: Christ Is Born

Seven centuries later God remembered the sign he had given to Ahaz, and he fulfilled the words perfectly—*virgin* and *Immanuel*. By the power of the Holy Spirit, Mary, a virgin, became pregnant with a son. The Holy Spirit overshadowed her and the power of God came upon her, and she conceived a son, fully human and fully divine—Jesus Christ our Lord (Luke 1:34-35). The word *Immanuel* was fulfilled by the incarnation of Jesus Christ; "The Word became flesh and dwelt among us" (John 1:14). "Since the children have flesh and blood in common, Jesus also shared in these" (Heb 2:14). He was God with us and God for us (Rom 8:31), and he became the focus of all saving faith. In him alone is fulfilled the words, "If you do not stand firm in your faith, then you will not stand at all" (Isa 7:9). He is with us in companionship through all our trials, for he has said, "I will never leave you or abandon you" (Heb 13:5). But by far the greatest deliverance Jesus will work for us is on judgment day, when he will claim us as his own; he will not abandon us on that day but will say, "I know you; you are mine. Enter into the joy of your salvation!" He will deliver us from death and hell and bring us safely into his eternal kingdom. All other deliverances are as nothing compared to that one.

Central Lesson: In What Are You Trusting?

The central lesson of this chapter is this one question: In what are you trusting? The various trials and crises of your life will reveal the true answer to this question, and it's not always flattering. As you face lesser trials of financial struggles, health problems, or relationship issues with family members or friends, does your heart flutter and are you shaken like trees in a strong wind, as Ahaz was, or do you have a growing stability in faith in Christ? The ultimate trial we all will face is judgment day. What we rely on now for lesser trials is related directly to what we will be trusting in for the salvation of our souls. Romans 1:17 says, "The righteous will live by faith," and that faith must be in Jesus Christ. He is Immanuel, God with us, our only Savior.

Reflect and Discuss

1. How do our reactions to lesser trials reveal what we're really trusting in?
2. How does the image of a tree shaken by the wind capture well the life of someone who has no faith in Christ? How does it also capture at times the immaturity of some believers during some trials they face?
3. How can we learn to be more stable in our faith in Christ? (See the context of Eph 4:14 and Jas 1:6 to help answer this question.)
4. How does God show amazing grace and patience with a wicked man like Ahaz? How does Ahaz, in effect, throw it back in God's face?
5. What is the significance of the statement, "If you do not stand firm in your faith, then you will not stand at all" (v. 9)?
6. What is the significance of the display of God's sovereignty in this chapter, especially in verses 6-7?
7. Discuss the three issues related to the Isaiah 7:14 prophecy discussed above. How do you resolve these three questions?
8. How is the word and concept of *Immanuel* (God with us) comforting to you?
9. How is Christ the perfect fulfillment of Isaiah 7:14?
10. How did the ultimate invasion of Judah by Assyria show the terrible end of Ahaz's failure to trust in the Lord?

Two Paths to Eternity

ISAIAH 8

*I will wait for the L*ORD, *who is hiding his face from the house of Jacob.*
I will wait for him. (Isa 8:17)

Main Idea: People travel to their eternal destiny by two paths—one of
light and one of darkness.

I. **Two Paths to Eternity**
II. **Terrifying Context: Assyria Invades the Region.**
    A. Phase 1: Assyria comes to rescue.
    B. Phase 2: Assyria comes to destroy.
    C. Phase 3: Assyria comes to be destroyed.
III. **The Way of Light**
    A. A life in God's strong grip
    B. A life listening to God's word and warnings
    C. A life apart from the crowd
    D. A life of fear and fearlessness
    E. A life resting in the true sanctuary
    F. A life guided by God's laws
    G. A life inquiring of God
    H. Ultimately, a life of faith in the Lord
IV. **The Way of Darkness**
    A. A life spent rejecting God's gentle provision
    B. A life of rejoicing while others suffer judgment
    C. A life of stumbling over God and being snared by him
    D. A life of false spiritual guidance
    E. A life of spiritual famine and restless roaming
    F. A life of rage and cursing
    G. Ultimately, a life of darkness now and eternally
V. **Christ (Immanuel), the Only Way**

Two Paths to Eternity

I n 1916 Robert Frost wrote his most famous poem, "The Road Not
Taken," describing a quandary he found himself in. He was walking

through a beautiful forest in the autumn, enjoying himself until he came to a fork in the road; which direction should he go? After a time of wrestling based on uncertainty about the two destinations, he decided in the end to take the road less traveled, and, he said, "that has made all the difference" ("The Road Not Taken," 75).

Jesus Christ describes even more poignantly a far more significant choice—two paths, one leading to heaven, the other to hell:

> Enter through the narrow gate. For the gate is wide and the road broad that leads to destruction, and there are many who go through it. How narrow is the gate and difficult the road that leads to life, and few find it. (Matt 7:13-14)

So also, in Isaiah 8 there are two ways to live woven together side by side. The Bible teaches that there is one way, and only one way, that leads to heaven, and his name is Jesus (John 14:6). It was true in Isaiah's day, as they looked forward to God's promised Messiah, and it will be true to the end of time.

Terrifying Context: Assyria Invades the Region

As we saw in Isaiah 7, Ahaz and Judah were terrified by the prospect of an alliance between Israel and Aram. God warned Ahaz not to give way to fear but to trust him. Instead, Ahaz made a political alliance with Assyria to deliver him from these enemies (2 Kgs 16:7-9). That's like a mouse, threatened by a rat, turning to a ravenous alley cat for assistance. The cat is only too delighted to gobble them both up!

Assyria is dealt with in Isaiah 8 in three phases. In phase 1 Assyria comes to the "rescue" of Judah by destroying her enemies Israel and Aram. Verses 1-4 center on the mysterious name Maher-shalal-hash-baz: "Speeding to the Plunder, Hurrying to the Spoil." In the past, God spoke through the prophets both by their words and their lives. In each of these ways God gets this message out to the people through Isaiah. First, he is told to write this name on a large scroll so that people could read it. Second, Isaiah and his wife (the prophetess) had a son whom the Lord commanded to be named "Maher-shalal-hash-baz." The message is that Assyria is going to sweep in and swiftly conquer the two dreaded enemies. The boy born with this long name will become, like Immanuel in Isaiah 7, a living timepiece for the fulfillment of God's purposes through Assyria. Before the boy is old enough to say "Dada" or "Mama"—generally six to twelve months—the wealth and plunder of the two feared kings will be carried off by the king of Assyria. Judah will be spared but only temporarily!

In phase 2 the Lord has more work to do through Assyria: judgment will come on Judah as well. In verse 6 God gives reasons: The people have rejected the "slowly flowing water of Shiloah" and have rejoiced over Rezin and the son of Remaliah. The king of Assyria is likened to an overflowing, powerful river, impressive in its dominance. So the gently flowing water of Shiloah (a pool outside of Jerusalem) represents God's quiet and steady provision for and protection of his people, but the people have tragically rejected it, turning instead with awe and lust toward the perceived power of Assyria. They also rejoiced in the demise of the two nations they dreaded. The Hebrew word translated "rejoiced" implies a great exaltation, a gloating over the destruction of Israel and Aram. A German word captures this: *Schadenfreude*, delight in other people's misery. God hates it because it is basically arrogance; not "There but for the grace of God go I," but rather "Ha! They're finally getting what they deserve!" or "Better you than me!"

So, because of this attitude, God is bringing the king of Assyria with all his pomp, like a river that overflows its banks. It will flood the land of Judah and go right "up to the neck" (v. 8). The flood will destroy the entire land but will spare the head (Jerusalem), a very clear and accurate prophecy of the deliverance of Jerusalem described in Isaiah 37.

This brings us to phase 3: the destruction of Assyria. The flooding river would love to have drowned the head (Jerusalem and King Hezekiah), but God stopped it cold. Phase 3 is clearly described in 8:9-10: any Gentile nation who makes a plan to destroy God's people will themselves be destroyed. This is the power of the word *Immanuel*: God is with us, to protect us from annihilation. So Assyria will itself be annihilated because they came against Judah and sought to destroy it.

So, "God is with us," but who is the "us"? Many citizens of Judah would be slaughtered in phase 2, when the Assyrian river of destruction floods "up to the neck." Who is the "us" God fights for, the "us" included in the word *Immanuel*? The rest of the chapter is devoted to answering that vital question.

The Way of Light

The way of light is described in a variety of ways in Isaiah 8. Verse 11 says, first, it is a life in God's strong grip. God spoke to Isaiah with, literally, "the power of the hand" on him. This strong grip is a sense of the presence of almighty God to shield and protect at every moment but also to guide. Like a godly father putting his strong hand on the shoulder of his toddler son to keep him from running into the street, so the way of light involves this mighty grip of God day by day. Jesus, our good Shepherd, takes hold of each believer in Christ (John 10:28) and leads him or her powerfully through life, ultimately to heaven. So the apostle Paul says in Philippians 3:12 that he daily makes every effort to take hold of heavenly perfection because he also has been taken hold of by Christ Jesus.

Second, the way of light consists in listening to God's Word. Again, in verse 11 not only did the Lord put his strong hand on Isaiah; he also spoke a word of warning to him. Christ's sheep listen to his voice (John 10:27) speaking through the written Word and by the power of the Spirit within. It keeps us from following the way of those other people (Isa 8:11-12).

Thus, third, the way of light is a way apart from the crowd. We march to the beat of a heavenly drummer. We do not fear what they fear (v. 12), and we do not love what they love. It is a life of separation from the world (2 Cor 6:17), not thinking as they think, living as they live, or touching the unclean things they touch.

Fourth, the way of light is a life of a fear that drives out all other fears. Verses 12-13 say, in effect, "Fearing the holy God, we will fear nothing else. But if we don't fear him, we need to fear everything else!" Ahaz and Judah were terrified of Israel and Aram, and their hearts fluttered like trees in a wind. They should have feared the Lord; then they would have feared nothing that could possibly happen. Jesus said plainly, "Don't fear those who kill the body but are not able to kill the soul; rather, fear him who is able to destroy both soul and body in hell" (Matt 10:28).

Fifth, the way of light is a life lived safely in the sanctuary of the Lord's protection. Verse 14 says, "He will be a sanctuary." That means a refuge, a safe haven, like Noah's ark in the flood—a place to flee to when the waters rise. Ultimately, this is a life lived in the shelter of Christ's atoning work on the cross.

Sixth, the way of light is a life lived in a pathway completely bounded by God's Word. Verse 16 says, "Bind up the testimony. Seal up the instruction among my disciples." God's disciples are the ones who listen to the testimony and instruction of his laws. Verse 20 commands them to "Go to God's instruction and testimony!" This is the straight way that leads to heaven, completely bounded left and right by God's perfect laws. Christ perfectly obeyed the law of God for us, and his righteousness is ours by faith. But having been justified by faith, the law's requirements are then fully met in us as we live by the power of the Spirit (Rom 8:4). The way of light is not lawless but gladly submissive to God's perfect laws.

Seventh, the way of light is a life spent inquiring of God (v. 19). We need guidance about the future, and unlike the dark pagans who go to mediums and spiritists, we simply ask God for wisdom (Jas 1:5). It is a life of submissive prayer, saying, "Lord, what is your will for me?"

Eighth and ultimately, it is a life lived by faith in the Lord. Verse 17 says twice, "I will wait for the Lord." Even if it seems he is hiding his face from the house of Jacob, even if great trials and purifying judgments come—still, "I will put my trust in him." Jesus is the final Immanuel, the one whom we must trust continually.

The Way of Darkness

By contrast, the way of darkness is described in this chapter as well. It is a life spent rejecting God's gentle provision, "the slowly flowing water of Shiloah" (v. 6). This rejection of God, exchanging the fountain of living water for the cracked cisterns that can never satisfy, is the fundamental and most shocking sin Israel ever committed (Jer 2:13).

Second, the way of darkness is characterized by a mocking delight in the sufferings of others (v. 6) rather than taking the occasion of those judgments to look inwardly and repent deeply, knowing one deserves the same kinds of judgments. People tend to watch some criminal on trial, some politician who gets caught with a high-priced prostitute, or some athlete who gets caught with drugs, and cluck their tongues self-righteously and say, "Serves them right!" This self-righteousness is the enemy of our souls, as Jesus pointed out in Luke 13:1-5. Unless we too repent, we will all likewise perish!

Third, the way of darkness is a life of stumbling over God and being snared by him (vv. 14-15). Instead of fleeing to Christ for salvation, people stumble over the stumbling stone (Rom 9:32). They can't believe in the doctrine of the incarnation and are offended by the cross. So they end up being crushed by him and snared by him rather than being saved by him.

Fourth, the way of darkness is a life of false spiritual guidance. People are essentially spiritual, and if they reject the true God who is Spirit (John 4:23-24), they will seek some supernatural "voice," some spiritual "guidance" that often comes in the costume of the occult. Isaiah 8:19-20 speaks of those who consult mediums and spiritists, who seek to consult the dead on behalf of the living, instead of going "to God's instruction and testimony!" Rejecting God's Word, they go after demonic voices "who chirp and mutter." And why can't the dead speak to the living? Because the evil dead are too busy screaming in agony in hell, and the righteous dead know that God has spoken adequately in the Word. Instead, it is demons who impersonate the dead and deceive those who consult them.

Therefore, the way of darkness is, fifth, a life of spiritual famine and restless roaming (v. 21). Like the devil who roams the earth (Job 1:7) and homeless demons who restlessly roam through arid places seeking rest (Matt 12:43), these dark people become demonic themselves. They roam through the land, famished for true food, and, enraged, they look upward and curse God. When they look at life on earth, they see only distress, darkness, and the gloom of affliction.

Sixth, and ultimately, such a dark, demonic life can only end in an eternity of thick darkness in hell. Jesus will say, "Depart from me, you who are cursed, into the eternal fire prepared for the devil and his angels!" (Matt 25:41). And they will be thrown into outer darkness where there will be nothing but "weeping and gnashing of teeth" (Matt 25:30).

Christ (Immanuel), the Only Way

As we have mentioned throughout this chapter, the key to everything is Immanuel (v. 8), Jesus Christ, who alone fulfills all the images of this chapter: He is the way of light, and he will judge the way of darkness. He is the refuge to which we flee, and he is the rock of stumbling over which the children of darkness stumble and are snared (vv. 14-15). In the end, we must put our trust in him (v. 17) for the salvation that he alone can give. It also behooves us to assess the course of our lives and be sure that we are on the way of light and not the way of darkness. There are two ways and only two ways. Christ alone leads to heaven.

Reflect and Discuss

1. Comment on the two methods that God used to speak through the prophets in the Old Testament era—their words and their lives (Heb 1:1).
2. Describe the three phases of the Assyrian invasion traced out in this chapter.

3. How do these three phases show the complexity of God's plan and its wisdom? How do they show the sovereignty of God over the events of human nations?

4. Comment on the precision of the prophecy saying that the Assyrian invasion will be like a river that overflows its banks and rises "up to the neck."

5. Compare the two ways to live in Isaiah 8 with the teaching of Christ in Matthew 7:13-14.

6. As you look at the attributes of the way of light in Isaiah 8, how do you see these things lining up with the New Testament's description of the life of a true Christian?

7. How should we understand the role of the law, God's instruction, in the Christian life (vv. 16,20)? Why is it true that we who have been rescued from the law must now live out the law every day by the Spirit?

8. What is the significance of the way of darkness being characterized by the rejection of the "slowly flowing water of Shiloah"? Why do people reject God and go after other sources of protection and guidance?

9. How do you see the occult flourishing in our day?

10. How is Christ (Immanuel) the fulfillment of the themes of this chapter? Why is it vital for each person to line himself up with the characteristics of the way of light versus the way of darkness to be sure that we are truly alive in Christ?

The Eternal Kingdom of the Prince of Peace

ISAIAH 9:1-7

For a child will be born for us, a son will be given to us, and the
government will be on his shoulders. He will be named Wonderful
Counselor, Mighty God, Eternal Father, Prince of Peace. (Isa 9:6)

Main Idea: The deity and humanity of Jesus Christ and the nature of his
kingdom are clearly predicted.

I. **A Light in Darkness (9:1-2)**
II. **The Source of Joy: A Stunning Victory (9:3-5)**
III. **The Surprising Conqueror: Natural, Yet Supernatural (9:6)**
IV. **The Kingdom of Christ (9:7)**
   A. The identity of the King: Jesus Christ
   B. The wealth of his kingdom: increase and peace
   C. The nature of his kingdom: prophetic, secure, holy, and
      eternal
   D. The power of his kingdom: the zeal of the Lord Almighty

---

In every epoch of history, humanity has sought a righteous form of
government, but the depravity in every nation has made it impossible.
The pharaohs of Egypt enslaved people to build their pyramids. The
Assyrians introduced new depths of human brutality into government,
leaving piles of corpses behind them. The Greeks under Alexander the
Great sought to spread the fruits of Greek wisdom, but the despotic
Greek kings that followed him left a trail of defilement in the pages
of history. The Roman Empire brought stable government and a great
road system, propped up with the overwhelming power of their legions.
The barbarian hordes swept across Europe from the icy northland and
the steppes of Asia and put out the lights of culture and of government
for centuries. The "divine right of kings" dominated Christendom in
Western Europe during the Middle Ages with its feudal system, but the
government was only as good or bad as the king's moral character. The
American Revolution sought to break away from monarchy and establish a government "of the people, by the people, for the people," in

Abraham Lincoln's famous words; but the government established here has proven to be far from perfect, corrupted as it is by the sinful hearts "of the people." The twentieth century saw an experiment in governmentally forced sharing for the supposed benefit of the poor, called Communism, and it has proven a gross economic, social, and moral failure all over the world. Representative democracy, with all of its weaknesses and corruptions, still remains the best the human race has developed; but as Winston Churchill said famously, "Democracy is the worst form of government, except for all those other forms that have been tried from time to time" (*By Himself,* 574).

Isaiah 9:6-7, one of the most famous passages in the entire book, answers these hopes and dreams of the world, for it predicts a perfect ruler who will reign forever and ever over a prosperous and peaceful realm. This is Jesus Christ, the perfect Ruler of the world, and the government will be on his shoulders.

A Light in Darkness
ISAIAH 9:1-2

Isaiah 8 ended in the darkness and gloom of a corrupt and wicked people who were seeking occult wisdom from mediums and rejecting the wisdom of God, people who were roaming the earth in angry despair and cursing God. The land of Zebulun and Naphtali, Galilee of the nations (Gentiles), is called a humbled land, a "people walking in darkness," a people living "without hope and without God in the world" (Eph 2:12).

Suddenly, God says, "Let there be light!" and there is light! This was nothing less than the light of the glory of God in the face of Christ (2 Cor 4:6). Jesus came in the power of perfect teaching and of signs and wonders, beginning in the dark region of Galilee. "The people walking in darkness have seen a great light" (Isa 9:2), and Jesus called himself "the light of the world" (John 8:12). He revealed himself first in the synagogue in Galilee, saying that the Spirit of the Lord was on him, not only to be a light shining in a dark place but to recover sight for the blind by releasing prisoners from darkness, in direct fulfillment of the messianic prophecy of Isaiah 61. He also performed his first miracle in Cana of Galilee, changing water into wine. After that, Jesus poured out a river of miracles in Galilee (Matt 4:23-25), the beginning of the unquenchable light of Jesus radiating out into Satan's dark world.

The Source of Joy: A Stunning Victory
ISAIAH 9:3-5

Because of this light shining into darkness, the people respond with overpowering joy. The nation is enlarged, and the people rejoice as on a day when a great war has ended in total victory, with abundant plunder for everybody. The joy is likened to the day of Midian's defeat, a famous story from the era of the judges, when Gideon defeated the overwhelmingly oppressive Midianites without a sword in his hand (Judg 6–7). At that time Israel was powerless to save itself and was enslaved by the Midianites. God caused the terror of the Lord to come on them when the light from Gideon's scant "army" of three hundred men ripped through the darkness. The evil forces of Midian turned on themselves and imploded, destroying one another. As a result, the "oppressive yoke and the rod on their shoulders, the staff of their oppressor" was shattered (Isa 9:4), and all trampling boots and bloodied garments were destined for the fire (v. 5). In the same way, the death and resurrection of Jesus Christ has defeated Satan's seemingly unbreakable yoke of sin and death. Satan's dark kingdom has been routed by implosion—Satan turned his evil weapon of death on Jesus and by killing him destroyed his own kingdom. And we who were enslaved by Satan through fear of death have been released to serve God in joy (Heb 2:14).

The Surprising Conqueror: Natural Yet Supernatural
ISAIAH 9:6

This one verse contains perfect proof of the deity of the Messiah, the doctrine of the incarnation, which was the stumbling block for the Jewish opponents of Jesus. The surprising conqueror who works the stunning victory of verses 1-5 is revealed to be a child given, a son born, described unforgettably in a string of four couplets that mingle his humanity and deity in marvelous balance. The humanity of the Savior is established in the first words: "For a *child* will be born for us, a *son* will be given to us" (emphasis added). The fact that he has come "for us," to benefit us, is also established in these words. As the glorious angel said to those shepherds outside Bethlehem, "Today in the city of David a Savior was born *for you*" (Luke 2:11; emphasis added). So the surprising conqueror will be a child born, a son given. The mingling in Christ of weakness like a lamb and power like a lion is also revealed in Revelation 5:5-6, the infinite mystery of the "frailty" of the incarnate God.

On the shoulders of this child is laid the weight of the government of his people. He at last is the answer to the quest for a perfect and lasting government. His shoulders will bear that weight, and they will not buckle. As Jesus said, "All authority has been given to me in heaven and on earth" (Matt 28:18).

Next comes the mysterious series of four couplets, four pairs of two words linked, a mingling of supernatural and natural, of God and man.

Wonderful Counselor: the word translated "wonderful" refers to the ability to work supernatural signs (Exod 3:20); the word *counselor* refers to the giving of wise advice, as advisors to the king would do (2 Sam 16:23). Jesus came both to do signs and wonders and to give wisdom by his teachings.

Mighty God: the word *God* ascribed to someone who is a child born absolutely clinches the doctrine of the incarnation—Jesus was a human baby who was also called "Mighty God." The word translated "mighty" was a common one for powerful men, warriors who could carry the day by the power of their military prowess (Judg 11:1); it is a natural word but still descriptive of great power. But the word translated "God" (Hb *el*) was absolutely divine, the most common word in the Hebrew Bible for deity.[4] These words show the infinite power of Jesus Christ, our Savior, who is an omnipotent warrior and who will someday return to earth to slay all his enemies with the sword coming out of his mouth (Rev 19:11-16).

Eternal Father: Again, a mingling of the natural with the supernatural. The title *father* is obviously an everyday word, but to couple it with the word *eternal* makes it supernatural—a father whose going forth is from eternity past (Mal 5:2) and who will continue a father forever. Ascribing fatherhood to Jesus is unusual, given that we usually reserve it for God the Father; but Jesus does play a fatherly role toward his disciples, for he often used "son" or "daughter" when addressing others affectionately (Matt 9:2; Mark 5:34).

Prince of Peace: Jesus reigns as a *prince*, a common word for a government official (Isa 34:12; 49:7), but he will be a ruler who brings peace and is characterized by peace. This is the very thing that most warlike conqueror kings can never bring about, but Jesus speaks peace to his disciples after his resurrection victory (John 20:19,21,26) and previously

---

[4] Assuming *el*, *eloah*, and *elohim* are all forms of the same root and taking *yhwh* as a proper noun, not a word for deity.

had said, "Peace I leave with you. My peace I give to you. I do not give to you as the world gives. Don't let your heart be troubled or fearful" (John 14:27). Most of all, Jesus gives eternal peace with God by his death on the cross (Rom 5:1).

The Kingdom of Christ
ISAIAH 9:7

So this is the supernatural yet natural conqueror who comes to rule. What is the nature of his perfect kingdom? Verse 7 describes it magnificently! The CSB says, "The dominion will be vast, and its prosperity will never end." That is a fine translation, but perhaps more dynamic is the more famous KJV: "Of the *increase* of his government and peace there shall be no end" (emphasis added). What is the "increase" of Christ's government? How is it that it will never end? The Hebrew word translated "increase" (or "vast") gives a sense of ever-growing abundance (7:22), of multiplication (Gen 1:28). So Christ's kingdom will be characterized by the never-ending multiplication of its prosperity. How can that be true in heaven, especially because there will no longer be babies born or any form of procreation (Matt 22:30)? I think that in heaven Christ's subjects will be morally perfect and will not forget anything they have learned; but they will still be learning, constantly growing in their estimation of the greatness of Christ's person and achievements. We will never stop increasing in our love for him and our passionate, knowledgeable worship of him.

He will reign on David's throne and over his kingdom, in direct fulfillment of the promises made to David (2 Sam 7:13,16). God promised David that a son from his own body would have a throne that God would establish forever. Jesus fulfills that by reigning as the Son of David (Matt 1:1) forever. And David himself will be on his face before his infinitely greater Son, worshiping him with the rest of the redeemed forever. Jesus will "establish and sustain it with justice and righteousness." His kingdom will be a perfect reflection of his own character, of which it is said in Hebrews 1:8-9, "Your throne, O God, is forever and ever, and the scepter of your kingdom is a scepter of justice. You have loved righteousness and hated lawlessness." In other words, a perfectly righteous King who loves righteousness and hates wickedness will make sure that those attributes will characterize his kingdom forever, protecting the poor and needy rather than exploiting them.

This kingdom was established the moment Christ came to earth, and it will never end. And what guarantees that these things will most certainly come to pass? "The zeal of the LORD of Armies will accomplish this." God's zeal for the glory of his Son will make this happen forever, and no power in heaven or earth or under the earth can stop it.

Application

Understand now, by faith, that the victory of Jesus Christ over sin and death is total and complete. He did it alone, no one helped him, so that all the glory would go to him. As in the day of Midian's defeat, he caused Satan's kingdom to destroy itself. He gives us the plunder forever: eternal life, peace, righteousness, good counsel. Rejoice greatly in this! Be certain that you are restoring your joy in Christ's victory over sin and death every single day. Say to your soul, "Why, my soul, are you so dejected? Why are you in such turmoil? Rejoice in the victory Christ has won for you!"

Meditate on the awesome titles given to Jesus Christ in this chapter: Wonderful Counselor, Mighty God, Everlasting Father, Prince of Peace. Allow each word to have a time in your meditation. Worship Jesus for each aspect of these titles.

Resolve to obey Jesus as your King more and more. This is by faith and by the power of the Spirit. Jesus is a ruler who has saved sinners from their rebellion against his rule. Submit fully to his authority.

Look forward to an eternity of learning more and more about Jesus: "of the increase of his government and peace there will be no end" (9:7 KJV). Heaven will not be a static, boring place but a place of rich discoveries of Jesus forever and ever.

Finally, share the gospel with others so that his kingdom might increase now, on earth, before the end of time comes.

Reflect and Discuss

1. How does this prophecy help prove the deity of Christ?
2. How is Jesus a light for a people walking in darkness? What is the nature of that darkness? How does Jesus shine in this dark world?
3. How is the defeat of Midian under Gideon a prophetic picture of Christ's victory over Satan at the cross (Judg 6–7; Heb 2:14)?
4. How does Jesus's resurrection victory bring joy like a harvest or military conquest? What is the spoil Jesus gives for his victory?

5. How does the combination of son/child and "Mighty God" prove the deity of Christ in verse 6?
6. What is the significance of the title "Wonderful Counselor"? How does it point to the two great aspects of Jesus's earthly ministry: mighty words and amazing deeds?
7. Does it seem strange to you to call Jesus "Everlasting Father"? How is Jesus like a father?
8. How is Jesus the "Prince of Peace"? How would you relate this to Romans 5:1? How about Philippians 4:6-7?
9. What does verse 7 teach you about the nature of Jesus's kingdom?
10. What is the significance of the statement in verse 7 that "the zeal of the LORD" will bring this about? What is zeal? How is God the Father zealous to establish the kingdom of his Son? What does this teach you about their relationship?

His Hand Is Still Raised

ISAIAH 9:8–10:4

In all this, his anger has not turned away, and his hand is still raised to strike. (Isa 10:4)

Main Idea: God's hand of wrath is raised to strike sinners with judgment, and the cross of Christ is the only refuge to which we can flee for escape.

I.   The Wrath of God: Pure, Holy, and Perfect
II. Judgment 1: Stubborn Pride Results in Invasion (9:8-12).
III. Judgment 2: Unrepentance Results in Leaders' Removal (9:13-17).
IV. Judgment 3: Growing Wickedness Results in Self-Destruction (9:18-21).
V.   Judgment 4: Social Injustice Results in Conquest (10:1-4).
VI. The Only Refuge: The Cross of Christ

The Wrath of God: Pure, Holy, and Perfect

On July 8, 1741, a substitute preacher stood up to preach a sermon in the parish church of Enfield, Connecticut. The preacher chose as his text Deuteronomy 32:35 (KJV), "Their foot shall slide in due time." It is a passage that makes plain the inevitability of God's judgment on sinners in Israel. The preacher laid out his doctrine clearly: "There is nothing that keeps wicked men at any one moment out of hell, but the mere pleasure of God. By the mere pleasure of God, I mean his sovereign pleasure, his arbitrary will, restrained by no obligation, hindered by no manner of difficulty." He then unfolded quite plainly the almost indescribable wrath of God against unredeemed sinners. The result of that sermon was extraordinary: people gasped in horror, pleading that there might be some escape from the seemingly inevitable wrath of God. Revival broke out that day in Enfield, and the sovereign grace of God rescued many from his own wrath through faith in Christ.

The substitute preacher's name was Jonathan Edwards, and his sermon, "Sinners in the Hands of an Angry God," became one of the most famous in the history of the American church. But some would say it was one of the most infamous sermons in the history of the American church, for many struggle to accept the underlying premise of Edwards's sermon: that God has a perfectly righteous wrath against sin, and that he steps into human history to pour out that wrath whenever he chooses. In 1961 Phyllis McGinley lampooned this view of God in a poem titled "The Theology of Jonathan Edwards":

> And, if they had been taught aright,
> Small children, carried bedwards,
> Would shudder lest they meet that night
> The God of Mr. Edwards.
> Abraham's God, the Wrathful One,
> Intolerant of error—
> Not God the Father or the Son
> But God the Holy Terror. (McGinley, *Times Three*, 19)

But every thoughtful Christian must ask, Does God act in human history bringing out righteous judgments on sinners for their sins? And do those earthly judgments portend a far more terrifying and eternal judgment in hell? The biblical answer to both questions is yes. And both are laid out plainly for us in the book of Isaiah. Isaiah 9:9–10:4 reveals a very clear declaration of a series of judgments God pours out on Israel for their sins. Four times in this section we have this powerful phrase: "In all this, his anger has not turned away, and his hand is still raised to strike" (9:12,17,21; 10:4). Isaiah is plainly saying that God's wrath is not easily extinguished; it is relentless, terrifying, inescapable. Isaiah is saying to Israel, "Yes, God has struck you very hard. But he isn't finished yet; there's still more to come!" This repeated assertion teaches us much about the wrath and judgment of God. But it also leaves the profound question, How then will his anger be removed? What will lower his hand so that he is no longer poised to strike sinners like us? Ultimately, this chapter points powerfully to the finished work of Jesus Christ on the cross as the only propitiation, the only atonement by which the wrath of God is satisfied and sinners like us reconciled to a holy God.

The Bible reveals that God is a passionate being, full of what we call emotions. He is not the God of the stoics, completely unaffected by the events of human history. Rather, the God of the Bible is a God filled with passions, including joy over a single sinner who repents (Luke 15:10). Our human emotions are a significant part of being created in the image of God. But because of sin, our emotions are badly polluted by the corruption of our hearts. This is especially evident in our anger, which James calls "moral filth" (Jas 1:21). Our anger is frequently like a mind-altering drug whose influence causes us to do shocking things for which we later tearfully repent. Not so with God. God is "slow to anger" (Exod 34:6) and exceedingly patient with sinners. But when the time comes for God to express his wrath, the display is terrifying and he is implacable, except by himself. Only God can stop God's wrath. But unlike ours, it is always pure and holy, absolutely consistent with his character and his stated purposes. And he never has cause to repent later of anything he does in his anger.

By the time of Isaiah, God had been provoked for centuries by Israel's stubborn sinfulness. In Isaiah 9–10 the time has come for God to raise his hand in anger and strike, and he does so again and again, with fearsome result. Four judgments fall on Israel in this chapter, always with just cause. And in the midst of it all, God calls on his people to turn to him in repentance and forsake the sins that brought about his wrath.

Judgment 1: Stubborn Pride Results in Invasion
ISAIAH 9:8-12

God had warned Israel ("Jacob" or "Ephraim") through his prophets repeatedly (v. 8) and has now brought some significant acts of judgment: "Aram from the east and Philistia from the west" have already devastated Israel (v. 12), leveling some buildings and cutting down some trees (v. 10). Amazingly, however, the people of Israel have not repented as they should have at this judgment (v. 13). Instead, they responded with arrogance of heart, saying that whatever was destroyed by these invasions, they would rebuild better than it ever was before. But the sinful nation has missed the point. These invasions did not come to improve Israel but to judge her for her many idolatries. God's anger has not yet been removed, and his hand is still raised to strike: Rezin's[5] adversaries are coming—the terrifying Assyrians!

Judgment 2: Unrepentance Results in Leaders' Removal
ISAIAH 9:13-17

Having struck the people with invasions from the Arameans and the Philistines, God called on them to repent, to turn to him who struck

---

[5] Rezin was king of Aram, Israel's enemy. See commentary on Isaiah 7.

them to seek the Lord of Armies (v. 13). This is a consistent pattern in Scripture: when God brings a judgment on his people, they are always called on to search their hearts and lives for the sins that caused that judgment and to return with grieving and repentance to the one who struck them. James 4:9-10 gives a clear pattern for us as Christians: "Be miserable and mourn and weep. Let your laughter be turned to mourning and your joy to gloom. Humble yourselves before the Lord, and he will exalt you." In Israel's case there was no such grief-filled humbling. So God must bring stiff-necked people even more severe judgments: he cuts off the leaders who brought the nation into these sins to begin with. God decrees the decapitation of the nation, its leaders and officials cut off; he also removes the prophets who were supposed to speak God's words to the people (vv. 14-15). As a result of their evil leadership, everyone is a godless evildoer. From the beginning of the history of the divided kingdom, the northern nation of Israel was led into sin by her first king, Jeroboam, who set up idols and commanded the people to go there to worship instead of to God's only legitimate temple in Jerusalem. After him, a series of bad kings and false prophets continued to mislead Israel. So God raises his hand to strike them and cut them off. Yet after all this, his hand is not lowered; it is still raised for the next strike.

Judgment 3: Growing Wickedness Results in Self-Destruction
ISAIAH 9:18-21

One thing that the Bible reveals about sin is that it metastasizes like cancer, growing larger and spreading rapidly throughout the body. Adam and Eve eat a piece of fruit in Genesis 3; Cain murders his brother early in Genesis 4; later in Genesis 4 Lamech takes two wives and murders a man for insulting him; and by Genesis 6 the thoughts of people all over the earth were only evil all the time. So it was in Israel. In Isaiah 9:18-21 we have a wickedness that burns like a fire and makes the whole forest go up in smoke. People don't care about their relatives and neighbors; all hearts are grown cold and hard with sin (v. 19). Their lustful cravings for meat (v. 20) are so overpowering they are even pictured as feasting on their own flesh. This may be a metaphor for self-destructive brother-to-brother conflict, Manasseh against Ephraim, Ephraim against Manasseh, both of them against Judah. As they are living like this, God is scorching the land with his wrath (v. 19), trying to bring them to repentance. The wicked become like chaff for the fire, going up in smoke under the wrath of the Lord Almighty.

Judgment 4: Social Injustice Results in Conquest
ISAIAH 10:1-4

In the final paragraph of this section, Isaiah exposes the social injustice that was enraging the Lord's heart. The leaders were making unjust laws to strip the poor, widows, and orphans of their meager possessions rather than protecting and providing for them (v. 1). This outrageous injustice further inflamed the heart of God, moving him to bring judgment from far away—a distant nation would come and bring a devastating "day of punishment" (v. 3), and what would those mighty tyrants and oppressors of the poor do then? Where could they run and hide from the uplifted hand of Almighty God (v. 4)? What good will the plunder they have taken from the poor do them on that day when they are enslaved or killed? For God's hand is still raised, ready to strike even more fiercely.

The Only Refuge: The Cross of Christ

In 10:3 Isaiah asks the question that should burn in every heart after reading this section of Scripture, with its repeated statements of God's wrathful hand continually raised: "What will you do on the day of punishment when devastation comes from far away? Who will you run to for help?" Is there a refuge from the terrifying wrath of God? The judgments described in this section are actually as nothing compared to the infinite, eternal wrath of God poured out on sinners in hell (Rev 14:10-11). There, unforgiven sinners will forever experience God's raised hand, striking them in righteous wrath for their sins. Is there a refuge to which we can fly to escape hell? The consistent teaching of this chapter and of the Bible is that only God can turn his own wrath away. But the magnificent good news of the gospel is that God has provided in Jesus Christ a refuge to which we can run and hide! Jesus Christ is the propitiation for our sins (Rom 3:25; 1 John 2:2); he is the one who drank the bitter cup of God's wrath (Matt 26:39). Flee to him! Escape to him! Christ is the only refuge, the only hiding place from the coming wrath.

Reflect and Discuss

1. Why is it vital for us to understand properly the biblical doctrine of the wrath of God?
2. Why do you think so many seek to undercut or change this doctrine by asserting that God has no such wrath against sin?
3. How do the judgments of God against the nation of Israel stand as a permanent example of his character and his intentions for every nation?
4. What is the significance of the repeated phrase, "In all this, his anger has not turned away, and his hand is still raised to strike"?
5. What are the various judgments that God brings in this section of Isaiah?
6. What are the reasons given for the various judgments of God in this section?
7. How does this section of Isaiah reveal God's passion for the poor, widow, and orphan?
8. Why do leaders come under special judgment?
9. How does this chapter point to the finished work of Christ as the only refuge from God's raised hand of wrath?
10. How is hell infinitely worse than any judgment of God that he works on the earth?

The God Who Tests Motives

ISAIAH 10:5-34

But this is not what he intends; this is not what he plans. It is his intent to destroy and to cut off many nations. (Isa 10:7)

Main Idea: God uses Assyria to punish Israel, then he judges Assyria for doing it. Why? Because of their motives.

I. God's Surprising Messengers: The Assyrian Army
II. God's Even More Surprising Message: Woe to Assyria!
III. The Key Issue: "What He Intends" (10:7)
IV. Assyria's Motives Displayed (10:7-14)
V. Assyria's Judgment Described (10:15-19,24-34)
VI. Israel's Future Foretold: "The Remnant Will Return" (10:20-23).
VII. True Deliverance Worked by Christ

One of the most difficult aspects of Christian theology is to understand how God's eternal plans, made from before the foundation of the world, are carried out to the letter while at the same time God holds all people accountable for their actions. Though the complete solution to this problem will elude us, Isaiah 10 gives us a big piece of the puzzle. In this chapter God raises up the Assyrian army as the rod of his anger to judge his people, Israel. Then God judges Assyria for doing the exact thing that he dispatched them to do! How is it just for God to use evil people to do key aspects of his eternal plan then to judge them for doing the exact thing that he ordained for them to do? The key piece of the puzzle comes in verse 7: What did the Assyrians intend? What was in their hearts during their actions? Isaiah 10 reveals that God judges people for their motives. A faith-filled meditation on Isaiah 10 will result in a far more mature understanding of the way God rules human history and judges the human actors in his play.

God's Surprising Messengers: The Assyrian Army

In verse 6 God says of Assyria, "I will send him against a godless nation." This is a doubly surprising statement. First, the "godless nation" is the northern kingdom of Israel, the descendants of Abraham, his chosen friend. They are called "godless" because they have rejected the true God and have embraced idols. Second, God chooses to send Assyria, generally regarded as an even more wicked nation than Israel, to punish his own people. It is so difficult to conceive of the wicked Assyrian nation "on mission" from God, but so they are—unwittingly, however! God calls Assyria "the rod of my anger," saying that the staff in their hands is his wrath. For God to "send" such an evil nation against his people is so stunning! It teaches us that God is the ruler of all nations, including the most powerful and the most wicked. God sits "enthroned above the circle of the earth; its inhabitants are like grasshoppers" (Isa 40:22). God moves his little finger, and massive nations mobilize. God has a work to do, not only against the northern kingdom of Israel but also against Mount Zion (Jerusalem; 10:12). And that work will be brutal; God is sending the Assyrians against the objects of his rage to trample them and seize plunder. Why? Because both Israel and Judah have broken his covenant and thrown his laws behind their backs (Neh 9:26).

God's Even More Surprising Message: Woe to Assyria!

But God has an even more shocking message for Assyria, the rod of his anger: Woe to you for doing it! God is going to judge the Assyrians for the very actions he is sending them to do. How could that possibly be just? How we struggle with such questions! But there it is plainly in verse 5: "Woe!" And he is even more plain in the rest of the prophecy: "But when the Lord finishes all his work against Mount Zion and Jerusalem, he will say, 'I will punish the king of Assyria for his arrogant acts and the proud look in his eyes'" (v. 12). Verses 16-19 describe the destruction of Assyria by a terrifying wasting disease. So God uses Assyria, and then he judges them severely for doing the very thing that he ordained.

The Key Issue: "What He Intends"
ISAIAH 10:7

The key piece to this timeless theological puzzle is found in verse 7: "But this is not what he intends; this is not what he plans. It is his intent to destroy and to cut off many nations." God rightly judges Assyria not for what they did but for their motives behind their actions. They are just as godless in slaughtering Israel as Israel was in their idolatries. The motive of the Assyrians had nothing to do with the glory of God or his righteous rage against the godless nation of Israel. They were not angels of vengeance, swinging the sickle of God's wrath out of holy zeal for God's honor, as the angels in the book of Revelation do, for then they would have been guiltless for the exact same actions (cf. Phinehas in Num 25). The Assyrians have no zeal for the glory of God, and therefore God judges them for the very actions he ordains. God searches hearts and minds and gives to each person what he deserves (Rev 2:23). Anything that does not come from faith is sin (Rom 14:23; Heb 11:6).

Assyria's Motives Displayed
ISAIAH 10:7-14

So if the glory of God was not the motive of the Assyrians, what was? In verses 7-14 Isaiah is clearly laying out the mind-set of the Assyrian empire builders: their purpose was to destroy and cut off many nations for their own glory and pleasures. They arrogantly boast that all of their commanders are like kings (v. 8), and Samaria (Israel) is no different than any of the small nations they have already conquered (Calno, Carchemish, Hamath, and Arpad; v. 9). Verse 12 makes plain the arrogance in the hearts of the Assyrian king and his commanders—they have a satanic pride bordering on self-worship. They believe that everything they have accomplished militarily has been done by their own wisdom and strength for their own glory (v. 13), giving no credit to the God who held in his hand their life-breath and all their ways (Dan 5:23). Their arrogance is breathtaking, and God will not allow it to go unpunished.

Assyria's Judgment Described
ISAIAH 10:15-19,24-34

God makes it plain in verse 15 how offensive Assyria's pride is in his sight. Assyria is merely a tool in God's omnipotent hand, like an ax he's using to chop down a tree. How, then, can the ax boast against the one wielding it? How ridiculous is human pride, when apart from God we can't even take a single breath! We are merely like a wooden rod in his hand; he is the true actor in history. So God speaks his verdict against arrogant Assyria: they will die by a wasting disease; all their powerful warriors will burn up by fever and die in a single day (vv. 16-18). Later, in Isaiah 37, we will have the fulfillment of this judgment. But it is this passage that tells us why a hundred and eighty-five thousand Assyrians died in one night at the hand of the angel of the Lord. The result of that wasting and burning disease will be that Assyria's "forest" (warriors) will be so few that a child could count them (v. 19). This is something God will do out of zeal for his own glory (v. 17).

God then comforts the remnant of his people in verses 24-34 with details of Assyria's defeat. He tells them not to be afraid of the Assyrians because God will deal with them in the end (vv. 24-25). God's anger against his people will abate, and his wrath will then turn to the destruction of Assyria. On the day that God deals with Assyria, the yoke of Assyrian tyranny will fall from their necks. Verses 28-32 give a travelogue of the impending invasion of Judah, as step by step the Assyrian juggernaut gets closer and closer to Jerusalem. But all they will be able to do to that protected city will be to shake their fist at it (v. 32). God will slaughter them before the very walls of Jerusalem as a forest is laid low by an ax.

Israel's Future Foretold: "The Remnant Will Return"
ISAIAH 10:20-23

By contrast, God will preserve a remnant of his people. The word *remnant* appears in each of verses 20, 21, and 22. The remnant is chosen by God's grace (Rom 11:5), and it is for their benefit that God does all of this. After the Assyrian invasion, the godly remnant will have learned never again to trust in the power of human armies. By the eternal plan and sovereign power of almighty God, a remnant would return to the Lord (v. 21). Tragically, though the physical descendants of Abraham were as numerous as the sand of the sea, only a remnant would return because God had decreed an overwhelming and righteous destruction.

These words are incredibly significant in redemptive history. The apostle Paul quotes them in Romans 9:27-28 to explain why only some Jews were believing in Jesus. Throughout Israel's history, only a small portion of the nation were genuine believers. Unbelieving physical descendants of Abraham have always been as "godless" as the Assyrians and all the other pagans. And in Isaiah 10 God makes it plain that he will wipe out both the godless Hebrews and the godless Gentiles alike. But in Christ there is a remnant chosen by grace from both Jews and Gentiles (Rom 11:5; see also 9:24). That remnant will return to a genuine and lasting trust in the Lord and will dwell in the perfect and final "promised land": the new heaven and new earth.

True Deliverance Worked by Christ

The Old Testament context of this chapter can obscure how timeless these themes are. Every single day, the sovereign plan of God is unfolding. In God's mind, that plan has been worked out down to the smallest detail, even before the foundation of the world. It involves many evil people doing things that are contrary to his laws, but all of them part of God's wise and complex plan. The most evil thing that has ever happened on earth is the crucifixion of Jesus Christ. Many evil people did many evil things to bring about Christ's death—all of them were planned by almighty God before he created the universe. Isaiah 10 tells us quite plainly how God could ordain that Judas Iscariot could betray Jesus for thirty pieces of silver, and yet he could condemn Judas for such an act. Jesus said concerning Judas, "The Son of Man will go just as it is written about him, but woe to that man by whom the Son of Man is betrayed!" (Matt 26:24). How could that be just? How could Judas act in the preordained way ("just as it is written") and still have the "woe" stated over him, having it be said by Jesus, "It would have been better for him if he had not been born"? According to Isaiah 10:7, it all has to do with Judas's motive: love for money (John 12:6). God judged him for his motives, just as he will do to every person who ever lived. Our biggest problem is that we cannot survive such scrutiny. Our motives naturally are no better than those of the "godless" Jews or the vicious Assyrians or the money-loving Judas.

The greatest yoke of bondage (v. 27) in human history is sin. In Christ alone can that yoke be broken and fall from our necks. Christ's death on the cross and his resurrection from the dead is the true deliverance that he works for the remnant chosen by grace. Amazingly, God will then judge the remnant based on Christ's motives and actions (not ours), his perfect righteousness imputed to us by faith.

Reflect and Discuss

1. How is the problem of divine sovereignty and human responsibility addressed in this chapter?
2. What are the two surprising aspects of God's statement that he will "send" Assyria against a "godless nation"?
3. Why is it frequently troubling to people that God uses wicked men to achieve holy ends?
4. On what basis does God say he will judge Assyria for doing the very thing he sent them to do?

5. Why is God so concerned about the motives of our hearts?
6. What is ultimately the only proper motive for every action (1 Cor 10:31)?
7. How does the arrogance of the Assyrians get exposed in this chapter? How do we struggle with similar attitudes of pride as are displayed in verse 13? Why does God hate such pride?
8. How should this chapter humble us?
9. How does this chapter relate to the statement Jesus makes about Judas in Matthew 26:24? Specifically, how does the question of motive raised in Isaiah 10:7 help us understand how God could judge Judas for doing the very thing he had ordained Judas to do?
10. How does verse 27 point to the deliverance worked by Christ?

The Perfect Nature of Christ's Glorious Kingdom

ISAIAH 11

On that day the Root of Jesse will stand as a banner for the peoples. The nations will look to him for guidance, and his resting place will be glorious. (Isa 11:10)

Main Idea: The perfect future reign of Jesus Christ is described, with its humble beginnings, its irresistible power, its absolute justice, its perfect peace, and its universal reach to the ends of the earth.

I. **The Humble Beginning of Christ's Kingdom (11:1)**
II. **The Divine Power of Christ's Kingdom (11:2-3)**
III. **The Absolute Justice of Christ's Kingdom (11:3-5)**
IV. **The Perfect Peace of Christ's Kingdom (11:6-9)**
V. **The Universal Reach of Christ's Kingdom (11:10-16)**

Every four years American voters have to weigh and evaluate a new array of grandiose promises made by candidates aspiring to the office of president. Those with a sense of history will be familiar with the broken promises made in these campaigns:

- Woodrow Wilson's pledge in 1916 to keep the US out of the "Great War" (World War I), broken in 1917 with the declaration of war on Germany.
- Hebert Hoover's pledge in 1928 to end poverty in America, famously promising to put "a chicken in every pot and a car in every garage." This promise was broken within one year by the worst economic depression in the history of this country.
- Franklin Roosevelt's pledges in 1932 to maintain balanced budgets and to decrease government spending by 25 percent, as well as his pledge in 1940 to keep the US out of World War II—all of them broken.
- George H. W. Bush's campaign pledge, "Read my lips: no new taxes." The pledge was famously broken in his 1990 budget compromise to reduce the federal deficit.

Throughout history people have sought the perfect society and the perfect government to rule it. The yearning for this explains why people so consistently believe new promises of a grand vision of government. But the amazing promises of Isaiah 11 for the kingdom of Jesus Christ are far more glorious, and certainly more eternal, than all of the governmental promises in history.

The Humble Beginning of Christ's Kingdom
ISAIAH 11:1

The perfect kingdom and its perfect King emerged from quite a humble origin. Nothing could be more bleak than the picture of a stump where once a mighty tree flourished. Verse 1 speaks of a shoot coming up from the stump of Jesse, who was King David's father. So the tree of Jesse refers to the promise made to David to have his descendent sit on an eternal throne (2 Sam 7:12-13). But because of their sins, God exiled Judah, and the promises made to David seemed to have come to nothing. After the exile to Babylon, the names in Jesus's kingly genealogy in Matthew 1 are obscure. The tree of Jesse had become a stump. But God willed that there be life in the roots of that stump, as he said he would in Isaiah 6:13. And out of this totally humbled obscurity would come a "shoot" and a "branch" to fulfill the promises to David. This prophecy will be restated plainly in Isaiah 53:2: "He grew up before him like a young plant and like a root out of dry ground." The humble origins of the most glorious King and kingdom in history were these: a conquered people in a lowly backwater of the Roman Empire—obscure, poor, powerless.

The Divine Power of Christ's Kingdom
ISAIAH 11:2-3

However humble were the origins of this supernatural Branch coming from the lineage of Jesse, yet he would be perfectly anointed with the Spirit of God for his task as King. The word "Christ" (Hb "Messiah") literally means "Anointed One," and the oil poured on the head of a king represented the outpouring of the Spirit on him for his task. Jesus was perfectly and completely anointed by the Spirit. It can be observed that there is a sevenfold description of the Spirit in these verses: he is the Spirit of the Lord, of wisdom and of understanding, of counsel and of strength, of knowledge and of the fear of the Lord (v. 2). This sevenfold Spirit represents the perfection of Christ's anointing, and it is repeated in the Trinitarian vision in Revelation 1:4 ("the seven spirits before his throne"). This anointing of Jesus shows comprehensive wisdom and power—the two attributes an effective king needs.

Yet all of this wisdom and power does not in any way challenge the overarching authority of almighty God, as human kings usually do in their arrogance. Rather, King Jesus will "delight . . . in the fear of the LORD" (v. 3). That means that the exaltation of Christ is actually an exaltation of God himself.

The Absolute Justice of Christ's Kingdom
ISAIAH 11:3-5

Jesus judges perfectly, not relying on his five senses but reading people's hearts by the standard of absolute truth. Therefore his judgment will always be perfectly righteous because he seeks to please the Father (John 5:30). Because Jesus delights in the fear of the Lord, he has wrapped righteousness and faithfulness as a sash around his waist (v. 5); and by this wisdom and power he will judge the poor righteously and slay the wicked powerfully—with merely the command from his lips. Thus, in Christ's kingdom righteousness will be perfect and crime will be gone forever. Scripture teaches that Jesus will be the Judge of the whole earth, and every human being who has ever lived will stand before him to be judged (Matt 25:31-32; John 5:22; 2 Cor 5:10). At that judgment, Christ will weed out of his kingdom all those guilty of lawlessness and will destroy them eternally in hell (Matt 13:41). Those saved by his grace will shine in perfect righteousness forever.

The Perfect Peace of Christ's Kingdom
ISAIAH 11:6-9

Human governments and societies cannot be characterized by perfect peace because of the seething wickedness of the natural heart (Isa 57:20-21). Because of the righteousness and power of Christ's judgments, there will only be perfect peace forever in his kingdom. Verses 6-9 capture that peace in powerful imagery. These well-known verses are favorites for those who teach a literal millennium, the thousand-year reign of Christ physically on earth. The doctrine of the millennium comes from

Revelation 20:1-7; it is distinct from the eternal state (the new heaven and new earth) in that there is still natural life, including births, sin, and death.[6] This passage speaks of infants playing beside the cobra's pit and not being harmed (v. 8). So also animals that would naturally have been enemies (wolves and lambs, leopards and goats, calves and lions) will live in complete harmony with each other, the predator no longer consuming the prey. However, all of these things could still be true in the eternal state as well—all except the existence of infants. So whether these verses refer to the millennium or the eternal state, they will most certainly be literally fulfilled in Christ's future kingdom—a kingdom of almost indescribable tranquility. The consummation of that kingdom is captured powerfully in verse 9: "The land will be as full of the knowledge of the LORD as the sea is filled with water." No longer studying how to kill one another or feed their own lusts, redeemed sinners will study the Lord's glory in all aspects of a magnificent creation.

The Universal Reach of Christ's Kingdom
ISAIAH 11:10-16

Verse 10 stands as a pinnacle for the glorious spread of the gospel of Jesus Christ to the ends of the earth: this humble King, the Root of Jesse, will stand prominently before the eyes of all the nations on the face of the earth; and his resting place will be glorious. As we've seen in Isaiah 2, people from all over the earth will stream to that banner, loving and worshiping Jesus Christ as the fulfillment of all their aspirations for a perfect king and a perfect society. The land he rules will radiate with his glory, and all creation will glow with astonishing beauty. Christ will reach out his sovereign hand to gather the scattered children of God and make them one (John 11:52). In Isaiah 11:11-16 their nations of origin are listed as "Assyria, Egypt, Pathros, Cush, Elam, Shinar, Hamath, and the coasts and islands of the west." These localities symbolize the geographical extent of the spread of the gospel, beginning in Jerusalem and to the ends of the earth (Luke 24:47; Acts 1:8). The streaming of "his people" will be like the original exodus of Israel from Egypt (vv. 15-16), only this time it will include Jews and Gentiles alike.

---

[6] See commentary on Isaiah 65:17-25.

Application

We must learn not to judge God's work by mere external appearance. The Jews and the lineage of Jesse seemed to be completely cut off, but God ordained an infinite glory to arise from the stump of Jesse. So also Christ's kingdom, so silently and imperceptibly advancing among the meek and lowly of the earth, cannot be assessed by the five senses. We who have embraced Christ and entered his kingdom should be fully dedicated to advancing the gospel by proclamation, not looking for utopian societies to come by flawed human governments. Every presidential campaign carries the usual promises, and most of them fail in the end. Christ's promised kingdom is far more glorious and can never fail.

Reflect and Discuss

1. How does this chapter address the hopes of all humanity for a perfect government and a perfect society?
2. Why is it impossible for human governments (kings) to make good on their grand visions for a perfect society? Why are Christ's promises different and better than theirs?
3. What is the significance of the image of a shoot coming up from the stump of Jesse? How is it easy for us to underestimate what God is doing in the world when we judge by mere appearance?
4. How does Isaiah 11:1 relate to Isaiah 53:2? How does Christ fulfill each of these verses by his humble birth and absence of physical splendor?
5. How does the sevenfold Spirit of God perfectly endow Jesus to reign over his kingdom? How do these words point to a perfect combination of wisdom and power?
6. Why are wisdom and power indispensable for a perfect King? How would love fit into those attributes?
7. How do you understand the promises of verses 6-9? Do you see a description of the millennial reign of Christ here? Or could this be the eternal state? The problem with the first: there seems to be no end mentioned in the text, but the millennium will come to an end; the problem with the second: how can there be infants in the eternal state?
8. What does it mean to delight in the fear of the Lord? How do these words seem contradictory? How does Jesus perfectly harmonize them and make the fear of the Lord delightful?

9. How does the promise that the earth will be "as full of the knowledge of the LORD as the sea is filled with water" point to the glories of life in Christ's eternal kingdom?
10. How does verse 10 point to the advance of the gospel of Jesus Christ to the ends of the earth? What details come in verses 11-16 that help us understand the spread of the gospel among Gentile nations?

Celebrating God's All-Conquering Grace

ISAIAH 12

On that day you will say: "I will give thanks to you, LORD, although you were angry with me. Your anger has turned away, and you have comforted me." (Isa 12:1)

Main Idea: Here is a short psalm of praise for God's saving work for us in Christ, coupled with a rousing call to energetic effort in proclaiming the gospel worldwide.

I. **For the Praise of His Glorious Grace**
   A. God's ultimate goal: his glory
   B. God's second highest goal: our joy in him
   C. What grace had to conquer
   D. Praise: the healed from insanity to healthy delight
II. **Our Personal Theme: "God Is My Salvation" (12:1-2).**
   A. Personal salvation, personal praise
   B. God's wrath satisfied
III. **Our Corporate Pleasure: Joyful Satisfaction in God (12:3)**
   A. Something shared
   B. Deep satisfaction
   C. Ongoing refreshment for eternity in Christ
IV. **Our Universal Mission: Magnifying the Greatness of God (12:4-6)**
   A. Evangelism: proclaiming among the nations the greatness of God
   B. Worship: immersed in the greatness of God

For the Praise of His Glorious Grace

God does all this magnificent work of salvation for the praise of his glorious grace (Eph 1:6). But what is that grace? And what will it have overcome in the end to bring all of God's elect to a perfect state in that perfect world? Scripture reveals that God's highest priority in our salvation is his own glory. His second highest priority is our perfect blessedness: filled with joy in eternally perfect souls and bodies. Isaiah has traced out quite clearly the foul river of wickedness that our human natures have pumped out for centuries. In chapter 1 God had to put up with the empty machinery of cold-hearted religiosity. Isaiah 2 revealed God's hatred for the arrogance of idolatry. Chapter 3 laid open the filth of bad leadership: corrupt judges, magistrates, and kings. Isaiah 5 made plain through six woes God's revulsion at greed, excess, mockery of God, redefining of truth, false wisdom, and a drunken, corrupt justice system. Isaiah 6 showed that even the best of us, a prophet like Isaiah, feels completely undone by an unclean life under the gaze of such a holy Lord. Chapters 7 through 10 clearly described God's righteous devastation of Israel and Judah by invading forces. By the time we get to the magnificent vision of the messianic kingdom in Isaiah 11, we may rightly wonder how a holy God could give an unholy and wicked people such a majestic and beautiful Savior as that chapter describes. Isaiah 12 is the only appropriate reaction of the people of God to such "glorious grace."

Our Personal Theme: "God Is My Salvation"
ISAIAH 12:1-2

God speaks to us through his prophet, telling us that in the day of the Lord each of his redeemed will give personal praise to God for his amazingly gracious salvation. We will thank God for turning his holy and just wrath away from us. This passage clearly points to the propitiation Christ worked (Rom 3:25; 1 John 2:2), the turning away of God's wrath by giving a sacrifice. On judgment day, and for eternity beyond that day, all the redeemed in Jesus will give our direct praise to the God of our salvation (Isa 12:2). Because we will in that day praise God for our salvation, we are able to put our faith in him now and not be afraid of anything. God will be our ongoing strength for the journey the rest of the way.

Our Corporate Pleasure: Joyful Satisfaction in God
ISAIAH 12:3

Isaiah also speaks of the joy we will have in drawing "water from the springs of salvation" (v. 3). Isaiah is filled with images of cool, satisfying streams in the wasteland from which thirsty wanderers drink and are refreshed (32:2; 35:6; 43:19-20; 44:3-4). Jesus perfectly fulfills these images, as he spoke to the Samaritan woman at the well: "Whoever drinks from the water that I will give him will never get thirsty again. In fact, the water I will give him will become a well of water springing up in him for eternal life" (John 4:14). So, as we make our toilsome way through the wilderness of this world, we are free to drink from Jesus at any moment through the Holy Spirit (John 7:38).

Our Universal Mission: Magnifying the Greatness of God
ISAIAH 12:4-6

The rest of this brief chapter covers what we should be doing for the rest of our fleeting lives on earth: giving thanks to our Lord, proclaiming his name among the nations, celebrating his deeds among the peoples. This is nothing less than worldwide mission work, exalting the achievements of God the Father through the perfect work of his Son, Jesus Christ. We are to declare to all peoples that God's triune name is exalted and that everyone who calls on that name will be saved. Each "citizen of Zion" (v. 6) will do this worship-filled mission work, and we will experience the greatness of God in our midst both for now and all eternity.

Application

This chapter is a brief but delightful interlude of rich worship and praise to God for his amazing grace in turning away his wrath and pouring out compassion on us. It is therefore a call to us to fill our mouths with praise and thanksgiving now, to worship him in spirit and in truth, to live every moment of our lives in thankful praise to the God of our salvation. It is secondly a call on us to be passionately and fruitfully engaged in evangelism and missions, declaring among the nations of the earth the greatness of Jesus's achievements at the cross and empty tomb. Finally, it is a promise of rich future blessings when our present worship by faith and by the Spirit will be consummated in heaven.

Reflect and Discuss

1. How does this chapter give us ample reasons for praising God?
2. How does it point to our heavenly future worshiping God with people from all over the earth?
3. How should a rich meditation on this chapter conquer complaining and teach us the discipline of giving thanks in all circumstances?

4. What is the significance of the reference to God's anger being turned away? How does it relate to the concept of propitiation in Romans 3:25 and 1 John 2:2?

5. How would a meditation on the fact that "God is my salvation" humble us completely, fulfilling the statement, "Let the one who boasts, boast in the Lord" (1 Cor 1:31)?

6. How does this brief chapter call on us to sing?

7. How does verse 3 point to Jesus's encounter with the Samaritan woman at the well (John 4:4-30)? How does it also connect with Jesus's statement in John 7:25?

8. How do verses 4-6 strongly move us to evangelism and missions?

9. What is the connection between evangelism/missions and joyful worship? How does joyfully praising God fit well in an evangelistic encounter?

10. How does verse 6 connect with the promise that we will dwell eternally in the very presence of God in the heavenly Jerusalem (Zion)?

The End of the World: Babylon's Past and Future Destruction

ISAIAH 13

Babylon, the jewel of kingdoms, the glory of the pride of the Chaldeans, will be like Sodom and Gomorrah when God overthrew them. (Isa 13:19)

Main Idea: God predicts the fall of Babylon almost two centuries before it happened.

I.   **Babylon's Symbolic Role in Redemptive History**
 A.   Babylon, Rome, and Revelation
 B.   The constant threat of "the world"
II. **God Summons an Army against Babylon.**
 A.   God's sovereign actions in history
 B.   God raises an army and darkens the stars.
III. **The Invaders Named**
 A.   The "Medes": their history
 B.   Detailed prophecy centuries in advance
IV. **Desolation Decreed, Then Fulfilled**
 A.   Babylon overthrown like Sodom
 B.   The decree fulfilled, centuries later

Babylon's Symbolic Role in Redemptive History

All Christians have three relentless enemies that constantly wage war against our souls: the world, the flesh, and the devil. Peter calls Satan our personal enemy who prowls around like a roaring lion, seeking someone to devour (1 Pet 5:8). Paul says that the "flesh," our indwelling sin, drives us constantly to do the very thing we hate doing (Rom 7:18-20). John writes clearly of the "world," with its relentless assault through the lusts of the flesh and of the eyes, and the pride in one's lifestyle (1 John 2:16). The "world" that John writes about is made up of real, living people whose decisions and actions are controlled by the devil and their own flesh. These people all make their own poisonous contributions to the noxious brew that is the "world": perhaps a non-Christian politician running for the highest office in the land;

or an increasingly ambitious leader in a restless Muslim nation, eyeing a small neighboring country that has resources his nation needs; or a terrorist masterminding the next suicide attack; or the publisher of a pornographic magazine thinking of branching out into the smartphone market; or an actor willing to do anything on film to further his or her career; or a marketing consultant urging a "bolder approach" to marketing clothes to teens; or a financial expert writing a column on "how you can be far richer than you ever dreamed"; or a motivational speaker telling spellbound audiences ten irrefutable laws for success.

This roiling cauldron of rebellion against the rule of almighty God is a vicious, relentless, alluring, cold-hearted enemy to the soul; it is the enemy territory through which every pilgrim for Jesus is making his way to heaven. It has a symbolic name in the Bible: *Babylon*.

In its simplest meaning, Babylon was the name of an ancient city in Mesopotamia on the Euphrates River. What has traditionally been called the tower of Babel (Gen 11) was actually a tower in the nascent city of Babylon, its inhabitants refusing to accept God's authority from the very start. From that city arose a mighty empire that conquered the world. From it came an army that conquered the promised land, tore down the walls of Jerusalem, and burned God's temple to the ground. Babylon was the enemy of God's people.

Isaiah 13 is the clear prophecy of the fall of Babylon, but astonishingly Isaiah wrote about it a full century and a half before it occurred. So Isaiah saw vividly the conquest of the literal city on the Euphrates. But Isaiah 13 speaks of God's relentless wrath poured out on "Babylon," the enemy of his people; it would be fulfilled again and again through the history of the world because from the ashes of one Babylon, rising like a wicked, God-hating phoenix, would come the temporary glory of the next "Babylon." When the apostle Peter wrote his epistle from Rome, he called that city "Babylon" (1 Pet 5:13). Each God-hating "Babylon" would not literally originate from that same city, but it would have all the same attributes as far as God was concerned. Not until the end of the world would the final "Babylon" be crushed with the second coming of Christ (Rev 18–19).

God Summons an Army against Babylon

First, throughout Isaiah 13, God's activity as the secret initiator of history is emphasized. God tells what he is doing, how he is acting, who he is raising up to do what, etc. Verse 3 is plain: "*I* have commanded *my* consecrated ones; yes, *I* have called *my* warriors, who celebrate *my* triumph, to execute *my* wrath" (emphasis added). So also verses 11-13 (emphasis added):

> I *will punish the world for its evil.* . . . I *will put an end to the pride of the arrogant and humiliate the insolence of tyrants.* I *will make a human more scarce than fine gold.* . . . I *will make the heavens tremble.*

This is God's sovereign activity throughout this chapter. In verses 2-4 God is summoning an army from the nations to overthrow another Gentile nation, Babylon, the land of aristocratic "nobles" (v. 2). The invasion and conquest is the "day of the LORD," a cause for abject terror (vv. 6-9). But then Isaiah's language reaches up to the heavens saying the sun, the moon, and the stars will all be darkened. Jesus used this same language to speak of the celestial portents that will immediately precede his second coming (Matt 24:29-30). Thus the first fall of Babylon is a mere dress rehearsal for the final one (Rev 18–19).

The Invaders Named

It's astonishing to marvel at Isaiah's far-reaching prophetic vision. At the time when this oracle against Babylon was written (ca. 725 BC), Babylon was just a city chafing under the yoke of the mighty Assyrian Empire. The Medes were allies with Babylon in finding opportunities to resist the Assyrians. But by the power of the Holy Spirit, Isaiah looks down the corridors of time and predicts the fall of Babylon at the hands of the Medes (v. 17) almost two centuries later (539 BC). The Medes grew and developed their culture in what is now central Iran, east of Mesopotamia in the Zagros Mountains and the high plateaus east of that mountain range. As early as 836 BC, the Assyrians referred to them as enemies. In 612 BC the Medes joined the Babylonians to crush the last vestiges of the Assyrian Empire. Here in Isaiah 13:17, the Lord decrees that he is going to "stir up" the Medes against Babylon, and they will not be bought off with silver or gold. So God is looking beyond the first empire (the Assyrians) *and the second* (the Babylonians) to the third empire, the Medes and Persians. God is eternal, standing over the entire stretch of time and able to declare the end from the beginning.

Desolation Decreed, Then Fulfilled

God goes beyond merely identifying the invader who will defeat Babylon. He predicts the level of devastation that will befall Babylon in her ultimate doom. Babylon, the jewel of the kingdoms, will be overthrown by God like Sodom and Gomorrah (v. 19). There will be few survivors; the refugees will flee, only to be found and stabbed by a sword (vv. 14-15). The cold-hearted Medes will even slaughter their children before their very eyes (vv. 16,18). Babylon will be left a howling wilderness, never to be inhabited again. Not even nomadic Arabs will pitch their tents there (v. 20). Instead, it will be a haunt for owls, ostriches, and wild goats (v. 21). This desolation is a clear picture of how empty all the enemies of God will be when his judgment has run its course.

Interestingly, in God's wisdom, the fulfillment of this decree of desolation came in stages, not all at once. Darius the Mede conquered Babylon in 539 BC, as recorded in Daniel 5, but essentially left it intact. By the time of Alexander the Great, Babylon was still opulent enough for him to desire to make it the capital of his empire. In 323 BC, after his conquests in India, he returned to Babylon, despite the warnings of his soothsayers that Babylon was a cursed city that he should avoid (Cantor, *Alexander the Great*, 142). Alexander decided to enter the city and to go ahead with his grandiose plans for rebuilding Babylon. But suddenly, God's sovereign will intervened; Alexander died in Babylon, tradition tells us from a fever brought on by a drunken binge. After Alexander, Babylon quickly hurtled toward God's decreed desolation through the various Greek kings that ruled the region. By the time the Roman emperor Trajan went to visit the infamous Babylon in AD 116, he was disappointed when he arrived at the site; it was only a wasted pile of rubble. The ruins of ancient Babylon were not discovered until relatively modern times—that's how totally desolate the place had become. God's decree had been fulfilled. Babylon still has not been rebuilt.

Applications

The lessons from the "Oracles of the Nations" will be emphasized in the upcoming chapters of this commentary, but they are always worth meditating on. Overall, we must embrace and celebrate the absolute sovereignty of God over the flow of human history. We must see how God used these mighty Gentile empires to chastise his people for their sins but how he also judged each of them for their own wickedness. We must learn not to despair when the temporary ascendency of the mighty enemies of God bewilders us and tempts us to wonder what God is doing. We should stand in awe of God's extraordinary ability to decree the distant future and make everything occur exactly as planned. We should study the theme of "Babylon" in the Bible and realize that it represents the God-hating world system, organized militarily and/or economically for vast power; and we should "come out of her, so that [we] will not share in her sins or receive any of her plagues" (Rev 18:4). We should realize that Jesus Christ fights against the spirit of "Babylon" in every generation by his Word and his Spirit, and that he will overthrow the final form of Babylon with the sword coming from his mouth at his second coming (Rev 19:15). So, we should guard our hearts from the "lust of the flesh, the lust of the eyes, and the pride in one's possessions" (1 John 2:16), for because of these things the wrath of God is coming on this world. Christ alone can rescue his people from being destroyed with Babylon.

Reflect and Discuss

1. How are 1 Peter 5:13 and Revelation 18 clear indicators that "Babylon" in the Bible represents more than only the city on the Euphrates but also a spirit of worldly rebellion against God that arises generation after generation?

2. How does John's warning in 1 John 2:16 relate to the warning of Revelation 18:4? How do we heed these warnings?

3. What are the lessons from the "Oracles against the Nations" listed above? How could those lessons be an encouragement to us today?

4. How does Isaiah 13 (specifically v. 17) show God's amazing power to predict the future, even down to small details?

5. How is God the central actor in this chapter? (See especially what God says he will do in vv. 3,11-13.)

6. What reasons does God give in this chapter for overthrowing Babylon?

7. How would this chapter be a great encouragement to the Judeans who would be exiled to Babylon a little less than a century and a half later?

8. Why do you think God decreed the total desolation of Babylon, such that it would never be rebuilt?

9. Why do you think God willed that the desolation should be fulfilled over many centuries, little by little, rather than all at once?

10. How is the fall of Babylon that is predicted in this chapter a dress rehearsal for the second coming of Christ?

God's Sovereign Plan to Destroy Satan's Puppet Kings

ISAIAH 14

Shining morning star, how you have fallen from the heavens!
You destroyer of nations, you have been cut down to the ground.
(Isa 14:12)

Main Idea: This chapter predicts the fall of the "king of Babylon" in language so soaring that it implies judgment on Satan, the power behind every evil throne, as well as on his human puppets.

I. **The Power Behind Every Evil Throne**
   A. Satan the puppet master
   B. Satan condemned through his puppet
   C. The satanic ambition of the king of Babylon
II. **The Power Above Every Evil Throne**
   A. God's sovereign power to rule and to judge
   B. God's direct actions on the king of Babylon
   C. God's expulsion of the arrogant king
III. **God's Sovereign Plan: The Eternal Joy of His Chosen People**
   A. The "plan" and the "hand" (14:24-27)
   B. The joy of the redeemed
   C. The taunt over fallen oppressors
   D. Peace at last
IV. **No Tyrant Stronger Than Death**
   A. All tyrants die physically.
   B. All tyrants die eternally.

The Power Behind Every Evil Throne

Isaiah 13 clearly prophesies the fall of Babylon, but we looked deeper and saw it refers *both* to the literal city of Babylon *and* to the God-hating, self-exalting "spirit of Babylon" that pervades every empire in human history. Isaiah 14 focuses on the "king of Babylon," the one who pushed the empire to its dizzying heights of domination. Obviously, in every great human empire there must be great human leaders. So we can take the "king of Babylon" to refer at least to that leader. But the language of verses 12-15 goes far beyond that which we would expect for that of a merely human leader. The KJV translation of verse 12 is one of the most famous in the whole book of Isaiah: "How art thou fallen from heaven, O Lucifer, son of the morning!" "Lucifer" is how Jerome translated the Hebrew expression ("shining one, son of the dawn") into Latin. The Latin word "Lucifer" literally means "light bearer," and it was the common name for Venus, seen to be the morning star. Throughout the history of interpretation of this passage, many have seen this as a poetical reference to Satan, the chief fallen angel and leader of the rebellion against God. The "king of Babylon" is said to have "fallen from the heavens." He is called a "destroyer of nations." His ambitions were to "ascend to the heavens" and to set his throne "above the stars of God." Ultimately, he desired to make himself "like the Most High." There are five "I will" statements in this staggering boast, showing a soaring ambition to challenge and even supplant almighty God.

So behind any human "king of Babylon" we must see the "puppet master," Satan, who invisibly dominates world history by controlling the tyrants who do his bidding. Satan is a master of disguises and delights in remaining hidden as he makes evil leaders dance to his wicked tune. He masqueraded as a speaking serpent in the garden of Eden, so God correspondingly spoke his curse to Satan *through the disguise* of the serpent. So also in Isaiah 14, Satan masquerades behind a human puppet—the real "king of Babylon"—so God speaks Satan's judgment through that alias. It is the exact same approach that God takes to decreeing judgment on the "king of Tyre" in Ezekiel 28. In both cases (Isa 14; Ezek 28) we have lavish language that exceeds the boundaries of that which would ordinarily be spoken of a merely human king. Satan desires to remain hidden behind every evil throne, moving evil leaders to do his bidding by his clever temptations and evil schemes. So, he is able to intoxicate his human puppet-slave with similarly outrageous ambitions, as so many of these tyrant-kings thought themselves deities soaring to the heavens in their all-conquering ambitions. Alexander the Great thought he was the incarnation of Zeus Ammon, integrating the chief deities of Greece and Egypt. The Caesars were worshiped as gods. Hitler was worshiped as a messiah by the German people. These tyrants all embraced these delusions, delighted in them, and murdered those who opposed them. They craved and accepted worship.

But these human tyrants have been mere puppets on a string; their ambitions and actions have been the responses to promptings by the power behind every evil throne—Satan, the "god of this age" (2 Cor 4:4), the "ruler of the power of the air," the "spirit now at work in the disobedient" (Eph 2:2). Some of these tyrants, like Adolph Hitler, have secretly embraced occultic powers; others, like Mao and Stalin, denied the very existence of Satan. No matter. They were all dancing on the end of strings held by dark intellect far above their own. Isaiah 14 addresses these human tyrants directly, but it also speaks to the puppet master, Satan, and consigns them all to the same fate—tormented in the final Sheol, which is "the eternal fire prepared for the devil and his angels" (Matt 25:41).

The Power Above Every Evil Throne

The tone of Isaiah 14 is one of unbridled celebration; it is a triumphant victory song by a formerly oppressed people over the tyrant(s) who have oppressed them. The "king of Babylon" is said to have caused "pain, torment, and . . . hard labor" (v. 3); he was a raging oppressor (v. 4) whose scepter dominated lesser kings and struck the nations of the world with "unceasing blows" and "relentless persecution" (v. 6). But now this seemingly undefeatable tyrant has been thrown down by the sovereign power of almighty God, the power above every evil throne. The Lord's power over the "king of Babylon" is plain throughout the chapter: in verse 5 it is the Lord who breaks his scepter; in verse 15 God casts him down from his lofty throne to Sheol. The justice and judgments of the Lord pervade this chapter. In the context of the later oracle against the Assyrians, verse 26 clearly declares God's sovereign power: his **plan** prepared for the whole earth, his **hand** stretched out over all nations. God is the power *above* all evil thrones, including Satan's.

God's Sovereign Plan: The Eternal Joy of His Chosen People

God's wise plan and sovereign hand (vv. 26-27) are ultimately for the eternal joy of his chosen people. Though Israel and Judah had rebelled against God and been subjugated by these tyrant kings—one "king of Babylon" after another—God will settle them in their own land and rule over their oppressors in power (vv. 1-2). Even better for us as Gentile believers in Jesus—we who have become "Abraham's seed, heirs according to the promise" (Gal 3:29)—are the foreigners who will unite (v. 1) with Jacob and Israel in the promised land and ultimately in the new heaven and new earth. We will look with triumph forever on the wicked oppressors who dominated us on earth, and we will sing the taunt song of Isaiah 14:3-21. While we live, Satan orchestrates the world system to assault our souls every day with temptations to deny Christ. In some parts of the world he orchestrates worldly temptations to allure us with appeals to pleasure. This is the "king of Tyre" aspect of the puppet master (Ezek 28). In other parts of the world he orchestrates tyrants to beat on the bodies and take the lives of God's chosen people. This is the "king of Babylon" aspect of the puppet master (Isa 14). But in the future God will cast down both types of enemy, and God's people will be forever at rest and at peace, singing their triumph over them all.

No Tyrant Stronger Than Death

In the end all tyrants must succumb to one simple reality: all existence comes from almighty God, for "in him we live and move" (Acts 17:28). When God wills to bring the death penalty on the "king of Babylon," there is nothing the king can do to stop it. God spoke each of these beings into existence, and he can bring each one down to Sheol forever and ever. The human tyrants all succumbed to death one after the other:

- a Babylonian king, drunk and sluggish in his purple-covered bed as Median warriors storm in to kill him while he sleeps;
- a Roman caesar whose word made nations tremble and convulse, being assassinated with a dagger between his ribs by one of the Praetorian guards as he leaves the coliseum;
- a Nazi dictator in a concrete bunker putting a bullet in his head while Russian troops burn his capital around him, his corpse being dragged outside, doused with gasoline, and set ablaze in total ignominy;
- a Soviet potentate, wheezing and gasping as he chokes out his last few breaths and dies in a seizure; and
- a Chinese communist chairman, lying helpless in his bed, stricken with a heart attack and trying to speak but unable to make anything but a hoarse whisper.

None of these world conquerors can defeat the final enemy, death.

And on judgment day Satan himself will be no more able to resist God's final decree on him than any of his human puppets. The final puppet will be the beast from the sea of Revelation 13, the antichrist. He will be the most powerful of all the satanic rulers, yet both Satan and the beast will be consigned to the lake of fire on that final day (Rev 20:10). There they will burn alike forever—no difference between them. This is the second death (Rev 20:14), and no tyrant will be strong enough to escape it.

Application

These verses strip the disguise from Satan and his puppets. Here we see the world as it really is—a mortal enemy to our souls. We who have trusted in Christ by faith have become sons and daughters of Abraham and stand as heirs of the world (Rom 4:13). At present, our souls are assaulted all over the world by Satan's wicked schemes—the allure of the "king of Tyre" with his pleasure-promising merchandise, and the brutality of the "king of Babylon" with his threats of persecution, torture, and death. Isaiah 14 gives us the ability to see through these disguises, perceiving behind the puppet thrones the evil puppet master who causes them to dance to his tune. Even better, it causes us to see above every evil throne the power of Jesus Christ, whose second coming glory will destroy the final puppet king, the antichrist, "with the breath of his mouth and . . . the appearance of his coming" (2 Thess 2:8). Meditation on this chapter will help us to humble ourselves before Christ daily, resisting all prideful, satanic temptations to usurp God's throne. It will cause us to live as meek servants of the true King, whose sovereign plan is for our eternal joy and peace. It will cause us to laugh at the supposedly irresistible power of the world's tyrants and to trust fully in the wisdom of God's eternal plan and the power of God's omnipotent hand.

Reflect and Discuss

1. How does Satan act as a puppet master behind each successive "king of Babylon"?
2. How does this tricky masquerade on Satan's part line up with his use of the serpent in the garden of Eden? How do both God's judgment of the serpent in the garden and his judgment of the king of Babylon in Isaiah 14 point to his intention to deal with the real power behind those physical opposers: Satan?
3. How do both the "king of Babylon" passage in Isaiah 14 and the "king of Tyre" passage in Ezekiel 28 seem to be talking about

Satan? How do these two realms add up to the allure and threat of the "world" against our faith in Christ—the temptations of Tyre (worldly goods and pleasures) and the threats of Babylon (military domination and tyrannical oppression)? How is Satan behind both?

4. How does this chapter expose the satanic pride that vaunts itself against the throne of God? What do the five "I will"s of Isaiah 14:13-14 show of his pride? If God is so powerful as to be beyond any threat by Satan or any other ambitious rebel, then why does God hate this kind of pride so much?

5. How would meditating on this chapter give us clarity in dealing with the brutality of the tyrants of our world?

6. How does the sovereignty of God and his wisdom in verses 26-27 rule over all of Satan's puppet-master schemes and those of the puppets themselves?

7. Why is it appropriate for the formerly tormented people of God to sing such a taunt against the "king of Babylon" after his fall?

8. How does Revelation 20:10 relate to Isaiah 14? If the "beast" (the antichrist) is the final version of the "king of Babylon," how is the fact that he is sharing the same fate as Satan in Revelation 20:10 a perfect fulfillment of Isaiah 14?

9. How could meditation on this chapter help us resist temptation to be worldly?

10. How does this chapter help us to pray for the persecuted church?

The Raging of the Nations Stilled by God's Judgment

ISAIAH 15–18

The nations rage like the rumble of a huge torrent. He rebukes them, and they flee far away, driven before the wind like chaff on the hills and like tumbleweeds before a gale. (Isa 17:13)

Main Idea: God rules over the raging, turbulent sea of the nations to accomplish his purpose: salvation extending to the ends of the earth.

I. **The Central Issue: The Wise Plan and Sovereign Hand of God (14:26-27)**
    A. God's wise plan and sovereign hand (14:26-27)
    B. The oracles against the nations: general principles

II. **The Oracle against Moab: Run for Your Lives (15:1–16:14)!**
    A. Moabite refugees fleeing from terror
    B. Weeping for the refugees
    C. The great advantage of refugees
    D. The only refuge: Christ

III. **The Oracle against Damascus and Ephraim: The Raging Nations Stilled (17:1-14)**
    A. The raging of the nations described
    B. The judgment on Damascus and Ephraim
    C. The root cause of the judgment: idolatry
    D. The effect of the judgment: genuine faith in God
    E. The raging of the nations: quieted at last

IV. **The Oracle concerning Cush: God Delights in the Ethiopians (18:1-7).**
    A. Envoys from Cush
    B. The message to the peoples of the world
    C. Gifts sent from the ends of the earth
    D. New Testament fulfillment: the Ethiopian eunuch

The Central Issue: The Wise Plan and Sovereign Hand of God
ISAIAH 14:26-27

From Isaiah 13 to 23 we have a series of oracles God gives against Gentile nations. The people of God have been warned in Isaiah 1–12 that devastating judgments are coming on the promised land because of their consistent rebellion against God's covenant. But God wanted to assure his people that these Gentile nations soon to be flooding in were totally under his sovereign control. The central fact of human history is that the God of the Jews is no tribal deity, no localized god who rules over this hill or that mountain or some aspect of nature like the clouds or the harvest. Instead, Isaiah proclaims a God who rules twenty-four hours a day, seven days a week, year after year, century after century over every square inch of earth and over the small and great events of history—a God who has made a plan for the whole world and brings it about by his irresistible power.

So God strengthens the faith of his people by giving Isaiah a series of clear oracles against the nations in Isaiah 13–23. The cumulative impact of these many oracles is the clear and multifaceted message God sends to his people, timeless and relevant in every age: (1) God is absolutely sovereign over all nations; (2) all nations are sinful and corrupt in his sight, worthy of his judgments; (3) do not trust in the power of nations or seek to make a saving alliance with them, but rather trust in God for protection; (4) do not question God's justice or power when, for a time, these nations gain an ascendency over God's people—the nations are still under God's power and will be judged in the end; (5) fear God and obey his commands, for no individual or nation will be able to stand before such a holy God without his redemption.

Isaiah 14:26-27 focuses on God's plan and God's hand. God's **plan** is infinitely wise, made before the foundation of the world and founded on God's omniscience. Nothing can ever surprise God; every single detail of human history has been thought through, and the best outcome for the glory of God has been determined. This infinitely wise plan would be worthless, however, apart from the sovereign **hand** of God to put it into practice. The hand of God stretches out over every nation, and no one is able to turn it back. God gets everything he wants because he is almighty, infinitely more powerful than all nations combined.

Opposing God is the raging of the nations, like a churning turbulent sea. Isaiah 17:12-13 captures this with perfect clarity:

Ah! The roar of many peoples—they roar like the roaring of the seas.
The raging of the nations—they rage like the rumble of rushing water.
The nations rage like the rumble of a huge torrent. He rebukes them,
and they flee far away, driven before the wind like chaff on the hills
and like tumbleweeds before a gale.

Later, the prophet will shine his light deeper into the hearts of the people to understand the reason for all this raging turbulence: "'But the wicked are like the storm-tossed sea, for it cannot be still, and its water churns up mire and muck. There is no peace for the wicked,' says my God" (57:20-21). This raging, turbulent sea of the nations is caused by the restless wickedness of their own hearts: lustful, covetous, prideful, angry, ambitious. They do not know the God of peace, so they can never know the peace of God. Therefore, the nations are frequently portrayed as a turbulent sea. In Daniel 7 four great beasts come out of a raging sea, representing four terrifying human empires. In Revelation 13 Satan (the dragon) stands on the shore and calls forth from that turbulent sea "the beast," the antichrist who will rule the nations in blasphemous pride. Isaiah 17:12-13 gives us confidence that, no matter how turbulent and powerful the nations may seem, God rules over them for his glory.

The Oracle against Moab: Run for Your Lives!
ISAIAH 15:1–16:14

Documentaries of World War II have depicted seemingly endless lines of European refugees fleeing Hitler's war machine: pathetic columns of people with a similar haunted and terrorized look on their faces. For example, an elderly woman in France in the summer of 1940 is seen pushing a baby carriage loaded with a framed painting, a lamp, and a party dress—all she had left of her former life before the Nazis invaded. This is the image we have of refugees: terror-stricken people clinging to scraps left over from a formerly comfortable and prosperous life, now running for their lives.

That is the picture depicted in Isaiah 15–16: the tiny Gentile nation of Moab was crushed by some unnamed invading force, and they ran for their lives, a terrified little flock of refugees seeking asylum in Judah, their ancient enemy. It is a picture of salvation in Christ for every person who flees the wrath to come and finds refuge in the former enemy, almighty God.

The Moabites were descended from another refugee family, Lot and his daughters, who fled the destruction of Sodom and Gomorrah and sought refuge in a cave. The daughters thought the human race had been wiped out, so they got their father drunk and had sons by him. The older daughter's son was named Moab—"from father" (Gen 19:30-38). The Moabites were historical enemies of Israel and Judah; the law of Moses forbade any of them to enter the assembly of the Lord (Deut 23:3-6). These are the people who are running for their lives in Isaiah 15–16. The historical circumstances of these chapters are unclear, but it is possible that Assyria invaded them sometime around 715 BC, causing the tragic scenes described here.

The picture in these short chapters is bleak: Ar and Kir, two powerful Moabite cities, are destroyed in one night (15:1); Moab resorts to her false god, Chemosh, and prays at his temple and high places (15:2; 16:12), but to no avail. Nothing is left for the survivors but to run for their lives with whatever possessions they can carry (15:5,7). The slaughter is so terrible that Moab's rivers are flowing with blood (15:9). They run from one attacker only to find another waiting for them like a lion crouching ready to pounce (15:9). Moab's women are the most pitiable of the refugees, like birds pushed from the nest (16:2). The end is quite near for the Moabites; within three years Moab will be completely stripped of all power and be left totally feeble (16:13-14).

Amazingly, Isaiah weeps for Moab's tragic refugees (15:5; 16:9-11), just as Jesus wept over Jerusalem (Luke 19:41-44) and the apostle Paul wept for spiritually lost Jews who were persecuting him (Rom 9:1-2). This opens the door for insight into God's amazing compassion for his enemies. Paul makes it clear that, while we were still God's enemies, Christ died for us (Rom 5:8). Part of being God's enemy is the haughtiness, pride, arrogance, and empty boasting (Isa 16:6) that characterize the heart of sinners. But becoming a refugee on earth may be the only way to save such arrogant enemies: stripped of pride, military power, false religion, and possessions, they now plead for refuge and mercy from a former enemy, Judah.

Therefore, at this critical moment, Moab's refugees turn to their ancient foe, Judah, for assistance. They send lambs as tribute to Mount Zion (Jerusalem, 16:1) and plead with Judah to shelter them, to take in the pathetic refugees and not betray them to their conqueror (vv. 3-4). This is a beautiful picture of salvation in Christ. Like the Pharisees in John's day, we must "flee from the coming wrath" (Matt 3:7) that we have merited for our wickedness. But most people don't believe there is a "coming wrath," so they never flee. The only refuge from the coming wrath is the cross of Jesus Christ (1 Thess 1:10). Only spiritual refugees will be saved, those who run for their eternal lives into the waiting arms of a Savior who is both Jewish and a descendent of a Moabite woman, Ruth! And God orchestrates dire circumstances in the lives of his elect to strip them of false refuges and lead them to flee to Christ.

The Oracle against Damascus and Ephraim: The Raging Nations Stilled
ISAIAH 17:1–14

The next oracle from Isaiah went out against the ancient city of Damascus, the capital of Syria (also known as Aram), another Gentile enemy of Judah. Damascus is the oldest continuously inhabited city on earth. It was founded more than one thousand years before Rome was settled in 753 BC. Damascus was one of the most strategic cities in the ancient Near East: it stood at the mouth of a natural funnel through which ran the only convenient land route between Mesopotamia and Egypt. It was also the base of operation for many Aramean raids against Judah, and therefore an implacable foe of the people of God. Isaiah 17:14 speaks of the "fate of those who plunder us and the lot of those who ravage us."

The oracle spoken against Damascus is clear: total devastation. Damascus will be leveled and no longer be a city; where once the city thrived, now flocks will graze with no fear (17:1-2). The Arameans will lose their kingdom entirely as a judgment from God (v. 3). But it is not only Damascus and Aram that will fall under God's judgment. Ephraim also will fall, treated in some ways as no more than a Gentile transgressor nation. They were allies against Judah, and they share judgment from God. Aram and Ephraim alike will waste away, fading like a diseased, emaciated body (v. 4). The pathetic survivors will be like a few berries left at the top of a fruit tree after harvest (v. 6).

It is so stunning to see descendants of Jacob treated no differently than Gentile sinners, but it is because they thought and behaved no differently. Verses 8 and 10 make clear that God was rejecting Ephraim because of the Asherahs and pagan incense altars they had made for worship. They had forgotten the God of their salvation and failed to remember the rock of their strength but trusted in gods that were no gods at all. So God would bring on them the same "disease and incurable pain" (v. 11) of his holy judgments.

Thus stripped of their false religion, at last the remnant of Israel would turn again to their Maker, casting their eyes of hope on the God of Israel (v. 7). But the language of Isaiah 17:7 is universal—not only an Israelite but "people" (Hebrew is *adam*, universal language for humanity) will turn away from idolatrous religion and cast their eyes on their Maker, who it turns out is also "the Holy One of Israel." The "turning of the eyes" to God by sinners all over the world is nothing less than repentance and faith, ultimately in the Savior, Jesus Christ.

Apart from that repentance and faith in the salvation of the Holy One of Israel, the nations rage and roar like a tempestuous sea (vv. 13-14), restlessly seeking something of joy and peace in their rebellious wandering from God. But they never find joy or peace; like Satan (Job 1:7) and demons (Matt 12:43) restlessly roaming the earth, they are tormented. They are driven like chaff before a gale, fleeing before the tempest of the wrath of God—sudden terror in the evening, desolation by morning. This is the fate of the rebellious nations who never come to repentance and faith in Christ.

The Oracle concerning Cush: God Delights in the Ethiopians
ISAIAH 18:1–7

Whereas Isaiah 13–17 proclaims strong oracles of judgment against Babylon, Assyria, Moab, Aram, and Ephraim, Isaiah 18 glows with a marvelous prophecy about the salvation of the people of Cush—modern-day Ethiopia. One of the surprising elements of this chapter is the evident delight God has in the people of Cush—"a nation tall and smooth-skinned . . . a people feared far and near, a powerful nation with a strange language, whose land is divided by rivers" (v. 2).

We live in a world of astonishing ethnic diversity. The human race is a mosaic of various genetic differences: height, skin color, hair type, eye color, shape of nose, etc. On top of these evident differences are the remarkably varied cultural differences of language, dress, social mores, rituals, etc. From a biblical point of view, these striking differences are all the more amazing when we consider that God made every nation on earth from one man (Acts 17:26). The differences between the ethnicities have come about by the magnificent variety God built into the genetic code of the first man, Adam, a variety in which God delights. But pride between the ethnicities comes from sin. Ethnicity is from God; racism is from man. Racism may be defined as the belief that one ethnicity is inherently superior to another. Closely linked to racism are all sorts of prejudice, oppression, and injustice that one group of people has foisted on another because of ethnic differences. Isaiah 18 stands above this wickedness and shows the delight God has in people from all ethnic backgrounds. Even more delightful is the sovereign grace of God in electing "a vast multitude from every nation, tribe, people, and language, which no one could number" to stand before the heavenly throne of Jesus dressed in white (Rev 7:9). Isaiah 18 gives us a beautiful foretaste of that worldwide harvest of people.

So who were these people who dwelt in the land of Cush? The Nile River valley was formed as its water cut through sandstone and limestone, making cataracts—waterfalls—that interfere with navigation and serve as natural boundaries for the Nile Valley peoples. The region of the Fourth Cataract was settled by the Cushites, descendants of Cush, the oldest son of Ham after the flood of Noah (Gen 10:7).

Isaiah 18 begins with a command for swift messengers to go to a land "of buzzing insect wings beyond the rivers of Cush" (vv. 1-2). This land is more than 1,500 miles away from Judah, and these Cushite people have sent envoys to Jerusalem to discuss an alliance. By lightweight boats the Cushite messengers travel swiftly. They are tall, smooth-skinned, strikingly beautiful. The ancient historian Herodotus said that the Cushites were "the tallest and handsomest men in the whole world" (*Histories* 3.20.1, 216). The average height of some Ethiopian tribes is 6'4", the tallest in the world. They have skin naturally free from hair, and they are feared far and wide as powerful warriors.

In Isaiah 18:3-6 God gives a message to every people group all over the world, including these Cushites. God usually looks on human history quietly, from his lofty dwelling place, "like shimmering heat in sunshine" (v. 4). But now God is going to unfurl a banner and announce with trumpets something magnificent for the entire human race. The spreading grapevine that is the ravenous Assyrian Empire is about to be pruned so severely that nothing will be left but that which mountain birds of prey can feed on (vv. 5-6). The whole world, which had been trembling at the spreading power of Assyria, will be astonished instead at the power of God through his tiny nation of Judah. This certainly refers to the slaughter of 185,000 Assyrian troops by the angel of the Lord outside the walls of Jerusalem.

As a result of that awesome and shocking victory, gifts will be sent from the ends of the earth, from Cush to Mount Zion, the place of the name of the Lord Almighty (18:7). These gifts were sent to congratulate King Hezekiah at his stunning victory (2 Chr 32:23), but they are a typological picture of the worldwide worship that the ultimate King, Jesus Christ, will receive from every tribe, language, people, and nation. This is a major theme in the book of Isaiah: God's awesome acts in history centered around Judah and Israel are meant to make his name great among the nations so that all nations will fear him and worship him eternally.

Many prophecies tell of the people of Cush sending gifts of worship to God in Jerusalem: Psalms 68:31 and 87:4 and Zephaniah 3:9-10. This is just a part of God's saving intention toward people from every nation on earth. In Acts 8 we see the fulfillment of this in the amazing account of the conversion of the Ethiopian eunuch. Based on the prophecies of Isaiah, this Cushite man was led to faith in Jesus Christ by the witness of Philip. He believed and was baptized, and then he returned to Cush to spread the gospel to his fellow countrymen. Church history tells us this was the beginning of the Coptic church. And in the future, "a gift will be brought to the LORD of Armies from a people tall and smooth-skinned." That gift will be eternal worship at the throne of Christ Jesus!

Applications

These chapters depict God's sovereign power over the nations, his infinitely wise plan and his omnipotent hand (14:26-27). It is vital for us as Christians to trust entirely in the God who thus rules over human history. The nations are restless, full of rage, completely unable to find peace in their wandering rebellion against God. We must not live like that. We must find rest in God alone, trusting in him to give joy and peace, even while we suffer at the hands of such restless empire builders. We must not be faithlessly anxious over the restless churning of current events on earth. But we must learn to weep with compassion over the judgments God brings on sinful people as Isaiah did in 15:5 and 16:9-11. We must also see the futility of the idolatrous world systems of worship. The Jews were allured by the gods of the nations, and we also will be tempted to live for idols. We must continually return to the only true God and do his will while we live. We must see God's sovereign hand in allowing a remnant of Jews to survive his judgments, such as the few berries at the top of the fruit tree at harvest. Only by the sovereign power of God do the Jews even still exist on earth. And we must delight in God's purpose to save people from distant lands like the Cushites. We ought to delight in the varied attributes of the ethnicities and know that God delights in any morally neutral distinctives among them. But let us allow biblical truth to destroy the racism that is no more than a form of idolatrous self-worship. From one man all nations of the earth were born, and by one man all the elect from all nations on earth will be redeemed.

Finally, we should seize the opportunity to minister to refugees in the name of the Lord. The ongoing turmoil of nations all over the earth—wars, Islamic terrorist groups, natural disasters—results in a steady stream of refugees who have to flee their countries and seek protection somewhere else. According to a recent United Nations report, the number of refugees worldwide is more than sixty-five million, the highest recorded in history (Yeung, "Refugee Crisis"). The church of Jesus Christ should be there, ministering to these desperate people and allowing them to see in Christ their true Refuge.

Reflect and Discuss

1. Why is it vital for Christians to understand God's wise plan and mighty hand for the nations (Isa 14:26-27)?
2. How are these (God's plan and hand) displayed in these oracles about the nations in Isaiah 15–18?
3. What is surprising about Isaiah's obvious compassion for Moab in Isaiah 15:5 and 16:9-11? How is it also displayed in Jesus weeping over Jerusalem (Luke 19:41-44) and Paul weeping for unbelieving Jews (Rom 9:1-2)?
4. Why is it necessary for us as Christians to develop this same kind of compassion for others who are suffering God's judgments on earth?
5. What are the spiritual advantages for refugees? How do these experiences strip individuals of pride and other obstacles that are keeping them from coming to Christ? On the other hand, how could the exact same sufferings actually cause some people to feel bitter against God?
6. How is the Moabite refugees' seeking help from Judah a picture of salvation in Jesus?
7. What is the significance of Isaiah 17:12-13 for describing the present world scene? How do we still see the tendency of the nations to be like a restless, turbulent sea?

8. How is that restlessness much like Satan in Job 1–2 and the demons Jesus describes in Matthew 12:43?
9. How does Isaiah 18 show God's delight in the people of Cush? How does this delight help destroy racism? What is racism? How are Christians uniquely positioned to crush racism by our biblical doctrine and our love for believers from all over the world?
10. How are the gifts brought to the Lord Almighty by the people of Cush (Isa 18:7) a picture of the salvation that will extend to the whole earth and the universal worship that the nations will give God through Jesus Christ?

Egypt's Judgment Results in Egypt's Salvation

ISAIAH 19–20

When they cry out to the LORD because of their oppressors, he will send them a savior and leader, and he will rescue them. The LORD will make himself known to Egypt, and Egypt will know the LORD on that day. (Isa 19:20-21)

Main Idea: God judges Egypt, completely stripping her of pride in every area—militarily, economically, politically, religiously—so that he can save some Egyptians by Christ.

I. **Egypt's Comprehensive Judgment (19:1-16)**
   A. The Lord's wrath against Egypt (19:1)
   B. The Lord's judgments on Egypt in all areas (19:2-15)
   C. Egypt's strength sapped completely (19:16)
II. **The Shame of Relying on Egypt (20:1-6)**
   A. Judah's temptation to run to Egypt (30:1-7)
   B. Isaiah's strange mission (20:1-4)
   C. The shame of all who rely on Egypt and not on God (20:5-6)
III. **The Glorious Future of Egypt and the World (19:17-25)**
   A. A reminder: God's saving intention toward all nations (Gen 12:3)
   B. The transformer: a savior from God to Egypt (19:20-22)
   C. Transformed fear: the fear of the Lord, the beginning of wisdom (19:17)
   D. Transformed cities: swearing allegiance to the Lord Almighty (19:18)
   E. Transformed religion: an altar to the Lord in the heart of Egypt (19:19)
   F. Transformed hearts: a new life in Christ (19:21)
   G. Transformed relationships: worshiping as one people on the earth (19:23-25)

Egypt's Comprehensive Judgment
ISAIAH 19:1-16

There was a time when Egypt was the most powerful nation on earth. Now she is a third-world country, ranked 102nd in the world in terms of per capita economic strength. There was a time when Egypt's pyramids represented the towering achievement of human technology. Now they stand as ancient reminders of how far Egypt has fallen. There was a time when Egypt's armies were the most feared on earth, when she could project her power anywhere she chose in that region of the world. Now Egypt isn't even ranked among the top fifteen most powerful militaries in the world. How the mighty have fallen!

Egypt, however, shouldn't feel singled out in this matter; the same is true of Assyria, Babylon, Greece, Rome, Hungary, Mongolia, Spain, France, England, and Germany—all of whom had the opportunity to dominate the world for a brief time but who now are humbled by the judgments of God. In the historical relay race of the "Rise and Fall of the Nations," no one nation has the dominant position for long. Egypt's fall as depicted in Isaiah 19–20 is a lesson and a warning to any nation with aspirations to rule the earth.

But the ultimate message of Isaiah 19–20 is not God's judgment on Egypt; rather, it is the glorious future that some Egyptians will have in sweet fellowship with some Assyrians and some Israelites in eternal fellowship in the kingdom of Christ! God's judgments in these two chapters merely clear the way for God's mercies on his elect people. The humbled and elect remnant of Egypt are in God's view when he says, "Egypt my people . . . are blessed" (Isa 19:25). Astonishing! God calls Egypt "my people"! Only the new covenant of Christ can bring this miracle about. And that is the final result of the story in these two chapters.

Still, before the blood of the Lamb can redeem any sinner or any nation, first they must be humbled. Isaiah 19:1-16 shows the comprehensive humbling of Egypt under the judgments of God. A consistent message of Isaiah is how much God hates human pride. Egypt was proud of every area of her society, so God systematically judges Egypt in all areas, leveling her completely. God is pictured as riding on a swift cloud and coming to Egypt in judgment, making her idols tremble before him (v. 1). Then God unleashes comprehensive judgments: on Egypt's politics, resulting in civil war (vv. 2,4); on Egypt's religion, showing the emptiness of seeking counsel from idols and from the dead (v. 3); on

Egypt's economy, by drying up the Nile River, resulting in agricultural failure and economic collapse (vv. 5-10); on Egypt's supposed wisdom, exposing her counselors as the fools they are (vv. 11-15); and on Egypt's military, causing her might to be stripped and her people to tremble "like women" (v. 16).

The Shame of Relying on Egypt
ISAIAH 20:1-6

While the strongest pronouncement of these judgments is to Egypt herself, God is also sending a message to Judah and to any small nation that, threatened by the vicious Assyrian Empire, is tempted to rely on Egypt for help. Judah should know better, but Isaiah 30:1-7 clearly reveals emissaries traveling across the desert with money to buy an alliance with Egypt. We will speak more in due time about that sinful unbelief on Judah's part. But other small nations in that region were also tempted to turn trembling to Egypt's might for aid from the Assyrians. Isaiah 20, one of the strangest chapters in the whole book, shows God's command to his prophet, Isaiah, to act out Egypt's humiliation by going around naked and barefoot for *three years* as a sign against Egypt and Cush. The message was clear: Egypt is no refuge against the terror of the Assyrian Empire and its expansionist ambitions. Assyria will defeat Egypt and humiliate her completely. Then all the people will realize how foolish it is to rely on the strength of man and not on God.

The Glorious Future of Egypt and the World
ISAIAH 19:17-25

The glowing center of these chapters, however, is not a word of judgment but rather a word of salvation. Isaiah 19:17-25 are some of the most delightfully clear prophecies in the Old Testament of God's saving intentions for the whole world. God chose Abraham and called him out of Ur of the Chaldees, promising that through him all peoples on earth would be blessed (Gen 12:3). God has never forgotten that intention to save a remnant from every tribe, language, people, and nation (Rev 7:9). In these magnificent verses God goes so far as to bless Egypt by calling her "my people" (Isa 19:25). How that must have shocked any narrow-minded, Gentile-hating Jews throughout history as they read the bold words of this visionary prophet!

Having leveled Egypt's pride by his comprehensive judgments, God speaks clearly of his intention to send a Savior to Egypt (vv. 20-22):

> *When they cry out to the LORD because of their oppressors, he will send them a savior and leader, and he will rescue them. The LORD will make himself known to Egypt, and Egypt will know the LORD on that day. They will offer sacrifices and offerings; they will make vows to the LORD and fulfill them. The LORD will strike Egypt, striking and healing. Then they will turn to the LORD and he will be receptive to their prayers and heal them.*

This is such an amazing passage! God's judgments on Egypt have the ultimate purpose of calling his chosen people among the Egyptians to saving faith in him. God promises to send the humbled Egyptians "a Savior and Leader." By capitalizing these words, I show my interpretation: it must be Jesus Christ. Perhaps these words may be fulfilled by some human king who will later deliver them from the bondage of Assyria. But the vision here is so sweeping—including a perfect harmony between Egypt, Assyria, and Israel (vv. 23-25)—that only salvation in Christ can work it. There is no record in history of these verses being fulfilled by any human governmental leader. Isaiah 19:17-25 pictures a transformation so spectacular, reaching to the core of people's hearts, that only Jesus by the Holy Spirit can bring it about. He alone is the "radiance of God's glory" (Heb 1:3) who will perfectly make God known to the peoples of the world, including Egyptians (Isa 19:21). Jesus is the Transformer!

And what are the transformations? Isaiah 19:17 pictures a fear of the God of Israel, a "fear of the LORD [that] is the beginning of wisdom" (Prov 9:10). Isaiah 19:18 pictures transformed cities that will speak the language of Canaan and swear loyalty to Yahweh. Verses 19-20 speak of a transformed religion, with an altar built to the Lord in the heart of Egypt and a pillar to the Lord erected near her border. Verses 20-21 speak of the transformed hearts of the Egyptians, calling on the name of the Lord for salvation, making vows and offering sacrifices to the true God.

Ultimately these transformations (which are also going on in Israel and Assyria) will end the terror of one nation moving out militarily to conquer another. Isaiah 2:4 predicts the day when nations will forge their swords into plows and will never again attack other nations. Isaiah 19:23-25 predicts the same thing, with a highway uniting Egypt and Assyria so they can worship together with Israel, all worshiping the one true and living God. Some commentators think these words will be fulfilled in the millennial reign of Christ on earth, while others simply extend them into eternity in the new heaven and new earth. In either case, they stand as a magnificent answer to the problems of this present age of national arrogance, idolatry, and empire-building militarism. And they show that God's adopted people include Gentiles, as the apostle Paul makes plain in Romans 9:25: "I will call Not My People, My People, and she who is Unloved, Beloved." Egypt was at one time excluded, but God will call the elect from that nation and every nation "my people" for all eternity.

Application

This chapter teaches us again God's power to judge even the mightiest nations comprehensively. God can touch any nation's economic lifeline (the Nile River, in Egypt's case) and render her a pauper nation. God can level any nation's politics and send her into civil war. God can strip any nation of military power and render her totally weak. God can humble any nation's wise counselors and reveal them to be fools. Thus it is vital for the people of God not to trust in any human power but in God alone. This is a warning to all arrogant empire-builders on earth to fear the Lord alone and humble themselves before him.

This chapter also teaches the redemptive purposes of God's judgments, how God strikes in order to heal (19:22), to cause previously independent people to cry out to him for deliverance. It shows that God's saving intention through Christ extends to all Gentile nations on earth.

Therefore, Christians in every nation should learn to look on their nation's political enemies differently than unbelieving policy makers do. God will put an end to the strife of all nations by slaughtering his unbelieving enemies all over the world and by redeeming his elect to become one people. Thus we should pray for the spread of the gospel to the ends of the earth and show how, in Christ, ancient foes can become brothers and sisters.

Reflect and Discuss

1. How does this chapter display the awesome power of God to destroy any nation on earth? What image does 19:1 give of the power of God?

2. What are the aspects of God's comprehensive judgments on Egypt in 19:2-16?

3. What is the redemptive purpose of these judgments according to 19:22?

4. How can we also learn to see God's redemptive purposes in the judgments he may bring into our lives?

5. How should a deep reflection on 19:23-25 destroy nationalism among Christians and cause us to think more like global Christians than as citizens of this or that country?

6. Why would a nationalistic, Gentile-hating Jewish person (1 Thess 2:14-16) find Isaiah 19:25 so troubling? How should it cause such a person to repent and delight in the salvation of Gentiles?

7. How does 19:20-22 predict the coming of Jesus Christ?

8. What do you think of God's strange mission for Isaiah in 20:1-4? Why would God command Isaiah to do such a difficult thing? Do you think he would be arrested and locked up as a crazy man in our time if he obeyed such a command? How is it a display of the variety of ways God spoke through the prophets (Heb 1:1)?

9. Why do you think God hates it when his people trust in Egypt or anything on earth rather than in him alone? What do you think modern Christians may be trusting in rather than God?

10. What do these chapters teach you about the future unity of the people of God in heaven (Rev 7:9)?

Babylon and Its Allies Are No Refuge for God's People

ISAIAH 21

My people who have been crushed on the threshing floor, I have declared to you what I have heard from the LORD of Armies, the God of Israel. (Isa 21:10)

Main Idea: Babylon and its allies are enemies of God and thus no refuge for God's people.

I. **Trusting in Babylon: A Devastating Mistake (21:1-2,10)**
   A. A message of warning—and comfort—to God's people
   B. Assyria the threat, God alone the refuge
   C. The way of the world: Babylon betraying, then betrayed by, its allies

II. **Isaiah's Amazing Reaction (21:3-4)**
   A. Isaiah overwhelmed
   B. Compassion on the lost

III. **Disaster Destroys the Party (21:5).**
   A. Overwhelming desire for pleasure even in the face of death
   B. The fulfillment: Belshazzar's idolatrous feast (Dan 5)
   C. Historical testimony: Herodotus's account

IV. **Babylon Has Fallen; Don't Fall with Her (21:6-10)!**
   A. The scene shifts: Israel receives news.
   B. "Babylon has fallen, has fallen!"
   C. Final warning: Don't share Babylon's fate.

V. **Edom and Arabia Are No Refuge Either (21:11-17).**
   A. Edom: a land silenced by judgment
   B. Arabia: a land overrun by refugees
   C. Remaining refuge: only the glory of the Lord

Trusting in Babylon: A Devastating Mistake
ISAIAH 21:1-2,10

I n the world, but not of it." This is a perpetual struggle for the people of God in this present evil age. God's people are constantly tempted to trust in human power (here represented by Babylon and its allies, Edom and Arabia) rather than in God, who should be our only refuge (Isa 8:13-14).

The tiny kingdom of Judah was under constant threat of invasion from Assyria, and therefore they were tempted to seek refuge in alliances with similar nations who were also threatened. Isaiah 19–20 was given to persuade Judah not to trust in Egypt. So also Isaiah 21 was given to Judah to tell her what the future held for Babylon. Like Egypt, Babylon would be destroyed one day. So verse 10 says that God's people would be "crushed on the threshing floor" by Assyria (in 722 BC) and Babylon (in 586 BC). In between, Judah would be tempted to make an alliance with Babylon against Assyria. Merodach-baladan, king of Babylon, would send emissaries to King Hezekiah for just such a purpose. Isaiah would tell King Hezekiah that someday Babylon would become the enemy of Judah, carrying off all her valuables and many of her people (Isa 39).

But in chapter 21 Isaiah sees even beyond this to the eventual fall of Babylon at the hands of the Medes and Elamites (Isa 13). Babylon, in its struggle against the Assyrian Empire, would make allies of smaller nations like the Medes and the Elamites. But, when the time was ripe for Assyria to be toppled by the growing Babylonian kingdom under Nebopolassar (625 BC), Babylon turned from ally to traitor, from friend to conqueror, and the Medes and Elamites were trampled by this new empire—Babylon.[7] Babylon would rule the region for three generations, but in due time the Medes would rise with their allies, the Persians, and conquer Babylon. So a whirlwind of destruction would sweep in on Babylon (21:1); the former traitor would now be betrayed, the former looter would now herself be looted. Elam would rise to attack, and Media would rise to lay siege, and together they would put an end to all the groaning caused by wicked Babylon (Pfeiffer, *Old Testament History*, 472–73; Bright, *History of Israel*, 360). This is the way of the world, as once subjugated people rise to conqueror their oppressors, only to become oppressors themselves.

---

[7] For an excellent overview of the history of Assyria's fall at the hands of the Neo-Babylonian Empire, see Pfeiffer, *Old Testament History*, 341–43.

Isaiah's Amazing Reaction
ISAIAH 21:3-4

Isaiah reacts to this prophetic insight with remarkable sorrow over Babylon. Just as he had earlier shown compassion for the Moabites (15:5; 16:11), so now Isaiah's body is wracked with pain, his heart filled with anguish and sheer terror for Babylon (21:3-4). As we noted in Isaiah 15–16, compassion for those under the judgment of God is godly.

Disaster Destroys the Party
ISAIAH 21:5

Astonishingly, in verse 5 Isaiah foresees (centuries in advance) the details of Babylon's fall. Specifically, it is during a feast in which tables are prepared, carpets spread out, and people eat and drink that the slaughter comes. Isaiah even seems to give the Babylonian princes military advice: "Rise up, you princes, and oil the shields!"

This feast occurred during the siege of Babylon by the Medes and Elamites, which makes it all the more amazing. During a siege, the people usually do absolutely everything necessary to conserve food and water. But the arrogant Babylonians, who had stockpiled huge quantities of food to withstand a siege for years and whose water needs were supplied indefinitely by the ever-flowing Euphrates River (Herodotus, *Histories* 1.190, 102), could stand on walls 76 feet thick and 304 feet high (*Histories* 1.178, 97) above their besieging enemy and mock them, then retire to the banqueting halls and drink themselves into drunken oblivion, confident of their security.

The idolatrous feast is recorded for us as history in Daniel 5, where Belshazzar, the final king of the Babylonian Empire, held a feast with his nobles and princes and drank toasts to the gods of wood and stone, using vessels stolen from the temple of God in Jerusalem. Suddenly, the fingers of a hand appeared and wrote the epitaph of Belshazzar's reign: *Mene, mene, tekel,* and *parsin*—God has numbered your days and brought them to an end; God has weighed you on the scales and found you wanting; God is going to give your kingdom to the Medes and Persians.

What happened next was foretold clearly by Jeremiah the prophet decades beforehand:

> *While they are flushed with heat, I will serve them a feast, and I will*
> *make them drunk so that they celebrate. Then they will fall asleep*

> *forever and never wake up. This is the LORD's declaration. . . . I will*
> *make her princes and sages drunk, along with her governors, officials,*
> *and warriors. Then they will fall asleep forever and never wake*
> *up. This is the King's declaration; the LORD of Armies is his name.*
> (Jer 51:39,57)

The drunken feast was essential to Babylon's fall, for her walls were only vulnerable where the Euphrates River went under them. Alert soldiers could easily guard that weak spot, but God made them all drunk, first with arrogance then with wine. They staggered drunk to their beds and collapsed there. Meanwhile, according to Herodotus, the Medes diverted the Euphrates until the water was only thigh deep, and they came in under the walls (Herodotus, *Histories* 1.190–91, 102–3). Then they swooped into the houses of the warriors and princes and slaughtered them while they lay drunk in their beds. Isaiah and Jeremiah saw it all by prophetic eye long before it occurred.

Babylon Has Fallen; Don't Fall with Her!
ISAIAH 21:6-10

In verses 6-10 the scene shifts from the place of the arrogant feast to a watchman waiting on the walls of (perhaps) Jerusalem to receive the news. The watchman waits and receives the dramatic news of the fall of Babylon (v. 9), the news that Isaiah's downtrodden people have been longing to hear (v. 10). But the key for them is to avoid falling with Babylon. As God has made plain, Babylon is falling because of her wicked idolatries. So the timeless warning to the people of God concerning Babylon is given again: "Come out of her, my people, so that you will not share in her sins or receive any of her plagues" (Rev 18:4).

Edom and Arabia Are No Refuge Either
ISAIAH 21:11-17

The chapter ends with two brief oracles against other Gentile nations: Edom ("Dumah") and Arabia. Allies of Babylon, ready to welcome refugees fleeing the falling city with food and water (v. 14), they wait breathlessly through the night for the terror to end; but one terror follows another. In short, there is no refuge on earth from God's judgments; find refuge in God alone.

Applications

We should all stand amazed at the astonishing detail of Isaiah's prophecy. His prophetic eye sees beyond the immediate threat of Assyria, and even beyond the rise of the Babylonian Empire, to the fall of the Babylonians at the hands of the Medes and Elamites. God alone knows the future, and he has revealed enough of the future to us in the pages of Scripture that we will be wise for salvation through faith in Christ Jesus (2 Tim 3:15). There is no refuge from the wrath and judgments of God on earth—nowhere to run, nowhere to hide. The only refuge is faith in Jesus Christ. Until the end of the world, the people of God will often feel like flotsam and jetsam on the waves of history. One mighty nation will rise to conquer the previous one, and God's people are usually merely along for the ride. But the elect from every nation are the centerpiece of God's purpose for history, not merely debris on the waves. God's people will often be crushed on the threshing floor of God's judgments, with cause to grieve over our sins. We are warned in this chapter not to trust in Babylon or to share in Babylon's demise. Our citizenship is not earthly but heavenly. So, while we wisely should pray for and seek the welfare of our earthly nation (Jer 29:7), we should also know by prophecy that it will someday be destroyed. Christ alone is our final refuge. So let us live in purity, free from the idols that will bring about the "fall of Babylon." Let us spread the gospel of Christ in light of that coming judgment.

Reflect and Discuss

1. What does this chapter show about the rise and fall of the world?
2. How should Christians live in this world given these facts? How are we to be "in the world, but not of it"? How would you relate this to Philippians 3:20 and Hebrews 11:13-16?
3. What do you make of Isaiah's remarkable reaction to the prophecy against Babylon (vv. 3-4)? How do you explain it? How is it related to Jesus weeping over Jerusalem (Luke 19:41) and Paul weeping for unbelieving Jews (Rom 9:2)? If so, what does this teach us about compassion for the lost?
4. How does the history of the fall of Babylon, together with the details covered above from Isaiah 21:5, Daniel 5, and Jeremiah 51, make you marvel at the accuracy of prophecy? How was the drunkenness of the Babylonians essential to the fall of Babylon?

5. What does the fact that the Babylonians wanted to party the night they were conquered show about human nature?
6. How does Isaiah 21:6-9 relate to Habakkuk 2:1 as well as to all of Habakkuk 2?
7. What do the oracles against Arabia teach us as well? How is it that even small nations like these are subject to such judgments from God?
8. How does this chapter teach us to live a holy life in this present age?
9. How does it point to the need to spread the gospel and be passionate about missions?
10. Do you see your present nation as a form of Babylon in some ways? If so, how? If not, why not?

When God Calls You to Mourn for Sin, Don't Party Instead

ISAIAH 22

Let us eat and drink, for tomorrow we die! (Isa 22:13)

Main Idea: God calls on the citizens of Jerusalem to fast and repent; instead, they party and die.

I. **Jerusalem: Besieged like Any Other Sinful City (22:1-8a)**
   A. The context: God's judgments on all sinful nations
   B. Bitter surprise: Judah and Jerusalem no different than Gentile sinners
   C. The valley of vision: Jerusalem more accountable because of prophets
   D. The siege described
   E. Isaiah's overpowering reaction

II. **What Jerusalem Should Have Done: Faith and Repentance (22:11-12)**
   A. The visions of the prophets warned Jerusalem of this for centuries.
   B. Now current events verify the prophets' warnings.
   C. Isaiah told the people what to have: faith and repentance.

III. **What Jerusalem Did: Faithless Preparations and Feasting (22:8b-11,13)**
   A. Faithless military preparations
   B. Self-indulgent feasting

IV. **God's Solemn Response: This Sin Will Never Be Forgiven (22:14).**
   A. A shocking response to shocking actions
   B. The unforgivable sin: attacking the means of grace

V. **Jesus Christ: Our Sovereign and Immovable Support (22:15-25)**
   A. The range of God's piercing vision: from national to individual focus
   B. Shebna: arrogant official seeking worldly security
   C. Hilkiah: humble servant exalted by God
   D. Christ: the fulfillment of the promise

Jerusalem: Besieged like Any Other Sinful City
ISAIAH 22:1-8A

This chapter displays a stunning judgment from God against his own people for this statement: "Let us eat and drink, for tomorrow we die!" God swore that this sin would never be wiped out. In our pleasure-loving age it's easy to misunderstand that verdict and think the God of the Bible is against all human pleasure. But the fact is, God created us for eternal pleasures in his presence (Ps 16:11). And Jesus likened heaven to a wedding banquet prepared by a king for his son in which the oxen and fattened cattle have been butchered and everything is prepared (Matt 22:1-14). So why does God pronounce such a dire judgment on feasting in Isaiah 22?

The context is God's oracles of judgment on the Gentile nations of Assyria, Babylon, Edom, Arabia, and Egypt. God's wrath-filled justice toward the wicked pagans of the earth would have brought delight to any patriotic Judahite. But suddenly, in Isaiah 22 the shocking verdict comes like a thunderbolt: God threatens Jerusalem with destruction just like any Gentile nation. In fact, they are actually much worse than the Gentile sinners. Because Jerusalem had been so clearly instructed and warned by the prophets (including Isaiah), they were even more accountable and guilty for their sins.

So in verses 1-3 Isaiah describes a deadly siege to come on Jerusalem. The city is filled with tumult and revelry: a city of laughter and lust, of eating, drinking, and making merry, of bloodshed, covetousness, and greed, of sexual immorality and idolatry. What should have been the "Faithful City" (Zech 8:3) was the Party City. But it was so no longer; under the wrath of God, it would become the Dead City. And the perished will not have died through valiant struggle in battle but by famine and plague as in a siege.

Amazingly, the invaders of Isaiah 22 were identified by name: Elam and Kir (v. 6). The exact same people who would later help to destroy Babylon (21:2) would join in the invasion of Judah and the siege of Jerusalem. As it turns out, the invading power would not be the dreaded Assyrians but the Babylonians. Strangely, Isaiah lists the Elamites as taking part with the Babylonians in the assault on Jerusalem before they would turn later to destroy Babylon as well. Thus the events of Isaiah 22 *precede* those of Isaiah 21!

So "the Lord GOD of Armies had a day" in store for Jerusalem (v. 5) in which he would judge them for their sins. As a result of this, Isaiah is once again moved to an emotional reaction (v. 4), as he had been earlier concerning Moab and Babylon (Isa 15–16; 21). However, here his grief is more intense because this is his own people and his own city that were being destroyed by God's wrath.

What Jerusalem Should Have Done: Faith and Repentance
ISAIAH 22:11-12

Isaiah was plain: "On that day the Lord GOD of Armies called for weeping, for wailing, for shaven heads, and for the wearing of sackcloth" (v. 12). This is the only proper response to the river of wickedness that had flowed from the corrupt hearts of the inhabitants of Judah and Jerusalem. God wanted them to repent with great grief over their sins and "look to" the Lord in faith (v. 11). So he called on them to do this as they saw the Babylonians approaching. This is what they should have done. But what did they do?

What Jerusalem Did: Faithless Preparations and Feasting
ISAIAH 22:8B-11,13

Instead of deep, heartfelt repentance, instead of sackcloth and mourning, instead of looking to the Lord in faith to meet the coming threat, Jerusalem made faithless military preparations and feasted. When they should have been mourning, they celebrated. When they should have been trusting in God, they trusted in themselves. The military planners prepared for battle, trusting in the weapons in their arsenal (called "the House of the Forest"); they shored up their defenses and stored up their water. But they did not look to (trust in) the God who created the water pool long ago (v. 11). A city or nation can make all the preparations it wants; if God is against them, it doesn't matter what they do, for disaster is imminent.

As the Babylonians approached, the citizens of Judah and Jerusalem should have been asking themselves and the Lord why this Gentile power was even coming their way to begin with. They should have understood that God had promised to bring Gentile armies to discipline his people for their idolatries if they failed to keep his laws (Deut 32:21-25). They should have mourned for their sins. But instead they faithlessly prepared for battle. And then, when all their preparations were complete, they filled their bellies with meat and wine and celebrated. They said,

"Let us eat and drink, for tomorrow we die!" (v. 13). Paul quoted this exact expression in 1 Corinthians 15:32 as he was working through the implications of life if there is no resurrection from the dead. If this life truly is all there is, then mindless hedonism, grabbing as much pleasure as possible while living in the moment, is the only reasonable course.

God's Solemn Response: This Sin Will Never Be Forgiven
ISAIAH 22:14

The response from the Lord is solemn and terrifying: "This iniquity will not be wiped out for you people as long as you live" (v. 14). It's as though God says this is an unforgivable sin. The wrath of God will be poured out, and there will be no atonement. But why such a terrifying response from our loving and forgiving God? Certainly it is true that no sin is so great that it cannot be covered, given the infinite value of the shed blood of Jesus Christ. But the real issue has to do with how God works salvation in sinful hearts. God calls on sinners to repent and provides the means of grace by which sinners can avail themselves ultimately of the finished work of Christ on the cross. But if instead of repentance and faith the sinners harden their hearts and go exactly the opposite direction, if they party instead of mourning, there is no other way of salvation available.

Jesus Christ: Our Sovereign and Immovable Support
ISAIAH 22:15-25

The rest of the chapter shows a shift from the national warning he gives a century and a half ahead of time to an individual warning given to a man who lived in Isaiah's time. God's Word covers the entire range of human experience, from the global to the individual. Global issues arise from the tendencies of individual human hearts. The universe is made up of atoms. So human history is made up of individuals.

In verses 15-25 God addresses the sinful selfishness of a specific man, Shebna, the palace steward, who had arrogantly misused the prerogatives of his office to carve out a privileged place for himself, including a luxurious crypt where he would ultimately (so he supposed) be buried with full honors. Instead, Isaiah prophesies that he would lose his position of power and be hurled to die in a foreign land. In his place God would raise up a faithful and godly official, Eliakim son of

Hilkiah (v. 20). God would clothe Eliakim with Shebna's robe and sash and install him in power to serve God's people in Jerusalem and Judah (v. 21). But then this prophecy soars above Eliakim, for God promises to place on his shoulder the key to the house of David: "What he opens, no one can close; what he closes, no one can open." God will establish this man as a firm peg for his father's house, and everything will hang on him—all the descendants of his father's house (vv. 23-24). But even he will be sheared away (v. 25) when he also dies.

These verses show the relationship between actual leaders in Judah's history and the ultimate fulfillment in Christ. Judahite history was made up of godless leaders, like those in verses 1-14 and Shebna, as well as of godly, capable leaders, like Eliakim. But ultimately, good and bad will all be sheared away, and all that will be left is Jesus Christ, the King of kings and Lord of lords. The words of verse 22 are ascribed to the resurrected and glorified Christ in Revelation 3:7. He is the one who holds the key; what he opens, no one can close; and what he closes, no one can open. Unlike any human leader (good or bad), now that Christ has risen from the dead, he cannot die again. He is an infinitely strong peg that can never be sheared away. Everything hanging on Christ will be held securely for all eternity.

Application

The strongest application of this chapter is for the people of God to learn how to mourn for sin and how to trust fully in Christ. Mourning for sin is never easy, but it is truly part of the Holy Spirit's work in us as we continue to struggle with sin. There's nothing wrong with wanting to be happy, to celebrate, to eat and drink and be merry. But when God calls on us to mourn, we must not party instead. Many Christians, under conviction of sin, try to take a shortcut back to God: a quick prayer, a brief bowing of the head, a shallow promise never to do it again. But in many cases God is calling us to a far deeper work of mourning and trusting. James 4:9 was written to Christian people to "be miserable and mourn and weep." Sometimes that is the healthiest thing a person can do. Ask God to search you and know you and show you if there is any deep-seated sin pattern that is destroying your life. When the Spirit reveals it to you, do not go too quickly on to happy feelings. Ultimately, trust in Jesus, the firm foundation for your life. Hang everything on him, and he will never let you go.

Reflect and Discuss

1. In our fun-loving age, so saturated with ways to please our senses, how is the message of this chapter ("When God calls you to mourn for sin, don't party instead!") a particularly needed one? Why is it hard for us to accept this message?

2. How does James 4:9 especially support this message?

3. What is the significance of the apostle Paul quoting Isaiah 22 in 1 Corinthians 15:32? How do non-Christians live out this hedonistic philosophy, "Let us eat and drink, for tomorrow we die"?

4. How can we Christians use these concepts to preach the gospel to people who are living for earthly pleasures?

5. What do you make of the fact that God laid all of this out so plainly to Judah through Isaiah the prophet more than 150 years ahead of time?

6. What does this chapter show about the nature of the sinful human heart, especially in the faithless preparations and celebrations?

7. What are some ways that we can go deeper in repentance when the Spirit convicts us of sin? How do we tend to take shortcuts and seek quick fixes so that we can feel good again in our walk with the Lord?

8. How would Psalm 139:23-24 help us in going deeper to do genuine heart work under the painfully thorough convicting work of the Holy Spirit?

9. What do you learn about wicked and godly leadership from the examples of Shebna and Eliakim?

10. What does Revelation 3:7 (quoting Isa 22:22) teach you about Jesus Christ? How is Jesus's power to open doors that no one can shut essential to the advance of the gospel, especially into closed countries where Christianity is illegal?

The Merchants of Tyre Stripped of Their Glory

ISAIAH 23

Who planned this against Tyre, the bestower of crowns, whose traders are princes, whose merchants are the honored ones of the earth? The LORD of Armies planned it, to desecrate all its glorious beauty, to disgrace all the honored ones of the earth. (Isa 23:8-9)

Main Idea: Isaiah speaks an oracle against the wealthy, powerful trading city of Tyre, a symbol for the worldly lust for materials that still dominates our world.

I. **Tyre Described: A Wealthy Merchant City**
   A. Two patterns of world dominance: military and economic
   B. Tyre described: a wealthy merchant city
   C. A heavily protected fortress

II. **Tyre Exposed: A Satanic Stronghold**
   A. Ezekiel 28: the "king of Tyre" condemned
   B. Like Isaiah 14: Satan the puppet master over economic dominators

III. **Tyre Destroyed: A Divine Punishment**
   A. The punishment declared by Isaiah the prophet
   B. The punishment described in greater detail in Ezekiel 26
   C. The punishment decreed by almighty God
   D. The reason for the decree: the humbling of all human pride
   E. Tyre to be rebuilt only to fall again and again
   F. The final fall of Tyre: Revelation 18

IV. **Tyre Evangelized: A Triumph for Christ**
   A. Tyre more bearable on the day of judgment than Capernaum
   B. Tyre visited by Christ; an early Gentile trophy won (Mark 7:24-30)
   C. A growing church in Tyre: Acts 21

Tyre Described: A Wealthy Merchant City

Every year, various large ports vie for the honor of being called the "busiest port in the world." Since 2005, Shanghai, China, has claimed the title based on cargo tonnage: over 500,000 tons of cargo flow by sea through Shanghai every year (AAPA, Port Rankings). The flow of materials through such massive and frantically busy ports like Shanghai and Singapore, Hong Kong and Rotterdam is essential to our international economy; the sea has always been the easiest and most inexpensive way to transport goods. For this reason, large cities have almost always grown by large bodies of water or large rivers. Tyre's dependence on the sea is the focus of this prophecy.

Tyre represents human striving after wealth, the material possessions that will make its people comfortable and happy, prosperous and satisfied. Though each of these possessions is a good gift from God, like any created thing, each can become an idol, the center of human existence. Thus Tyre represents idolatry. It also represents human pride, the great enemy of God.

In Isaiah 23 God speaks through his prophet Isaiah a word of destruction against the busiest seaport of Isaiah's time—the city of Tyre.

Two great patterns of dominance are in world history: military and economic. The "four beasts" of Daniel 7 represent militarily dominant, world-crushing empires. These world conquerors build up their military strength and skill; they stockpile weapons and train vast armies, all to satisfy the lust for conquest that flames the heart of their ambitious king. When the time is right, they sweep over their borders and invade the peaceful dwelling places of their neighbors and plunder them (Ezek 38:11-12). Assyria, Babylon, Medo-Persia, Greece, and Rome all represent this kind of dominance.

Tyre, on the other hand, represents the other kind of dominance: economic. This is a worldwide empire of trade. It is built not by terror and death but by smooth talk and a warm handshake. The Tyrian traders were experts at setting up trade relations with all the regions around the Mediterranean Sea. They gained the confidence of the rulers and forged trade alliances with the merchants in some nation, and soon the ships of Tyre had yet another trading partner by which to become even wealthier. Little by little, they became the hub of all commerce on the Mediterranean, and by their widespread trade they became fabulously rich.

So what was Tyre? Tyre was a port city on the eastern coast of the Mediterranean Sea, in modern-day Lebanon. It was established approximately twenty-eight centuries before the birth of Christ by the sea-faring Phoenicians. Originally, it consisted of two distinct urban centers—one on the mainland and one on a pair of rocky islands just off the coast, like Alcatraz in the San Francisco Bay. King Hiram of Tyre had connected these two islands by means of an embankment and had also brought drinking water to the island port city. The island port city had two harbors, one on the north side and the other on the south; the northern harbor was acclaimed to be one of the best harbors in the eastern Mediterranean. It was from this base that the ships of Tyre (and her neighboring sister city, Sidon) began sailing out into the waters of the Mediterranean to seek trading partners, and they found them. Ezekiel 27:3-25 lists the trading partners of Tyre in detail, likening Tyre itself to a trading vessel made of materials from all over that part of the world. A quick survey of that chapter shows how extensive were the trade routes of the Tyrian ships.

With such a stunning flow of cargo and wealth through Tyre, it seemed best to the kings of Tyre to make the city a powerful fortress, to protect its vastly alluring wealth. In many places in Scripture, Tyre is called a "fortress," quite difficult to capture, even to attack. In fact, the island city's walls went right down to the sea! How do you attack a seafaring nation whose walls prevent any access whatsoever and that can be constantly resupplied by sea? If you try to besiege them, they can get food and water and military supplies by sea at night; if all you have is a land-based army, you have no chance of destroying the island fortress.

Historically, Tyre had a good relationship with Israel. King Hiram of Tyre provided materials for David to build his palace (2 Sam 5:11) as well as vital materials and craftsmen to King Solomon to build the temple of the Lord (1 Kgs 5:1). The latter verse even speaks of the great love that Hiram had for David. But as time went on, Tyre eventually showed itself to be an enemy of God's people. In Ezekiel 26:2-3 God says he is against Tyre because they had delighted in the ruin of Jerusalem. So God said he would bring many nations against Tyre as a judgment. This is exactly what Isaiah 23 had foretold!

Tyre Exposed: A Satanic Stronghold

In order to get a fuller picture of Tyre, however, we must look behind the externals to the true power behind Tyre. As we saw in the commentary on Isaiah 14, two prophecies in the Old Testament concern the fall of Satan: Isaiah 14 and Ezekiel 28. Amazingly, both of them are, on the surface, oracles of judgment against human kings: the king of Babylon (Isa 14) and the king of Tyre (Ezek 28). But, as we made clear in Isaiah 14, these powerful men are merely puppets, dancing on the strings held by the puppet master, Satan. Satan is called the "god of this age" (2 Cor 4:4), the most powerful ruler on earth. He boasted to Jesus that all the kingdoms of the world and their splendor had been given to him, and that he could give them to anyone he wanted to (Luke 4:5-6). Yet, he remains hidden, invisible, the "ruler of the power of the air" (Eph 2:2). So, if the two great patterns of world domination are military and economic, it seems reasonable that the true "king of Babylon" and "king of Tyre" is Satan and that the human kings are merely puppets. How wise for God to speak the words of judgment to the tricky, invisible puppet master through his puppets. They will share the same fate, both languishing in the lake of fire (Rev 20:10).

In Ezekiel 28 the oracle speaks words that soar beyond the ordinary level of speech addressing a human king. The "king of Tyre" was "in Eden, the garden of God" and was "the seal of perfection, full of wisdom and perfect in beauty" (vv. 12-13). This "king of Tyre" was "anointed guardian cherub" on the holy mountain of God, but when his heart became proud because of his beauty, God cast him down to the earth (v. 17). There, the wicked "king of Tyre" corrupted himself by his wide-spread trade.

Thus do the puppet master and the human puppet come together. Satan moves the economic levers, motivating human rulers with the lust of the eyes and yearning for power and glory. They become like him in pride and soaring ambition; and, like him, they come under eternal judgment from God Almighty. In our age the economic megapowers exert in some ways even more influence on the hearts and lives of human beings than do the military. Whether the commodity is oil, wheat, steel, textiles, medicines, high-tech electronics devices, or even money itself, the CEOs, executive boards, and multinational conglomerates shape life on this planet. They set prices and quotas, stimulate covetous desires for individuals and economic vitality for nations, and in some cases decide who lives or dies, and even more powerfully, what they live or die for! Satan is the hidden power behind these thrones, whether they even know he exists or not. Scripture alone exposes Tyre for what it really is: a satanic deception in direct conflict with the holy God.

Tyre Destroyed: A Divine Punishment

The judgment from God is plainly described in this chapter. Isaiah the prophet declares it in verses 1-6, powerfully depicting it as news that reaches Tyrian trader vessels that are nearing their home port from distant Tarshish (possibly in Spain) with yet another rich cargo. The message comes from Cyprus that Tyre has been demolished; her beautiful harbor is gone. So also Sidon has been demolished in the same onslaught. Everything is leveled. The news spreads throughout the Mediterranean Sea's network of trading partners: news reaches Egypt, and the farmers of the Nile will no longer have a market for their grain (vv. 3,5). The destruction of Tyre is even more clearly described in Ezekiel 26:3-14: Nebuchadnezzar, king of Babylon, will destroy the mainland city of Tyre (v. 8); he will make it a bare rock, flat on top (v. 4); fishermen will spread nets over the site (v. 5); the debris will be thrown into the water (v. 12); ultimately, Tyre will never be rebuilt (v. 14).

Isaiah makes it clear that this devastation is no accident of fate or of the ebbs and flows of human history; no, it is a direct judgment from a holy God. Isaiah 23:8-9 states it openly:

> *Who planned this against Tyre, the bestower of crowns, whose traders are princes, whose merchants are the honored ones of the earth? The* Lord *of Armies planned it, to desecrate all its glorious beauty, to disgrace all the honored ones of the earth.*

So also verse 11 says that God stretched out his hand over the sea and made its kingdoms tremble. From these verses it is also plain why God did it: to humble all human pride, to lay low all human glory. Tyre's soaring ambition, like that of the king of Babylon, was a direct challenge and affront to God; so also the merchandise of the nations was an idolatrous system that supplanted God in the hearts of consumers. So God planned a judgment against Tyre to humble human glory.

God planned it, decreed it, and then brought it to pass. Babylon that was itself humbled at one time by Assyria (v. 13) would be God's initial instrument for attacking Tyre. In verses 15-17 it is revealed that Tyre will be humbled, stripped, and laid bare for seventy years. But then she would be rebuilt and again take up her trade with the nations. This would begin the cycle of Tyre's destruction that would continue for many centuries. Nebuchadnezzar's Babylonians did drive his army in a hard campaign against Tyre (Ezek 29:18-20) but would have little to show for it. The majority of Tyre's wealth slipped away by ships to distant ports, and the land-based army of the Babylonians won the city but lost their plunder. An aspect of the prophecy against Tyre was thus yet to be fulfilled: destroyed completely, *never again to be rebuilt.* Three centuries later Alexander the Great came along the coastline, determined to take everything from Tyre. With brilliance and persistence, by recruiting a navy and by scraping the land-based city down to bare rock (as Ezek 26:4,14 predicted) and using the rubble to build a causeway from the mainland, Alexander was able to take the city and all its rich plunder. Alexander then razed the city, and it has never been rebuilt to this day.

But ultimately, according to Isaiah 23:18, the wealth of Tyre will go to the godly. The meek will inherit the earth, and the sons and daughters of Abraham will be heirs of the world (Matt 5:5; Rom 4:13). The final fall of "Tyre" (the spiritual heir of the literal city) will be included in the fall of Babylon in Revelation 18, when the same scenes that are depicted in Isaiah 23 are reenacted: traders and mariners stand afar off and mourn and lament her destruction because her markets are closed and no one will buy their goods anymore (Rev 18:11-13), and sea captains and sailors will see the smoke of her destruction and lament that the time of making wealth through her trade will be over (vv. 17-19). Then will the spirit of Tyre, the marketplace of the nations, be crushed forever.

Tyre Evangelized: A Triumph for Christ

Yet, in the grace and mercy of God, some of the people of Tyre were chosen for salvation, and they will celebrate God's glory and inherit the wealth of the earth through faith in Christ. Several vignettes from the New Testament give us a sense of this sovereign mercy. In Luke 6:17-20 Jesus Christ preached and healed a great number of people from all over Judea, Jerusalem, and the coast of Tyre and Sidon. Then Jesus actually went up to that region and ministered in the vicinity of Tyre (Matt 15:21-28; Mark 7:24-30). A Syro-Phoenician woman from Tyre came to him and pleaded with him to heal her demon-possessed daughter, and he did, a foretaste of the greater grace that would come later. By the time of the book of Acts there was a church at Tyre that met with Paul and sent him on in his work (Acts 21:3-6). How sweet is the grace of God to move through the wreckage of Tyre's lust and greed and create some true gems—people who will spend eternity praising God for grace in Christ.

Applications

Christ alone has the power to rescue us from idolatry, from the greed that comes out of the commerce of the nations. The spirit of Tyre is still alive today. You can see it as you sit by the bay in Shanghai and watch all the cargo ships steam out to the ports of the world. You can see it as you walk down the aisles at Walmart or Best Buy. Jesus said, "Watch out and be on guard against all greed, because one's life is not in the abundance of his possessions" (Luke 12:15). It is for us as Christians to live boldly free from materialism in this present evil age; to be generous with our money, storing up treasure in heaven; to be suspicious of our flesh's desire for the next new electronic device. It is for us to see Satan's hidden presence behind the economic ebbs and flows of human history and to understand that God will judge it finally in the end (Rev 18). It is for us to heed the warnings against worldliness in James 4:4 and 1 John 2:15-17, and to use the things of this world while not being addicted to them (1 Cor 7:29-31). As we consider the issue of worldwide evangelism, we should realize that the consumerism and false joy of the materialistic West has preceded us on the mission field. Coca-Cola is more widespread than the gospel of Jesus Christ. We will have to battle the lie of materialism everywhere we go, even in the poorest nations. Isaiah 23 is a prime place to start, pointing to God's judgments on Tyre as proof of his hatred of worldliness.

Reflect and Discuss

1. Why do you think God is so zealous to destroy Tyre and its busy trade and teeming markets? How does Tyre represent idolatry and human pride?
2. What does this chapter teach you about human nature, human desires, human pleasures, and human pride?
3. What does this chapter teach you about God—his power, plans, and purposes?
4. How does Ezekiel 28 expose the true "king of Tyre" in the same way that Isaiah 14 exposes the true "king of Babylon"?
5. How does Satan manipulate the world economy to suit his wicked purposes? What are Satan's purposes for the markets of the world?
6. How is God's plan for Tyre unfolded in world history? If God intended to destroy Tyre so that it would never be rebuilt, why did it take centuries to accomplish it?

7. What connection do you see between Tyre and Babylon in Revelation 18? What verbal similarities do you see between Isaiah 23 and Revelation 18?
8. How is this chapter a general warning to Christians against the consumerism that dominates our lifestyles?
9. How do we as Christians combat the "spirit of Tyre" (worldliness, lust for possessions) that we see in our hearts and lives?
10. How does this issue affect missions and the spread of the gospel to the ends of the earth?

Judgments for the Earth, Joy for the Righteous, Glory for God

ISAIAH 24

They raise their voices, they sing out; they proclaim in the west the majesty of the LORD. Therefore in the east honor the LORD! In the coasts and islands of the west honor the name of the LORD, the God of Israel.
(Isa 24:14-15)

Main Idea: God's ongoing judgment of human cities one after another culminates in the destruction of the final version of the rebellious "City of Man" by the glory of Christ's second coming.

I. **The Judgments of God on the Whole Earth (24:1-6)**
   A. "Isaiah's apocalypse": a sweeping vision for human history
   B. God's judgments extended to all nations and all peoples (24:1-2)
   C. The reason for the devastation: human sin (24:5-6)
   D. Yet in wrath, God remembers mercy (24:6).

II. **The End of Worldly Joy (24:7-12)**
   A. Pursuit of escape in worldly pleasure shut down by God (24:11)
   B. The destruction of the City of Man (24:10-12)
   C. A constant cycle of invasion/destruction
   D. All suffering in some sense a judgment from God

III. **The Reactions of the Righteous (24:13-16)**
   A. The godly remnant (olives and grapes) (24:13)
   B. Two very different reactions by the righteous

IV. **Outside of Christ, Inescapable Judgment (24:17-22)**
   A. They will run, but they cannot hide or escape.
   B. A fine filter, and none can slip through (24:17-18).
   C. The whole earth will be destroyed (24:19-20).
   D. Satanic powers will be judged with their earthly puppets (24:21-22).

V. **The Finale: God's Glorious City (24:23)**
   A. City of Man removed; City of God remains forever.

B. The new Jerusalem: Mount Zion and Jerusalem become truly one.
C. The new universe has a new light source: the glory of God in Jesus.

The Judgments of God on the Whole Earth
ISAIAH 24:1-6

As we come to this chapter we are entering a new section of Isaiah's prophecy. The unifying theme of Isaiah 13–23 has been God as the sovereign ruler of the nations—for his own glory, for the judgment of the wicked, and for the salvation of the righteous. Now, Isaiah 24–27 serves as a glorious capstone for this section:

- Isaiah 24: God's judgment generally on the whole earth
- Isaiah 25–27: The delight of the righteous in God's defeat of death, the redemption of Israel, and the fruitfulness of the world

Isaiah 24 is a very complex and detailed chapter; it covers the destruction of the whole earth and the establishment of God's open reign in Jerusalem. Because of these grand and glorious themes, and because the total destruction of the earth is in view, some have called this chapter "Isaiah's Apocalypse" (Motyer, *Prophecy of Isaiah*, 200). It speaks in generic terms about many judgments from the Lord that would occur from Isaiah's time onward, including our present day, all of them dress rehearsals for the final drama described so powerfully in the book of Revelation. A key concept for biblical eschatology comes from this statement from Jesus: "As the days of Noah were, so the coming of the Son of Man will be" (Matt 24:37). "As it was, so it will be": past events are dress rehearsals for final events. Redemptive history will continue in repeatable patterns until these events are consummated in the second coming of Jesus Christ. So in Isaiah 24 we have judgments (plural) from God on the whole earth because of human sin; those judgments follow a certain pattern, likened to the fall of a walled city: "*The city* of chaos is shattered; every house is closed to entry" (v. 10; emphasis added); "Only desolation remains in *the city*; its gate has collapsed in ruins" (v. 12; emphasis added). "The city" represents what Augustine called the "City of Man": the sum total of human society and experience, the "world."

That the city represents all of human society is increasingly true: in 2008 it was established that 50 percent of the world's population lives in urban settings; by the year 2050 it will surpass 66 percent (UN, "World Urbanization Prospects"). But whether urban or rural, the "City of Man" represents all of humanity.

Isaiah 24 depicts the fall over and over again of aspects of the City of Man, usually by other people invading and destroying them.

So in the fifth century when Attila the Hun was sweeping through Europe and destroying one village after another, he was called the "Scourge of God"; the destruction was seen to be God's judgment for sins. So also with the Vikings in the tenth century and Genghis Khan and the Mongol horde in the thirteenth century. Conqueror after conqueror, sweeping in to batter gates to pieces and destroy buildings; people giving up joy and music and drinking and dancing, cowering behind the barred doors of their homes, hoping to survive, but there would be no escape. Isaiah 24 depicts this pattern that earth's people will experience again and again until Jesus returns.

The chapter begins with a sweeping statement: God is stripping the earth bare and scattering its inhabitants (v. 1). It begins with two dramatic words in the original Hebrew, "Look, the LORD." By faith in the prophetic word, we are to see God's activity in these judgments, as if the chapter pulls back a veil that had hidden his activity. God is not a tribal deity, concerned only with Israel and the tiny promised land. His judgments range over the whole surface of the earth and over every era of human history.

And there is no escape from the net of God's judgments. Verse 2 makes it plain that God's judgments extend to "people and priest alike, servant and master, female servant and mistress, buyer and seller, lender and borrower, creditor and debtor"—no one escapes. The entire surface of the earth will be stripped completely bare (v. 3), and the whole earth will mourn, wither, and waste away (v. 4). The reason for the judgment is the wickedness of the human race (v. 5). People have defiled the earth, so God rises to judge the polluters (Rev 11:18).

Yet in all this wrath, God still remembers mercy (Hab 3:2). Though "only a few survive" (Isa 24:6), there is nevertheless a remnant that God preserves for salvation. They are a picture of the elect, chosen by grace, whom God rescues from the wrecks of time by the cross of Christ.

The End of Worldly Joy
ISAIAH 24:7-12

As we've seen in Isaiah 21–22, people are always seeking escape from God's judgments in sensual pleasures. The night Babylon fell, Belshazzar was feasting (Dan 5). So also in secular history: while the Red Army was conquering Berlin in 1945, the remnants of the wicked Nazi regime were partying in Hitler's bunker before committing suicide. In Isaiah 24 we see this so clearly—the yearning for joy and revelry, music and drinking, eating and carousing. But God has shut it all down completely (vv. 7-9). The noise of the revelers comes to an end; the last song has been sung (v. 8). The sinners in the "City of Man" must face the judgments of God sober, and they will be slaughtered themselves: only desolation is left in a once-populous city (v. 12).

In all this horror there are no accidents, there is no bad luck, no fate. Every time a city has been destroyed by a conquering army it is in some sense a judgment from God. As Jesus said in Luke 13:1-5, unless every sinner on the face of the earth repents, they "will all perish as well." The sinners in the cities that weren't destroyed in Germany in 1945 were no better in God's sight than the ones who lived in Dresden or Berlin, which were leveled by the Allies. Every destruction is a message from God: repent or perish!

The Reactions of the Righteous
ISAIAH 24:13-16

As the "City of Man" is destroyed, the righteous among the human race have two very different reactions, both reflected in verses 13-16. First, the godly are depicted as a tiny remnant (a few olives or grapes) who lift their voices in triumphant worship, celebrating the majesty of the Lord. Because of thousands of years of successful missions spreading the gospel of Christ, this chorus of praise extends from west to east, from the distant islands of the west to the ends of the earth. This is one valid reaction: unbridled joy in the Lord, the mighty Warrior, who has destroyed his enemies completely.

On the other hand, Isaiah represents an opposite reaction by a godly man. In verse 16 he grieves and laments the details of this vision. He feels like his body is wasting away because of the judgments of the Lord that are yet to be unleashed on the earth. Perhaps Isaiah is lamenting all the damage the treacherous have yet to do on the earth, like Elisha weeping in advance of Hazael's destructions (2 Kgs 8:11-12). The earth will be viciously convulsed before the Lord returns, and much suffering is still to come.

Outside of Christ, Judgment Is Inescapable
ISAIAH 24:17-22

In verses 17-22 Isaiah makes it plain that God will weave his net with fine mesh, and no one will escape. "Panic, pit, and trap" await the people of the earth, and whoever escapes the one will be caught by the second; whoever escapes the first two will be swallowed by the third. Like an earthquake, when the very ground beneath your feet is convulsing, there is no refuge, nowhere to hide (vv. 18-20). These terrifying verses show a comprehensive level of destruction that will ultimately be fulfilled only in the awesome events depicted in the book of Revelation. Outside of Christ, there is no escape possible.

As the earth itself is being judged, the Lord also will punish the "army of the heights in the heights" and the "kings of the ground on the ground" (vv. 21-22). This refers to Satan and the demonic "evil, spiritual forces in the heavens" (Eph 6:12) and to the human rulers who dominated people under their power. So both the demonic puppet masters and the human puppet kings will be judged on that final day. Verse 22 mentions a dungeon in which some of these "army of the heights" and "kings of the ground" are held until the time comes for final judgment (Matt 8:29; 2 Pet 2:4).

The Finale: God's Glorious City
ISAIAH 24:23

The final verse in this awesome chapter depicts the Lord of Armies reigning as king on Mount Zion in Jerusalem, putting his glory on display before the elders. Some believe this refers to the millennial reign of Christ in Jerusalem; others see it finally fulfilled in the new Jerusalem depicted in Revelation 21–22. The City of Man will be purified, with only the redeemed left. The City of God will descend and become the City of Man, with the God-Man, Christ, at the center of the union. And how glorious that will be!

Application

All phases of the City of Man, erected for the glory of man, will be laid waste: first, by one another, in an ongoing cycle of invasion and destruction, one rising empire supplanting the previous; second, by the second coming of Christ. He will bring the final judgment of God, to which all of these smaller dress rehearsals have been pointing throughout history. Because this is so, we should live as aliens and strangers on earth, looking ahead to a "city that has foundations, whose architect and builder is God" (Heb 11:10). We should be faithful in preaching the gospel to the ends of the earth so the worldwide worship of the Lord by the remnant (Isa 24:14-16) may come to pass. By faith we should flee to Christ, who is the only refuge from the coming wrath. Like Isaiah, we should weep for the misery yet to come, for it will be dreadful. But in the end, we should celebrate the glory of the Lord who will be reigning in Zion (the new Jerusalem) forever.

Reflect and Discuss

1. How does the expansive vision of this chapter teach us to look on the ebbs and flows of history?
2. Matthew 24:37 says, essentially, "As it was, so it will be." How was the destruction of Berlin by the Russians in 1945 a dress rehearsal for the destruction of the earth right before the second coming of Christ?
3. What did Augustine mean by "The City of Man" and "The City of God"? How does this chapter depict the destruction of "The City of Man"?
4. How does this chapter depict the end to all empty, earthly joy (alcohol, music, revelry, etc.)?
5. How do verses 14-16 depict the fruit of missions?
6. Why does Isaiah grieve and mourn in verse 16?
7. How does this chapter depict the impossibility of escaping the judgment of God? How could we use these verses to preach the gospel to people?
8. What do verses 21-22 teach about the judgment of satanic forces and human rulers alike?
9. How does verse 23 depict the final glory of God's reign? How does it harmonize with the vision of the new Jerusalem in Revelation 21–22?
10. How does this chapter help motivate us to evangelism and missions?

God Will Swallow Up Death Forever

ISAIAH 25

On this mountain he will destroy the burial shroud, the shroud over all the peoples, the sheet covering all the nations; he will destroy death forever. (Isa 25:7-8)

Main Idea: We find four themes of praise in God's magnificent actions: executing his wise plan in history (v. 1), converting violent nations to worship him (vv. 2-5), swallowing death forever in the resurrection of Jesus Christ (vv. 6-9), and condemning arrogant nations by his justice and power (vv. 10-12).

I. **Praise God for Carrying Out His Wise Eternal Plan (25:1).**
   A. God's eternal plan
   B. The praise of his glorious grace
   C. God's perfect faithfulness
II. **Praise God for Converting Violent Nations (25:2-5).**
   A. The "City of Man" destroyed
   B. God revered by violent nations
   C. A sweet history of the violent being converted
III. **Praise God for Swallowing Up Death Forever (25:6-9).**
   A. "Original sin": the shroud of death covering all nations
   B. One of the clearest prophecies of the resurrection
   C. A rich banquet spread: death swallowed up forever
IV. **Praise God for Condemning Arrogant Nations (25:10-12).**
   A. The reprobate nations drowned in God's judgment
   B. Eternity free from the wicked

Praise God for Carrying Out His Wise Eternal Plan
ISAIAH 25:1

Before the foundation of the earth, God had crafted a perfect plan for the universe. God's eternality, perfect wisdom, omnipotence, and zeal for his own glory combined to fashion this perfect plan. One of the staggering things about the omniscience of God is that it means he never learns anything. If God can learn something, it means God didn't know it before he learned it, and that would mean God wasn't omniscient. So all of human history was completed in God's mind before he spoke anything into existence. God's zeal for his own glory means that God's plan was crafted to maximize his glory, to put his attributes radiantly on display. But without an audience, what would be the point? God created beings who could know and delight in his glory and give him praise for it. God's love would pour out to his creatures—human beings—who could enjoy him in a love relationship. It was out of love that God wanted to give to people the greatest gift he could give—himself! God wanted us to be as happy as he is by enabling us to delight in the grand display of his perfections in creation and in history.

But sin entered the universe in a mysterious way, twisting the minds of people so they "worshiped and served what has been created instead of the Creator" (Rom 1:25). With the entrance of sin came the just penalty for sin: death (5:12-14; 6:23). The death penalty was a universal disgrace to the human race, a shroud that covered all nations. In Isaiah 25 the removal of this disgraceful shroud is proclaimed and celebrated! Amazingly, the entrance of sin into God's perfectly good universe actually increased the display of God's glory, for it enabled him to unfold a plan of redemption though his Son, Jesus Christ. For eternity, the redeemed will study the history of God's grace to sinners like us and be swept up in self-forgetful worship!

God's perfect plan for history involves a meticulous sequencing of events—first this, then that, then the next four things, etc.—resulting in a marvelous tapestry of glory. Therefore, Isaiah 25 celebrates four great elements of God's actions in history: (1) executing his wise plan in history (v. 1), (2) converting violent nations to worship him (vv. 2-5), (3) swallowing death forever in the resurrection of Jesus Christ (vv. 6-9), and (4) condemning arrogant nations by his justice and power (vv. 10-12). Because God does all this "to the praise of his glorious grace" (Eph 1:6), it is best to cast each heading in the language of exuberant praise.

Praise God for Converting Violent Nations
ISAIAH 25:2-5

The first element of that wise plan is somewhat surprising. In Isaiah 24 we saw God crush the "City of Man," the self-glorying empire building that has characterized history. Isaiah 25:2 picks up that same theme again, saying that part of God's ancient plan is turning the fortress of "barbarians" into piles of rubble, never to be rebuilt. But suddenly in verse 3 God reveals that his purpose in destroying these cities is so that "a strong people will honor [him]. The cities of violent nations will fear [him]." This speaks of the power of God to convert formerly terrifying enemies into genuine worshipers: Nebuchadnezzar, the murderous tyrant (Dan 4:34-35); the Roman centurion who crucified Jesus (Mark 15:39); Saul of Tarsus, who began the day breathing out murderous threats against the Lord's disciples and ended the day a Christian (Acts 9:1-8). This power to transform world conquerors into genuine worshipers has been played out again and again in history. Courageous missionaries have faced death and persecution to spread the gospel to one terrifying, war-loving people after another: world-conquering Romans, scimitar-wielding Muslims, fierce Viking warriors, head-hunting cannibals, Amazonian tribes, communist party officials behind the Iron Curtain, etc. Heaven will be full of formerly vicious warriors who became disillusioned and sat on piles of rubble in their home cities after returning home from lost wars, who later found Christ after their worldly dreams of conquest were shattered.

Until the violent are converted, God must protect his beloved people from the storm of their vicious attacks, so verses 4-5 depict the refuge God is from their onslaught. The delight of his people comes when God at last stills the song of the violent by either converting them or crushing them, as he does at the end of the chapter.

Praise God for Swallowing Up Death Forever
ISAIAH 25:6-9

Isaiah 25:6-9 is one of the clearest predictions in the Old Testament of the resurrection of Jesus Christ from the dead. Romans 5:12 teaches that sin and death spread to all human beings in Adam. The entire human race is covered with shame because of this death penalty. Isaiah 25:6-9 depicts a lavish feast spread by the Lord of Armies, a banquet with the best of wines and choice meats. This feast is spread "for all the peoples," for the entire human race, laid out "on this mountain." It is a metaphorical feast, for it consists of God destroying the burial shroud that covers all nations—death itself. The verse plainly says that God will "destroy death forever." The Hebrew word translated accurately by most versions ("swallow up") gives the picture of an overwhelming defeat of death, like the earth swallowing up the enemies of God. God uncovers the face of the corpse and speaks the word of resurrection, removing the disgrace of his people from the whole earth. They rise in power, never to die again. The disgrace of sin and death has been swallowed up in victory (1 Cor 15:54).

Clearly this has been fulfilled in the death and resurrection of Jesus Christ. He is the death Conqueror, and by his death and resurrection alone are these words fulfilled. "On this mountain," Mount Zion (Jerusalem), Jesus wins his victory over death once for all. And he speaks the clear promise to the human race: "I am the resurrection and the life. The one who believes in me, even if he dies, will live" (John 11:25). This is the most lavish feast in history—eternal life through faith in Christ!

Praise God for Condemning Arrogant Nations
ISAIAH 25:10-12

The chapter ends in a strange way, with Isaiah speaking words of condemnation against Moab, who probably represents the reprobate among the nations, those who will never believe. God will bring down Moab's pride as if he were a swimmer drowning in a dung pile. Part of the joy of heaven will be that God will weed out of his kingdom everything that causes sin and all those who do evil (Matt 13:41). We will feast in peace, free from the assaults of the arrogant.

Applications

As noted, this chapter gives four magnificent themes for us to use in praise to God. In light of these, we should live confidently in this world, knowing that God, in his wisdom, has crafted a marvelous plan. We should pray that he will carry out faithfully every detail of his plan. We should live utterly fearless lives in the face of death, for wicked oppressors still stalk the earth, many of whom will be converted by the grace of God. And we should long for the day when the wicked will either be converted or be destroyed by the power of God.

Reflect and Discuss

1. What four actions does this chapter focus on as grounds for heart-felt praise for God?
2. What do Ephesians 1:6,12,14 teach us about God's motives for his redemptive plan?
3. How does Isaiah 25:1 point to God's perfect eternal plan? How does God show perfect faithfulness in carrying out his eternal plan?
4. Why do some people struggle with the concept of God having fashioned a plan for all things from before the foundation of the world (Eph 1:11)?
5. What surprising act of God is celebrated in Isaiah 25:3? How is it an encouragement to missionaries who are facing daunting challenges in bringing the gospel to a violent and resistant people?
6. What is the banquet that God spreads in verses 6-8? How is the swallowing up of death forever like a rich banquet?
7. How is death a disgrace for all people? How does faith in Christ remove that disgrace?
8. How is the death and resurrection of Jesus Christ the fulfillment of these verses?
9. How does verse 9 help us to praise God?
10. What do verses 10-12 speak about? How does God's treatment of Moab show his power?

A Song of Salvation for the Peace of the Oppressed

ISAIAH 26

*You will keep the mind that is dependent on you in perfect peace, for it is trusting in you. Trust in the L*ORD *forever, because in the L*ORD*, the L*ORD *himself, is an everlasting rock!* (Isa 26:3-4)

Main Idea: God speaks a promise of perfect peace in the midst of great suffering for the people of God.

I. **A Song of Trust in God (26:1-6)**
    A. A song to be sung by the suffering
    B. A tale of two cities consummated
    C. The perfect peace of the City of God
    D. The total destruction of the City of Man
II. **A Lament While Waiting for Salvation (26:7-18)**
    A. Walking in righteousness, waiting on the Lord
    B. The purpose of God's judgments: an education in righteousness
    C. God glorified in crushing tyrants and enlarging the nation
    D. Lamenting the weakness of the people
III. **The Joyful End: Resurrection and Deliverance (26:19-21)**
    A. The magnificent promise of the resurrection
    B. Hiding in the meantime

A Song of Trust in God
ISAIAH 26:1-6

In Isaiah 24–27 the suffering people of God who are going through the fires of oppression at the hands of vicious tyrants are given two great encouragements: (1) God is actively ruling right now, measuring out the victories of the wicked and limiting the damage they can do to his beloved people; (2) God will someday crush all the oppressors and set up an eternal kingdom in which he will reign gloriously over all his people.

As we've seen, Isaiah 24–25 gives triumphant prophecies of final victory by the Lord over all tyrants who oppress God's people in this world. But Isaiah 26 teaches God's oppressed people how to celebrate right now, before the final victory has come, when the oppressors are still trampling the poor with bloody, hobnailed boots. Isaiah is dealing realistically with the "right now" for the people of his day and beyond; they are dominated by earthly oppressors, carried off into exile by either Assyria or Babylon. These massive, city-based empires seem unconquerable; the future for Israel and Judah looks very bleak indeed. How then can God's people sing a song of celebration when it seems like the tyrants are winning all the battles? Isaiah 26 is a song of realistic praise for God's present protection and future deliverance for his suffering people.

It begins with a faith-filled look ahead to "that day," when God will at last throw down the "City of Man" and all its oppression, as described in Isaiah 24–25. "On that day" the people of God will be singing the celebration song, a song of triumph for the mighty "City of God," a strong and glorious city with walls and ramparts, with mighty gates standing open, so only the righteous nation that has remained faithful to God can enter (Isa 26:1-2). This city is the eternal city described so vividly in Revelation, the "new Jerusalem" whose gates of pearl always stand open to allow the righteous from all the nations on earth to enter (21:25).

Because of this secure future, God is able to keep in perfect peace those whose minds are steadfast, who are continually trusting in God (Isa 26:3). Here we Christians are exhorted to trust continually in the Lord Jesus Christ in all circumstances.

A Lament While Waiting for Salvation
ISAIAH 26:7-18

There is a toilsome journey for the righteous to travel in this sin-cursed world before we come into our inheritance, and verses 7-9 give a beautiful recipe for the righteous while we travel. God makes the path of the righteous level by his commands and his judgments; the smoothest path through this world is obedience to the laws of God. Verse 8 teaches that God's name and fame should be the top desires of our hearts. But while we seek to live obedient lives and spread the name of the Lord Jesus to the ends of the earth, we are still waiting on the Lord, yearning for him to reveal himself to us and to the wicked. So we trust in God's sovereign rule over the wicked of the earth. The purpose of God's judgments is to teach the world his righteousness. But the wicked constantly misinterpret the lessons, blind to the implications of God's wrath poured out on other wicked people (vv. 9-11).

Meanwhile, God's people continue to seek God's glory and to do good works in the world. But as we do, we come to understand the profound truth of verse 12: all of our good works were done only by the power of God in us (John 3:21). The saddest part of our journey in the world is acknowledging our idolatries, when other lords have ruled our affections (Isa 26:13); but God works genuine repentance in us to restore us to him alone. Ultimately, God's judgments crush all tyrants, but God continues to sustain and enlarge his people (vv. 14-15). The nation of Israel was restored to the promised land after the exile, but this is merely a picture of God's ultimate saving work in his people throughout redemptive history. Not by our own strength has the nation of the elect survived and increased in this dangerous world, for the people of God who suffer under his discipline can barely whisper a prayer; they do not bring salvation to the earth (v. 18). This is a powerful picture of the weakness of Israel in the Old Testament and the church in the new. God alone can finish his saving work in the world.

The Joyful End: Resurrection and Deliverance
ISAIAH 26:19-21

Isaiah 26:19 is one of the clearest prophecies of the bodily resurrection of the dead in the Old Testament. Though God's people die in the judgment of Adam, though our bodies sink back into the dust from which we came (Gen 3:19), yet "the earth will bring out the departed spirits." Taken together with Isaiah 26:18, it is clear that God alone can save sinners from the penalty of their sins. We have no plan, no strategy, no power to raise our own bodies from the grave. But Jesus Christ has made a promise to sinners that should melt our hearts and fill our mouths with exuberant praise: "I am the resurrection and the life. The one who believes in me, even if he dies, will live. Everyone who lives and believes in me will never die" (John 11:25-26). Someday the dead will rise in radiant glory to give eternal praise to Jesus who gave them life; they will "awake and sing"!

In the meantime, God's people must hide for a little while until the storm of God's judgments on the wicked of the earth has passed by (Isa 26:20-21). The wicked will continue to shed the blood of the righteous, as Cain did to Abel. But someday the earth will disclose that blood, and the unrepentant wicked will be brought to judgment for their crimes. Isaiah 26 is a magnificent chapter for the redeemed to cling to while riding out the convulsive storm of redemptive history.

Application

Isaiah 26:3 is one of the great verses in the Bible on an abiding peace in the midst of afflictions. The doctrine of our salvation is a secure foundation for our peace. We have an objective status of peace with God through our justification by faith in Christ (Rom 5:1), and we can never lose that. Beyond that objective peace, however, there is a subjective sense of peacefulness that we should have by keeping our minds fixed on Christ. If our minds continually depend on Christ, we will have a continual experience of peace in him; if trials and anxieties divert our minds from Christ, we can temporarily lose our peacefulness. Philippians 4:6-7 teaches the same thing:

> *Don't worry about anything, but in everything, through prayer and petition with thanksgiving, present your requests to God. And the peace of God, which surpasses all understanding, will guard your hearts and minds in Christ Jesus.*

If we cast our burdens on God through prayer, we will find the peace of God guarding our hearts and minds in Christ Jesus, just as Isaiah 26 pictures salvation like a walled fortress, with high gates and ramparts.

Reflect and Discuss

1. How does this chapter fit into the flow of Isaiah 24–27?
2. How does it give a realistic and yet encouraging outlook on the suffering and the sustaining grace God's people will experience in this world?
3. What does verse 3 promise to the people of God in this world?
4. What is "perfect peace"? How does God promise to keep his people at peace in this world?
5. How does verse 3 relate to Philippians 4:6-7?

6. What practical advice does Isaiah 26:7-8 give to help God's people in their toilsome journey through a world of spiritual enemies?
7. Why are the wicked unable to see the mighty hand of God lifted threateningly against them (v. 10)?
8. How should we learn to give God full glory for all of our good works (v. 12; John 3:21; 15:5)?
9. How is Isaiah 26:19 a clear prediction of the general resurrection of bodies from the earth?
10. What practical advice do verses 20-21 give to the persecuted church in the world?

The Lord—a Warrior and Vinekeeper—Saves His Sinful People

ISAIAH 27

In days to come, Jacob will take root. Israel will blossom and bloom and fill the whole world with fruit. (Isa 27:6)

Main Idea: The Lord shows his great power as a warrior and a vinekeeper, so his people will fill the world with fruit for his glory.

I.   **The Wicked Serpent Is Slain (27:1).**
   A.   The epic battle: the Lord versus Leviathan
   B.   Who is Leviathan? What is the sword of the Lord?
   C.   Already and not yet
II. **The Vineyard Fills the World with Fruit (27:2-6).**
   A.   The vineyard of Israel, fruitful at last!
   B.   All enemies thrown down
III. **The People Are Punished by Measure but Only to Purify (27:7-11).**
   A.   Israel will be struck, but those who strike her will be struck harder.
   B.   Israel's bitter punishment purges her of sin.
   C.   Israel's cities are made desolate.
IV. **The Elect Are Gathered by Trumpet Call One by One (27:12-13).**
   A.   The people of God threshed by judgment
   B.   The people of God gathered by trumpet
   C.   The people of God assembled to worship
V.   **The Gospel of Jesus According to Isaiah 27**

The Wicked Serpent Slain

ISAIAH 27:1

The chapter opens with an awesome battle between two ancient enemies: the Lord vs. Leviathan. Like a heavyweight title fight, this battle is observed by angels and men as the central struggle in the universe. But the Lord's victory is proclaimed here from the beginning, for the battle is between two infinitely unequal foes. Who is Leviathan? In this chapter the beast is described as a twisting, hissing serpent, a "monster that is in the sea." The Lord brings judgment on this coiling serpent, putting it to flight with his "relentless, large, strong sword."

Some Old Testament scholars have noted the similarities of this battle with the mythological struggle in the Babylonian creation myth, the *Enuma Elish* (Pritchard, *Ancient Near Eastern Texts*, 66–68).[8] But there was no need for Isaiah to reach for a Babylonian myth. The Bible itself uses such imagery to picture God's power over pagan nations. In celebrating the destruction of Pharaoh's army in the Red Sea crossing, Psalm 74:13-14 says to the Lord, "You divided the sea with your strength; you smashed the heads of the sea monsters in the water; you crushed the heads of Leviathan; you fed him to the creatures of the desert." So what is Leviathan? It seems reasonable to understand the "sea monster" both as the Gentile empires that rise out of the sea to destroy God's people (Dan 7) and as "the ancient serpent, who is called the devil" (Rev 12:9). The serpent motivates the Gentile empires to invade Israel with a long, marching army like a twisting, hissing serpent. The Lord is able to defeat Leviathan with the "relentless, large, strong sword" of his word (see Heb 4:12). Therefore, Isaiah 27:1 represents the power of God to destroy his enemies (Satan and wicked empires) by his powerful word. This is a victory that has already been won through Jesus, and it will be won again at the end of the world. It is "already and not yet."

The Vineyard Fills the World with Fruit
ISAIAH 27:2-6

Verses 2-6 depict the nation of Israel (Jacob) as an abundantly fruitful vineyard. In contrast to the disappointing vineyard of Isaiah 5:1-7, this time the vineyard of the Lord will be worthy of a sweet song of celebration. The Lord will protect it and water it continually (v. 3). He is done being angry at his people and now speaks a word of comfort and blessing to a people formerly under his judgment. He will purge the vineyard of thorns and briers (symbols of the curse—Gen 3:18), guaranteeing its fruitfulness. Even though formerly his enemies, he urges his people to take hold of him for strength and make peace with him (vv. 4-5). As a

---

[8] Motyer also has a good extended discussion on Isaiah's use of mythology (*Prophecy of Isaiah*, 408–10).

result, Jacob will take root in the rich soil of God's grace and "fill the whole world with fruit" (v. 6).

The People Are Punished by Measure but Only to Purify
ISAIAH 27:7-11

These verses depict the good effects of God's stern punishments of Israel. God decrees a bitter exile under the domination of Gentile nations, but even this punishment is measured. God did not punish Israel as he punished the nations that punished Israel. Those nations God eventually gave over to total extinction—not a remnant was left. But God preserved a remnant among the Jews (Isa 1:9), which he did not do among the Assyrians and Babylonians. The purpose of this punishment was to create a heart separation between the people and their idols. By exile, the people would learn to hate the pagan altars and Asherah poles that had caused God's wrath; they would purge the land of those wicked emblems of paganism, crushing the altar stones like chalk with a fiery zeal. Exile would result in the cities of Israel and Judah (including Jerusalem) being completely deserted. But even in the severest judgments, God still remembered mercy.

The Elect Are Gathered by Trumpet Call One by One
ISAIAH 27:12-13

"In that day," when God is dealing so directly with Israel, he will thresh his people throughout the promised land (from the northern to the southern boundaries). Threshing involves separating the wheat from the chaff, and God would "clear his threshing floor and gather his wheat into the barn. But the chaff he will burn with fire that never goes out" (Matt 3:12). The Israelites will be tested and threshed "one by one," and no one will escape the careful judgment of God. When the people of God are threshed, he will then send out a trumpet call (Num 10:3) to assemble the remnant that is left from Assyria and Egypt to gather at the holy mountain in Jerusalem to worship the Lord.

The Gospel of Jesus According to Isaiah 27
So many of the themes of Isaiah 27 prefigure the saving work of Jesus Christ. It was Christ whose death destroyed Satan, "that ancient serpent," and freed his people from death (Heb 2:14-15; Rev 20:2). It was Christ's

resurrection and the irresistible power of the advancing kingdom of Christ that continues to crush Satan under our "beautiful feet" (Rom 10:15; 16:20). At his second coming Jesus will crush the final pagan empire of the antichrist and consign both the beast and the devil to the lake of fire, triumphing over them both by the harsh, powerful sword that comes from his mouth—his word (2 Thess 2:8; Rev 19:15; 20:10). It is Christ who guarantees the fruitfulness of God's vineyard by being the vine, and we are the branches (John 15:1-8). God says in Isaiah 27:4, "I am not angry." But only in Christ's work of propitiation is the wrath of God finally averted from the people of God (Rom 3:25). In Christ alone are the remnant of Israel, chosen by grace, finally saved (Rom 11:5). And in Christ alone are the scattered people of God gathered together with the trumpet call of the gospel, assembled to worship God in the new Jerusalem (John 11:51-52; also Matt 24:31).

Applications

We should understand and celebrate each detail of the way Christ has defeated Satan, is defeating him, and will continue to defeat him. We should seek to bear fruit for the glory of God through abiding in Jesus (John 15:1-8). The fruit of our lives should extend to the ends of the earth, especially in our zealous efforts to advance the gospel of Jesus Christ to unreached people groups. We should also be zealous to crush the idolatry in our lives—worldliness, sexual immorality, greed, etc. Finally, we should be part of God's clear "trumpet blast" to the nations, calling the elect from every tribe to faith in Christ, for that great day of assembly, for the worship of God and of the Lamb in the new Jerusalem.

Reflect and Discuss

1. How should verse 1 motivate us to study and master God's Word so we can wield it as a spiritual sword (Eph 6:17) in battling sin and Satan more effectively?

2. How can we understand the great suffering our persecuted brothers and sisters are experiencing around the world in light of this chapter?

3. How would you contrast Isaiah 5:1-7 with 27:2-6? Why does the first vineyard of God fail so miserably and the second one succeed so handsomely?

4. How can Christians come to a fuller realization of God's assertion about us: "I am not angry" (v. 4)?

5. Read verse 6 in light of John 15:1-8. What is the "fruit" that God wants to see in our lives?

6. How does verse 6 point to the fruit of the gospel around the world in the advance of missions?

7. How does verse 7 show that God deals differently with his chosen people in the world than he does with the wicked? How are their punishments far more severe than ours?

8. How is idolatry still an issue for Christians now as it was for Israel in the Old Testament?

9. How do verses 12-13 show God's faithfulness to Israel after the exile? How does his power to regather them by a trumpet blast give you reason for worship?

10. How does the gospel of Jesus Christ draw together all the themes of this chapter?

Self-Salvation versus Salvation in Christ

ISAIAH 28

Therefore the Lord GOD said: "Look, I have laid a stone in Zion, a tested stone, a precious cornerstone, a sure foundation; the one who believes will be unshakable." (Isa 28:16)

Main Idea: People try to save themselves from death by their own efforts. But Christ alone is the rock of refuge, and whoever trusts in him will never be shaken.

I. **A Fading Crown on a Drunkard versus a Glorious Crown on the Remnant (28:1-6)**
   A. The warning to Judah: the fall of drunken Ephraim
   B. The impending judgment on Ephraim: a fading crown thrown down
   C. A glorious crown on the head of the remnant
II. **God Speaking through the Prophets versus God Speaking through Judgment (28:7-13)**
   A. The key moment: hearing the prophetic word of the Lord
   B. Mocking the word of God, then God speaking more clearly
III. **The Shaky Foundation of Self-Salvation versus the Solid Rock of God's Salvation (28:14-22)**
   A. The "covenant with Death": self-salvation
   B. God's sure foundation: Christ, the Rock laid in Zion
   C. The final warning: catastrophe approaching
IV. **The Parable of the Farmer (28:23-29)**
   A. The primary lesson: God knows what he's doing.
   B. The secondary lesson: God teaches all science.

A Fading Crown on a Drunkard versus a Glorious Crown on the Remnant

ISAIAH 28:1-6

Isaiah chapters 28, 29, 30, 31, and 33 all begin with "Woe," the prophetic word of warning that God's judgment is coming. In this chapter

God cites the judgment about to fall on the northern kingdom of Israel, called "Ephraim." He yearns that the southern kingdom of Judah would take to heart the lessons from that judgment. The Lord speaks of the pride of Ephraim, a crown of splendor on the heads of drunkards. The image is repulsive: Ephraim is like a drunkard, slumped in his banquet chair; he is sleeping, drooling, with a faded crown of past glory set crookedly on his head. God warns plainly: "Woe to those overcome with wine." God lavished on the Israelites a land flowing with milk and honey (Deut 11:9-12), but this rich fertility corrupted them. The people became gluttons, drunkards, and idolaters, forsaking the fear of the Lord. So the Lord was about to bring on Ephraim "a strong and mighty one" (the king of Assyria) like a devastating hail storm and a flood. Ephraim's "majestic" drunkards would be thrown down by the judgment of God.

In stark contrast, God intends to lift up the godly among the remnant of his people and be for them a crown of eternal glory on their heads. God himself will be for them a source of strength to enable them by faith to turn back the battle—Assyria's invasion—at the gates of Jerusalem.

God Speaking through the Prophets versus God Speaking through Judgment
ISAIAH 28:7-13

The key moment in the life of any human being on earth is this: the hearing of God's prophetic word. Faith comes by hearing the message (Rom 10:17), but if the message is not believed, it only hardens the heart of the one who hears. In Isaiah 28:7-13 the Lord exposes the wickedness of priests and prophets (probably in Jerusalem) who are themselves (like those in Ephraim) overcome by wine and reeling from beer. Though the lips of a priest ought to give godly instruction (Mal 2:7), the priests and prophets of Judah were drunkards who rejected the word of the Lord. What came out of their mouths was both literal and spiritual vomit.

Even worse, they openly mocked the word of the Lord coming from Isaiah. Arrogantly, when they heard Isaiah's words, they asked, "Who is he trying to instruct? Infants just weaned from milk?" They actually took to mimicry: verse 10 comes across more powerfully in Hebrew: *tsav latsav, tsav latsav, kav lakav, kav lakav.* A literal translation is, "Law after law,

law after law, line after line, line after line." But in our expression perhaps it is more like, "Blah, blah, blah, yadda, yadda, yadda." Mockery.

What comes next is terrifying: God effectively says, "So . . . or *All right, then* . . . since you reject my plain speaking through Isaiah, I will speak to you in the tongues of foreigners. When the Assyrians are trampling your land and commanding in their language the slaughter of your people, you will understand what I've been trying to say to you through Isaiah's 'baby-talk.' And decades later, when the Babylonians in their Chaldean tongue are commanding the temple to be set ablaze, you'll 'get it.'" Simple lesson: If you don't listen to the verbal warning, you will get the real-life fulfillment. Then you'll be drunk with terror, not with wine (v. 13). All of this because you rejected the sweet place of rest (salvation) God had established—simple faith in him (v. 12)!

The Shaky Foundation of Self-Salvation versus the Solid Rock of God's Salvation
ISAIAH 28:14-22

Having rejected God's place of rest, they had no choice but to craft their own refuge for the coming storm of Assyria. The mocking leaders of Jerusalem claim to have "made a covenant with Death" (v. 15), crafting a refuge that will protect them from the imminent "overwhelming catastrophe." This covenant probably refers to the alliance with Egypt, which Isaiah will attack in chapters 30–31. Isaiah calls this self-salvation "falsehood" and "treachery." God will sweep away their false refuge and dissolve their covenant with Death (vv. 17-20). There is no possible refuge from the judgment of God other than the grace of God.

Instead of self-salvation by a false refuge, God established a genuine salvation by a stone he lays in Zion. Isaiah 28:16 is quoted three times in the New Testament to refer to Jesus Christ: Romans 9:30-33 and 10:9-13 and 1 Peter 2:6-8. Jesus Christ is a "tested stone," a "precious" stone, a "cornerstone." He is infinitely valuable, absolutely secure, a perfectly righteous stone worthy of being the foundation of your life. Whoever trusts in this precious, tested cornerstone will be "unshakable" and will survive the storm of God's wrath.

And that storm is coming! Isaiah says God is going to rise and do an "unexpected work" (v. 21), as he did at Mount Perazim and at the valley of Gibeon (two places where David defeated the Philistines with God's direct intervention). Strangely, now God will directly intervene to destroy his people in judgment rather than to save them. The only possible refuge is to stop mocking the word of God (v. 22) and to trust in the tested, precious stone God lays in Zion.

The Parable of the Farmer
ISAIAH 28:23-29

The chapter ends with a parable about a farmer. It teaches the same lesson in two phases: In phase 1 (plowing and planting), the farmer knows when to stop plowing and start planting; one doesn't go on plowing forever. In phase 2 (harvesting and threshing), the farmer knows when to stop threshing the grain and to start grinding it to make bread. In both cases, all of his knowledge has come from almighty God (vv. 26,29). It was God who taught the farmer his agricultural skills, and by that knowledge he knows when "enough is enough." How much more does God know what he's doing when it comes to judging his people. When it is time for the judgment to come, it will come; when it is time for the judgment to end, it will end.

We should also embrace a rich secondary lesson here concerning God's mysterious activity in the development of all human science. Just as God teaches farmers the science of agriculture, so the God who made the universe secretly teaches the human race all branches of science, especially in its "Eureka!" moments of discovery. This is true whether the scientist acknowledges God or not.[9] (See Isa 45:5, where God leads Cyrus even though he does not know God is doing it.)

Applications

First, in our day of affluence, when our soil keeps producing rich crops and our businesses keep turning handsome profits, we must guard our hearts against not only drunkenness but also against overindulgence of every kind. Second, we must see that the most crucial moment in any

---

[9] The history of science is full of "Eureka!" moments in which flashes of insight popped into the scientist's mind and greatly advanced research and knowledge. The word *eureka* itself means, "I have found it!" and was spoken by Archimedes when he discovered the concept of specific gravity. Newton's apple falling and giving him insights on gravity and Alexander Fleming's "chance" discovery of penicillin in 1928 serve as other examples. Here I am contending that, based on Isaiah 28:26-29, God secretly teaches the scientist the right way.

person's life is at the hearing of any word from Scripture. If we hear and obey, we will be blessed. But if we hear and mock, God may well speak to us more plainly in his providential judgments in life. Heed the word, or live the judgments!

The centerpiece of all prophetic words is Christ. The "overwhelming scourge" that sweeps through human history is death itself. If we think we can rely on some self-salvation, some "covenant with Death," to escape, we are deluded. This includes good works, foreign religions, and atheistic rationalization ("Death is just the biological end of life"). Jesus Christ is the refuge, the place of repose (v. 12) and the precious, tested cornerstone (v. 16). If we trust in him, we will never be shaken— not by any trial in life and not even by death itself.

Finally, we must see the hand of God in all human knowledge— all science (agricultural and otherwise) comes ultimately from God (vv. 26,29). To him alone be the glory for physics, mathematics, chemistry, cosmology, biology, and every branch of knowledge.

Reflect and Discuss

1. How does the drunkenness of Israel stand as a timeless warning to a wealthy nation of the dangers of overindulgence in the blessings of God?

2. How is Israel's "fading crown" a warning of the fleeting nature of all human achievements? How is God a "crown of glory" to all true believers in Christ?

3. How does the mocking of the Word of God in this chapter still go on in our day?

4. What is the significance of this statement: "If we don't learn from verbal warnings, God will speak to us in daily life"?

5. How does verse 12 relate to Matthew 11:28-30?

6. What are some ways that people in our age try to "make a covenant with Death"?

7. Why is it impossible to escape the judgments of God except by the grace of God in Christ?

8. What does verse 16 teach us about Jesus Christ?

9. What is God's "unexpected work" in verse 21?

10. How do verses 26 and 29 prove that all human knowledge, all branches of science, come from God's secret instruction, whether we acknowledge him or not?

God Acts Powerfully to Cure Spiritual Hypocrisy

ISAIAH 29

These people approach me with their speeches to honor me with lip-service—yet their hearts are far from me. (Isa 29:13)

Main Idea: God uses a very painful cure—the siege of Jerusalem—to heal his people of the heart disease of spiritual blindness and hypocrisy.

I. **God Humbles Jerusalem and Her Enemies to the Dust (29:1-8).**
   A. God humbles complacent Jerusalem by a siege (29:1-4).
   B. God humbles her ruthless enemies by his sudden appearance (29:5-8).
   C. God's enemies are bitterly disappointed.
II. **God Exposes the Root Issues (29:9-16).**
   A. Willful spiritual blindness (29:9-12)
   B. Cold-hearted, hypocritical worship (29:13-14)
   C. Worldly wisdom (29:14-16)
III. **God Transforms His People from All Effects of Sin (29:17-24).**
   A. Amazing promises! A full deliverance for the people of God
   B. Image after image of God's lavish work of restoration

God Humbles Jerusalem and Her Enemies to the Dust

ISAIAH 29:1-8

In this sin-cursed world most therapies for disease and injury in medical science involve hurting the body in order to heal it. All surgeries involve cutting through healthy tissue to reach the unhealthy. Radiation and chemotherapy both involve doing massive harm to the body to kill the cancer growing within the patient. Dentists regularly drill through healthy enamel to get to the decay exposed by x-rays. Physical therapists put their patients through agonies to retrain atrophied muscles and make them healthy and useful again. In a similar way, the Great Physician of Souls must often hurt his people in order to heal them.

In Isaiah 29 God deals severely with his people in Jerusalem; he humbles them to the dust by bringing a siege on them; then, suddenly, he turns and humbles their enemies also to the dust by showing up with wrath and power. In this chapter God exposes the heart issues in his people that brought on this judgment from God centuries ago, and we find that we struggle with the same sins they did. And as God works in our lives, he will seek to achieve the same purpose as in theirs: healing our hearts—from coldness, complacency, dry religion, formalism, spiritual dullness, and worldly wisdom—resulting in a people wholeheartedly passionate for his glory. To accomplish this, God must do some strange work in our lives; he must hurt us in order to heal us.

In act 1 of the drama (vv. 1-4), God addresses the sins of "Ariel" (Jerusalem, "the city where David camped"). He rebukes them by commanding that their endless cycle of religious festivals go on like a machine while he humbles them to the dust by a fiery trial, a siege. After that siege, Jerusalem will be so abased that she will barely be able to whisper a prayer.

But suddenly, act 2 changes everything (vv. 5-8). The besieging forces that are arrogantly assaulting Jerusalem will themselves be humbled to the dust by almighty God. He will break out powerfully against them in "thunder, earthquake, and loud noise, storm, tempest, and a flame of consuming fire" (v. 6). Many foes of God have dreamed of exterminating God's people by genocide only to find themselves rudely awakened, their dream evaporated like a nighttime mist (v. 8). So also in this case: Assyria assumed they would soon be dancing over the corpses of Hezekiah and his rag-tag remnant. But the angel of the Lord went out and slaughtered 185,000 of their soldiers, and the dream died that very night (Isa 37:36-37).

God Exposes the Root Issues
ISAIAH 29:9-16

The question presses on any of God's people whom he severely hurts: "Why, O Lord? Why are you doing this to me?" Scripture is able to stand with clarity in the suffering of God's people and tell us why he must hurt us in order to heal us. Though the heart issues may differ from person to person, a relatively small number of common themes arise in every generation. Among them are spiritual blindness, cold-hearted worship, and worldly wisdom.

In verses 9-12 Isaiah speaks powerfully to the spiritual blindness of the people of Judah. They stagger around drunk but not from strong drink. They are blind because they do not understand the words of Isaiah's prophecy; they stagger because they are in terror at God's judgment through Assyria. The prophecy is like a sealed scroll: those who should have been skilled enough in the laws of God to understand Isaiah's prophecy (priests and prophets) cannot read it because it is sealed. The rest of the common people cannot read at all. No one understands what God is doing by bringing these vicious Gentile warriors to destroy their cities and ravage their lands. The words of the prophecy are a sealed scroll. God would have to speak more clearly by means of the invasion itself (Isa 28:11).

In Isaiah 29:13 God exposes the coldness of their hearts toward him. They are going through the motions of all their religious machinery, for Hezekiah had restored the lawful patterns of temple worship (2 Chr 29). But just because the king was wholeheartedly pursuing the Lord doesn't mean the people were. As in Isaiah 1:11-15, there was an endless trampling of the courts of the temple with meaningless offerings and hypocritical festivals. The people honored God with their lips, but their hearts were far from him. Their lukewarmness in worship was despicable to God; it was the ground of their astonishing judgments from God in verse 14. In Jesus's day the scribes and Pharisees carried on the hypocritical spirit of their forefathers. They were meticulous in their religious observances, but Jesus exposed their hypocrisy by quoting this verse in reference to them (Matt 15:7-9).

The third cause of Judah's painful judgment from God is in Isaiah 29:14-16: worldly wisdom. Hezekiah's counselors were pouring this "wisdom" into his ears, effectively saying, "We must not be naïve; we must make an alliance with Egypt to survive Assyria!" Perhaps these plans were being formed in secret, even hidden from the king. However, "No creature is hidden from [God], but all things are naked and exposed to the eyes of him to whom we must give an account" (Heb 4:13). These perverse people have forgotten that they are merely the clay and God is the omniscient potter who will expose all their sins.

God Transforms His People from All Effects of Sin
ISAIAH 29:17-24

The chapter ends with a cascade of gracious promises from the Great Physician. God will work a full deliverance for his chosen people to rescue them from their own cold hearts. God promises to level the forests of Lebanon (the humbling of human pride) and to turn it instead into a fertile field for his glory. God promises to give spiritual hearing and sight to formerly deaf and blind people, so they will at last hear the words of his scroll and see him by faith. The result of this faith will be genuine spiritual joy; having been humbled by the judgments of God, they will drink at a fountain of "joy after joy" (v. 19). Ruthless oppressors (the wicked among Judah itself as well as the Gentile invaders) will vanish, removed by God's terrifying power. The true sons and daughters of Abraham, the godly remnant of Jacob, will see their own children as the evidence of the supernatural power of God. In the end, the transformation of former rebels into humble disciples is the centerpiece of God's healing work.

Applications

First, we have the same disease. We can be quite complacent in our religious lives, mindlessly doing out of habit what should be done out of passion. We can honor God with our lips while our worldly hearts remain far from him.

Second, the Great Physician is Jesus, able to heal spiritually diseased people through repentance and faith (Luke 5:31-32). But genuine repentance from these deep-seated heart issues never comes easily. The Great Physician must bring into our lives deep pains, bitter sufferings, to get at such profound heart sins. So . . .

Third, we should expect painful trials, knowing that Jesus must hurt us to heal us. We should learn to hate anything that makes us distant from God. Jesus shed his blood on the cross to save us from all sins, including religious formalism, hypocrisy, deadness of heart, worldly wisdom, and secret sins. We should plead with him to heal us, however painfully, by trials and by the Holy Spirit.

Reflect and Discuss

1. What timeless lessons does Isaiah 29 have for the people of God in every generation?
2. Why is it vital to accept the three premises given in the application section above? (1) We share the same heart sins as they did; (2) Jesus is the Great Physician; but (3) the therapies for heart sins will be painful.

3. How do you see religious formalism in the Christian church of our day?

4. What is the significance of the fact that so many medical remedies must hurt the body in order to heal it? How does that also ring true in our spiritual lives?

5. How is the Scripture frequently like a sealed scroll to people (vv. 9-12)? Why is that their fault, not the Bible's?

6. Jonathan Edwards said, "In nothing is vigor in the actings of our inclinations so appropriate as in religion, and in nothing is luke-warmness so odious" (Edwards, *A Treatise*, 238). How does this quote relate to Isaiah 29:1,13?

7. Why is Isaiah 29:13 one of the most important verses in the Bible on worship?

8. What should we do if we see that our hearts are "far from God"?

9. How do we display "worldly wisdom" in our lives?

10. What awesome words of grace do you see cascading in verses 17-24? How do these promises relate to our Christian lives?

God Saves His Stubborn Children from Self-Salvation

ISAIAH 30

For the Lord GOD, the Holy One of Israel, has said: "You will be delivered by returning and resting; your strength will lie in quiet confidence. But you are not willing." (Isa 30:15)

Main Idea: God condemns the stubborn strategies of Israel for self-salvation through Egypt and promises salvation by his grace for believers and fiery wrath for his enemies.

I. **Woe to Those Who Make Plans to Save Themselves (30:1-7)**
   A. Woe to stubbornly rebellious children
   B. Their sin: making plans that don't come from God
   C. Envoys to Egypt bring nothing but shame.
II. **Woe to Those Who Want God's Prophets to Speak Pleasant Lies (30:8-17)**
   A. The prophetic word is written down.
   B. "Tickle our ears; don't convict our hearts."
   C. God's invitation to security is rejected.
   D. The future for rejecters is dark.
III. **Transforming Grace to Those Who Wait for the Lord (30:18-26)**
   A. The hinge verse (30:18)
   B. Salvation flowing step by step from grace
   C. A people transformed and a world transformed
IV. **Terrifying Wrath to the Enemies of God (30:27-33)**
   A. A terrifying foretaste of God's final wrath
   B. God's wrath upholding God's name
   C. Topheth: a picture of hell

Woe to Those Who Make Plans to Save Themselves
ISAIAH 30:1-7

As we read this chapter, it is easy to struggle with its relevance to us. Ancient Judah was facing the terrifying prospect of an imminent invasion by an overwhelmingly superior foe—Assyria. In this dire situation they had four options: (1) submit to the Assyrians without a fight and suffer the consequences for the rebellion they had already put up against Sennacherib, (2) wage war against the Assyrians (resulting in almost certain death for most of the people), (3) make an alliance with another Gentile nation—probably Egypt—who might be able to save them from the Assyrians, (4) humbly repent of their sins and seek a miraculous deliverance from the Lord. However distant it may seem from us, fundamentally Judah's choice is much like the one we face every day. Will we try to control our circumstances by making our own plans for self-salvation? Or will we submit to God in repentance and trust in his power to save us from all our foes? God's counsel has never changed: "You will be delivered by returning and resting; your strength will lie in quiet confidence" (v. 15). Only by turning to almighty God in repentance and resting in his mercy and power can we be saved from his wrath. But every generation of sinners is tempted to find some other way, a path of self-salvation.

The lesson of Isaiah 30 is to reject all stratagems of self-salvation and to live by repentance and rest, to learn to face all the small and great trials of our lives by faith in God. This lesson is vital because an enemy is coming that is far more powerful than the Assyrian army: death. And no "separate peace" can be made with death, no ally can be hired that will help at all. Now as then, by faith in Christ alone can we survive that invasion.

Judah's efforts to find a path of self-salvation by forming an alliance with Egypt are utterly repugnant to God. So he speaks a word of "Woe!" to his stubbornly rebellious children. Poignantly, Isaiah's vision describes the journey of the "animals of the Negev" (the desert between Judah and Egypt), the donkeys or camels who carry gold for the emissaries to buy Pharaoh's protection. But Egypt can do nothing to save Judah—she will be named "Rahab Who Just Sits." In the same way, people who trust in good works, religion, or morality for salvation will be utterly disappointed.

Woe to Those Who Want God's Prophets to Speak Pleasant Lies
ISAIAH 30:8-17

At the core of this people's rebellion is their rejection of the prophetic word of God. God commanded Isaiah to write the words of his prophecy down so that it would testify against them that "They are a rebellious people, deceptive children, children who do not want to listen to the LORD's instruction" (v. 9; see Acts 7:51). Such people only want to have their ears tickled with "flattering things" and "illusions" (v. 10). They yearn for their prophets to fill their minds with positive messages. The last thing they want is to be confronted by the "Holy One of Israel" (v. 12). Every generation of God's messengers feels this same pressure: to seek to please the audience with pleasant messages. False prophets say things that everyone likes, so everyone speaks well of them (Luke 6:26). They refuse to confront the people in their sins and call them to repentance.

Isaiah likened their efforts to build their own refuge by sugary prophetic words to hiding behind a high wall poorly constructed, which will crumble in an instant (vv. 13-14). Instead, God offered them refuge in him if they would only repent and rest in him by faith (v. 15). But tragically, they refused. They have their own plans of self-salvation. If the alliance with Egypt fails, the walls of Jerusalem will protect them. If the walls fall down, they plan on fleeing on horseback. But it is impossible to escape God's judgment by any means other than God's grace: "You say, 'No! We will escape on horses'—therefore you will escape!—and, 'We will ride on fast horses'—but those who pursue you will be faster" (v. 16). God always gets the final word. The end of this stubbornness will be the total desolation of Judah.

Transforming Grace to Those Who Wait for the Lord
ISAIAH 30:18-26

Verse 18 is a glorious hinge. Up to this point, we read nothing but God's disapproval of the attitudes and actions of his people. But God is still yearning to show them mercy, rising to show them compassion. He waits until just the right moment and then takes sovereign initiative to pour out grace on his sinful people: "All who wait patiently for him are happy."

The first step in the salvation journey is in verse 19, as the Lord works in them to call on him for salvation. God knows exactly what we need for salvation, but he will not act until we call on him to do it. We see this in Jesus's healing of Bartimaeus. This man was crying aloud, "Have mercy on me!" and everyone in the crowd knew exactly what this blind man wanted. But Jesus stood in front of him and said, "What do you want me to do for you?" (Mark 10:51). So also in Isaiah 30:19, God waits on the people to cry for help. As soon as he hears, he saves!

The next step is in verses 20-21: God radically transforms the hearts of his people to hear and obey his word. They will hear their Teacher's voice speaking plainly to them, "This is the way. Walk in it." This is ultimately fulfilled in the new covenant promise of the indwelling Holy Spirit, "the Spirit of truth [who] will guide you into all truth" (John 16:13), who writes God's laws in the minds and hearts of his people then compels them to walk in that way (Ezek 36:26-27; Rom 8:4; Heb 8:10-11). Their rebelliousness ends when their hearts are so transformed.

The next step occurs when, under the transforming influence of the Spirit of God, the people defile their formerly precious idols, casting them away forever in holy zeal (v. 22). The redeemed people of God then live only for the glory of his name.

The final step of salvation refers to the land, cursed and damaged because of human sin. In the narrow focus, verses 23-26 refer to the restoration of the land of Judah after the Assyrian invasion. The promised land will be healed, the rain will fall, the rivers and streams will flow freely, the harvests will be rich and abundant, the livestock will be richly fed, and even the sunlight and moonlight will be brighter and more beautiful than ever before. But these words must find their ultimate fulfillment in the new heaven and new earth, that perfect world freed forever from the curse of decay and death (Rom 8:21).

Terrifying Wrath to the Enemies of God
ISAIAH 30:27-33

The final section of this chapter is one of the most terrifying depictions of the wrath of God in the writings of the Old Testament prophets. Verse 27 says literally, "The name of the LORD comes from afar," meaning that the wrath of God is poured out for the sake of his name. The approach of the name of the Lord is with fiery emblems of wrath and terror (v. 27). His breath pours out a rising torrent of fire on all nations. He sifts all nations in a sieve of destruction, and all are consumed. Verse 28 specifically teaches God's power to orchestrate the history of nations to achieve their just destruction. The devastation of Assyria is only one example. The destruction of all wicked, oppressive nations will result in an overflowing celebration by the people of God (v. 29). Verses 30-33 depict in vivid language a fire pit, called Topheth, where the torrent of God's wrath sets ablaze kings and whole nations that have rebelled against him. It is a clear foretaste of hell, the lake of fire, described so vividly in Revelation 14 and 20.

Perhaps the corpses of the 185,000 Assyrian troops that God slaughtered were collected and burned in the valley of Ben Hinnom, the smoldering garbage pit outside the walls of Jerusalem. Jesus used this as a vivid picture of hell (Matt 10:28; Gk *gehenna*). This will be the final image of the book of Isaiah: "They will see the dead bodies of those who have rebelled against me; for their worm will never die, their fire will never go out, and they will be a horror to all mankind" (66:24). Though God works salvation for sinners with amazing grace, he also will pour out a river of fire on all his enemies.

Applications

This chapter has powerful themes pointing to the gospel of Jesus Christ. The ultimate threat we face is not an Assyrian invasion but death and eternal condemnation in hell. Woe to any person who thinks he can escape that judgment by clever means of self-salvation. God wants us to forsake those efforts and flee to Christ. God still makes the same gracious offer as he did to Judah in verse 15: in repentance and quiet faith in Jesus comes our rest and our refuge; there is no other ("Come to me, all of you who are weary and burdened, and I will give you rest," Matt 11:28; "There is salvation in no one else, for there is no other name under heaven given to people by which we must be saved," Acts 4:12). God is still longing to be gracious to all sinners who call on his name in faith (Isa 30:18). And God works the same steps of salvation now as then: He moves us to call on his name, he transforms our hearts to obey his Word, he puts the indwelling Spirit in us to guide our steps moment by moment, and he will transform the universe and make it glorious. This is the gospel we must proclaim to all the nations, telling them all there is one way, and only one way, of escape from the coming wrath of God: faith in Christ.

Reflect and Discuss

1. Why do you think God was so offended by the efforts of Judah to seek an alliance with Egypt?
2. How do non-Christians seek self-salvation? How do Christians sometimes seek self-salvation from lesser trials other than in God?

3. Read 2 Timothy 4:3-4 and compare it with Isaiah 30:10-11. Why is it vital for pastors to resist the temptation to satisfy people's itch to hear what they want to hear? Why must they continue confronting people with the Holy One of Israel?

4. How is verse 15 a particular comfort to you? How can we as Christians learn to rest more deeply and trust more fully in Christ?

5. Read verse 18 again. What does it mean that God waits and rises to be gracious to us? How is the fact that God is a God of justice a comfort to us, especially in light of the cross?

6. How does verse 19 urge us to call on the Lord in the midst of our afflictions? Why do we tend to hesitate and to solve the problems ourselves?

7. Read John 16:13. What does that teach you about the ministry of the Spirit? How could the indwelling Spirit's ministry be like verse 21 of our chapter?

8. How could verse 21 be abused, so that people say, "The Spirit told me to _____," but they are not living according to the Word?

9. How do verses 27 and 33 give a powerful depiction of the wrath of God in hell? How does this make you feel about the salvation Christ has worked for us?

10. Why do you think some Christians struggle with the idea of a place of eternal torment where sinners are punished by the wrath of God?

Trust in God, Not in Your Schemes and Idols

ISAIAH 31

Woe to those who go down to Egypt for help and who depend on horses!
They trust in the abundance of chariots and in the large number of
horsemen. They do not look to the Holy One of Israel and they do not
seek the LORD. (Isa 31:1)

Main Idea: God declares his judgment on those who trust in idols and
proclaims his wisdom and power to save his people—those who cast
away their idols.

I. **Woe to Those Who Trust in Egypt Rather Than God (31:1-3)**
   A. The key question: In what are you trusting?
   B. Impressed by Egypt's wisdom and power, forgetting God
II. **The Greatness of God's Power Both to Destroy and to Deliver
    (31:2-5)**
   A. God's credentials as a Savior
   B. Like a lion, God will devour; like a mother eagle, God will
      protect.
III. **A Call to Repentance: Turn from Idols to the Living God (31:6-7).**
   A. Return to the God against whom you have rebelled.
   B. You will defile and discard your idols.
IV. **Thus Says the Lord: Assyria Will Fall (31:8-9).**
   A. Clear decree: Assyria will fall.
   B. A sword not of man will devour.

Woe to Those Who Trust in Egypt Rather Than God
ISAIAH 31:1-3

Isaiah 31 proclaims quite a plain message to Judah in Isaiah's day and
a timeless message to the church of Jesus Christ: God is putting all his
power on the line to save his people; woe to you if you trust anything
but him. In Isaiah's day King Hezekiah and his counselors were tempted
to trust in Egypt for military salvation from Assyria, as we've seen in

Isaiah 30. The powerful Egyptian cavalry and the wise Egyptian counselors were an alluring false "savior."

God spoke these oracles to Judah through the prophet Isaiah while Hezekiah was seeking to purify their religion, getting rid of the evil high places where the Jews were worshiping in a pagan manner. Unfortunately, Hezekiah's counselors, terrified of Assyria, felt they needed human help to survive. So they thought the best thing they could do was to send gold down to Egypt to hire Egyptian cavalry. And this deeply offended God. In Isaiah 31:1 God speaks a word of "Woe" against those who trust in Egypt's powerful and plentiful horses and chariots but who do not "look to" (trust in) the Holy One of Israel for salvation. In verses 2-3 God is essentially comparing résumés with Egypt, saying, "I also am wise . . ."! "Also"? God's wisdom soars infinitely above that of every man that ever lived (Rom 11:33). If Hezekiah or any of his counselors needed wisdom, they should have asked God, who gives wisdom to all generously and ungrudgingly (Jas 1:5), not sought the "wise" counselors of Pharaoh who "give stupid advice" (Isa 19:11). Also, God's power extends infinitely beyond that of any human warrior, even one riding a horse! The Egyptians are mere mortals, and their horses are mere flesh (31:3). But God speaks and never retracts a single word; he acts and brings about disaster. He is the only one to fear and the only one to seek.

The Greatness of God's Power Both to Destroy and to Deliver

ISAIAH 31:2-5

God is able to bring disaster on everyone who opposes him and his people, no matter how mighty they may seem (vv. 2-3). His indomitable courage and power are pictured in verse 4 as a lion that roars over his prey, completely unconcerned by the shepherds who seek to intimidate him. The lion keeps tearing and devouring, and the shepherds can do nothing to make him afraid. So it is with God and his enemies: when God wants to devour, nothing in heaven or on earth can stop him. Conversely, when God wants to protect, he is like a hovering mother eagle that cannot be moved from protecting her young (v. 5). The omnipotent Ruler of the universe is everything—humanity is nothing by comparison. So why trust in Egypt for deliverance?

A Call to Repentance: Turn from Idols to the Living God
ISAIAH 31:6-7

Based on these words of woe and of assurance, God now calls on his people to turn away from their idols in repentance and to return to him (v. 6). Assyria would not have even been coming had it not been for their idolatries and sinful rebellion. His people's hearts were "far from" God (Isa 29:13), and they had acted it out by open rebellion. Now through the prophet God was calling on them to return to him. Essential to this is rejecting the idols of silver and gold their sinful hearts had devised and their sinful hands had crafted. God is at war with idolatry throughout the book of Isaiah, and the battle was far from over.

Thus Says the Lord: Assyria Will Fall
ISAIAH 31:8-9

God gives a final and clear prediction of the fate of Assyria: They will fall by the sword, but it will not be held by a human warrior. God will supernaturally intervene and slaughter Assyria, and Egypt's "help" will be displayed to have been utterly useless. In God every single human being lives and moves and exists (Acts 17:28), and when God wills the death of either a single individual or an entire empire, nothing can stop it. Assyria will walk into a raging inferno of wrath in Jerusalem, and they will be completely consumed (v. 9). Beyond their clear defeat at Jerusalem, Assyria's "rock" (their citadel, even their empire) will "pass away" (v. 9).

Applications

As it was then, so it is for us; we face earthly trials that expose the true basis of our confidence, our true "savior":

Health: When you are faced with the terror of a life-threatening disease, your true "savior" will float to the surface in your thought process. If as you try to sleep, you comfort yourself with thoughts of the advances of medical science, that is your "savior."

Finances: When the economic experts are predicting a severe recession, and your company has already laid off 30 percent of the workforce with more layoffs expected, when you look ahead to the cloudy future, your true "savior" will float to the surface of your thoughts. If your dominant thought is, *At least I have a year's worth of salary saved up*, then that is your savior.

Our God is a jealous God; he wants to be our only Savior. He wants our entire trust to be placed solely in him. As Joseph Hart wrote in 1759 in his hymn, "Come Ye Sinners, Poor and Needy": "Lo the incarnate God ascended pleads the merit of his blood. Venture on him, venture wholly, let no other trust intrude." Any trust but in Jesus (the "incarnate God") is as unwelcome as a home-wrecking lover vying for the affections of your spouse. To purify our trust, God brings smaller trials into our life to show us what we are really trusting in. Ultimately, we must learn through every trial on earth to trust wholly in Jesus Christ. Small trials (a winter flu, a marital conflict, a fender-bender, losing your wallet, etc.) are training opportunities for the final one: death and judgment. We must seize every one of those trials to purify our faith and rest on Christ alone.

Nations also must learn to trust in God ultimately for "national security." It is certainly wise for governments to promote their national defense by military strength, but Isaiah 31 teaches us never to trust in that strength for ultimate security. The world governments spent $1.6 trillion on their militaries in 2015; the United States spent $596 billion, 36 percent of the world's total (Perlo-Freeman et al., "Trends"). It is very easy for Christians in the US to trust in the power of the military and not in the Lord.

Reflect and Discuss

1. How do we apply the lessons of God's "woe" on alliances with Egypt to our daily lives, especially during trials?

2. What are some common trials that we face, and what would be the equivalent of an "alliance with Egypt" in each of those cases (e.g., medical issues, financial troubles, marital problems, parenting problems, unemployment, single people seeking a spouse, childless couples seeking a child)?

3. How could a nation's military spending become an idol that lures people away from trusting in the Lord?

4. Egypt was renowned for her wise men and counselors. What is God saying about his wisdom in verse 2? Why is it easy to forget how wise God is and to seek wisdom from other sources?

5. What does this image of God as a dauntless lion (v. 4) teach you about him? How can God's complete fearlessness before humans give us courage as well?

6. How are God's wisdom and power—on display when he slaughtered the Assyrians—even more on display at the cross of Christ?

7. How would you define an idol? What are modern versions of idols?

8. How can we throw our idols away in actual practice? What would cause us to hate our idols and reject them, returning to a love relationship with Christ?

9. How does this chapter show us the amazing power of predictive prophecy?

10. As you prayerfully reflect on what you are trusting in the most, how could Psalm 139:23-24 help you see your own idolatry?

The Righteous King and Outpoured Spirit Transform the World

ISAIAH 32

The result of righteousness will be peace; the effect of righteousness will be quiet confidence forever. (Isa 32:17)

Main Idea: God reveals his vision for a new society in which kings and rulers, transformed by the Spirit, reign under Christ.

I. **God's Purpose: Noble Rulers Instead of Wicked Ones (32:1-8)**
   A. A righteous king, godly rulers (32:1)
   B. A vision for a new society (32:2-5,8)
   C. The old society exposed (32:5-7)
II. **God's Purging: Judgment Clearing the Building Site (32:9-14)**
   A. Dire warnings of judgment
   B. Complacent women shuddering at judgments
   C. The rich fields and crowded cities cursed
III. **God's Power: The Outpoured Spirit Producing a Harvest of Righteousness (32:15-20)**
   A. "Until the Spirit from on high is poured out on us" (32:15)
   B. The effects of the Spirit: transformed hearts and transformed society (32:16-17)
   C. Peace and prosperity (32:18-20)

God's Purpose: Noble Rulers Instead of Wicked Ones
ISAIAH 32:1-8

Two major themes in Isaiah 32 resonate with our current world situation. First, we see the corruption of rulers who use their positions of leadership in government for selfish purposes. Forms of corruption vary but include bribery, extortion, cronyism, nepotism, patronage, graft, and embezzlement. Corruption may facilitate criminal enterprise such as drug trafficking, money laundering, and human trafficking. All over the world and throughout history, there are many examples of governmental corruption:

- Nigeria: More than $400 billion was stolen from the treasury by Nigeria's leaders between 1960 and 1999.
- Haiti: After the tragic earthquake in Haiti on January 12, 2010, endemic corruption siphoned off billions of dollars of aid that was sent for the suffering victims.
- Prohibition-era Chicago: Gangster Al Capone ran the town; many of the police leadership and the politicians were involved in some way with Capone; Mayor Big Bill Thompson was on Capone's payroll and was called "the best mayor money could buy."

The second major theme is how the power of the Holy Spirit can change everything, making leaders godly and making society richly blessed. However, this is not a utopian vision for what can happen in this world; it is a foretaste of the new heaven and new earth. It is also a call for Christian leaders to use their positions of power to bless their people in the pattern of Christ.

Proverbs 29:2 unites these themes: "When the righteous flourish, the people rejoice, but when the wicked rule, people groan." As the old saying goes, "Power tends to corrupt, and absolute power corrupts absolutely" (Dalberg-Acton, "Letter"). Yet theologically, this isn't quite right. The human heart was already corrupt, but power gives an opportunity to draw out and increase the corruption as leaders glut their flesh on the "good stuff" of the world: food, gold, beautiful houses overlooking spectacular scenic vistas, luxurious possessions, soft clothes, fine furniture, etc. Almighty God has absolute power and is never corrupted by it! What is the only remedy to the corruption of human government? It is the kingdom of God displayed in the incorruptible Son of God and empowered by the Spirit of God.

The chapter begins with some difficulty of interpretation: Who is the "king" who will reign righteously, and who are the rulers who will rule justly? I think it is best to see this chapter as God's ideal society after judgment has cleared away the wickedness. The pattern for the righteous king is ultimately Jesus, called the "King of kings" (Rev 19:16), who rules over human rulers who seek to please him with how they rule. Isaiah 32:2 speaks of how these rulers use their positions to shelter the needy from the storms and heat, how they are like streams of water in the desert. Clearly, these rulers are not ruling in a perfect world (like the millennium or the new heaven and new earth) because their protection and provision are so sorely needed by the people they are governing. So we can see here the effects of the reign of Christ by the power of the Holy Spirit on human rulers who seek to glorify God in their governance.

In that beautiful new society "those who see" (prophets) will see true visions clearly, and the teachers of the Word of God will speak clearly and faithfully his truths to the people. The minds of those who listen to their words will grasp their truths and take them to heart (vv. 3-4). The people will recognize the difference between a godly leader and a scoundrel (v. 5). The wicked leaders of the past were ungodly fools whose corrupt minds resulted in corrupt plans and corrupt words (vv. 6-7). By stark contrast, the noble leaders of the new society yearn to use their positions for good, to bless those entrusted to their care. They make noble plans and carry them out (v. 8).

God's Purging: Judgment Clearing the Building Site
ISAIAH 32:9-14

In order to make room for this new society, God must clear away the old corruption. Verses 9-14 focus on "complacent women" who end up beating their breasts because of the devastation that is coming on their delightful fields and crowded cities. These lovers of luxury are overconfident in their wealth, unconcerned for the poor and needy, and certain that their present lifestyle will continue indefinitely. But their judgment rushes on them "in a little more than a year" (v. 10). The judgment is devastating: the delightful fields and fruitful vines will produce thorns and briers (v. 13; see Gen 3:18); the palace and crowded city will be left desolate, a place for flocks to graze (v. 14). The now humbled women will beat their breasts, stripping off their rich clothes and donning sackcloth instead (vv. 11-12).

God's Power: The Outpoured Spirit Producing a Harvest of Righteousness
ISAIAH 32:15-20

The new society described in this chapter can only come about by the Holy Spirit's transforming power. Verse 15 shows this plainly: the desolation of the city and the thorns and briers in the fields will continue until the Spirit is poured out from heaven. The leveling of a formerly bad society does not necessarily give way to a godly one in its place. The piles of rubble in bombed-out Europe after World War II were grounds for all kinds of anarchistic acts: vigilante squads wreaked vengeance on Nazi collaborators in France; 20,000 people were summarily executed by their countrymen in northern Italy in the final weeks of the war; in eastern Poland and western Ukraine rival nationalist groups carried out an undeclared war of terrifying brutality resulting in the deaths of thousands more (Lowe, *Savage Continent*, xiii–xiv, 75ff). Only if the Spirit is poured out from on high will anything good rise up on the rubble of the past government.

In the Bible the Spirit is often likened to water, and the verb frequently used for the giving of the Spirit is "pour" (Isa 44:3; Joel 2:28-29; Acts 2:33; 10:45; Rom 5:5). The Spirit is "poured out" like water or "placed" on the hearts of the people, transforming them and moving them to obey God's laws (Ezek 36:27); and that is the key to the changes in society predicted in this chapter. Why does God use the verb "pour" when speaking of the gift and influence of the Holy Spirit? Perhaps it has to do with an ongoing influence as time progresses, as life unfolds, so the Spirit's activity is more like a river continuously flowing from heaven to earth rather than a lightning strike that makes a single, instantaneous impact. The Spirit flows into a ruler's heart, and he continuously seeks to render judgments and provide for and protect the poor and needy as the holy King Jesus would have him do.

So, as the "Spirit from on high is poured out on us," the desert will be transformed into an orchard that seems like a forest. Righteousness will be the direct result of the Spirit's influence, and that righteousness will produce "quiet confidence forever" (Isa 32:16-17) and prosperity (v. 20). This vision for a new society starts with transformed leaders, imitating the king who reigns righteously (v. 1).

Applications

Jesus is the embodiment of the righteous king of verse 1. Under his perfect rule, other kings and lords do their ruling in imitation of him. Jesus is the perfect shelter from the storm, the only refuge from the coming wrath of God. He also is the final provision for our souls, the river of the water of life and the bread from heaven that supplies our deepest needs. In imitation of him, Christian rulers—whether kings or prime ministers or governors or town council members—can use their positions of power not to line their pockets by corruption but to provide for and protect the poor and needy and to render right judgments. The final images of rich harvest and peaceful security can be realized on earth to the degree that leaders as well as citizens are filled with Christ's Spirit. They will find final consummation in the new heaven and new earth.

Reflect and Discuss

1. How does this tendency toward selfishness in government officials reveal the nature of the human heart? How is it only by the power of the Holy Spirit of God that such corruption can ever be finally remedied?

2. How is this chapter a display of the maxim, "Power tends to corrupt, and absolute power corrupts absolutely"? Why isn't that maxim true about Christ and about Spirit-filled rulers?

3. Who is the "king" of verse 1? What evidence is there that this verse is talking about a human king like Hezekiah and not the coming King, Messiah? Who are the "rulers" or "princes" of verse 1?

4. How do verses 1-8 give a vision for a new kind of society?

5. How does verse 2 give a picture of what a ruler should be for the people he governs?

6. How does the wicked ruler misuse his position in verses 6-7? How does the godly man desire to use his position in verse 8?

7. How do verses 9-14 speak of the coming desolation of the land? Why is that desolation necessary to prepare the land for the coming righteous society?

8. What vast changes do you see in verses 15-20?

9. What is the role of the Holy Spirit in producing those changes (Ezek 36:25-30)?

10. How do verses 15-20 describe a beautiful and righteous society? How is verse 17 a great picture of the fruit of the Spirit (Gal 5:21-22)?

A Magnificent Vision of the King in His Glorious Triumph

ISAIAH 33

Your eyes will see the King in his beauty; you will see a vast land.
(Isa 33:17)

Main Idea: This chapter gives a magnificent vision of the victory of King Jesus over all his foes, giving hope to all who trust in him.

I. **Lookout Mountain: A Magnificent Prophetic Vision**
   A. Lookout Mountain: the magnificent view
   B. Context: Assyrian treachery
   C. Comfort: the prophetic vision
   D. Outcome: sinners in Zion tenderly warned then graciously encouraged

II. **You Will See the Destruction of the Treacherous (33:1-6).**
   A. Woe to the treacherous destroyer: what goes around comes around.
   B. Judah finally cries out to the Lord.
   C. God is Zion's treasure: the fear of the Lord is the key.

III. **You Will See the King Arise in Power (33:7-16).**
   A. The present anguish: a broken treaty (33:7-9)
   B. "Now I will rise up," says the Lord (33:10-12)!
   C. Zion's terror-filled question: "Who may dwell with such a God?" (33:14-16)

IV. **You Will See the Beauty of the King and His Kingdom (33:17-24).**
   A. Promise 1: Your eyes will see the King in his beauty.
   B. Promise 2: Your eyes will see a vast land.
   C. Promise 3: Your eyes will no longer see the wicked.
   D. Promise 4: Your eyes will see Zion perfectly governed.
   E. Promise 5: Your sins will be forgiven.
   F. Promise 6: You will be rich.

Lookout Mountain: A Magnificent Prophetic Vision

At the northwest corner of the state of Georgia, Lookout Mountain rises 2,389 feet above sea level. From its peak, it is said that one can see seven states, though actually the curvature of the earth lowers the farthest three of those states below the horizon. Isaiah 33 is a prophetic Lookout Mountain, with a far more magnificent view. The chapter is saturated with rich themes rooted in Isaiah's immediate circumstances but timeless in their applications. It employs visionary language of what the people of God will "see" (vv. 17,19,20) even in the distant future—and nothing dips below the prophetic horizon because these things have been decreed and announced centuries in advance by almighty God.

The immediate historical context for Isaiah and Judah should be well known to us by now: the threat of Assyrian domination. King Hezekiah and the people of Judah have been trembling under that threat for years and have sought many escapes. Now at last, with nowhere else to turn, Hezekiah and Judah turn to the Lord—as they should have done from the beginning. They now trust in the Lord and cry out to him for deliverance. The vision of this chapter describes what occurs when God rises to vindicate his glory and save his people. The vision stretches out to include the destruction of the wicked, including both "sinners in Zion" and barbarian invaders. The vision covers the future radiant beauty of the King of Zion and of the magnificent land he will rule. The vision ends in the perfect government of Zion and the absolute blessedness of her people.

This magnificent view is a double-edged sword, for the same holiness that motivates God to destroy wicked nations like Assyria also motivates him to purge out sinners from Zion (God's visible people on earth). Thus, this chapter both warns God's people to repent and encourages them with blessed hope for the future.

You Will See the Destruction of the Treacherous
ISAIAH 33:1-6

The chapter opens with a word of "Woe!" to the treacherous destroyer (v. 1). Assyria is not mentioned by name because this is a transferable promise covering every generation of treacherous tyrants, whoever they may be and whenever they may live. The immediate circumstance is Assyria's intention to destroy Jerusalem despite a treaty of alliance. Ahaz had faithlessly made an original treaty with Assyria (2 Kgs 16:7), but all that accomplished was to increase Assyria's interest in eventually conquering Judah. Hezekiah trusted the Lord enough to break the treaty with Assyria and stop making the payments of a vassal state to her overlord (18:7). Assyria responded as any tyrant would: by invading Judah and conquering many of her cities (v. 13). At that point Hezekiah wavered in his trust in the Lord and sought to buy off the Assyrians with silver and gold (vv. 14-16). Assyrian King Sennacherib accepted the payment, implying that he would break off his invasion and leave Judah alone. But he did no such thing. He made it plain that he would soon be coming to Jerusalem to conquer it as well. Sennacherib thus acted treacherously and broke the agreement. This is described in verses 7-9 of Isaiah 33: the "messengers of peace" (Hezekiah's envoys to Sennacherib) are weeping because of this treachery; they return to Hezekiah with the terrifying news that Assyria will be destroying all the cities of Judah and slaughtering her people. So Hezekiah and Judah now have nowhere else to turn. Their attempts to buy military help from Egypt have failed. Their attempts to buy off Sennacherib and Assyria also have failed. Now that all these efforts have failed, they turn to the Lord. Isn't it amazing that God would lower himself to want such bargain-basement repentance and faith? How greatly does turning to God as a last resort dishonor the one who should be our first and only Savior! But God lowers himself and accepts it.

He speaks that word of woe on the treacherous destroyer (in this case, Assyria; v. 1). Basically he says, "What goes around comes around." God decrees that when the destroyer has stopped destroying, he will be destroyed; when he has stopped betraying, he will be betrayed. So Sennacherib was treacherously betrayed and murdered by his own sons (see Isa 37:38), and Assyria was treacherously destroyed by her former vassals Elam and Babylon (Pfeiffer, *Old Testament History*, 341–42).

Verses 2-6 display the newfound faith and trust of the people of God in this terrifying situation. God has blocked them in, and they must at last turn in faith to him. They cry to him for grace, knowing they don't deserve his deliverance. The fear of the Lord is Zion's treasure; and fearing him, they need fear nothing else.

You Will See the King Arise in Power
ISAIAH 33:7-16

As we've seen, verses 7-9 reflect the terror caused by the news that Sennacherib will act treacherously and come to destroy Jerusalem. In verses 10-12 God rises up in power to exalt himself by destroying the treacherous and turning their wicked schemes back on them. The report of God's awesome power will reach the ends of the earth (v. 13).

But such a vision of God's holy power causes the people of God on earth (Zion) to tremble with terror. The "sinners in Zion" (v. 14) realize that they have no more right to stand before such a holy God than do the Assyrians. In December 1740 Jonathan Edwards preached a powerful sermon based on Isaiah 33:14 entitled "Sinners in Zion Tenderly Warned." In it he asked the question of that verse: "Who among us can dwell with a consuming fire? Who among us can dwell with ever-burning flames?" The "consuming fire" is the holiness of God, and we sinners are like combustible chaff. The surface of the sun is said to be more than 10,000 degrees Fahrenheit, and the closest a NASA probe could be able to get to it is four million miles away. At that staggering distance, the temperature is an astonishing 2,600 degrees Fahrenheit (Butler, "Solar Probe Plus")! Just as the sun exists in unapproachable heat, so God dwells in unapproachable light (1 Tim 6:16). God's holiness is like the raging inferno of the sun, and none of us sinners can survive it. The prophetic Word calls all the people of Zion to look inward, see the corruption of our sins, and flee to Christ. For all who humbly repent, the perfect righteousness of Christ will be imputed to them by faith alone, for Christ alone has perfectly lived out the righteousness of verses 15-16. Then, by his Spirit working in us, such a pattern of life can be increasingly ours by faith.

You Will See the Beauty of the King and His Kingdom
ISAIAH 33:17-24

The magnificent vision from the top of this "Lookout Mountain" of prophecy ends with a cascade of promises to the true people of God. First, their own eyes will see the King of Zion in his beauty. The greatest beauty our eyes will ever see is the radiant Christ, seated on his throne in the new Jerusalem; and that vision will complete our salvation (1 John 3:2).

We will also see a "vast land," the perfect new heaven and new earth. However, we will *not* see the wicked people who made life such a horror on earth (Isa 33:18-19). The days of their terrorizing will be over forever. Instead, we will see Zion now consummated in eternal glory. It will be a rich land, flowing with rivers; it will be a secure city, not a movable tent. It will be a place of perfect government, where Jesus Christ will reign. Verse 22 amazingly traces out the branches of human government: the judicial, the legislative, and the executive. In the United States Constitution these three branches are separated from each other in a system of checks and balances because "Power tends to corrupt, and absolute power corrupts absolutely" (Dalberg-Acton, "Letter"). But Jesus Christ is the perfect King, and he cannot be corrupted by anything. He is our Judge, he is our Lawgiver, he is our King. The government will be perfect in his hands. Praise God the fourth title is added: Savior! If all Jesus was for us was Judge, Lawgiver, and King, we would all be justly condemned. But by his atoning work, his fourth title of Savior makes the other three titles something we will yearn to see in eternity. By God's grace, the final promise of this amazing chapter is of full forgiveness of sins (v. 24).

Applications

The best application of this visionary chapter is to stand on it as "Lookout Mountain" and turn slowly, gazing at each theme in turn.

- We should rest confidently in God's power to turn the wicked treachery of nations like Assyria back on their own heads.
- We must see how God blocks us in (as he did to Judah) until we have nowhere else to turn; thus, we come to reject all our efforts to buy off our attackers, instead humbly crying out to God alone for salvation (v. 2).
- We must understand that God's awesome power to exalt himself in history is so that the peoples of the world may call on his name for salvation (vv. 10-13).
- We must be active in evangelism and missions, making certain that people to the ends of the earth may hear of God's mighty acts of salvation in Christ and be saved.
- We must tremble before the holiness of such a God and ask the question of verse 14: How can a sinner like me dwell with the consuming fire of God's holiness? We should fear the judgment

of God and flee to Christ alone. This theme should cause all the "sinners in Zion" (unregenerate church members) to be warned and flee genuinely to Christ and stop playing religious games.

- We should examine our lives and be sure the holiness of verses 15-16 characterizes us.

- We should cherish the cascading promises of verses 17-24, of our future perfect blessedness in the new Jerusalem, the capital city of the new heaven and new earth. We will see Jesus face to face; we will look out on a perfected earth; we will no longer see any wicked people; we will delight in the perfect government of King Jesus; and we will be rich in our forgiveness. Let this vision fill you with hope!

Reflect and Discuss

1. How is Isaiah 33 like a prophetic "Lookout Mountain"? What themes fill this chapter and fill the minds of all who believe its words?

2. How does 2 Kings 18:13-16 help us understand Isaiah 33:7-9 and the historical context?

3. How does this chapter speak a timeless warning to all treacherous destroyers (not just Assyria)?

4. How does verse 2 give all sinners a great prayer to pray to the Lord for salvation?

5. What attributes of God and of Christ flow in this chapter?

6. What motive does God give for rising up and exalting himself in verses 10-13?

7. What is the significance of the phrase "sinners in Zion"? If "Zion" means God's visible people on earth, how could verse 14 speak a word of warning to unregenerate church members?

8. How is God like a consuming fire? How does that idea drive us to the cross of Christ for salvation?

9. How should the promises of verses 17-24 fill us with hope as well as with energy for personal holiness and for witness to the ends of the earth?

10. How could the various offices of Christ mentioned in verse 22 (Judge, Lawgiver, King, Savior) be an excellent outline to a gospel presentation?

God Warns the Whole Earth of the Wrath to Come

ISAIAH 34

All the stars in the sky will dissolve. The sky will roll up like a scroll, and its stars will all wither as leaves wither on the vine, and foliage on the fig tree. (Isa 34:4)

Main Idea: God warns the nations on earth of his coming judgment on the whole earth and on all the armies of the earth, with Edom as a symbolic representative of God's enemies.

I. **God Summons the Nations to Listen (34:1).**
   A. Doomsday scenarios underestimate what will come.
   B. God graciously warns all nations.
   C. God's word is sufficient for their salvation.

II. **God's Wrath Is on All Nations and Their Armies (34:2-4).**
   A. God has an overwhelming wrath; no nation is exempt.
   B. Overwhelming slaughter includes heaven and earth.

III. **Edom Represents God's Enemies (34:5-15).**
   A. Edom is a historical and representative nation.
   B. God upholds Zion's cause.
   C. Edom's judgments are a foretaste of hell.

IV. **God's "Scroll" Is Written, and Every Line Will Be Fulfilled (34:16-17).**
   A. God's "scroll" is his sovereign plan.
   B. Wild animals overtake Edom.
   C. All the days ordained for each nation are already written in God's book.

V. **Isaiah 34 Prepares Us for the Second Coming of Christ.**
   A. The signs in the heavens: the "falling of the stars"
   B. The gathering of the kings of the earth and their armies for slaughter
   C. Deeper issue: deliverance from hell

God Summons the Nations to Listen
ISAIAH 34:1

People are constantly fascinated by doomsday scenarios, ruminations on what future catastrophes await the human race:

- Some huge meteorite will hit the planet and make the human race instantly extinct.
- Radiation blasts from solar flares will heat up the earth's core to such a level that life on earth will be impossible.
- A gamma-ray burst from elsewhere in the galaxy could make its way to earth and end it all.
- The destruction of the earth's ozone layer will produce rampant global warming that will lead to the extinction of the human race.
- The eruption of a super volcano could disrupt the earth's climate enough to wipe out humanity.
- A supervirus will become airborne and wipe out the human race by disease.
- Some nation or terrorist group will use thermonuclear weapons to trigger a worldwide conflagration resulting in total annihilation.
- Overpopulation will cause a depletion of the earth's food sources resulting in widespread starvation.
- Robots designed with superior artificial intelligence and mechanical power will rebel against the human race and wipe us all out.
- An evil genius will create some doomsday machine that will detonate and destroy the earth.
- Aliens will invade and conquer our race with their superior intellect and technology.

Anyone who watches enough movies or reads enough fiction will be able to line up these doomsday scenarios with popular depictions. Yet amazingly, however horrific any of these depictions may be, all of them actually *understate* the danger to the human race because every single one of them leaves out the most terrifying threat of all: the just wrath of an almighty and omniscient God. No doomsday scenario crafted by the imagination of some literary genius will ever supersede what the Bible proclaims about the future of our race and of our planet. Isaiah 34 gives a powerful foretaste of the terrifying future of the human race and the universe.

The chapter begins with God summoning the whole earth to warn everyone about the universality of his coming wrath (v. 1). This is sheer grace from a holy God; he is not obligated to give such warnings, but he gives them for the salvation of his chosen people from every nation. The elect will heed these warnings and flee to Christ; the reprobate will scoff and blow them off.

God's Wrath Is on All Nations and Their Armies
ISAIAH 34:2-4

We learn two lessons: (1) God has an overpowering wrath against sin; (2) this wrath is against every single nation on earth without exception. There is not one righteous nation on earth whose leaders and policy makers exist for and render all decisions simply for the glory of God and of Christ. Jesus asserted, "Anyone who is not with me is against me, and anyone who does not gather with me scatters" (Matt 12:30). So any president, prime minister, dictator, or king who makes decisions and sends forth his nation's armies on some mission, if their motive is not the glory of Christ, God is against them. Therefore, God's wrath is against every single army on the face of the earth. He will "set them apart for destruction" (v. 2).

The prophecy goes far beyond this, for the words reach into the heavenly realms to throw down the celestial bodies and to roll up the heavens like a scroll (v. 4). These words may speak of Satan's demonic army being routed by God's angelic army and hurled down or of the total destruction of the present universe, including the stars, in order to make way for the new heaven and new earth. Hebrews 1:10-12 makes it plain that the heavens will be rolled up and changed like a robe, and Isaiah 34:4 also predicts it.

These verses have an "already and not yet" aspect to them. In every generation God's wrath moves out against all the godlessness and wickedness of every nation and individual, and God's use of one wicked nation to punish another wicked nation has been a major theme of the tapestry of human history. When Hitler's Nazi armies were slaughtering and being slaughtered by Stalin's Soviet armies, it was a partial fulfillment of this prophecy. But the fullest and final fulfillment is yet to come; it will immediately precede the second coming of Christ, as we will see in a moment.

Edom Represents God's Human Enemies
ISAIAH 34:5-15

The prophecy of Isaiah 34 goes from the universal to the specific in one sense in verses 5-15, as the words focus on Edom, the ancient foe of Israel. Edom was the nation descended from Esau, the twin brother of Jacob. Edom was a literal, historical nation, frequently at war with Judah and Israel. Here they are called by God, "the people I have set apart for destruction" (v. 5). Verse 6 also specifically mentions Edom, as well as Bozrah, which was the capital city of that small nation.

Yet in Scripture, Edom (Esau) is also representative of the reprobates of the earth, those who live and die as rebels against God. In Malachi 1:2-4 God uses his consistent settled judgments against Edom as evidence of his electing love toward the Jews, the descendants of Jacob. The statement "I loved Jacob, but I hated Esau" (Mal 1:3) is chosen by the apostle Paul to teach the doctrine of unconditional election and reprobation in Romans 9:13. So in Isaiah 34 it is reasonable to see Edom as not only a historical nation but a representative one: God's wrath falls on the reprobates from every tribe and nation on earth.

God declares that when his sword has "drunk its fill in the heavens, it will then come down on Edom and on the people I have set apart for destruction" (v. 5). So God will punish the satanic forces behind the reprobate nations on earth then descend to punish their earthly slaves. The slaughter will be overwhelming, as the prophecy uses gory sacrificial language to depict the carnage: there will be a "great slaughter in the land of Edom" (v. 6).

Significantly, verse 8 links the slaughter to God's zeal to uphold Zion's cause against her earthly enemies. Again and again, God makes plain his commitment to punish those who persecuted his people. In his complex plan he allows the "Edom" nations of the earth to trample his people for a time (Dan 7:23-26); but God ordains the final triumph of his people by his own personal intervention from heaven, ultimately in the second coming of Christ. Verses 9-10 depict the devastation of Edom in language that gives a foretaste of hell itself. The smoke rising forever from Edom's burned-out land prefigures the smoke rising eternally from the lake of fire in Revelation 14:10-11. To fulfill his careful plan, God stretches out over Edom a measuring line of total destruction (Isa 34:11); the words are reminiscent of the total chaos of the universe in Genesis 1:2: "Now the earth was formless and empty." In effect, God is saying he will speak Edom out of orderly creation; total desolation will be her lot.

God's "Scroll" Is Written, and Every Line Will Be Fulfilled
ISAIAH 34:16-17

The final insight from this terrifying chapter comes in understanding the eternal plan of God for all this destruction. Though the final verses speak of wild animals and birds nesting and finding mates, the real focus is on the "scroll" of the Lord (vv. 16-17). This is the language of the sovereign plan of God, a plan written down in detail before the foundation of the world. God has written his scroll, and every line will be fulfilled, including where "sand partridges" and "birds of prey" will mate and lay their eggs (v. 15).

Isaiah 34 Prepares Us for the Second Coming of Christ

Isaiah 34 prepares the earth for the second coming of Jesus Christ. In Matthew 24:29-31 Jesus quotes Isaiah 34:4 about the stars falling from the sky and the heavenly bodies being shaken. Revelation 6:12-17 is filled with similar images. When the sixth seal is broken, the stars fall to the earth like late figs from a fig tree, and the sky recedes like a scroll. Revelation 17:13-14 speaks of the ten earthly kings who submit to the antichrist ("the beast" of Rev 13) and who wage war against the Lamb (Jesus Christ) and his followers. Revelation 19:11-21 depicts plainly the second coming of Christ in this context, returning to rescue his people from the terror caused by the antichrist and his wicked henchmen, the "kings of the earth, and their armies" (v. 19) who are gathered to wage war against Jesus and his army. They are slaughtered without mercy by the sword coming from the mouth of Jesus as he rides on his white horse, descending from heaven. The gruesome chapter ends with the birds of the air coming to feast on the flesh of the wicked armies of the nations that assembled to fight Jesus. This is the final consummation of the themes of Isaiah 34:2, God's wrath against all the unbelieving nations on earth.

Applications

Everyone must be warned to flee the wrath to come by trusting in Christ. The messengers of the gospel should regularly refresh their minds with how terrifying will be the wrath of God against his enemies and should warn the nations as Isaiah has done here. We should also understand the reasons for the universality of God's wrath against the nations. There is not a political nation on earth that exists solely for the glory of God and of Christ. This should make every Christian be somewhat suspect of overweening patriotism. We must remind ourselves again and again that "our citizenship is in heaven, and we eagerly wait for a Savior from there, the Lord Jesus Christ" (Phil 3:20). Finally, we should study the doctrine of the end times and the second coming of Christ and get ready for the vicious worldwide persecution that will accompany that age under the antichrist. We should get our children and our disciples ready for that suffering, confident of final triumph by the return of the King.

Reflect and Discuss

1. How do the doomsday scenarios of Hollywood compare with what is depicted in Isaiah 34 and the book of Revelation?
2. How is this chapter actually a display of God's grace and patience toward his enemies?
3. What stark descriptions of judgment are displayed in verses 2-4? What language is used?
4. Do you think verse 4 refers to Satan and his wicked army in the heavenly realms, to the actual stars in the sky, or both?
5. How is Edom both a historical nation and a representative one? In Scripture, what does Esau/Edom represent (Mal 1:2-4 and Rom 9:10-13; also Heb 12:16)?
6. According to verse 8, what is the motive given for the slaughter? How is God upholding Zion's cause?
7. What images fill verses 9-10? How are these verses like a foretaste of hell (Rev 14:10-11)?
8. What does God's "scroll" represent in verses 16-17? How is it comforting that God has carefully determined details of human history and written them in his "book" before anything began (Ps 139:16)?
9. How do these verses prepare us for the second coming of Christ (Matt 24:29-31)?
10. How could meditation on this chapter, especially verses 1-2, keep us from excessive patriotism and nationalism?

The Cursed Universe Restored to God's Original Purposes

ISAIAH 35

The wilderness and the dry land will be glad; the desert will rejoice and blossom like a wildflower. It will blossom abundantly and will also rejoice with joy and singing. The glory of Lebanon will be given to it, the splendor of Carmel and Sharon. They will see the glory of the LORD, the splendor of our God. (Isa 35:1-2)

Main Idea: God restores the cursed universe and suffering humanity to their original purposes by the redemption plan achieved in Christ.

I.   **Creation Transformed: From Sterile Desert to Fruitful Garden (35:1-2)**
   A.   Human sin leads to a cursed desert.
   B.   The blooming of the desert is a supernatural, gracious, sovereign act of God.
   C.   God's glory is fully on display.

II. **People Transformed: From Cursed Weakness to Blessed Strength (35:3-7)**
   A.   Human weakness is a curse from the fall.
   B.   The message of the gospel is the only encouragement.
   C.   Christ's miracles are a foretaste of future strength.
   D.   The desert blooming is both a symbol and the reality of salvation.

III. **The Transforming Event: "Your God Is Coming to Save You" (35:4)**
   A.   The key to everything: Christ intervenes to save.
   B.   The coming of Christ changes the cursed universe.
   C.   A Scripture reading in Nazareth is a message of fulfillment.

IV. **The Journey of the Transformed: A Highway of Holiness (35:8-10)**
   A.   The "Way of Holiness" is described here.
   B.   The "Holy Way" is the "Way" of salvation.
   C.   Progressive sanctification is essential to true salvation.

V.   **The Destination of the Transformed: Glorious Zion (35:10)**
   A.   The final destination of the highway: Zion
   B.   The joy of their arrival and of their eternity

Creation Transformed: From Sterile Desert to Fruitful Garden
ISAIAH 35:1-2

We live in a world that is constantly groaning under the weight of human sin. When Adam fell into sin in the garden of Eden, God cursed the garden and indeed the world. Where the garden once bloomed in magnificent glory, it soon shriveled into thorns and thistles. Though God in his goodness allowed a great deal of beauty to survive, the transformation of the earth to a cursed desert is part of his just penalty for human sin. Romans 8:19-23 makes it plain that creation is groaning under this curse every single moment, locked in "bondage to decay." This corruption is depicted often in the book of Isaiah as a fertile field that has been turned into a wasteland.

Sadly, the drama of the cursing of Eden was replayed to a smaller degree in the promised land. When Israel entered the promised land under Joshua, it was described in magnificently lush terms, "a land flowing with milk and honey" (Deut 11:9). But God went on to warn Israel that if they failed to keep his covenant, he would curse the land by commanding the clouds not to rain on it.

> *The sky above you will be bronze, and the earth beneath you iron. The LORD will turn the rain of your land into falling dust; it will descend on you from the sky until you are destroyed.* (Deut 28:23-24)

This has come about because of the sinfulness of Israel, as God warned them before they entered the land.

More painful is the profound cursing of the human race itself. Our bodies are wracked with diseases that attack every single organ and bodily function. Eyes that were created to see the glory of God's light are blind; ears that were created with marvelous complexity to hear the various sounds of God's creation are deaf; legs that were astonishingly crafted with strength and flexibility are paralyzed. Deeper than that, our minds are corrupted with constantly sinful thoughts, and our hearts delight in evil. Left to ourselves, both we and this world will continue to groan under corruption and become more and more bereft of blessing.

But Isaiah 35 stands as a glorious prophecy of God's intention to transform this cursed world through Christ. The chapter begins with the desert rejoicing and blossoming like a rose, singing praise songs to the God of salvation (vv. 1-2). Formerly stripped of its glory by human sin, it has now been lavishly replenished. Verse 2 says the glory and splendor of Lebanon, Sharon, and Carmel will be given to it. The restored earth will proclaim at every moment the glory of God. When the redeemed walk the surface of the new earth, it will radiate not with sunlight but with the glory of God in Christ (Rev 21:23). The earth will at last be liberated from her bondage to corruption and brought into the glorious freedom of the children of God (Rom 8:21).

People Transformed: From Cursed Weakness to Blessed Strength
ISAIAH 35:3-7

And that freedom will ultimately be total. Physical perfection for every redeemed human being awaits the consummation of Isaiah 35. Blind eyes, deaf ears, lame legs, and mute tongues are all devastations brought on by human sin. Death itself is the ultimate curse, for in death every eye is blind, every ear deaf, every leg paralyzed, every tongue stilled. But a time is coming when all of this human degradation and cursed weakness will be radically transformed. Isaiah 35 is a message meant to be proclaimed to those still languishing under the curse. The messenger (Isaiah then, each believer now) is under orders from almighty God to take these words as a healing balm to the nations. With these words we are to strengthen the weak hands and steady the shaking knees, encouraging Christians with the promise of final salvation (v. 3; see Heb 12:12). The promises of God are given to strengthen the weak for the journey that still awaits us on the "Highway of Holiness."

God here promises a new order in which all the effects of sin and death will be removed forever. When God said, "Let there be light," he also said, "Let there be sight." Blindness thwarts God's purpose for light. Isaiah 45:18 says that God did not create the world to be empty but formed it to be inhabited. In the same way, God did not create the eye to be blind or the ear to be deaf. The marvelous intricacy of the eye must find its fulfillment in sight, and the goal is that the one who sees may give God glory for the magnificent beauty of creation. In the new order there will be no blind eyes, no deaf ears, no lame legs, no mute tongues. Every single human being will function as God intended in creation; joy will fill their hearts as they look on a universe similarly redeemed from the curse—water flowing where once was desert.

The Transforming Event: "Your God Is Coming to Save You"
ISAIAH 35:4

These words so obviously go infinitely beyond anything that happened in the Old Testament that they must refer to the salvation God wrought in Jesus Christ. The actual physical restoration of the remnant to Jerusalem under Ezra and Nehemiah comes vastly short of the promises here. Actually, it was bitterly disappointing to them in many ways (Ezra 3:12-13; Neh 1:3-4). The words of Isaiah 35:1-7 were looking ahead to a transformation that had not yet occurred. And verse 4 points plainly to the transforming event: "Here is your God; . . . he will save you."

This can be none other than the work of God in Jesus Christ, the Savior of the world. In Christ alone are the promises of Isaiah 35, "Yes!" and "Amen!" (2 Cor 1:20). Our God has come to save us in Christ's incarnation, sinless life, wonder-working ministry, perfect teachings, atoning death, and bodily resurrection. So will our God come to finish this saving work in us and for us by the second coming of Christ and the new heaven and new earth. At that time Christ will raise our bodies from the dead (1 Cor 15:21-58), completing his triumph over every curse mentioned in this chapter. Only then will these promises find their fulfillment.

The miracles of Christ's first coming were merely signs pointing to this glorious consummation. A sign is not the reality, just as a highway sign declaring how many miles it is to New York City shows you haven't yet arrived there. Every healing Jesus ever did in his life has been in some way reversed by death. The eyes of the man born blind that Jesus healed in John 9 are presently closed by death. The ears of the deaf man that Jesus opened by sighing and saying, "Ephphatha!" (Mark 7:34) are presently closed by death. The legs of the paralyzed man who was lowered through the roof that were strengthened by Jesus's power (Mark 2:12) are now made motionless by death. So also the tongues of every mute person that Jesus healed are now stilled by death. Those miracles did not solve the true problem of the human race—death. But they were infallible signs of a total healing that God intends to give every believer in the resurrection! Then alone will the glories of Isaiah 35 be fulfilled. Death is "the last enemy to be abolished" (1 Cor 15:26). And when death is abolished by the full redemption of our bodies at resurrection, then creation itself will forever be liberated from its bondage to decay and be brought into the glorious freedom of the children of God (Rom 8:21-23).

But Isaiah 35:4 also speaks of vengeance and retribution, for these will also be consummated at the second coming of Christ, as Isaiah 34 has made plain. The wicked will be winnowed out of God's glorious kingdom, and only the redeemed will be there.

The Journey of the Transformed: A Highway of Holiness
ISAIAH 35:8-10

But we are not there yet! We still groan inwardly as we wait eagerly for the redemption of our bodies (Rom 8:23). In the meantime, we must travel a Holy Way in order to arrive at that glorious destination. This picks up on the glorious theme of holy pilgrimage that would have been so familiar to Judah. Three times a year God's people were required to travel from their homes to Jerusalem for national worship. The pilgrimage of Isaiah 35 is far more significant, however, for it ends in heaven.

The descriptions of the highway in verses 8-10 are very significant. First, the name—the "Holy Way" or "Highway of Holiness"—implies the need for absolute purity from sin. The central command concerning this is found in Leviticus 11:44 (and many other places): "Be holy because I am holy." As 1 John 1:5 says plainly, "God is light, and there is absolutely no darkness in him." So the Highway of Holiness is characterized by people who "walk in the light as he himself is in the light" (1 John 5:7), loving righteousness and hating wickedness.

The Highway of Holiness is an exclusive way, and only the righteous may travel on it. The unclean cannot travel on it. This exclusive way refers to the atoning work of Jesus Christ, for only faith in the blood of Christ shed on the cross can cleanse a guilty soul from sins. The positional cleansing of the soul from sin by faith in Christ is called justification. The Highway of Holiness follows this cleansing; it is the journey of sanctification—of progressive growth in practical righteousness—that inevitably follows justification. As Romans 6:19 says, "Just as you offered the parts of yourselves as slaves to impurity, and to greater and greater lawlessness, so now offer them as slaves to righteousness, which results in sanctification."

The Highway of Holiness is also a protected and secure way: Even if people are occasionally foolish, they will not wander off it; no lion will travel there, nor will any vicious beast; only the "redeemed" (Isa 35:9-10) will travel on it. This term clearly points to the purchase made by Christ in blood for each of the pilgrims who travel the Highway of

Holiness, and everyone who begins the journey will most certainly finish it (cf. Rom 8:29-39).

The Destination of the Transformed: Glorious Zion
ISAIAH 35:10

The final destination of those traveling the Holy Way is Zion, the City of God, where God and man will dwell together. The thrice-annual pilgrimages to Jerusalem in Israel's spiritual calendar were shadows and prophetic foretastes of the journey that all the redeemed must travel to enter the true Zion, the new Jerusalem, where they will at last enjoy the full salvation purchased for them by the blood of Christ (Rev 21:4).

Applications

See in the person and work of Jesus Christ the fulfillment of this chapter. It is in Christ that God's original intention for the universe and for human beings will at last be realized after the long nightmare of sin's curse has ended. By Christ will the deserts literally flow with water and spring to life with vegetation. So also through Christ will the human body lose all weakness, disease, and death, and Christians will live forever in perfect happiness. In Christ is the "Holy Way," for as he said in John 14:6, "I am the way, the truth, and the life. No one comes to the Father except through me." Christ's miracles were literal fulfillments of this chapter but also mere signs of a reality not yet ours, a reality only consummated when all the redeemed will receive their resurrection bodies. So see all of these promises in Christ alone, and walk every day in the hope and holiness that are ours in Christ.

Reflect and Discuss

1. How does the image of a desert being transformed speak both about our spiritual transformation in Christ and the physical transformation of the universe coming in the new heaven and new earth?
2. How are Christ's miracles signs, like signposts on a highway, pointing to the final destination?
3. How do verses 3-4 give us a clear pattern for the encouragement of discouraged and weak Christians—whether discouraged at some medical struggle or at some spiritual issue (like sin)?

4. How do verses 5-6 speak directly about the wonder-working power of Jesus Christ?
5. How does the image of a "Holy Way" (vv. 8-10) picture progressive sanctification, as in Romans 6:19?
6. How does John 15:2-3 help explain how only the clean can travel on the Holy Way, but the whole purpose of that Way is to become more and more clean? How does justification relate to sanctification in this issue?
7. How is the Holy Way bounded on each side by the law of God (Rom 8:4)? How does the Spirit help us obey the requirements of God's law?
8. What does Isaiah 35:10 teach you about the joys of heavenly life?
9. How can we use this chapter to strengthen our hope in heaven and build up others who are struggling with discouragement in the Christian life?
10. How does this chapter predict the physical side of redemption (the resurrection body and the new heaven and new earth)?

On Whom Are You Depending to Defeat the Evil Tyrant?

ISAIAH 36

What are you relying on? (Isa 36:4)

Main Idea: The taunts of the royal spokesman of the Assyrian army before the walls of Jerusalem picture Satan's assaults on our souls.

I.   **A Foretaste of the Greatest Battle in History**
    A.   Climactic showdown: good versus evil
    B.   Historic context
    C.   An intimidating evil tyrant
II. **The Crisis Comes at Last: Assyria Invades Judah (36:1-3).**
    A.   Sennacherib shows his power.
    B.   God judges Judah.
III. **Psychological Warfare: The Spokesman's Intimidating Speech (36:4-17)**
    A.   The royal spokesman's mission: talk Judah out from her fortress
    B.   Wave upon wave of intimidating talk
        1.   "Can mere words save you?"
        2.   "Egypt is a splintered staff."
        3.   "The Lord won't deliver you; he is offended at you!"
        4.   "You are militarily pathetic."
        5.   "If you refuse, you will suffer."
        6.   "If you surrender, you will thrive."
IV. **Blasphemy: The Spokesman's Fatal Error (36:18-22)**
    A.   Evil overreaches itself.
    B.   "Not only *won't* the Lord deliver you; the Lord *can't* deliver you!"
    C.   The greatest power in the universe is God's zeal for his own glory.
V.   **Central Question in Life: What Are You Relying On?**
    A.   The royal spokesman's two striking statements
    B.   The key issue in life: What are you relying on?
    C.   Splintered staffs that will pierce

A Foretaste of the Greatest Battle in History

We come at last to the climactic showdown between good and evil played out in the pages of Isaiah's history. Christians are not dualists; we do not believe that good and evil are equal and opposite. We believe that God is infinitely more powerful than Satan and his evil minions. The fact that an omnipotent God allows Satan not only to continue to exist but also temporarily to harm God's people will perpetually be one of the most perplexing issues of theology. Only by embracing Scripture can we make some sense of the twists and turns of history.

Ultimately, this awesome struggle between Assyria and Judah is a picture of God's salvation for us in Christ: his intervention to rescue a people from Satan's tyranny, a people who had no chance at all of defending themselves. In 1682 John Bunyan published *The Holy War*, an allegory of the spiritual warfare Christians face in this world that is dominated by Satan and his spiritual forces of evil. It pictures a walled city called "Mansoul" under siege by Diabolus (Satan), with five gates allowing access to the city: Eye-gate, Ear-gate, Mouth-gate, Feel-gate, and Nose-gate. These represent our five senses and Satan's assault on our souls by means of sensual temptations. In *The Holy War* it was at Ear-gate that Diabolus made his first attack to gain entrance, and by means of his wicked and clever words the inhabitants of the town were deceived and allowed him in (Bunyan, 256–57).

For Christians, it is helpful to read Isaiah 36–37 with a similar eye to analogies, to see in the walled city of Jerusalem a type of our souls and to see in the *rabshakeh* ("royal spokesman") a type of the devil, who uses an array of words to intimidate, allure, insult, and persuade the inhabitants of the town to open up and thereby be enslaved and killed by him. Yet as we look at these chapters analogically, we must not disregard the genuine history of it all. There really was an Assyrian invasion of Judah, a tyrant king named Sennacherib, a godly king named Hezekiah, and a cowering remnant of Judahites who could not save themselves from enslavement and death. And God really did intervene in space and time and slaughter 185,000 Assyrian troops. Biblical history is often both literal and analogical. In this way, it speaks to every generation of Christians whose souls are under constant assault by the devil. And only the angel of the Lord, Christ, can slaughter our enemy.

The Crisis Comes at Last: Assyria Invades Judah
ISAIAH 36:1-3

For thirty-five chapters Isaiah has been preparing God's people for this crisis—exposing the sins that caused it, warning that it would come, predicting the limitations of it, speaking of God's judgment on both Judah and Assyria. Now the prophecy becomes history. Sennacherib, the newly crowned king of Assyria, led his mighty army down the eastern coast of the Mediterranean Sea, subduing other small kingdoms: Tyre and Sidon, Ammon, Moab, Philistia. It seemed that nothing could stop the Assyrian juggernaut (Pfeiffer, *Old Testament History*, 336). Finally, Assyria invaded Judah and conquered all her fortified cities except Jerusalem. The tiny remnant of Judah cowered behind Jerusalem's formidable walls. Because siege warfare was so costly, Sennacherib sent his royal spokesman with a sizeable detachment to Jerusalem to try to persuade Hezekiah and Judah to surrender without a fight.

Psychological Warfare: The Spokesman's Intimidating Speech
ISAIAH 36:4-17

With intimidation and insult, the royal spokesman begins to speak to Hezekiah's delegation. He calls Sennacherib "the great king, the king of Assyria." He was the mouthpiece for his master like the prophet of a god: "The great king . . . says this." He then begins to chop down Hezekiah and Judah's grounds of confidence, one stroke at a time.

He begins by asking a key question: "What are you relying on?" In his mind there is no possible answer. But like a master intimidator skilled in the arts of psychological warfare, he seeks to get inside the heads of the people of Judah. He asserts that their military strategy is nothing more than "mere words." Isn't it interesting it is all the royal spokesman is using at that moment! This man is seeking to undermine Hezekiah's words with his own words. Then he addresses the possibility of Egypt coming to aid Judah. Remarkably, the royal spokesman says the same thing God has been saying: Egypt cannot save you. He calls Egypt a "splintered reed of a staff that will pierce the hand of anyone who grabs it and leans on it" (v. 6).

Finally, the royal spokesman goes for the jugular: their faith in the Lord. He mixes error with truth in his verbal assault, saying that Hezekiah removed the Lord's high places (the Lord hated them) and commanded that the people worship at one altar (true), and that the Lord commanded Assyria to invade (sadly true). He also mocks the military weakness of Judah, saying that even if Assyria were to supply Judah with horses, they would not have enough skilled men to ride them. What hope could they possibly have?

At this point, the royal spokesman raised his voice even louder and sought to crush the confidence that the warriors on the wall had in Hezekiah and in the Lord. He said Hezekiah was trying to deceive them that the Lord would deliver them. He urged them to surrender, promising them peace and prosperity if they did. Here he is most satanic, promising pleasure in return for enslavement. Of course, the Assyrians were notorious for breaking such promises and leaving cities in ashes with piles of heads stacked high.

Blasphemy: The Spokesman's Fatal Error
ISAIAH 36:18-22

But here, evil overreaches itself, as it always does. Just as Satan overreached his power by seeking to ascend to sit on the throne of God (Isa 14:13-14), so the royal spokesman's words soared in an attempt to topple God's rule over the nations. He has already implied, "The Lord *will not* rescue you." He now moves into blasphemy: "The Lord *cannot* rescue you!" His logic is based on history: None of the gods of other nations has ever been able to deliver their lands from the hand of the king of Assyria, so why should the "god" of your puny land be able to do so? This blasphemy, especially since it was believed by Sennacherib and all the Assyrians, is the very thing that will bring down Assyria at the walls of Jerusalem. He has committed a fatal error, and God will respond to it by slaughtering his evil empire. The delegation that the spokesman addressed returned to Hezekiah with their clothes torn as a sign of their humiliation in the sight of the Lord. Their humble repentance and faith would be the conduit of the Lord's deliverance.

Central Question in Life: What Are You Relying On?

The blasphemous royal spokesman's words amazingly get to the central issue in life: "What are you relying on?" While this was an important military question, it is even more poignant spiritually, as a far greater tyranny threatens us: Satan, sin, death, and hell. As we face the overwhelming power of these vicious tyrants, we must feel the weight of the royal spokesman's penetrating question: "What are you relying on?" It seems we live in a world of people who are leaning on many different "splintered reeds" as they face the impending terror of judgment day. Islam, Buddhism, Hinduism, Mormonism, etc. will pierce those who lean on them—so will materialism, Darwinism, and academic philosophy. Those who are depending on their good works to save them will be pierced. Stunningly pierced will be those who leaned on a pale reflection of true Christianity—nominal Christians—who will find their superficial "commitment" to Christ was a fatally false hope. The piercing will begin with Jesus's words on that day: "I never knew you. Depart from me" (Matt 7:23).

It is eternally vital for each person to take stock of his or her true condition before God and ask, "What am I truly relying on to deliver me from Satan, sin, death, and hell?" The only true Deliverer is Jesus Christ.

Application: How Satan Assaults Our Minds

We end by reverting to the idea of Isaiah 36 as an allegory of Satan's assault on our souls by his alluring, insulting, persuading, intimidating words. Ever since the garden of Eden, Satan has sought to trap us by his words. In his approach to Eve (Gen 3:1-5) he used three timeless strategies of speech: (1) questioning God's word ("Did God really say . . . ?"); (2) contradicting God's word ("No! You will not die."); (3) employing partial truths to tell a bigger lie ("God knows that when you eat it your eyes will be opened and you will be like God, knowing good and evil"). Satan still does the same three things every day: causing people to doubt God's Word, contradicting things taught in God's Word, and crafting religious systems that incorporate some truths in overall systems that are false (like Islam's teaching of monotheism).

Beyond this, Satan loves to promise us a delightful life if we will just come out of our fortress of holiness and surrender to him. He seeks to undermine our will to fight by getting us to forsake holy resolutions. Someone who is seeking to stop drinking, stop using Internet pornography, or stop reacting with sinful anger, Satan will assault by intimidation: "Sin will always be your master; you're mine, I own you, and you will never get away. What hope do you have of resisting me? I will relentlessly come after you until you yield as you always have in the past!" His words flow like poison through the rivers of this world's thought systems, and some of the pollution inevitably seeps into the wellsprings of a Christian's mind. We must learn to "resist him, firm in the faith" (1 Pet 5:9).

Reflect and Discuss

1. How does John Bunyan's allegory *The Holy War* fit well with Isaiah 36? How is the royal spokesman a type (picture) of Satan in his assault on the human soul?

2. On the other hand, why is it important for us to embrace the significance of the fact that all of this actually occurred in human history?

3. How is Isaiah 36–37 the culmination of one of the major themes in Isaiah 1–39: the rise and fall of Assyria?

4. What does this chapter teach us about the sinfulness of the human heart?

5. What was the overall goal of the royal spokesman in front of the walls of Jerusalem?

6. How do the royal spokesman's words display a powerful form of psychological warfare?

7. How does the royal spokesman blaspheme and overreach himself?

8. How is the royal spokesman's question "What are you relying on?" a vital one for all Christians, who face the tyranny of Satan, sin, death, and hell?

9. What are some of the "splintered reeds" of false hopes with respect to the tyranny of Satan, sin, death, and hell?

10. How can we use this chapter to defeat the assault of Satan on our minds?

God Vindicates His Honor over an Arrogant Foe

ISAIAH 37

I will defend this city and rescue it for my sake and for the sake of my servant David. (Isa 37:35)

Main Idea: The battle between God and the king of Assyria comes to a head, and God wins effortlessly, symbolizing also Christ's defeat of our eternal enemies.

I. **Hezekiah's Humility: Disgraced, Humbled, Seeking Answers (37:1-4)**
   A. God's zeal for his own glory
   B. God's zeal for the purification of his people
II. **God's First Answer: Fear Not, the Blasphemer Will Die (37:5-7).**
   A. An immediate answer from God
   B. The blasphemer will die.
III. **The King of Assyria's Blasphemy: "Your 'God' Is No Different!" (37:8-13)**
   A. The arrogance of the king of Assyria
   B. "God is lying to you!"
IV. **Hezekiah's Prayer: "Defend Your Glorious Name, O Lord!" (37:14-20)**
   A. Hezekiah prays based on God's glory.
   B. Hezekiah prays based on God's covenant with Israel.
V. **The Verdict Comes Down from the King of the Universe (37:21-38).**
   A. God's mighty words
   B. God's mighty deeds

Hezekiah's Humility: Disgraced, Humbled, Seeking Answers
ISAIAH 37:1-4

For many unbelievers, the most powerful force for shaping world history is military might. History has been shaped by one world-dominating empire after the next: Egypt, Assyria, Babylon, Medo-Persia,

Greece, Rome, etc. It seems nothing can stop a conqueror at the head of an army sweeping across the earth to add to his realm. But the Bible reveals there is a power infinitely greater: God's zeal for his own glory. In Isaiah 37 these two forces come face to face, and God's effortless victory stands as a timeless lesson to the human race.

At the center of this victory is God's determination to purify his people from their sins so that they will glorify God alone. Despite Isaiah's many warnings, the people of Judah have persisted in many patterns of sin, and Hezekiah has continued to seek deliverance from Egypt instead of relying on God alone. Now at last, with the Assyrian army having conquered everything in Judah but Jerusalem, with the royal spokesman having proclaimed the intimidating speech recorded in Isaiah 36, with Hezekiah's delegation having returned with their clothes torn, Hezekiah has nowhere left to turn.

He begins by putting on sackcloth as a sign of humiliation before the Lord and going into the temple to seek the Lord. He also seeks answers from Isaiah the prophet. He urges Isaiah to pray to the Lord on behalf of the remnant that still survives, acknowledging that these actions are a just punishment from the Lord for the sins of the nation (v. 3). He also shows his one last shred of hope in this exceedingly dark situation: the words of blasphemy spoken by the royal spokesman. He is humble about this, for he knows that God doesn't always immediately act to vindicate his glory in a world of blasphemy, so he says, "*Perhaps* the Lord your God will hear . . . and will rebuke him" (emphasis added). Hezekiah represents the godliest response we can have in a time of humbling chastisement from the Lord.

God's First Answer: Fear Not, the Blasphemer Will Die
ISAIAH 37:5-7

Through Isaiah, God gives an initial answer to King Hezekiah's inquiries. God commands Hezekiah and the remnant not to be afraid because God has heard the blasphemous words of the underlings of the king of Assyria. God rules over mighty nations as powerfully as he rules over sparrows, and he is able to move kings to do his will: "I am about to put a spirit in him and he will hear a rumor and return to his own land, where I will cause him to fall by the sword" (v. 7). With ease, God will move the heart of this king for his own destruction (Prov 21:1).

The King of Assyria's Blasphemy: "Your 'God' Is No Different!"
ISAIAH 37:8-13

Verses 8-13 represent the final warning of Sennacherib to Hezekiah. Judah's purchased "ally," Egypt, has marched out to fight Assyria. Lest Hezekiah should gain any confidence from this, Sennacherib sends the letter recorded in the text. The letter reiterates the royal spokesman's blasphemies against the power of the Lord. But the letter gets far more insulting than the royal spokesman did. It basically says, "Do not let the God you are trusting in lie to you when he says he will deliver you from my hand." Shocking blasphemy! Not only does Sennacherib say that the God of Judah is impotent to stop him but that God is a liar and a deceiver when he says he will deliver them. The bottom line: "Your God is no different than the gods of any other nation."

Hezekiah's Prayer: "Defend Your Glorious Name, O Lord!"
ISAIAH 37:14-20

Hezekiah's response to this blasphemous letter is one of the most memorable and faith-filled reactions in Scripture. He takes the actual letter into the temple and spreads it out before the Lord. Then he prays with great faith and passion. He understands the far greater force in the universe than that of tyrant kings: God's zeal for his own glory. He addresses God in covenant language unique to Israel and Judah: Yahweh, Lord of Armies, is the God who made the universe and rules over every kingdom on the face of the earth, but he is also the God of Israel who is enthroned above the cherubim on the ark of the covenant. Hezekiah links the awesome power of God to the specific fortunes of Judah. As Isaiah will say a few chapters later, "God is enthroned above the circle of the earth; its inhabitants are like grasshoppers" (Isa 40:22). Hezekiah pleads with God to see and hear Sennacherib's blasphemies. He dismisses the "proof" that the Assyrians have cited that no god can stop them; he realizes that the gods of those other nations are nothing more than mere blocks of wood and stone. Hezekiah finishes by pleading with God for deliverance from the king of Assyria, not only for Judah's sake, but ultimately so that all the kingdoms of the earth may know that God alone truly is God.

The Verdict Comes Down from the King of the Universe
ISAIAH 37:21-38

The verdict now comes down from the Judge of the whole earth; it takes our breath away. It comes in two parts: God's mighty words (vv. 21-35) and God's mighty deeds (vv. 36-38). God speaks to Hezekiah first: "Because you prayed to me about King Sennacherib of Assyria . . ." God has not changed his plan because of Hezekiah's prayer, but rather God uses Hezekiah's prayer mysteriously to accomplish his preordained ends, and God includes Hezekiah ahead of time in what he's going to do. There are four parts to God's answer: (1) God promises to judge the blasphemer (vv. 22-29); (2) God promises to save his remnant (vv. 30-32); (3) God promises to deliver Jerusalem (vv. 33-35); and (4) God makes clear that he does all of this for his own glory (v. 35).

First, God promises to judge the blasphemer. God turns the arrogance of Sennacherib against him (vv. 22-29). Sennacherib, in effect, has said to Hezekiah, "Don't you know who I am? Don't you know what I have done to other nations? Why aren't you afraid of me?" God, in effect, turns the whole thing around: "Don't you know who **I am**? Don't you understand the infinite power at my disposal? Why aren't you afraid to blaspheme me?"

Next, God discusses the centerpiece of Sennacherib's argument: his recent history of military conquest. The king of Assyria has made outrageous claims: ascending mountains with his chariots, chopping down the cedars of Lebanon, drying up the Nile by merely stepping in it (vv. 24-25)! Now God pulls the curtain back and reveals the sovereignty of his rule over the nations of the earth: God asserts that all of their military successes have been preordained in his eternal plan (vv. 26-27). It is not only that they won because the gods of the nations are merely idols; they won because the God of the Jews ordained it. God ends by threatening Sennacherib with personal destruction because of his personal blasphemy. Verse 28 says that God tracks every single moment of his life and knows everything he is doing. If Sennacherib heard this prophecy and took it seriously, he should have been thoroughly unnerved. This verse is a clear threat from an omniscient and omnipotent God: God will drag him back to Assyria by the nose and there have him assassinated by his own sons.

God then offers tender words of assurance to Hezekiah and to the remnant of Judah that still survives (vv. 30-32). God promises to provide food for them as agricultural production steadily returns to normal. God's zeal for the welfare of his people will guarantee their survival.

Next, God makes his verdict clear concerning the Assyrian army and Jerusalem. In the original language five of the clauses in verses 33–34 emphasize what Sennacherib will *not* do: He will *not* enter this city; he will *not* shoot an arrow here; he will *not* come against the city with shield; he will *not* build a siege ramp against it; I repeat, he will *not* enter this city. Instead, he will return by the way he came. The sovereign God will defend this city by himself. Often God raises up his own people—mighty warriors—to win great victories. Or sometimes God causes confusion among the enemy so that they destroy themselves. Sometimes God raises up other nations to fight the people threatening his own people. But here God does it all by himself, as he said he would do: "Then Assyria will fall, but not by human sword" (Isa 31:8).

So this is the end of the Assyrian threat. For all the terrifying power of the seemingly undefeatable army of Assyria, God's simple word overrules all things. On the scales of human history, all the nations are like tiny weights: some weighing a gram, some weighing a tenth of a gram, some weighing a kilogram. But God weighs a trillion grams (and more!), and whatever side of the scales he comes down on, that side will win.

Finally, God reveals the motive behind all this: his own glory. Verse 35 makes plain that he will defend the city of Jerusalem for his own name's sake. He mentions David at this point as a foretaste of the Son of David, Jesus Christ. Because of the plan he has to redeem the world through Christ, he must defend Jerusalem from the Assyrians.

The mighty words of God lead to the mighty deeds of God. The angel of the Lord is dispatched, and in one night he slaughters 185,000 Assyrian troops. This staggering slaughter is approximately the total number of troops that fought on both sides of the battle of Gettysburg! It is quite possible that God used a quick-acting plague, a fever that burned up these warriors, as Isaiah 10:16 seems to indicate. But whatever the means were, the end was clear: death. The angel of the Lord in the Old Testament is frequently the preincarnate Christ (Gen 22:11; Exod 3:2). Here it is not so clear that it was Christ, but it seems to fit with the significance of this moment. Just as Jesus would one day return in glory to destroy the antichrist in Revelation 19 and rescue his people, so he does here.

The epilogue is stunning. Not only the macro-scale (185,000 Assyrian troops dead) but so also the micro-scale: a single blasphemer cut down. God's arm is immeasurably long; there is not a single square inch on this planet that God doesn't rule. He moves in Sennacherib's sons to assassinate their father while he is worshiping in the temple of his "god" Nisroch. This is the justice of God to Sennacherib: "You said I don't have power to save my people from you; the fact is, your 'god' doesn't have power to save you from me, not even on his own turf!"

Applications: Timeless Lessons from a Miraculous Slaughter

Let us list some of the timeless lessons of this chapter:

- God's glory is uppermost in his own affections.
- Therefore, God's actions are first for his name, and second for human salvation.
- God's power and knowledge are awesome.
- God is sovereign over the nations.
- God rules over the hearts of kings.
- The human heart is arrogant.
- God opposes the proud but gives grace to the humble.
- God answers humble prayer.
- God's wrath is terrifying.
- God's mercy to sinners is amazing.

Each of these deserves a full sermon!

A final word: The true tyrant threatening the people of God is sin ruling in death (Rom 5:21). God dispatches his only begotten Son, Jesus Christ, who defeats this terrifying foe, not by killing but by dying. To him alone be the glory.

Reflect and Discuss

1. How does this chapter show God's zeal for his own glory?
2. How would it affect our lives if we lived more consistently zealous for God's glory rather than concerned about human themes?
3. Why is it important to put the highest motive as God's glory rather than human salvation?
4. In what ways is God's awesome power on display in Isaiah 37?
5. Why is God's sovereignty over nations vital to his control of human history in general? How does this doctrine bring us great comfort?

6. How do the boasts of the Assyrian king show that he is really worshiping himself as a god? Why is it true that this same temptation to pride is in each of us as well?

7. "God resists the proud, but gives grace to the humble" (Jas 4:6; 1 Pet 5:5). What does it mean that God "resists" the proud? How is that seen in Isaiah 37?

8. How is Hezekiah's prayer an example for all believers to follow? What are some attributes of that prayer that we can learn from?

9. History shows that Sennacherib didn't die until more than twenty years later. How does this put the amazing patience of God on display? How are Romans 2:4-5 and Romans 9:22 explanations for God's amazing patience toward the wicked?

10. How does this chapter display the amazing grace of God to us in Christ?

God's Purpose in Illness and Healing

ISAIAH 38

Indeed, it was for my own well-being that I had such intense bitterness.
(Isa 38:17)

Main Idea: God heals Hezekiah from illness and teaches him humility and obedience by what he suffered.

I.   **The Scourge of Sickness**
    A.   The variety of sickness worldwide
    B.   In Adam we all sinned; in Adam we all die.
    C.   Christ's atonement is the only ultimate cure.
II. **Hezekiah's Misery and Prayer (38:1-3)**
    A.   Put your house in order because you're going to die!
    B.   Hezekiah's reaction
    C.   Hezekiah's prayer
III. **God's Promise of Healing and Its Fulfillment (38:4-8,21-22)**
    A.   God answers Hezekiah's prayer with an amazing promise.
    B.   God grants Hezekiah an amazing sign.
    C.   God uses medicine to work the miracle.
IV. **Hezekiah's Thoughtful Praise (38:9-20)**
    A.   Hezekiah displays bitterness toward God.
    B.   Hezekiah learns from his illness.
    C.   Hezekiah focuses on praise.
V.   **Central Lesson: From the Sickbed**

The Scourge of Sickness

This chapter ushers us into the sickroom of King Hezekiah that we may learn the painful lessons God taught him there. Here we see the mighty king reduced to a quivering, crying babe. Here we see the devastation of disease, a silent, invisible enemy, destroying life from within. Here we also see the power and goodness of God in healing Hezekiah but only after the disease has led Hezekiah to question God's love for him. Here we are led to ask the deepest questions of life, about God's goodness in our pain and suffering and his purpose in it. Why does he allow it—even bring it? Is God truly powerful enough to heal it? And if so, why doesn't he heal it every time? As always, Isaiah will ultimately point us to Jesus Christ, the Great Physician.

The fundamental truth is that, when Adam sinned, suffering and death entered the world (Rom 5:12). The gospel proclaims the parallel truth: "For just as in Adam all die, so also in Christ all will be made alive" (1 Cor 15:22). Christ is the Second Adam, and by his wounds all God's people are healed. But God has willed that death should be the last enemy to be put under Christ's feet, so every single person must face diseases and injuries while we live.

And those diseases and injuries are legion! There is not a single part of the human body (inside or out), and not a single bodily function, that does not have some recognizable array of diseases attacking it. The World Health Organization categorizes 12,420 disease categories in the International Classification of Diseases (ICD). There are seventeen main categories, including infectious and parasitic diseases (e.g., malaria); neoplasms (e.g., tumors); diseases of the blood and blood-forming organs (e.g., leukemia); diseases of the immune system (e.g., AIDS); diseases of the nervous system and sense organs (e.g., multiple sclerosis); and injuries and poisoning (accessed 1/12/2017, http://www.who.int/classifications/icd/en). Our sin-cursed planet is a seething cauldron of suffering and death. We can hardly imagine how many cries of pain or pleaded prayers to God for healing come every single day.

The ultimate solution to this river of suffering is the atoning work of Jesus Christ. Medical science may divert the flow of this river and stem some of its tributaries (e.g., smallpox has been completely eradicated), but everyone who lives will die of something. Isaiah 38 escorts us beyond Hezekiah's sickbed to the cross and empty tomb of Jesus Christ: "He was pierced because of our rebellion, crushed because of our iniquities; punishment for our peace was on him, and we are healed by his wounds" (Isa 53:5).

Hezekiah's Misery and Prayer
ISAIAH 38:1-3

The chapter opens with the news of Hezekiah's illness, which carried him close to death. Isaiah the prophet is dispatched to Hezekiah's sickbed to tell him to put his affairs in order because he is about to die (v. 1). But Hezekiah does not take this news well. Instead of trusting in the joy of eternal pleasures at God's right hand, Hezekiah turns his face to the wall and begins to weep. He also prays that God might remember all the faithful service and wholehearted devotion he's displayed throughout his life. This is not the best ground on which an individual should stand before a holy God. For us as Christians, the best place to stand is the perfection of the Savior, Jesus Christ. At worst, Hezekiah's prayer may imply that he believes God has dealt with him unjustly, that God owes him a better outcome after all the many ways he's served him. It is so easy for those in suffering to lose perspective!

God's Promise of Healing and Its Fulfillment
ISAIAH 38:4-8,21-22

God's fatherly love sees through the weakness of Hezekiah's faith and sends him a surprising message: God will add fifteen years to his life. Beyond that, God promises to continue to deliver Jerusalem from the king of Assyria (vv. 4-6). For this reason, some scholars believe that the events of Isaiah 38 actually *preceded* the events of Isaiah 36–37 (Oswalt, *Isaiah Chs. 1–39*, 674–75; Young, *Isaiah Chs. 19–39*, 508–9). However, Hezekiah's illness and miraculous healing are given in three different places in Scripture (Isa 38; 2 Kgs 20; 2 Chr 32), and in all three places, the order is Assyrian invasion/defeat, then Hezekiah's illness and healing, then the Babylonian envoys (Isa 39). Therefore, we should accept this sequence.

Actually, the promise of fifteen more years is what causes deeper issues. God had already told him to put his house in order because he would die from this illness; now it seems God has changed his mind based on Hezekiah's prayer. It is not easy to harmonize these two statements from an omniscient God, especially since Psalm 139:16 says that all our days were written in God's book before one of them came to be. It seems that Isaiah 38:5 is teaching us that (1) God can heal anyone at any time from any illness; and (2) "The prayer of a righteous person is very powerful in its effect" (Jas 5:16). Our God is a prayer-answering God. The original statement by Isaiah was not false, merely incomplete. It seems the fuller statement would be something like this: "Put your house in order because you are going to die unless you seek me in prayer and ask me to extend your life. But if you do, I will!" But it was best for Isaiah to leave that last part out and allow Hezekiah to decide to come to God in prayer. The bottom line is, we should not imagine that the omniscient God who never must learn a single thing that he didn't already know should change his eternal plans based on input from fallible human beings.

The account ends with how God worked the healing and with the astonishing miraculous sign God gave Hezekiah to bolster his faith (vv. 7-8,21-22). The fuller account of this is in 2 Kings 20:8-11. Hezekiah requests a sign (Isa 38:22; 2 Kgs 20:10), and in response God treats the stairway of Ahaz like a sundial but makes the shadow go backward, as though time had reversed. It is difficult to know how God did this—it is a miracle that defies any scientific explanation—but in any case, the Lord used this astonishing sign to bolster Hezekiah's faith at a critical moment in his life.

Hezekiah's Thoughtful Praise
ISAIAH 38:9-20

The rest of the chapter is given entirely to Hezekiah's amazingly thoughtful psalm of praise to the Lord who healed him. It recounts with tremendous emotion Hezekiah's journey of faith, from bitterly questioning the Lord because of his illness to seeing God's wisdom in bringing the affliction into his life.

From verse 9 it is clear this is a poem Hezekiah writes later, showing a mature reflection on his experience of illness and healing. In verses 10-14 Hezekiah recounts vividly his bitterness toward God for his suffering: he felt it was unfair that God was robbing him of the best years of his life, as though God were hunting him down like a lion to crush his bones.

But in verses 15-17 Hezekiah turns a corner. He realizes that God struck him with bitterness and anguish to humble him, to teach him to walk meekly before God for the rest of his life. Psalm 119 teaches the same lesson (vv. 67,71,75,92): affliction teaches humility and causes us to walk more carefully and obediently before the Lord. The promise of God spoken by Isaiah restored his hope and gave him life (Isa 38:16). Ultimately, it was for Hezekiah's well-being (Hb *shalom*; peace, welfare) that he experienced such intense bitterness. Hezekiah, like all great men, surely struggled with pride, but God designed the affliction of disease and this miraculous cure to humble him to the core of his being.

The final portion of Hezekiah's praise (vv. 18-20) gives his reason for deliverance—so that he might praise God for his faithfulness and power.

Central Lesson: From the Sickbed

The central lesson of the universal human struggle with sin and death is this: "The wages of sin is death, but the gift of God is eternal life in Christ Jesus our Lord" (Rom 6:23). As Hezekiah celebrated how God put his sins behind his back in forgiveness, that forgiveness comes only by Jesus Christ. And the forgiveness of our sins is our top priority, not the temporary healing of the body this side of death. When the paralyzed man was lowered through the roof to be healed by Jesus, Jesus saw their faith and said to the man, "Have courage, son, your sins are forgiven" (Matt 9:2). He was still paralyzed, but his true need had now been met! The desperate pressure that people feel for healing, for deliverance from the suffering of disease, can obscure the infinitely greater need for forgiveness of sins. A paralyzed but forgiven man will spend eternity walking and leaping and praising God in heaven. An Olympic runner who dies in his sin will spend eternity bound hand and foot in outer darkness, weeping and gnashing his teeth in agony. Jesus's physical healings proved his authority on earth to forgive sins (Matt 9:6-7), and they showed a foretaste of the fact that forgiveness of sins guarantees perfection in body after the resurrection from the dead.

Second, we should all heed the command Isaiah gave to Hezekiah: "Set your house in order, for you are about to die." It is appointed to each of us to die, and after that, to face judgment (Heb 9:27). We should live every day aware of our mortality, and we should flee to Christ for salvation and power to make the most of the limited time we have.

Third, we should embrace affliction as Hezekiah and the writer of Psalm 119 did, as working vast spiritual benefits in us: it humbles us and causes us to walk softly in God's laws.

Finally, we should use our own experiences in suffering to make us genuinely compassionate to others who are suffering (2 Cor 1:4). We should use the brief time we have in this life to alleviate all suffering we can but especially eternal suffering. We address physical suffering by giving the kind of ministry the good Samaritan did to the man he found bleeding by the side of the road. We address eternal suffering by proclaiming the gospel of Jesus Christ to the sufferers in the world so that they will never experience the infinitely greater torments of hell.

Reflect and Discuss

1. How is sickness part of the curse of the entire human race in Adam?

2. What do you make of the amazing variety of sicknesses (12,420 disease categories in the International Classification of Diseases)?

3. How do you understand this statement in Isaiah 53 about Christ: "Yet he himself bore our sicknesses, and he carried our pains; . . . and we are healed by his wounds" (Isa 53:4-5)?

4. What do you make of Hezekiah's reaction to Isaiah's news? Do you think Hezekiah shows a lack of faith here?

5. Do you think it wrong for Hezekiah to talk to God about how faithfully he'd walked with him all those years? Why or why not?

6. How do you harmonize God's statement in verse 1 ("you will not recover") with the promise of healing in verse 5? What does this teach you about prayer and God's sovereignty?

7. How do you understand the astonishing sign to Hezekiah of the reversal of the shadow on the steps of the stairway?

8. How does Hezekiah show the bitterness of his soul in this psalm (vv. 9-20)? Why do you think he is so angry and depressed about death?

9. What central lesson does Hezekiah seem to have gleaned from his sickness (vv. 15-17)?

10. How can we learn to suffer well, and how do we avoid displaying a lack of faith in God and in the resurrection by suffering illness as the unbelievers do?

The Tragic End of Shortsighted Faith

ISAIAH 39

*Then Hezekiah said to Isaiah, "The word of the L*ORD *that you have spoken is good," for he thought: There will be peace and security during my lifetime.* (Isa 39:8)

Main Idea: When Isaiah warned Hezekiah of the future exile to Babylon, Hezekiah showed no concern because he knew it wouldn't happen in his lifetime, a tragic display of shortsighted faith.

I. **God Left Him to Test Him: Hezekiah's Erratic Journey of Faith**
   A. Hezekiah is a "smoldering flax."
   B. "God left him to test him" (2 Chr 32:31).
II. **The Babylonian Envoys and Hezekiah's Foolish Pride (39:1-2)**
   A. Hezekiah's fame and pride
   B. Babylon a possible ally
   C. Hezekiah's prideful tour
III. **Isaiah's Interrogation of Hezekiah (39:3-4)**
   A. Isaiah's courageous intervention
   B. The word of the Lord speaks to every situation.
IV. **The Shocking Prophecy of the Babylonian Captivity (39:5-7)**
   A. Isaiah 39:6-7, a "hinge passage" in the book: from Assyria to Babylon
   B. The shocking details of the prediction
V. **Hezekiah's Shortsighted Reaction (39:8)**
   A. Hezekiah's stunning reaction
   B. Self-focus; no concern for the big picture
   C. Manasseh waiting in the wings!

God Left Him to Test Him: Hezekiah's Erratic Journey of Faith

Jesus's gentle skill in redeeming erratic sinners is prophesied in Isaiah 42:3: "He will not break a bruised reed, and he will not put out a smoldering wick." The "bruised reed" is the picture of frailty and the "smoldering wick" the picture of inconstancy. A smoldering wick is an apt description of the faith of King Hezekiah: a great man who, from time to time, displayed the noxious fumes of smoldering unbelief and pride. Hezekiah was mighty through faith to purge Israel's religion of its pagan high places—that is the fire of grace, but he smolders through unbelief when he should be trusting the Lord and not politics to save Judah. He walks with the Lord in daily piety concerning the laws of Moses—that is the fire of grace, but he smolders by hiring Egypt's cavalry and chariots. He is strong in faith to break from the king of Assyria and not send him tribute—that is the fire of grace, but when Assyria invades Judah he sends messengers with gold and silver saying, "I have sinned; withdraw from me!" When the climactic moment occurs in Isaiah 36–37 and Assyria comes to besiege Jerusalem, the fire of grace shines forth in Hezekiah's life most brightly: he humbles himself and prays one of the most God-centered prayers in the Old Testament. In Isaiah 38 we see the mingled fire again: when he falls sick, he whimpers and questions God's goodness to him, but in the end, he learns to walk humbly because of his affliction.

In Isaiah 39 we end Hezekiah's pilgrimage on a sad note. Second Chronicles 32:31 relates the story: "When the ambassadors of Babylon's rulers were sent to him to inquire about the miraculous sign that happened in the land, *God left him* to test him and discover what was in his heart" (emphasis added). Chilling. "God left him." What does that mean? Not at all that God abandoned him, but that God withdrew from Hezekiah relationally and experientially. He did it "to test him and discover what was in his heart." This severe test revealed Hezekiah's pride, self-centeredness, and lack of concern for the future of God's people.

The Babylonian Envoys and Hezekiah's Foolish Pride
ISAIAH 39:1-2

The historical background here is important. By this time the Assyrian invasion has already occurred, and news of the stunning victory of almighty God over 185,000 Assyrian troops has made its way throughout that entire region. The plunder left from the dead soldiers (who had completed the conquest of many smaller nations before they invaded Judah) was collected by Hezekiah and Judah, making them suddenly very wealthy. This event made Hezekiah's reputation, and many nations sent emissaries to him to congratulate him on this spectacular victory

(2 Chr 32:23). News of Hezekiah's illness and miraculous healing had only enhanced his reputation as a king under the special favor of heaven.

Babylon at that time was a subject city-state, dominated by the Assyrian Empire. Their king, Merodach-baladan, had been agitating militarily against the tyranny of Assyria. His rebellion was defeated by Sennacherib before Sennacherib turned to deal with the other vassal states in the Near East (Moab, Edom, Philistia, Syria, Israel, Judah, etc.) (Pfeiffer, *Old Testament History*, 336; Bright, *History of Israel*, 284–87). After the stunning defeat of Assyria at Jerusalem, Merodach-baladan sent emissaries to Hezekiah, undoubtedly for the purpose of discussing an ongoing alliance between them to continue weakening Assyrian domination. So these emissaries represented a severe test for Hezekiah because his usual Achilles heel was politics: trusting in alliances rather than in the Lord to deliver Judah—"God left him to test him and discover what was in his heart."

Hezekiah received the envoys from Babylon gladly and showed them everything in his treasuries and his armories: the gold, silver, spices, precious oil, weaponry—everything. It was a prideful tour and greatly dishonoring to God because evidently Hezekiah made no mention of the power of the Lord in defending and so enriching Judah. He (amazingly) took credit for the works God had accomplished! But what had Hezekiah done? When Assyria invaded, he begged for his life. When threatened with a terminal illness, he begged for his life again. What pride could there be in this?

Isaiah's Interrogation of Hezekiah
ISAIAH 39:3-4

I can picture Isaiah the prophet standing at the door of the palace, waiting with his arms crossed, a severe look on his face. He confronted Hezekiah with probing questions: "What did these men say, and where did they come to you from?"

Hezekiah gave a partial answer: "They came to me from a distant country, from Babylon."

Isaiah probed deeper: "What have they seen in your palace?"

Hezekiah answered truthfully, "They have seen everything in my palace. There isn't anything in my treasuries that I didn't show them." Isaiah's probing of what happened was only the beginning of God's dealings with prideful Hezekiah.

The Shocking Prophecy of the Babylonian Captivity
ISAIAH 39:5-7

Isaiah's shocking prophecy ranged far beyond the immediate circumstances. God predicted the coming exile to Babylon, the end of Judah in the promised land. Isaiah had already predicted the fall of Babylon in several prophecies (13:19-20; 21:9-10). But here the prophecy was enhanced: Judah herself would go into exile in Babylon. All the material treasures Hezekiah was so proud of would become plunder for the Babylonians. And even more stunning was that Hezekiah's own descendants will become *eunuchs* in the service of the king of Babylon.

Isaiah's prophecy here in this chapter stands as a hinge for the entire book of Isaiah. For the first major section of Isaiah, chapters 1–39, the focus has been Assyria. Now that Assyria is behind us, chapters 40–66 will focus much more on the exile to Babylon and the restoration of Judah from that exile.

Hezekiah's Shortsighted Reaction
ISAIAH 39:8

Hezekiah's reaction is almost as stunning as the prophecy itself. His statement is simple enough: "The word of the LORD that you have spoken is good." But it was the attitude of his heart that was so self-centered: "For he thought: There will be peace and security during my lifetime." God had earlier promised to add fifteen years to Hezekiah's life. During that time his only son Manasseh was born to him. By this time, the boy was being reared to replace his father. This prophecy of Isaiah seemed to concern a distant future. So, as far as Hezekiah was concerned, there was nothing to worry about; his own personal situation was set for the rest of his life. Hezekiah's selfish focus is so revealing and so convicting for the similar shortsighted faith of many Christians today. As long as their own immediate needs are met, and as long as they are going to heaven when they die, what else is there to worry about?

Applications

First, let us reset our focus on the only true hero of the Bible, Jesus Christ! Every other biblical hero has some pattern of sin that must be covered by the grace of God. But Jesus was sinless, and in him alone must we trust for salvation. Hezekiah was a great leader, but Jesus is a perfect Savior. And whereas Hezekiah seemed completely careless about future generations, Jesus shed his blood for generations of God's children who would not even be born for millennia after he died.

Second, see how God uses circumstances to search the hidden motives of the heart. God leaves us to test us and discover what is in our hearts. Jesus said, "Then all the churches will know that I am the one who examines minds and hearts, and I will give to each of you according to your works" (Rev 2:23). We should expect this and actually yearn for it: "Search me, God, and know my heart; test me and know my concerns. See if there is any offensive way in me; lead me in the everlasting way" (Ps 139:23-24). When our sinfulness is exposed, let us be humble enough to repent from it, seeking the full cleansing only Christ can give.

Third, notice how susceptible the human heart is to pride. God had miraculously delivered Hezekiah twice, and somehow Hezekiah was *proud?* How can that be? But Scripture reveals that it was so: "However, because his heart was proud, Hezekiah didn't respond according to the benefit that had come to him. So there was wrath on him, Judah, and Jerusalem" (2 Chr 32:25). We should learn to say at every moment, "Not to us, Lord, not to us, but to your name give glory" (Ps 115:1).

Finally, we should be warned about Hezekiah's lack of a multigenerational vision, not caring about what would happen to his great-great-great grandchildren. Psalm 78:2-7 makes this multigenerational vision clear, saying that we must declare the great works of God to our children's children so they, in turn, can declare them to a generation yet unborn. Godly fathers are passionate about the future of their families.

The tragic fruit of Hezekiah's lack of multigenerational vision can be seen in his wicked son, Manasseh, the worst king Judah ever had. After Hezekiah courageously tore down the high places that had plagued Judah for generations, Manasseh put them back up. Manasseh even went so far as to sacrifice some of his own children in the fire to Molech. Second Kings 24:3-4 makes plain that it was specifically for the sins of Manasseh that God sent Judah into exile to Babylon. It is possible that Manasseh even had Isaiah sawn in two, as some traditions teach us. Could it be that Hezekiah's lack of any concern for the future led him to be a derelict father who failed to impart to Manasseh a vision for the glory of God and the future of Judah? We must not let that happen to our children through a similar lack of faith-filled concern for what is coming in their future.

Reflect and Discuss

1. How is each believer like a "smoldering flax"? How does Scripture trace this out in Hezekiah's life?

2. What is the significance of the statement from 2 Chronicles 32:31, "God left him to test him and discover what was in his heart"?

3. How does God test us? How does it relate to John 15:5? Or to Revelation 2:23?

4. How should we learn to say Psalm 139:23-24 to God?

5. What motivated Hezekiah to show all his kingdom's treasures and riches to the Babylonian envoys? How does this reveal the allure of the world still in our lives?

6. What does Isaiah's confrontation of Hezekiah teach you about the ministry of the Word and the need to rebuke sinners?

7. How does Isaiah's prophecy of verses 6-7 stand as a "hinge" in the entire book of Isaiah?

8. How does this passage reveal that there are no truly perfect heroes but Jesus Christ?

9. How does this passage warn us about the danger of pride?

10. What is a "multigenerational vision"? Why is it vital for Christian parents to have? How does Psalm 78:2-7 speak to this? How is Hezekiah's attitude actually common among Christian parents today?

The Awesome Display of the Glory of God Saves Sinners

ISAIAH 40

Zion, herald of good news, go up on a high mountain. . . . Say to the cities of Judah, "Here is your God!" (Isa 40:9)

Main Idea: As the majestic glory of God in creation and redemption is proclaimed among the nations, weakened, idolatrous, dying sinners are saved, comforted, and strengthened.

I. **The Proclaimed Glory of God Comforts Sinners with Forgiveness (40:1-11).**
   A. The comfort: an eternal word saves dying sinners.
   B. The central message: "Here is your God!"
   C. The stunning range of God: omnipotent gentleness!
II. **The Immeasurable Glory of God Dwarfs the Cosmos and the Nations (40:12-26).**
   A. The immensity of God dwarfs the cosmos (40:12).
   B. The inscrutable wisdom of God humbles humanity (40:13-14).
   C. The infinite power of God towers over the nations (40:15-17).
   D. What can we possibly offer such a God (40:16-17)?
   E. God exposes the wretched folly of idolatry (40:18-20).
   F. God is actively sovereign over earth and heaven (40:21-26).
III. **The Limitless Glory of God Strengthens the Weary (40:27-31).**
   A. God never forgets his people (40:27).
   B. God strengthens his people (40:28-31).

The Proclaimed Glory of God Comforts Sinners with Forgiveness

ISAIAH 40:1-11

Isaiah 40 is one of the greatest chapters in the Bible. Its language travels to the distant boundaries of the universe, finding a limit to the stars. Its language also probes the arrogance of human pride, finding a limit to human life span, power, wisdom, and strength. The central theme of the chapter is the proclamation of the glory of God for the salvation of dying sinners. God is great—infinitely so—whether sinful humanity recognizes it or not. But the grace of God is unleashed into this sin-cursed and dying world specifically in this way: the eternal word of God proclaimed to sinners on the very topic of the glory of God. As sinners hear and believe that message, they are forgiven, comforted, and strengthened.

So the chapter begins with the urgent command of God to Isaiah, his prophet, and beyond him to all future messengers of the grace of God: "Comfort, comfort my people!" God wants Isaiah to tell them how determined he is to assure them of his forgiveness. The remnant of Judah, exiled in Babylon, will need to hear this message because they will be tempted to think God has forsaken them because of their sins (v. 27). God yearns that his crushed people, humbled and broken under his judgments, will see that atonement for their sins is God's final purpose. So God tells Isaiah to speak tenderly to Jerusalem to assure her that her warfare is over and that she has received ample atonement from the Lord for all her sins.

What a poignant moment in this glorious book! For thirty-nine chapters Isaiah has exposed the wicked corruptions of Israel and Judah. Now, at last, Judah is assured that full atonement is provided for all her sins. For Christians who stand much further along the unfolding story of redemptive history, we know that this atonement can only have been provided by the death of Jesus Christ on the cross.

That God had in mind the work of Christ on the cross even when inspiring these words by Isaiah is plain from verses 3-5, a prophecy ascribed in every Gospel to the forerunner of Jesus Christ, John the Baptist (Matt 3:3; Mark 1:3; Luke 3:4; John 1:23). John came to cry out in the wilderness, "Prepare the way of the Lord!" This was not the work of a civil engineer, making literal highways in the wilderness, leveling mountains and filling in valleys. John fulfilled these words by preaching powerful messages of repentance for sin, baptism as a symbol of repentance, and a clear identification of the Son of God in his atoning work: "Here is the Lamb of God, who takes away the sin of the world!" (John 1:29). The leveling of mountains was done by blasting away at the self-righteous Pharisees and Sadducees who felt no need of a Savior. The raising of valleys was done by giving hope to wretched sinners who felt no Savior was possible. So preachers today must do the same leveling and raising in their preaching: "Disturb the comfortable, and comfort the disturbed!"

The display of God's glory is nowhere greater than at the cross of Christ! There we see all the attributes of God radiantly displayed—his love, mercy, grace, wisdom, power, wrath, justice, patience, etc. So Isaiah 40:5 gives us the centerpiece of the gospel: "The glory of the LORD will appear, and all humanity together will see it, for the mouth of the LORD has spoken." In this "spoken word" of the Lord—the gospel of Christ—the glory of the Lord appears radiantly for all who hear and believe.

This comforting word of salvation is especially needed in our dying world. In Adam the whole world lies under the death penalty. All humanity is like grass, and all our glory withers like the flowers of the field (vv. 6-8). God wants his messengers to remind our arrogant race of this clear fact that we will all soon die. We flourish for a brief time: athletes win their gold medals, scientists do their research, young women perfect their beauty, conquerors build their empires. But human splendor all withers and dies in an instant when the breath of the Lord blows on it. By contrast, the glory of the Word of the Lord will never fade—it stands forever radiant and will outlast heaven and earth (Matt 24:35).

Zion (the people of God) is given the responsibility of loudly heralding this gospel from the highest mountain, beginning with the towns of Judah (v. 9): "Here is your God!" "Here [he] is" (Hb *hinneh*, traditionally "behold") depicts an unveiling. God is hidden from our sight by our spiritual blindness, but when the Holy Spirit unveils Christ in the words of the gospel, we are able to see in our hearts "the light of the knowledge of God's glory in the face of Jesus Christ" (2 Cor 4:6).

Though this unveiling of the glory of God reaches its climax in Christ, it has been on display throughout redemptive history. God's power over the rise and fall of the empires of humanity is a major theme in Isaiah 40, beginning in verse 10. Leading with the word "See" (*hinneh* again), Isaiah unveils God's power to establish his kingdom, to judge his enemies, and to reward his servants. Yet amazingly, this same God who rules so powerfully also gently gathers weak lambs in his arms and tenderly leads those that are nursing (v. 11). This astonishing range of almighty God reminds me of the day I observed a powerful hurricane blow through my town, felling a gigantic oak tree near where I lived. Yet later that day, after the storm was over, I felt the gentlest breeze on my face and watched that breeze barely flutter the leaves of a sapling! So it is with Christ. He is the Good Shepherd who calls to his sheep,

"Come to me, all of you who are weary and burdened, and I will give you rest . . . because I am lowly and humble in heart" (Matt 11:28-29). He is also the terrifying King of kings with eyes of blazing fire who returns on a white horse at the head of the armies of heaven and destroys his enemies with the breath of his mouth (2 Thess 2:8; Rev 19:11-16).

The Immeasurable Glory of God Dwarfs the Cosmos and the Nations
ISAIAH 40:12-26

The good news of forgiveness of sins is so difficult for sinners to believe that God lavishes a feast of words for the rest of the chapter to strengthen our faith. He leads by a series of six probing questions, all beginning with the word *who*. This is meant to humble the arrogance of humanity and put us in our place. God is so immense that he has measured the waters of the seven seas in his cupped hand, a staggering achievement because the ocean—more than six miles deep in places—dwarfs the tiny stature of a human being. If a person tried to scoop out even a bathtub full of water, it would probably take more than one thousand handfuls to empty the tub! Beyond this, God has marked off the cosmos with the breadth of his hand as well. Science has given us a sense of the staggering immensity of outer space, and we cannot conceive of the distances. The farthest any human being has ever traveled into space occurred when the astronauts of Apollo 13 were on the far side of the moon. Traveling at the same speed as the Apollo capsule, to reach our *nearest* star (Alpha Centauri, 4.3 light years away) we would have to travel 114,078 years. Cosmologists tell us the observable universe is 46 billion light years across (Lineweaver and Davis, "Misconceptions," 43). Isaiah says a few of God's handbreadths are all that it takes for him to measure it! God is also immense compared to the dry land on earth: he has gathered the dust of the earth in a measuring cup and weighed the mountains on a balance (v. 12). These anthropomorphic measurements relate not only God's immensity, power, and knowledge but also his ownership of all creation down to the smallest detail. God proclaims these words to give his people a sense of his power to accomplish their salvation through all the twists and turns of history.

Therefore, Isaiah speaks next of the infinite depths of God's mind. The universe testifies powerfully to the mind of the Lord: its complexity, immensity, power, balance, beauty, order. God uses this to challenge the human race: "Who has directed the Spirit of the LORD, or who gave him counsel? Who did he consult?" (vv. 13–14). I once heard Pastor Erwin Lutzer say, "Has it ever occurred to you that nothing has ever occurred to God?" God has never learned anything, and he never will. So no human being can teach God a single thing.

This is especially poignant in verse 14 when it says, "Who . . . taught him the paths of justice?" So often, the twists and turns of God's paths in redemptive history are difficult to follow. As Paul said, "How unsearchable his judgments and untraceable his ways!" (Rom 11:33). That literally means God's footsteps cannot be tracked by human reason—we can't follow his train of thought. So, God's orchestrating the slaughter by the Babylonians of all but a small remnant of his people might seem to some unjust and incomprehensible. The suffering of God's missionaries to bring the gospel to the ends of the earth seems harsh, and the eternity of the torments of the damned has been called unjust by many. How much more the death of Jesus on the cross under the wrath of God made no sense to those who had hoped he would be the Redeemer of Israel. But no one can teach God the paths of justice, for his commitment to justice is displayed by the cross (Rom 3:25-26).

The immensity of God is also proclaimed specifically over the nations, which are merely a drop from a bucket and dust on the scales compared to him (Isa 40:15). If a man were carrying a bucket of water to a garden and a drop spilled on the way, would he try to reclaim that drop from the ground? That's what the nations are in God's sight. That means two things: (1) the combined power of the nations will not be able to stop God's plan of redeeming his chosen people; (2) the combined wealth of the nations is not sufficient to honor God with a suitable offering (v. 16). Only the perfect sacrifice of Jesus Christ can equal the worth of God himself or cover the multitude of the sins of God's people.

Despite this greatness of God, arrogant people have consistently rebelled and made their own gods to worship. There is nothing in the universe to which God can be compared, but the puny minds and limited powers of craftsmen make "gods" that steal the affections of people away from God who deserves them (vv. 18-20). God lines up these pathetic idols alongside himself, the God who rules the universe. How laughable that these lifeless idols must be nailed down so they won't fall over (cf. 1 Sam 5:1-5)!

The true and living God needs no such help. Surely we have heard of him from the beginning of the world—his eternal power and divine nature are seen daily in creation (v. 22; Rom 1:20). This majestic God sits enthroned above the circle of the earth, and all its people are like grasshoppers before him. The combined power of the grasshoppers would not be enough to turn him aside for an instant, but rather he would just laugh at their feeble rebellion (Ps 2:4). The heavens themselves are dynamic, being stretched out continually by God, for science reveals that the cosmos is expanding. If God can do that, then the princes and the rulers of the earth are as nothing to him! He is the very one who knit these people in their mothers' wombs, and it is he who will take their final breaths from their mouths whenever he chooses. Their reign, however terrifying and seemingly powerful, is like a blink of an eye to him. As soon as they are planted, they wither and die (Isa 40:24). To the Judahites living in Babylon, they could read this and not tremble at the power of their Gentile captors.

So who can even remotely be compared to God? The gap between God and all created beings is infinite! God's power and knowledge absolutely dwarf anything the human race can muster. God gave to Adam the task of naming the animals, but he alone can name all the stars, and by his power alone not one of them is missing from the night sky. Cosmologists tell us hundreds of billions of *galaxies* are in outer space, each with billions of stars. God has named each star, able to tell the difference from one to another, and by Christ he keeps each one burning (Heb 1:3).

The Limitless Glory of God Strengthens the Weary
ISAIAH 40:27-31

The culmination of this stunning meditation on the greatness of God is provided to renew his weak, weary, and dejected people. God has already told them these things before (v. 28). But just as faith comes initially by hearing, so it is strengthened and nourished by hearing again. God's chosen people throughout history ("Jacob" and "Israel") have been tempted to think that their sufferings were hidden from God and their legal claim is passed over by God who has not noticed them, such as the unjust judge and the persistent widow (Luke 18:1-8). Ultimately, God will see that they get justice. In the meantime, however, God has promised to give strength to his weak and weary people as they endure the sufferings of sanctification and gospel advance in this world. The Lord, the Creator of the ends of the earth, never grows weary for an instant—he is the everlasting God! He perfectly understands the needs of his people and of the hour. He gives strength to the weary and strengthens the powerless at every moment (v. 29). God's people on earth need constant strengthening, whether we are elite soldiers or frail elderly people in a nursing home. God's words recorded in this chapter convince us that this incomprehensibly majestic God is bending all the powers of his might and his mind toward our final salvation. By hearing him speak, we find our hearts strengthened in amazing ways, and we will resume our journey for his glory: we will soar on wings as eagles, we will run and not become weary, we will walk and not faint.

Applications

The central application of this chapter is to trust in Christ, the Redeemer, whose blood alone can atone for our sins. In Christ God has provided double for all our sins (Rom 3:24-26).

Second, we should expect the need for daily strengthening of our faith. At the end of the chapter the Lord speaks to us a humbling word, saying that everyone should expect to grow weak and weary in the Christian life. It is only as we listen to God's messengers proclaiming the words "Here is your God!" that we will run and not become weary, we will walk and not faint. So we must be daily in the Word of God, and weekly under the hearing of faithful exposition of the Scriptures so our faith may be renewed.

Soaring above all this, however, is the simple concept that "God *is* the gospel!" The staggering majesty of God so unforgettably described in this chapter is the treasure we will be gazing at and gloating over in heaven forever. How rich we are to have this God—the God of Isaiah 40—as our eternal inheritance! We should be constantly meditating on the themes of God's majesty described here: his immensity compared to heaven and earth; his awesome power and sovereign control over the nations; his direct power over the princes of the earth; his inscrutable wisdom and the fact that no human being can ever be God's counselor. The greater God appears to us, the smaller our afflictions will seem.

This should also affect our prayer lives. We should pray all the more confidently to such a God as this because we know he can do anything. We should also pray all the more humbly knowing he can learn nothing from us.

Next, we should be reminded constantly of our mortality. Psalm 90:12 says we should number our days to gain a heart of wisdom. We are like grass, and all our glory is like the flowers of the field. We should not be dismayed at the ravages of aging—the mind's diminished powers, the face's fading beauty, the body's decreased powers. We should not seek to stem this inevitable tide by surgery or Botox treatments. Rather, we should set our hope fully on the grace to be given us when Jesus Christ returns.

Finally, we should seek to embrace the entire range of the personhood of God in this chapter: both his terrifying immensity and power and his astonishing gentleness to his weak sheep.

Reflect and Discuss

1. How would meditating on God's amazing attributes on display in this chapter help people go through times of suffering?

2. How do verses 1-2 point directly to the cross of Jesus Christ as the atonement for our sins?

3. How did John the Baptist fulfill the predictions of Isaiah 40:3-5? How can preachers of the gospel seek to level mountains and raise valleys now?

4. How is the glory of the Lord revealed in the restoration of the Jews to the promised land after Babylon? How is it more clearly revealed in the person and work of Jesus Christ?

5. Why is the humbling of verses 6-8 so necessary, especially because so many people try to fight the aging process?

6. How do verses 6-8 exalt the greatness of God's eternal Word? How does this passage relate to Matthew 24:35?

7. How is Isaiah 40:9 in many ways the centerpiece to the whole chapter? What does "Here is your God!" mean? Since God is invisible, how does the ministry of the Word fit into that?

8. How does verse 11 encourage you in your life? How does it relate to Jesus Christ and to his words in Matthew 11:28-30?

9. How does Isaiah 40:12-17,21-26 show the infinite greatness of almighty God?

10. How do verses 27-31 personally encourage you to seek God when feeling weary and weak?

Only God Can Tell Us What Will Happen

ISAIAH 41

Who told about this from the beginning, so that we might know,
and from times past, so that we might say, "He is right"? No one
announced it, no one told it, no one heard your words. I was the first
to say to Zion, "Look! Here they are!" And I gave Jerusalem a herald
with good news. (Isa 41:26-27)

Main Idea: The Lord challenges the idols to do what only he can do: predict the future and then carry it out. This reveals the uniqueness of the Bible as a record of fulfilled prophecies.

I. **The Lord Challenges Idols and Defeats Them!**
    A. Israel's sin: idolatry
    B. God's remedy: challenge the idols, control history, save his people.
II. **The Lord Stirs Up a Conqueror to Do His Bidding (41:1-7).**
    A. The summons to the whole earth: a contest between God and the idols (41:1)
    B. God's claim: orchestration of human history (41:2-4)
    C. The futility of idols as saviors (41:5-7)
III. **The Lord Defeats Israel's Enemies (41:8-16).**
    A. God's promises to Abraham's children (41:8-16)
    B. God's threat to Israel's enemies (41:11-16)
IV. **The Lord Transforms Nature and Refreshes His People (41:17-20).**
    A. Drought, both spiritual and physical
    B. God's promise through the spirit
    C. The regeneration of the earth
V. **The Lord Alone Determines and Declares the Future (41:21-29).**
    A. God's challenge to the idols: tell the future.
    B. God alone predicted Cyrus.
    C. God alone rules human history.

The Lord Challenges Idols and Defeats Them!

Non-Christians love to point out the fact that other religions are essentially the same as Christianity, having a holy book, a holy prophet, and a pattern of superior behavior. The skeptical world demands, "What makes your religion better than all the others?" One clear distinction is the uniqueness of the Bible. Skeptics may claim that many religions have sacred writings that they cling to: Islam's *Qur'an*, Hinduism's *Vedas*, Buddhism's *Buddhavacana*. So, how can Christians know that the Bible is unique in this crowded field of holy books revered by millions around the world? Our best answer is that only the Bible describes the person and work of Jesus Christ, whose uniqueness should be obvious: claiming to be God incarnate, sinless, teaching in ways that no one had ever taught, working miracles, and especially dying on the cross and rising from the dead on the third day—this last being witnessed by more than five hundred people.

But along with this is the uniqueness of the Bible in fulfilled prophecy. The Bible contains the words of dozens of prophets who spoke with amazing clarity about future events—as many as two thousand specific prophecies. In Isaiah alone there are hundreds of very specific prophecies about the nations of his day: Israel, Judah, Egypt, Moab, Ammon, Assyria, Babylon, and others. By contrast, if you research Islamic prophecies, you will come up with some vague generalities, not true prophecies. Buddhism and Hinduism are not known for making any specific prophecies about world events. The bottom line is this: only the Bible has this kind of fulfilled prophecy. Isaiah 41 clearly proclaims God's stunning power to take on the idols of the world, challenging them to a simple test: declare the future, then bring it to pass.

The context of this chapter is powerful. The God who sits enthroned above the circle of the earth controls human history for his own purpose (Isa 40:22). His sovereign power is directly applied to the salvation plan he has worked out for his people, and that includes the events that surround the return of Judah from exile in Babylon. Isaiah 39 predicted the exile to Babylon, and much of chapters 40–66 speak of God orchestrating the return from Babylon. But deeper than that, in this chapter God addresses the very sin that would lead to the exile to begin with: idolatry. God is jealous over the affections of his people as a husband would be over the affections of his wife. And if a rival comes calling, the jealous husband will rise up and challenge him. God's claim and challenge are this: I alone know the future, predict the future, and bring those predictions to pass.

The key concept behind this unique power of God to foretell the future is the sequencing of events that mark the unfolding of history. Verse 4 speaks of a linear view of history: "Who has performed and done this, calling the generations from the beginning? I am the LORD, the first and with the last—I am he." Jesus claims the same thing for himself in Revelation 22:13: "I am the Alpha and the Omega, the first and the last, the beginning and the end." The linear view of history is essential to the miracle of prophecy: first A, then B, then C. So it is in redemptive history: the call of Abraham must precede the slavery of Abraham's descendants in Egypt, and that slavery in Egypt must precede the exodus from Egypt, and on down to the smallest detail of history. Along with this is the clear limitation we humans have: "Don't boast about tomorrow, for you don't know what a day might bring" (Prov 27:1). Even tomorrow is veiled to us. So when God makes amazing predictions in the Bible and then brings them to pass, it is clear evidence of his existence and supremacy. In Isaiah 41 God exposes the idols for the frauds they are.

The specific topic here is the calling of "one from the east" who comes to do God's bidding in history (v. 25), ending in the restoration of the Jews to the promised land. Though in this chapter God does not tell us his name, he will in Isaiah 44–45: Cyrus.

The Lord Stirs Up a Conqueror to Do His Bidding
ISAIAH 41:1-7

God the Judge begins by summoning the whole earth to his courtroom (v. 1), an assertion of his authority over every nation on earth. He calls on these idolaters to "renew their strength," for they will need strength to face God on judgment day.

Next, God declares his power to orchestrate the events of history (vv. 2-4). He summons "someone from the east" to whom he hands over nations. God's direct involvement ensures that this one will conquer kings, turning them to dust with his sword. Cyrus the Great of Persia fulfilled these words. Cyrus himself goes "safely" (v. 3), not wounded by any of these battles. Great leaders frequently expose themselves with stunning courage on the battlefield. Alexander the Great vaulted alone over a wall of the Multanese Citadel in the eastern Punjab and was severely wounded (Hammond, *Genius of Alexander*, 172–73). At the battle of Princeton on January 3, 1777, George Washington rode within thirty yards of the British line on a large, white horse, leading his men boldly under a withering hail of British musket fire. An aide covered his own eyes with his cloak so as not to watch his chief's inevitable death (Lancaster, *Golden Book*, 98). Obviously if these great leaders had been killed, we would never have heard of them. But God willed for Cyrus to move safely from battle to battle, building the great Persian empire that would topple Babylon and release the Jewish exiles. This "one from the east" treads paths his feet have never walked before. History records that Cyrus crossed the Tigris River from the east and so entered the Babylonian Empire; he marched quickly and defeated the wealthy King Croesus of Lydia, conquering his capital Sardis (Herodotus, *Histories* 1.76–86, 44–49). So he came from both the east and the north. The specificity of this prophecy more than a century and a half beforehand is stunning.

God's direct activity in all this is the focus of verse 4: "Who has performed . . . this . . . ? I am the LORD." God is sovereign not only with this generation but with every generation in history. The Lord determines the times set for all peoples and the exact places where they should live (Amos 9:7; Acts 17:26). Cyrus the Great and his Persian Empire are just one example of this. Idolaters trembling at Cyrus's approach turn to their metal gods, which have to be nailed down so they won't topple (Isa 41:6-7)!

The Lord Defeats Israel's Enemies
ISAIAH 41:8-16

Verse 8 is a sharp contrast between Israel and the pagan nations of verses 1-7. Because of God's everlasting covenant with Abraham his "friend," he will take hold of Israel with his righteous right hand (vv. 8-10). God speaks plainly of the enemies of his chosen people in verses 11-16, assuring his weak children ("worm Jacob") that they will look in triumph over their once terrifying but now defeated foes (vv. 11-12). God will make Israel into a mighty threshing board, with many new teeth (v. 15). The mountains they thresh represent the looming obstacles the little worm Israel is facing, but those problems will become like chaff swept away before the wind. There will come a time when God's people will search for any enemies at all and find none.

Though we may see the immediate fulfillment of these words in the destruction of Babylon by Cyrus the Great, yet it is farfetched to say that under the Persian domination Israel will look for enemies but find none (v. 12). This language points ultimately to Christ's kingdom. Our real enemies ("mountains," v. 15) are spiritual, not political or military. Our sins are as mighty as mountains in their threat to our souls. So also Satan and his demons are arrayed against us, as are his human servants in this world. In Christ alone are all these spiritual threats defeated. By Christ's death and resurrection alone will verses 10-16 be fulfilled. Only after the second coming of Christ will Satan soon be crushed under our feet (Rom 16:20).

The Lord Transforms Nature and Refreshes His People
ISAIAH 41:17-20

The powerful image of a drought-stricken land, with people desperately seeking life-giving water, stands before us in these verses. It represents both a literal and a spiritual reality. The promised land was cursed by drought when Israelites violated the Mosaic covenant (Deut 28:23-24). Theirs was a land "flowing with milk and honey," richly blessed year round with abundant water. But because of their sins, God had turned this beautiful land into "barren heights" (v. 18), and its inhabitants were seeking water but finding none (v. 17).

Yet the deeper thirst is spiritual. As Psalm 63:1 says, "God, you are my God; I eagerly seek you. I thirst for you . . . in a land that is dry, desolate, and without water." Distance from God creates spiritual drought. But verses 17-20 here promise that God has power to turn the desert into gushing mountain springs. Though it is possible that God did this literally in the promised land after the exile, the real issue is of spiritual revival by the outpouring of the Holy Spirit. Isaiah 44:3 likens the outpouring of the Spirit on God's people to water poured on desert land. The flourishing plant life of our text (vv. 19-20) represents both the literal transformation of the earth ultimately by Christ in the new earth (Rom 8:20-24) and the spiritual transformation of his people by their faith in him.

The Lord Alone Determines and Declares the Future
ISAIAH 41:21-29

The chapter resumes God's jealous contest with the idols that have seduced the heart of his bride (v. 21). Like Elijah's duel with Baal on

Mt. Carmel, it is the Lord who determines the ground rules for the contest. In this case it is this: predict the future. The clear implication of this is that no created being—neither human, nor angel, nor demon—knows the future apart from the revelation of God. God is sovereign, and he decides what will happen in his universe. As we saw in Isaiah 7:7, God is able to veto any plan of even the mightiest movers and shakers on planet Earth. Conversely, as we saw in Isaiah 14:27, no one has the power to veto even the smallest of his plans. God has determined every twist and turn of history (Acts 17:26; Eph 1:11), including all the mighty emperors with their impressive conquests, the sparkling cities they would build, how long they would rule, what scientific advances they would sponsor, and what effect they would have on literature and language, music and culture. God is able to predict the future because he has already decreed the future, even to the smallest detail (like Cyrus's name). He is then supremely capable of bringing it to pass.

The idols can do nothing since they represent gods that don't exist. In the end, the living God mocks them, saying, "Do *something*, whether good or bad!" They stand there motionless, while God raises up world rulers like Cyrus (v. 25).

Applications

God's purpose in inspiring this chapter was ultimately the salvation of his own elect children. We are the ones who read the Bible with faith and marvel at its astonishing predictive prophecies. And by far the most important predictions God ever made center on Christ: his birth, life, death, and resurrection. The lesser prophecies about Cyrus and Alexander are not nearly as significant as those predicting Christ. Can Islam, Buddhism, Hinduism, Mormonism, or any other false religion compete in the contest God has set up in Isaiah 41? Let them bring forth their prophecies!

Deeper than that, we can take assurance from the fact that God does all this for his defenseless people—"worm Jacob." God called Abraham his "friend" in verse 8, and we were chosen to be his children by faith in Christ. So we can hold verse 10 to our trembling hearts as major events shake our world: "Do not fear, for I am with you; do not be afraid, for I am your God. I will strengthen you; I will help you; I will hold on to you with my righteous right hand." What a powerful promise to cling to if a child is fighting for his life in an ICU, a woman suddenly becomes a widow one dreadful afternoon, or a weak Christian minority in a predominantly Muslim country sees their nation invaded by militant Islamic forces. God is controlling large and small events to ensure that not one of his elect will be lost but that all will come to final salvation through faith in Christ. There will come a day when God Omnipotent will have removed all of our foes forever (v. 12).

Reflect and Discuss

1. How can we use God's amazing ability to predict and control events of human history in witnessing to unbelievers?
2. What does the contest that God initiates with the idols show about his jealous nature over our hearts?
3. How do verses 2-4 show God's sovereign activity in the military success of Cyrus the Great? How does it connect with Acts 17:26?
4. What does verse 4 mean to you when it says that God is with the first and the last of the generations in terms of sovereign control of human history?
5. What is the significance of God calling Abraham his friend? How does it relate to Christ calling us "brothers" after his resurrection (John 20:17)?
6. How would memorizing verse 10 and quoting it regularly to yourself help you in times of trial?
7. What comfort do verses 11-16 give concerning our final vindication before our enemies?
8. How do verses 17-20 (along with Isa 44:3) give us a sense of the Holy Spirit's work of revival on dry, distant souls?
9. How do verses 22-23 make it plain that only God can predict the future?
10. As you look at the events of our time, how could Isaiah 41 be a special comfort to all Christians around the world?

The Gentle King Establishes Justice on Earth

ISAIAH 42

[My servant] will not break a bruised reed, and he will not put out a smoldering wick; he will faithfully bring justice. (Isa 42:3)

Main Idea: The servant of the Lord, Jesus Christ, will patiently and gently build his kingdom with broken sinners, even as far as the distant islands.

I. **The Gentle King and His Irresistibly Advancing Kingdom (42:1-7)**
   A. The quiet gentleness of the servant of the Lord (42:1-3)
   B. The irresistible advance of his kingdom (42:3-7)
II. **The Message of the Kingdom Resulting in Joyful Praise (42:8-12)**
   A. The message of the kingdom: the holy glory of the Lord (42:8-9)
   B. The joyful response to the message (42:10-12)
III. **The Zeal of the Warrior God Rescuing His Captive People (42:13-17)**
   A. The terrifying zeal of a God who is no longer silent (42:13-15)
   B. Rescue for his people; shame for his enemies (42:16-17)
IV. **The Shameful Condition of God's Sinful People (42:18-25)**
   A. The shameful blindness and deafness of God's people (42:18-21)
   B. God's just punishment for sin: the plundering of Jacob (42:22-25)

The Gentle King and His Irresistibly Advancing Kingdom
ISAIAH 42:1-7

History is dominated by the building of one vicious kingdom after another, all erected for the glory of sinful men who used conquest to etch their names in bloody monuments to their ambition. They delighted in the weakness of their enemies and trampled them down like mud in the streets. But one day a gentle Jewish carpenter stood on trial before the most powerful empire on earth and proclaimed a different kind of kingdom than the world had ever seen. In effect, Jesus said to Pontius Pilate that day, "My kingdom is not of this world. If it were, my servants would have fought, because that's how worldly kingdoms are built. But my kingdom is of an entirely different nature, built by a quiet proclamation of truth" (see John 18:36).

The nature of this King and the irresistible advance of his kingdom were predicted more than seven centuries before that day in the words of the prophecy we are studying right now—Isaiah 42. In this astounding chapter, Isaiah introduces for the first time "the servant of the LORD." This title identifies the person and work of Jesus Christ four times in Isaiah: 42:1-7; 49:1-9; 50:4-9; 52:13–53:12. The interpretive challenge comes in the fact that sometimes God identifies his people (Israel or Jacob) in this same way—"my servant" (41:8-9; 43:10; 44:1-2,21; 48:20). In some of those verses God's "servant," Jacob or Israel, represents the godly remnant who are redeemed by God's power. But even in this chapter, sometimes God's "servant" is portrayed as sinfully rebellious, even blind and deaf (42:19). But the "servant of the LORD" in those four passages above is a single individual, sent to do God's will and save God's people. This is the first of those four breathtaking prophecies.

In verse 1 God introduces his servant as one whom he strengthens through the Holy Spirit and in whom he delights. This delight and the empowering of Jesus for public ministry by the Holy Spirit were proclaimed at his baptism, when the Spirit descended on Jesus like a dove (Matt 3:16) and the Father proclaimed his love for his Son. Just as Jesus did nothing apart from the will of his Father (John 5:19), so it seems he did no miracles apart from the power of the Spirit (Acts 10:38). Isaiah 42:1 also highlights that the Father chose Jesus to be his instrument to establish perfect justice to the ends of the earth by his crucifixion and resurrection. Peter makes plain that this choosing of Jesus occurred before the creation of the world (1 Pet 1:20) but that God revealed it in the unfolding of human history.

The goal of Jesus's mission for the Father is to "bring justice to the nations," which is made clear by the fact that the word *justice* or *judgment* appears in verses 1, 3, and 4, and that the coasts and islands wait for his instruction (Hb *torah*, "teaching" or "law"). Throughout the history of this sin-cursed planet, strong rulers have crushed weak people, denying them justice. God has written justice in the hearts of all human beings, so we are well aware when we are being treated unjustly. The distant islands wait for the reign of the kingdom of Jesus Christ, who alone can bring perfect justice.

What is truly amazing is *how* this King will establish his just reign. Verses 2-4 give a series of seven negative statements that capture the essence of the peaceful and gentle advance of the kingdom of heaven. First, he will not cry out or shout or lift up his voice in the streets. This refers to the harsh sound of tyranny, like a Nazi warrior yelling, "Schnell! Schnell!" to the terrorized citizens of a newly conquered city, commanding them to run onto a waiting train to a concentration camp. Or the strident sounds of a rabble-rousing dissident, who stands on a wall to harangue the populace with ideology demanding revolution. Jesus established his kingdom by speaking words of peace and truth to brokenhearted sinners.

The astounding gentleness of Jesus was predicted in verse 3: "He will not break a bruised reed, and he will not put out a smoldering wick." Both of these are meant to convey the frailty and brokenness of human beings suffering in this sin-cursed world. A bruised reed is hanging by a slender green strand; a smoldering wick is just about to go out entirely. So are human beings in their frailty. And whereas wicked empire builders welcome bruised reeds so they can trample them and smoldering wicks so they can extinguish them, Jesus is building his kingdom out of exactly those kinds of people. He can take weeping sinners who have lost all hope of salvation and all desire to live and whisper words of gospel power into their hearts. He said, "Have courage, son, your sins are forgiven" to the paralyzed man (Matt 9:2). He said, "Have courage, daughter, . . . your faith has saved you" to the bleeding woman (Matt 9:22). He spoke reassuringly to a grieving widow whose only son was being buried that day, saying, "Don't weep" (Luke 7:13), and then he raised her son from the dead. Dear reader, have you experienced the gentle words of Jesus pouring like honey into your desperate soul, assuring you of forgiveness, promising you heaven?

This kingdom will spread to the distant islands where people are waiting expectantly for it to come. But the advance of this kingdom will be gradual and difficult. The later "servant of the LORD" prophecies will make plain how much suffering the servant will have to undergo. Despite the fact that the progress will be quite slow and bitterly opposed, Jesus will "not grow weak or be discouraged" until he has established his kingdom even to the distant islands (v. 4).

Verses 5-7 reveal that the same God who created the universe will also spread the kingdom of Christ to the distant islands. Nothing can stop it! The Creator gives breath to the people who walk on the earth, and he can also give eternal life by his Spirit to anyone he chooses. So God gives the servant his commission: he has called Jesus for a righteous purpose and will take him by the hand to enable him to finish what he started. God the Father made his Son to be a covenant for the people and a light to the nations so that the eyes of the blind may be opened and prisoners released from the dungeons of sin. These are amazing words, for Jesus doesn't merely *proclaim* a new covenant to Israel and to the world—he *is* the new covenant. And Jesus doesn't merely open physical eyes to *see* physical daylight—he *is* the light of the world by which their souls will be illuminated forever. And though Satan has kept sinners bound in the prison of sin with chains they cannot break, he is impotent to stop Christ from rescuing his people from the dominion of darkness and transferring them into his eternal kingdom (Col 1:13; Luke 11:21-22).

The Message of the Kingdom Resulting in Joyful Praise
ISAIAH 42:8-12

The message of this kingdom is the glory of God in the face of Christ (2 Cor 4:6). So in Isaiah 42:8 the Lord proclaims his name and establishes that his glory is his own, never to be shared with another. The people who were in the darkness of spiritual prison cells until the message of the kingdom came were there because of idolatry. The gospel of Christ proclaims that the time has come for them to turn away from idols to serve the living God. This also reveals the deity of Christ, for the Lord said he will not share his glory and praise with anyone; but Jesus is "the radiance of God's glory" (Heb 1:3) and is worshiped just as the Father is (John 5:23). If Jesus were not God, these things could not be said of him.

By the time of Jesus's birth, God's credentials of prediction will have been established through the fulfillment of the prophecies of Cyrus (Isa 42:9). But now new things are springing up, and all that he has promised he will certainly fulfill. Fulfilled prophecy gives the gospel message tremendous credibility.

The only proper response to all this is worship! So verses 10-12 call on the people of the earth to sing a new song of praise for such a great salvation (Rev 5:9; 14:3). The ends of the earth and sailors are summoned to sing. Even the desert will shout with joy: the settlements of Kedar (the Bedouin tribes of Arabia, descendants of Ishmael; Gen 25:13) and the inhabitants of Sela (Edomites). What is so amazing about these names is that they represent people who have been hostile to Israel and to God. The sovereign grace of God will guarantee elect people from every tribe will be singing eternal praises for their salvation in Christ (Isa 42:12).

The Zeal of the Warrior God Rescuing His Captive People
ISAIAH 42:13-17

The meek gentleness of Christ should not mislead us into thinking that the King lacks power or zeal. Actually, this advancing kingdom will be opposed every step of the way by powerful enemies. So verses 13-15 picture God's terrifying wrath, which is as essential to the advance of this kingdom as is the gentleness of Christ. God "advances like a warrior . . . he roars aloud, he prevails over his enemies" (v. 13). Christ is a delightful Savior but also a terrifying enemy. God's apparent silence in the past is easy to misunderstand, but he was intentionally holding himself back from judgment on sinners who were opposing his kingdom (v. 14).

All of this power is for the purpose of saving his weak, frail people—of leading the formerly blind along paths they've never traveled before (v. 16). Again, this could refer immediately to the restoration of the remnant to the promised land, but the whole chapter is speaking of the kingdom of Christ. Verse 17 is a warning, however, to all who refuse the call; if they will not repent, they will be put to shame on that final day.

The Shameful Condition of God's Sinful People
ISAIAH 42:18-25

In this final section Isaiah was writing to Judah and Jerusalem before the fall into idolatry during the reign of Manasseh that would result in their degrading exile to Babylon. The events that would occur in their destruction and exile would be absolutely humiliating to God's people. But what is worse, they could mislead observers into misunderstanding God's purposes. It was not that God was powerless to stop the Babylonians or didn't see them coming. No, actually, God *brought* the

Babylonians to exact judgment on his blind and deaf "servant," Israel. The willful blindness of the Jewish nation was more despicable than the blindness of the Gentiles because God had made his law glorious in Israel's midst (v. 21). If there are two men who do not read and pay attention to a "Caution: Wet Floor" sign, and one is in a dark cave and the other in a brilliantly lit room, the blindness of the second is more clearly exposed than that of the first.

For this reason, God commanded the Gentiles to plunder his own people, putting them into dungeons with no one to rescue them (v. 22). The tendency among God's people is to hate the Gentiles and wonder why God has forsaken Israel. Instead, Isaiah wonders aloud who among his people will understand the true message here: God was judging Israel (Jacob) for their willful blindness, deafness, and disobedience (vv. 24-25). Only the humble and faith-filled among the remnant (Dan 9:1-19) would recognize that the holy God was doing this because of the sins of his people.

Applications

First, simply kneel before the humble and gentle King, Jesus Christ, and by faith enter his kingdom. Jesus is the fulfillment of these words, as Matthew 12:15-21 makes plain.

Beyond this, delight in the gentleness of Jesus in dealing with sinners like us. We have a difficult time believing God loves us when we're so sinful. Sometimes we feel like we're a damaged reed, barely holding on by a slender green thread. We feel like the work of grace in our hearts is a flickering, smoldering, smoky fire just about to be extinguished. We must learn to trust the exquisite skill of Jesus in binding up our broken hearts and fanning into a more vigorous flame the work of grace within us.

This should also teach pastors and other Christians how to deal with those feeling guilty for sin. We must learn to be skillful and gentle in counseling sinners to a vigorous and healthy walk with Christ. It's so easy to be judgmental and harsh in a toxic, self-righteous way.

For all of this, however, we must not underestimate how much power Christ exerts every day as a mighty warrior to destroy his enemies and rescue his chosen people. Christ is a gentle Savior but a terrifying adversary. Let us fear the Lord and warn rebellious sinners of the coming wrath.

Finally, we should delight in the spread of the gospel to the distant islands, including the Arab nations who are descended from Ishmael. Christians should continue to give full exertion to the spread of the gospel, even in Muslim nations and hard-to-reach places.

Reflect and Discuss

1. How is the spread of Christ's kingdom so different from the way human empires are built?
2. What is the significance of the term "servant of the LORD"? How does this describe Jesus Christ?
3. How does verse 3 ("he will not break a bruised reed, and he will not put out a smoldering wick") depict the gentleness of Jesus in dealing with brokenhearted sinners?
4. Why would it be good for all Christians to meditate on Jesus's gentleness with them?
5. Why would it be good for pastors and all Christian leaders to imitate Jesus's gentleness with brokenhearted sinners?
6. How does this chapter depict the spread of the gospel to the ends of the earth?
7. How can we harmonize God's wrath against his enemies with his gentleness in dealing with humbled sinners?
8. Why should worship characterize a healthy Christian life? How does this chapter depict that?
9. How would you summarize the message of verses 18-25? Why would it have been very hard for unrepentant but suffering Jews in Babylon to embrace the message in those verses?
10. How should this chapter drive us to personal involvement in missions?

God Glorifies Himself by Working a New Salvation

ISAIAH 43

Bring my sons from far away, and my daughters from the ends of the earth—everyone who bears my name and is created for my glory. I have formed them; indeed, I have made them. (Isa 43:6-7)

Main Idea: God displays his glory by rescuing his chosen people through the fire and water of his judgments, a new salvation, which he predicted and which is greater than the deliverance of Israel from Egypt.

I. **God Is Glorified by Rescuing His Children through Fire and Water (43:1-7).**
   A. God claims his children as his own (43:1).
   B. God promises protection for his children through the fire and water (43:2).
   C. God gives up the nonelect for the sake of his elect (43:3-4).
   D. God is glorified by calling his children from the ends of the earth (43:5-7).

II. **God's People Are His Witnesses That There Is No Other God (43:8-15).**
   A. God puts the "gods" on trial, again (43:8-9).
   B. God's people are God's witnesses: there is no other God (43:10-13).
   C. God will redeem Israel by destroying Babylon (43:14-15).

III. **God Works a New Salvation Greater Than the Old (43:16-21).**
   A. Remember the past: God saved Israel at the Red Sea (43:16-17).
   B. Forget the past! This new salvation will be even greater (43:18).
   C. God will make a way in the desert and streams for his people (43:19-21).

IV. **God's People Weary Him with Their Sins (43:22-28).**
   A. God's people have not wearied themselves in serving God (43:22-23).
   B. God's people have wearied God by their sins (43:24).
   C. God has covered his people's many sins for his own sake (43:25-28).

God Is Glorified by Rescuing His Children through Fire and Water
ISAIAH 43:1-7

These verses are some of the sweetest in the book of Isaiah to the suffering children of God in every generation. Isaiah looked ahead a century and a half to the condition of Judah in exile in Babylon and spoke first to them a message of God's loving redemption from the water and fire of his judgments. But it is right for Christians in every generation to receive deep comfort from these words:

> *I will be with you when you pass through the waters, and when you pass through the rivers, they will not overwhelm you. You will not be scorched when you walk through the fire, and the flame will not burn you.* (v. 2)

The "water" and the "fire" often represent God's wrath and judgment; it was by water that he destroyed Noah's generation, and it will be by fire that he destroys the world at the end of the age (2 Pet 3:10,12). But because God has chosen us, because he has redeemed us by the blood of Christ, because he has called us by name, *we are his.* He has linked the fullest display of his glory to our final salvation. And in Scripture, water and fire not only picture total destruction under the wrath of God but also purification from sin (Num 31:23; Isa 4:4; Ezek 36:25). God's people *pass through* the waters; the rivers will not drown them. God's people *pass through* the fire; the flames will not consume them. Rather, this kind of "fiery ordeal" (1 Pet 4:12) is specially designed by God to purify them of their wickedness (1 Cor 3:12-15). So it was with the Jews in their exile to Babylon, and so it will be in every generation of God's elect until they are totally purified from sin, eternally glorifying God in heaven.

The special electing love of God for his people is clearly on display in these verses, for God says powerfully, "I have called you by your name; you are mine"! It is not because we are any better than those not chosen, but simply because he loves us (v. 4). The Jews who went into exile were just as sinful as Gentile nations who died under the wrath of God. But God speaks from the framework of sovereign election when he says, "I have given Egypt as a ransom for you, Cush and Seba in your place," and "I will give people in exchange for you and nations instead of your life" (vv. 3-4). God is willing to bring his righteous judgments down on Egypt, Cush, and Seba but to deal by sovereign grace with his elect, not treating them as their sins deserve. Only in heaven will God's people understand the many ways the truth of these verses has unfolded as God has given up one person to arrest or slaughter so that his chosen people could escape. The ultimate fulfillment of this concept is in the doctrine of reprobation, explained by Paul in Romans 9:22-23. There Paul teaches that God created and sustains the reprobate so that the elect may know more fully the riches of his glory. He gives the reprobate in exchange for the elect eternally, that the elect may know how astonishing is his grace to them, for there is no intrinsic difference between them.

All of this should free God's people from all fear in every generation. Twice in these verses, God says to us, "Do not fear." He is working out his plan so that all who are called by his name may display his glory (v. 7). Thus the regathering spoken of in verses 5-7 cannot merely refer to the gathering of Judah from Babylon. The words soar beyond anything that happened under Cyrus the Great. Later in this chapter God will say that this redemption will be greater than what he achieved when he led Israel through the Red Sea and slaughtered Pharaoh's army. The small band of 42,360 (Ezra 2:64) that returned to Palestine under Cyrus's edict does not fulfill these verses. They came from the east (Babylon), not from all points of the compass. That regathering of the Jews to the promised land was a type, a shadow. The reality is found in Christ, specifically in the gathering of the elect from every nation by the call of the gospel of Jesus Christ. John said that Jesus would die for the Jewish nation and not for that nation only, "but also to unite the scattered children of God" (John 11:51-52). Therefore, Isaiah 43:5-7 displays the sovereign decree of almighty God to gather the elect from the ends of the earth under the call of the gospel, all who are called by his name, whom he created for his glory. And no fiery trial they undergo will destroy them, only purify them.

God's People Are His Witnesses That There Is No Other God
ISAIAH 43:8-15

Having established God's eternal purpose to gather his elect by the call of the gospel, God makes plain his will that they should be his witnesses in every generation. God is once again putting the "gods" on trial to prove his supremacy over them. The "blind" and "deaf" of verse 8 may refer to God's own people who will be gathered by his sovereign grace. All of the elect are called out of Satan's darkness into the marvelous light of the kingdom of Christ (Col 1:13; 1 Pet 2:9). At one time, the exiles of Judah were idolaters, "blind" and "deaf" to the glory of God, exchanging his glory for that of images. Now God summons all nations to assemble together for the great trial of the universe. He will challenge the idols as he has already done (Isa 41:21-28). No idol foretold the future, no idol orchestrated history to make the prophecies come true. The peoples from all over the earth can testify to the prowess of their idols, but they are all vain and worthless. God calls on his elect people to be his witnesses in every generation, to say, "Our God is *alive*! He alone predicts the future, then makes it come to pass!" The three verbs in verse 12 make God's achievement plain: "I alone declared, saved, and proclaimed." That is, God predicted what he would do, then acted powerfully in history to make it happen, and then spread the news about his accomplishments.

The Lord makes plain that no "god" was formed before him nor has any been formed after him (v. 10). So the message of God's solitary existence must be spread abroad over the surface of the earth to every nation and in every language. "You are my witnesses," says the living God. What an incredible privilege God has entrusted to his people in every generation! God is the only Savior (v. 11), as he made plain in the death and resurrection of his Son, Jesus Christ. He declares himself to be absolutely sovereign over all events of human history; when he acts, who is able to reverse it (v. 13)? So God will prove again when he causes the Babylonians to flee in the ships about which they had previously rejoiced (v. 14).

God Works a New Salvation Greater Than the Old
ISAIAH 43:16-21

This section contains the interpretive key to the chapter. The Lord calls to their remembrance the mighty deliverance he worked over Egypt at the Red Sea (v. 17). But then God commands them to forget the former things (v. 18) as he unveils amazing news with the word "Look" (v. 19). He is going to work a far greater salvation in the future, something that will cause the exodus to shrink in memory. He will make a way in the wilderness and rivers in the desert, even causing the wild animals to honor him. He will give refreshing drink to his chosen people, whom he formed for himself to declare his praise (vv. 20-21).

Though this event could be understood as the journey of the Jews from Babylon back to the promised land, it seems difficult to fathom how a walk of forty thousand on a dusty road could be greater than what God did in bringing several million Israelites through the Red Sea. Therefore, the restoration of the Jews to Jerusalem must be seen as a type or shadow of a far more glorious journey home—the salvation worked among all nations by Christ, bringing them to the Father (John 14:6). That awesome work of God will be so great that it will make the redemption of Israel from slavery in Egypt shrink in comparison.

The rivers flowing in the desert (vv. 19-20) speak of the gift of the Holy Spirit, as in Isaiah 44:3. The Spirit is often spoken of as if he were a liquid, "poured out" on God's people (Isa 32:15; Ezek 39:29; Acts 2:33; John 7:38-39). So these verses predict the blessings of the new covenant. And they go beyond present spiritual salvation to speak of the redemption of nature as well because the desert and the wild creatures are included in the celebration (Rom 8:19-23).

God's People Weary Him with Their Sins
ISAIAH 43:22-28

The chapter ends with a snap back to reality. In Isaiah's day the wicked idolatry that would result in the exile to Babylon had yet to take place. And even if one takes verses 22-28 to be God's message to the exiled Jews right before their restoration, their grievous neglect of godly duties convicts us all. God's commands are not a burden (1 John 5:3) in any case. But Judah had not called on God in prayer because they had become weary of God. They had not wearied themselves in their religious services to God, but rather they had wearied him with their sins (v. 24). "Aromatic cane with silver" represents costly sacrifice, and while God had not required that of them, they should have been cheerfully willing to give far more. But so often, instead of laying it all on the line for Christ, we are lazy and hold back and actually weary God with our sins, grieving the Holy Spirit (Eph 4:30).

Because of these sins, God would soon be judging Judah and Jerusalem (v. 28). Sin had been woven through the tapestry of every generation of Israel's history, and this holy God would soon be handing the sanctuary and Jacob over to total destruction. But we know that God's final word for his chosen people is not judgment but grace. So God reminds them that he is the one who sweeps our transgressions away and remembers our sins no more (v. 25). God will do all this "for [his] own sake," that is, "for the praise of his glorious grace" (Eph 1:6).

We were created for his glory (Isa 43:7), and so we will be redeemed for his glory.

Applications

The wisest way for twenty-first-century Christians to begin to apply this marvelous chapter is to take the advice given in verse 18: "Do not remember the past events, pay no attention to things of old." This doesn't mean to disregard past successes in redemptive history entirely. But some commentators on Isaiah 43 focus exclusively on the author's original intent (the author being Isaiah) and speak only about the restoration of the Jews after the exile. Yet the chapter points to a far greater achievement, that worked by Jesus Christ at the cross and by the Holy Spirit in spreading the gospel to the ends of the earth. Therefore, while we Christians should respect the historical setting for this chapter, within it we see clues that God meant to speak a word of great encouragement to every generation of his chosen people.

So, we should begin by personally treasuring the words God speaks to his chosen people in verses 1-7. We should hold up each phrase like a rare gemstone and press it to our hearts in delight. We should bask in the electing love of God, that God has both created us and redeemed us for his glory. We should feel the intense power of God's cry, "I have called you by your name; you are mine!" We should heed his command not to fear the fire or the water, realizing that God does not mean to condemn us by them but rather to purify us. We should memorize verse 2 for the next "fiery ordeal" (1 Pet 4:12) God chooses to bring us through and say those words to our souls when the fire of the ordeal seems to burn our earthly hopes to ashes. Perhaps we have heard the worst possible result from the cancer test; perhaps the same has happened to our spouse; perhaps we must attend the funeral for our toddler this afternoon, and our hearts are screaming to a sullen sky for some reason why; perhaps we have been unemployed for months, and no prospects are on the horizon; perhaps we are elderly, in an assisted living center, and no one ever seems to call. Whatever the fire or water through which we are passing, we should cling to the faith Isaiah 43 was written to give us.

We must also embrace the challenge in the chapter to be God's witnesses in an idol-saturated world. We should prove to the idolaters that only the God of the Bible has "declared, saved, and proclaimed" (v. 12). We should learn to marshal the evidence of fulfilled prophecies to prove that God alone is powerful over human history. There are no fulfilled prophecies in any other world religion.

Finally, we should humbly realize that nothing within us compelled God to choose us; it was merely because he loved us that we are precious in his sight (v. 4). We should realize that God does all of this mighty work on our behalf for his own sake, for his own glory. We were created for his glory (v. 7) and redeemed to praise his glory (v. 21).

Reflect and Discuss

1. How does this chapter display the greatness and majesty of God?
2. How does it display the electing love of God for his people?
3. How can we use the words of this chapter for hope and encouragement when we are going through the fire or the water of severe trials?
4. What is the significance of God saying, "I have called you by your name; you are mine" (v. 1)?
5. How do you understand verses 3-4? How do they relate to Romans 9:22-23?
6. Isaiah 43:7 is the only verse in the Bible that clearly declares that God created us for his glory. What is the significance of that concept? How can we live that out?
7. How does this chapter (especially in vv. 8-15) teach us to be witnesses for God in this present idolatrous age?
8. Why does God command us to forget the former things in verse 18? What saving work of God is greater than the Red Sea crossing?
9. How do verses 19-20 point to the work of the Holy Spirit? How does that help us to understand verse 21?
10. How do verses 22-28 convict you of sin? How does verse 25 encourage you about God's grace?

The Solitary God Ridicules Idolaters and Raises Up Cyrus

ISAIAH 44

Who, like me, can announce the future? Let him say so and make a case before me, since I have established an ancient people. Let these gods declare the coming things, and what will take place. (Isa 44:7)

Main Idea: God ridicules idolaters and exalts his supremacy over idols by predicting the rebuilding of Jerusalem and the temple by Cyrus more than a century and a half before it happens.

I. **God Promises to Pour Out His Spirit and Create His Children (44:1-5).**
   A. The Lord promises to pour out his Spirit on the dusty ground (44:1-3).
   B. The result: God raises up his children out of the dust (44:4-5).

II. **God Alone Can Explain the Past and Predict the Future (44:6-8).**
   A. No one is like God (44:6-7).
   B. God's challenge to the idols: explain the past and predict the future (44:7-8).

III. **God Ridicules Idol Makers (44:9-20).**
   A. Idol makers and idol worshipers will be shamed (44:9-11).
   B. God ridicules idolatry (44:12-20).

IV. **God Has Swept Away Our Sins Like a Mist, So Rejoice (44:21-23)!**
   A. God sweeps away our sins like a mist (44:21-22).
   B. All creation rejoices in the redemption of God's children (44:23).

V. **God Raises Up Cyrus to Rebuild Jerusalem (44:24-28).**
   A. God the Creator foils false prophecies and fulfills true ones (44:24-26).
   B. God commands Cyrus to rebuild Jerusalem and its temple (44:27-28).

God Promises to Pour Out His Spirit and Create His Children
ISAIAH 44:1-5

In this chapter God continues his battle with the idolatry that threatens to destroy his people. To win their hearts, he has to command their attention (v. 1). God alone shaped Israel from birth (as he did to each of us) (v. 2); so also God called the nation Israel into existence. He will never forsake Israel; he is ready to help. In verse 2 he calls them "Jeshurun," meaning "Upright," a stark contrast to their other name, "Jacob" ("Deceiver"). So God is conferring on sinful Jacob the imputed righteousness in which alone he can stand before a holy God. Christ will later purchase this righteousness at the cross.

God then makes the magnificent promise that is our only hope of survival: he promises to pour out his Holy Spirit like "water on the thirsty land and streams on the dry ground" (v. 3). This image should be familiar to us by now because we've also seen it in Isaiah 32:15; 41:18; and 43:20. Though we shouldn't deny that Adam's sin has turned fertile fields and lush gardens into wastelands and that God intends to reverse that curse in the new earth, yet the image here is primarily spiritual: the pouring out of water on the desert is clearly the gift of the Holy Spirit, poured into transformed human hearts. This is the new-covenant blessing that was bought by the blood of Jesus Christ.

The result of the outpoured Spirit is the raising up of children for God (vv. 3-5). That Israel would even have any descendants at all after Babylon is a gift of God's grace, as he said in Isaiah 1:9. But these verses go beyond that. The image of a stand of poplar trees flourishing by an abundant stream (Ps 1:3) reflects the promise of the Holy Spirit transforming hearts, children of God born not in the normal way but by the Spirit of God (John 1:12). This predicts the blessings of the new covenant (Ezek 36:26-28): a transformed people living in a transformed land for eternity. And this promise will extend to the Gentiles as well. Isaiah 44:5 speaks of three individuals who seek to outdo each other in expressing a new loyalty to the Lord, the God of Jacob. Like Cornelius and his family, they will receive the outpoured Holy Spirit by faith and become children of Abraham (Gal 3:7). So, as John the Baptist said, "God is able to raise up children for Abraham from these stones" (Matt 3:9)—or from the dust of a spiritual desert.

God Alone Can Explain the Past and Predict the Future
ISAIAH 44:6-8

As God continues to challenge the idols to a duel, he once again returns to the theme of proclaiming history—either explaining the past or predicting the future, as we've seen (41:21-28; 43:9-12). But it comes spectacularly to a head in the prediction of Cyrus by name in this and the next chapter. The greatness of almighty God is front and center as God deeply yearns to melt the hearts of his elect into awe. He says that he alone is "the first and . . . the last." Just as Jesus Christ said, "I am the Alpha and the Omega, the first and the last, the beginning and the end" (Rev 22:13). Unlike Eastern religions that assert the cyclical nature of history by reincarnation, the Bible teaches that history is linear, ordained by God before even a single event had occurred. God was "in the beginning" (Gen 1:1), and he will be there at the end as well; he also controls every single day in between. Therefore he alone can accurately lay out the past and predict the future. He challenges anyone who thinks he is like God to recount in careful order (the Hebrew verb means to lay out in careful rows or stacks) what has happened from the time he established "an ancient people." Though it might not seem supernatural to do this, a perfect history of the past is something only God can relate. To prove this, compare the accounts of different professional historians about D-Day or the signing of the Declaration of Independence. No two accounts would perfectly jibe.

But what is supernatural is to predict the future, laying out in detail what is yet to come. James 4:14 says, "You do not know what tomorrow will bring." But in Isaiah 44:28 and 45:1 God stunningly names Cyrus as the man who will set his exiles free, rebuild the towns of Judah, rebuild Jerusalem, and lay the foundation of the new temple. This is mind boggling because Cyrus would not be born until sometime between 600 and 580 BC, at least a century later! Did his parents really have a choice in naming their son? As Proverbs 16:1 says, "The reflections of the heart belong to mankind, but the answer of the tongue is from the LORD." God named that baby and then raised him up to astonishing power, as we will see in the next chapter.

God alone can do this. Events of history continually stun us, but nothing stuns God. So we should not fear anything (v. 8) because God has predicted everything we need to know about the future, and it will certainly come to pass.

God Ridicules Idol Makers
ISAIAH 44:9-20

Scripture only rarely depicts God as laughing. Three times in Psalms almighty God is said to laugh, and all three times it is at the wicked—a laughter of scornful judgment (Pss 2:4; 37:13; 59:8). Isaiah 44:9-20 is dripping with the laughter of God at idol makers and idol worshipers. The utter foolishness of worshiping and serving created things rather than the Creator is exposed and condemned by ridicule.

In verses 9-11 the Lord begins by giving his overarching verdict on idol makers and idolaters: they are nothing, and the things they treasure are worthless; all who witness on their behalf or yield to that temptation will be put to shame on judgment day.

In verses 12-17 God escorts us into the workshop of an idol maker. The first idol he makes is constructed of iron, the second of wood. But the material doesn't matter: the process itself is ridiculous. The iron-worker must labor over hot coals to make his metal god. Sweat pours from his face, and if he forgets to drink water or eat, he grows steadily weaker. How different is our God, who as the Creator of the ends of the earth never grows faint or weary (40:28); and those who worship him have their strength constantly renewed (40:31). But this ironworker sits at the end of a hard day of heating iron to a glowing yellow and pounding it on an anvil. He mops his brow and feels satisfied. He has made a god worthy of worship!

So also the carpenter does the same work but in wood. He measures with a line, marks it out with a compass, and shapes it with a chisel. Like a famous sculptor once said when asked how he made a magnificent statue of a horse: "I choose a block of marble, then cut away everything that doesn't look like a horse." So it is with the idol maker, and herein is the offense: he has an idea in his mind first, then cuts away everything that doesn't look like the "god." But we must see the arrogance in this; we the created have turned unfulfilled away from our glorious Creator, and we take his place, shaping a god out of our own imaginations. In the end all idolatry is just self-worship.

The satire goes beyond this, for the idol maker goes out into the forest to cut down cedars, cypress, or perhaps an oak. In order to have a lasting supply, he plants a grove of trees. (And the rain made it grow! God's activity cannot be avoided.) He chops down a likely tree for the idol, but he doesn't need the whole piece. So he cuts it in half; half he uses for a fire on which he can make his dinner—roasting his meat, which he eats and is satisfied. But the other half he uses to make a god, before which he bows down and says, "Save me, for you are my god." God repeats for emphasis: half for the fire, which he sees and enjoys; half for a god, "something detestable." Absolutely ridiculous!

The Lord summarizes both the idol and those who worship it at the end: their eyes are shut so they cannot see; their minds are closed so they cannot understand. In other words, you become like what you worship! These idolaters should stop and think about what is happening; they should open their eyes to the utter folly of it all. But they never do.

God Has Swept Away Our Sins Like a Mist, So Rejoice!
ISAIAH 44:21-23

Isaiah 44 stands as a permanent indictment against worshiping and serving a created thing rather than the Creator. He calls on Jacob/Israel to remember these lessons, and they should remember also that the Lord made Israel to be his servant and to worship him alone (v. 21). They must never forget God because God will never forget them.

And in his amazing grace, when they lurch into idolatry and then get evicted from the promised land into their just exile in Babylon, God will remember them there and will forgive them. In a beautiful image, God sweeps away their sins like a heavy cloud or like a morning mist. No matter how great or small their sins, they will be swept away! Therefore, God calls on his people to return to him in repentance, faith, and love, for he has redeemed them. This redemption, this buying of Israel out from bondage to sin, could only be paid for by the blood of the Son of God. This future purchase is vastly more significant than the prediction of Cyrus with which the chapter ends.

As a result of this redemption, all of creation will be liberated from its bondage to decay and its groaning for freedom and will break forth into joyful celebration (Rom 8:19-23). So the heavens are invited to rejoice and the depths of the earth commanded to shout; and the mountains, forests, and every tree will sing for joy. No longer will a woodsman come to cut them down and use them to dishonor God.

God Raises Up Cyrus to Rebuild Jerusalem
ISAIAH 44:24-28

In these verses God unleashes details of the amazing restoration he has planned, the return of the remnant of Israel from Babylon under Cyrus the Great. God reminds Israel that he is both its Creator from the womb and its Redeemer (v. 24). But more than that, he is the God who has made all things and who stretched out both heaven and earth by himself. This awesome and powerful God is the one who controls the events of human history. The idols cannot foretell the future, and if the idolatrous priests come out in their bizarre garb and begin to whisper and mutter and look at omens to make some startling predictions, God will expose them as the frauds they are. But the words of his true prophets will be confirmed.

So it is in this case: Isaiah has predicted that Jerusalem will be inhabited again and the towns of Judah will be rebuilt, her ruins restored (v. 26). Of course, this assumes the destruction of Judah and Jerusalem that hadn't even happened yet, but such is the astonishing power of Isaiah's prophetic vision. The temple would be leveled, all its golden articles taken to Babylon—all of that in the distant future. But Isaiah looked beyond that and saw a man named Cyrus, whom the Lord would raise up to rebuild it all. He would be God's "shepherd" (v. 28) to accomplish all his purposes, rebuilding Jerusalem as a stage for the final drama of redemption, the death of Jesus for the sins of his people.

Applications

We modern people do not literally carve graven images and bow down to them, yet we must understand how rampant idolatry is in our culture. We worship material things just as they did. There is no end to the mansions, restaurants, malls, websites, sporting arenas, universities, investment houses, and steel/glass skyscrapers that testify to our earthly lusts. The utter emptiness of such a lifestyle of delusion is exposed and ridiculed by this chapter as powerfully now as it was then. We must stop and think; we must reason with ourselves and with our idolatrous neighbors to present before our spiritual eyes the vast superiority of the living God's glory. We must drink in the Spirit's living water (by the gospel of Christ and by the Word of God) so that we may clear our brains of this magnetic delusion. We must see again the supernatural evidence of the Word of God in predictive prophecy: no idolatrous religion has such credentials. And we must proclaim the gospel of Christ to the ends of the earth, for no other message can make our sins and delusions disappear like the morning mist.

Reflect and Discuss

1. How does verse 3 point to the powerful effect of the outpoured Spirit on our thirsty souls? How does this verse give us strong evidence that all the "streams in the wasteland" imagery of Isaiah is referring primarily to the work of the Spirit on human hearts?
2. How should we personally seek refreshment through the pouring out of the Spirit?
3. What claim does God make in verse 6?
4. How does God support that claim in verse 7? How can we use the Bible's amazing prophecies to prove the uniqueness and superiority of Christianity to other world religions?
5. What is the purpose of verses 9-20? Why does God use a tone of ridicule here?
6. What aspect of idolatry do these verses primarily hold up to ridicule?
7. What are some examples of modern idols in our culture and age?
8. What great encouragement does verse 22 give us? How does it point to Christ?
9. What specific prophecy does God give in verses 26 and 28? How is the presence of the specific name "Cyrus" a clear example of a miracle, given that Isaiah lived a century before Cyrus was born?
10. How does this chapter strengthen your faith in the God of the Bible?

The Temporary Empire of Cyrus Serves the Eternal Empire of Christ

ISAIAH 45

Turn to me and be saved, all the ends of the earth. For I am God, and there is no other. (Isa 45:22)

Main Idea: God raises up Cyrus of Persia and gives him an empire so that the Jews will rebuild Jerusalem, so that the gospel of Christ may spread to the ends of the earth.

I. **God Grants Cyrus an Empire for the Salvation of His Elect (45:1-8).**
   A. God calls Cyrus his "anointed" and grants him an empire (45:1-3).
   B. God does this so that Cyrus, Israel, and the whole earth may know him (45:3-6).
   C. God alone creates success and disaster (45:7).
   D. The Lord makes righteousness spring up (45:8).

II. **God Rebukes Arrogant Human Questioning of His Plans (45:9-13).**
   A. Woe to him who quarrels with his maker (45:9-10)!
   B. Woe to him who questions God about his plans (45:11,13)!
   C. God created the universe; he knows what he's doing (45:12).

III. **God's Mysterious Plans for Gentile Salvation (45:14-17)**
   A. The subdued Gentiles will enrich Israel (45:14).
   B. God is a God who hides (45:15).
   C. God's plan is shame for idolaters, salvation for Israel (45:16-17).

IV. **God's Gospel Call to the Ends of the Earth: Turn to Christ (45:18-25)!**
   A. God's purposes will be fulfilled: an earth filled with worshipers (45:18-19).
   B. God's clear challenge to idolaters: God alone predicted these things (45:20-21).
   C. God's gospel call to the ends of the earth: turn to Christ and be saved (45:22-25)!

God Grants Cyrus an Empire for the Salvation of His Elect
ISAIAH 45:1-8

The supernatural prediction of Cyrus the Great by name more than a century before his birth stands as one of the most stunning proofs of the Bible's divine origin. No other world religion or cult has the credentials of this achievement to commend itself to the human heart. Because of the clearly supernatural power of specific prophecy, scholarly skeptics have suggested there was a later author of this portion of the book of Isaiah, the "Second Isaiah" (Bright, *History of Israel*, 355). But, given that in this section of this amazing book the Lord again and again presents his power to predict the future as clear evidence of his superiority to the "gods," it actually is reasonable to accept the argument that the God who created the universe governs human history and is able to predict what he will do, even centuries before he does it.

God reveals the name of the coming conqueror, Cyrus the Great, who will destroy the Babylonian Empire and build an empire of his own. This Cyrus will decree that the Jews return to the promised land and rebuild Jerusalem and the temple. God's purpose in all this, however, is far greater than a surprising prediction or even than his covenant love to Israel. God's ultimate purpose is the salvation through Christ of the elect from every nation, tribe, people, and language (Rev 7:9). God willed that "salvation is from the Jews" (John 4:22) and that the Savior of the world, Jesus Christ, should be born in Bethlehem in Judea (Mic 5:2) and die in Jerusalem in Judea (Luke 13:33). God also willed that the gospel of salvation through faith in Christ should begin in Jerusalem and spread to the ends of the earth (Luke 24:47). Thus God gave Cyrus a temporary empire so that God might ultimately give to Jesus Christ an eternal empire of souls from every nation on earth.

The Lord surprisingly calls Cyrus his "anointed" (Isa 45:1), a title usually reserved for the kings of the Jews. The Holy Spirit chose and anointed Cyrus to play a role in redemptive history as a type and shadow of the true anointed King—Jesus. God says that he takes Cyrus by the right hand and leads him to subdue nations and strip slaughtered kings. God promises to go before Cyrus and open doors, remove mountains, and cut through bars of iron and gates of bronze (Herodotus said Babylon had a hundred bronze gates, *Histories* 1.179, 97). No obstacle would deter Cyrus's powerful advance through that region of the world. Paul said plainly to the philosophers in Athens, "From one man [God] has made every nationality to live all over the earth and has determined their appointed times and the boundaries of where they live" (Acts 17:26; cf. Deut 2:20-23; Amos 9:7). So the fact that God went before Cyrus and specifically gave him the territories of one smaller nation after another is consistent with his actions throughout all history.

God promised to Cyrus the "treasures of darkness and riches from secret places" (v. 3), clearly referring to the plunder he would gain from these conquests. This included the fabulous wealth of Croesus, king of Lydia, whose land contained a river with rich gold deposits (Herodotus, *Histories* 5.101). This fabulous wealth and the power of a mighty empire would motivate a man like Cyrus, who did not know the Lord and did not act for God's glory (v. 5). It is important for us to understand that God directs the hearts of kings like a watercourse whatever way he chooses (Prov 21:1), whether that king acknowledges him or not. Yet, as Paul said to the Athenians, God does all these things "so that they might seek God, and perhaps they might reach out for him and find him, though he is not far from each one of us. For in him we live and move and have our being" (Acts 17:27-28). So in our text God promises to give Cyrus these rich treasures so that he would know that the Lord, the God of Israel, has called him by name (Isa 45:3). Now, there is no clear indication that Cyrus ever did repent and follow the Lord as the only God, forsaking all idols. True, he did give credit to Yahweh for his empire in the decree to rebuild Jerusalem (2 Chr 36:23; Ezra 1:2), which Josephus tells us that Daniel pointed out to him in the very words of this Isaiah scroll. But in the Cyrus Cylinder (a baked clay cylinder with Akkadian writing ascribed by archaeologists to Cyrus the Great), he gives credit to Marduk, the god of Babylon, in almost the same language he used for the Lord (D. W. Thomas, *Documents*, 357).

However, God's purpose goes far beyond one man. God intends to use Cyrus's conquests to advance his master plan for the salvation of the elect from every nation, including the Jews first. So God tells Cyrus plainly that he summons him by name for the sake of Israel, his chosen one (vv. 4-5). And beyond even Israel, God has his eyes on the elect from every nation, "so that all may know from the rising of the sun to its setting that there is no one but me. I am the LORD, and there is no other" (v. 6).

The absolute sovereignty of God over human history is essential to this plan. One empire rises from the rubble and ashes of the previous one; emperors become wealthy by plundering the coffers of people they have slaughtered. So verse 7 makes plain that God creates both light and dark threads in the tapestry of human history; God brings success (*shalom*, "prosperity") and also disaster (*ra*, sometimes translated "evil"). Because of this, some feel that Isaiah 45:7 teaches that God creates evil, and they struggle with such a view of God. But *shalom* has a fuller meaning of prosperity in all areas of life: health, happiness, abundant harvests, full granaries, and overflowing vats. Thus the opposite is not moral evil but disaster. So we must see verse 7 in the light of the couplets: the "evil" is the opposite of the "prosperity" and must refer to Cyrus's invasion. To the Medes and Persians under Cyrus, their military conquest is unmitigated "success"; but to the Lydians, Babylonians, Assyrians, and other conquered peoples, it is "disaster." And God does it all.

Verse 8 sums this theme up powerfully with a poetic call to the heavens to "shower righteousness" so that salvation and righteousness may spring up from the earth. Heaven initiates; earth responds.

God Rebukes Arrogant Human Questioning of His Plans
ISAIAH 45:9-13

Such a complex plan of salvation using Gentile emperors might have seemed preposterous to many Jews languishing in exile in Babylon, to those who refused to accept that God was chastising their wicked nation for its sins. They would be strongly tempted to argue with their Maker. God proclaims "Woe!" to all who would show this kind of disrespect. These verses stand as a timeless warning to the entire human race to refrain from arrogant questioning of God's sovereign plan. We are the clay; he is the potter. Actually, we are just pottery fragments, shattered by sin, among many such fragments on the ground. So how dare we question our Maker? It is absurd for us corrupt sinners with such a narrow perspective to question the King of the universe about the children he created with his own hands (vv. 11-12).

God was determined to raise up Cyrus to execute his righteous plan, and he will level all of Cyrus's paths so he can succeed. Cyrus is the one who will rebuild the city of Jerusalem and set the Jewish exiles free. But he will receive no price or financial reward for doing it. This action can only be explained by the sovereign activity of God on his heart; God "moved the heart" of Cyrus (Ezra 1:1,5 NIV), and so it was done.

God's Mysterious Plans for Gentile Salvation
ISAIAH 45:14-17

Here we have a clear sense of the glory and mystery of God's salvation plan. The wealth of Egypt, and of the Cushites and Sabeans, comes over to the Jews and becomes theirs. That verse 14 is speaking of the Jews and not of Cyrus can be seen in what these representative Gentiles say: "God is indeed with you!" (cf. Zech 8:23). In this verse the image is more forceful and almost a little disconcerting: are the Egyptians, Cushites, and Sabeans *enslaved* to the Jews? The verse says, "They will come over in chains and bow down to you." However, in the larger context of Isaiah's message we see the merchandise of wealthy Gentile nations being used to build and adorn the temple and the city of Jerusalem (Isa 60:7-14). This depicts the success of the gospel of Jesus Christ to the ends of the earth; the "riches" of these nations has to do with the delight Jesus will have in their Spirit-empowered, heart-felt worship. The "chains" they wear may either be the chains from which Christ will liberate them or the forcefulness/compulsion of the Spirit's drawing them to Christ: "No one can come to me unless the Father who sent me *draws* him" (John 6:44; emphasis added).

Such an awesome and complex plan draws our minds up to breathless wonder, to say with Isaiah, "Yes, you are a God who hides, God of Israel, Savior!" This "hiddenness" of God is in the secret councils of his eternal plan, and that same hiddenness and mystery caused Paul to cry out, "Oh, the depth of the riches both of the wisdom and of the knowledge of God! How unsearchable his judgments and untraceable his ways!" (Rom 11:33). God's ways are untraceable; truly he is a God who hides in mysterious providence.

God's Gospel Call to the Ends of the Earth: Turn to Christ!
ISAIAH 45:18-25

To accomplish this glorious plan, God must proclaim the truth to the ends of the earth (vv. 18-25). We see God's eternal purpose in verse 18. God did not create, shape, and form the world to be an empty wasteland (Hb *tohu*; "empty" in Gen 1:2). Step by step, throughout the account in Genesis 1, God prepared a place for the human race to live. Advocates of intelligent design have spoken of a "fine-tuned" universe just right for human life (Bradley, "The 'Just-So' Universe," 157–70). This is especially seen on planet Earth: the atmosphere, climate, water, soil, interactive ecosystems, and thousands of other factors are exactly what they need to be to sustain human life. God did not go to all that meticulous trouble so that he could wipe out all humanity in the end! So, though God will judge humanity for its sin, God has chosen a remnant from every nation on earth, and he will cleanse this sin-soiled universe with fire (2 Pet 3:10,12), resulting in a new heavens and new earth. He will populate that beautiful place with redeemed worshipers who will inhabit it for all eternity and give God the worship he deserves. All of God's original purposes will come true!

To make it happen, God must call to a world full of idolaters to seek him and find him. He does not dishearten people by saying, "Seek me in vain" (v. 19 KJV; Hb *tohu*), which is in fact the case for those who pursue "wooden idols . . . who cannot save." God does not speak from somewhere in a land of darkness, like the occultic pagan priests assert about their mysterious gods (8:19). God speaks openly and clearly through his servants, the prophets. Once again, he summons the idolaters (45:20) to come to a place of judgment, to contend for their "gods" and see if they can do what he is doing in this chapter: predicting actual historical events long before they happen (v. 21). The God of creation is the only one who can!

So he calls out to the distant lands in plain, gospel language: "Turn to me and be saved, all the ends of the earth. For I am God, and there is no other" (v. 22). The word *turn* implies a turning away from something and a turning to something else. First Thessalonians 1:9 says of the Christians in that pagan community, "You turned to God from idols to serve the living and true God." So also God commands every nation to turn "to me" (and away from idols), for all those idols are false, and he is the only true God. The promise is plain: "Turn to me and *be saved*, all the ends of the earth" (emphasis added). This salvation is more than from mere exile or from the evil of a powerful invasion by the Medo-Persian conqueror, Cyrus. The salvation is from the just wrath of God for our sins. And Jesus Christ's death on the cross purchased it for us. So those who live in the remotest regions will be commanded to believe the gospel of Jesus Christ for salvation.

To that end, God swears a solemn oath. He swears by himself because, as the author of Hebrews says, "he had no one greater to swear by" (Heb 6:13) and because he wants to give a sense of absolute certainty to his elect: "Every knee will bow to me, every tongue will swear allegiance" (Isa 45:23). This means that, in the end, the kingdom of God will win out and all rivals will be removed forever. This bowing of

the knee and swearing allegiance should be understood in two ways:
(1) by the elect, both now by faith and later in worship by sight; (2) by
the rebels, in cowering fear at the impending judgment that God's righteous wrath will pour out on them. Both groups will see plainly in the
end that "righteousness and strength are found only in the LORD."

It is vital for us as Christians to see how stunning is the fact that the
apostle Paul alluded to verse 23 and directed it to Jesus. Isaiah 40–48 is
fiercely monotheistic; the repeated message is that there is no one but
Yahweh, no one even remotely close to him. He will not share his glory
with another; he alone created the universe, and he alone is the Savior.
Before Yahweh alone will every knee bow; in Yahweh alone will every
tongue swear allegiance. And Paul ascribes these ideas to *Jesus Christ*:
"At the name of *Jesus* every knee will bow—in heaven and on earth and
under the earth—and every tongue will confess that *Jesus Christ is Lord*,
to the glory of God the Father" (Phil 2:10-11; emphasis added). The
sum total of this chapter is this: God the Father orchestrated the rise of
Cyrus the Great, going ahead of him in sovereign power, to give Cyrus
an empire; and God would move Cyrus to rebuild Jerusalem and the
temple. But God did this so that his far more glorious purpose could
be accomplished: the building of the empire of his only begotten Son,
Jesus Christ.

Applications

Obviously the greatest application for this chapter is to obey God's
command in Isaiah 45:22 to turn to Jesus Christ in repentance and
faith and find salvation in him. Nothing is more important than that.
And anyone who reads Isaiah 45 and finds its primary message in the
immediate circumstances of the restoration of the Jews to the promised land under Cyrus the Great has missed the whole point. God did
not create the world to be empty but rather to be filled with worshipers who would be righteous and exult in him. Only the gospel of Jesus
Christ can change sinners from the idolaters we were to the God worshipers we must be.

Second, we should stand in awe of God's awesome sovereign power
over the rise of Cyrus the Great to world-dominating power. God called
him by name more than a century before he was born. This gives us a
sense of how minutely God orchestrates history for his own ultimate
purposes. We should embrace that God controls the actions of great
"movers and shakers" in world history even though most of them never

acknowledge God. Of course, along with that, we should understand that the Bible is a miracle; the Bible violates the laws of nature in that it contains a record of actual prophecies that have been fulfilled as well others that have not yet come to pass but surely will. This sets both the Bible and Christianity apart from all the false religions of the world.

Third, we should embrace the deep truths of Isaiah 45:7 and take them to heart, no matter how difficult they are to accept. Some days may seem "light" to us, filled with prosperity and success. Others may seem "dark" to us, filled with what we think of as disaster. For the children of God, there are no disasters but only afflictions by which God is strengthening our faith (Jas 1:2-4). For the wicked, though they do not recognize God, everything they experience comes from his hand, and both the success and the disaster of world history are from the sovereign hand of God. As Christians, we are called on to grow up to full maturity doctrinally and accept that God does all these things, though his ways are often hidden (v. 15) and mysterious.

Fourth, as a direct corollary of this, we should learn to stop murmuring and questioning God when he afflicts us. We should humble ourselves before his infinite wisdom and power and not question what he does with us. We should meditate on the rebukes of verses 9-10 so that we are quiet under the mighty hand of God when we are suffering.

Finally, we should yearn for the day when people from distant lands (like the Egyptians, Cushites, and Sabeans) will be drawn inexorably to Christ, in chains of love and Spirit-led compulsion, and find salvation in him. This should make us yearn to be involved in the spread of the gospel to the ends of the earth, praying for unreached people groups to hear this gospel message and bow the knee to Christ by faith.

Reflect and Discuss

1. What does the fact that Isaiah the prophet mentioned Cyrus the Great by name more than a century before he was born teach you about God? What does it teach you about the Bible?

2. How do verses 1-3 harmonize with Deuteronomy 2:20-23; Amos 9:7; and Acts 17:26? What does this teach us about God's orchestration of human history and the rise and fall of every nation/kingdom/empire that there has ever been?

3. What makes Isaiah 45:7 a difficult verse to understand and accept? How does the commentary help bring understanding that God is not the author of evil, but he is the author of disaster?

4. What does verse 8 teach us about God's initiative in salvation? How does it relate to Isaiah 55:10-11?

5. How does Isa 45:9-10 convict you? When are you tempted to argue with your Maker? How could we learn to humble ourselves and not question God so much?

6. How does verse 14 point to missions? How does Isaiah 60:7-14 help shed light on it?

7. How does God "hide" (Isa 45:15)? How does this verse relate to the fact that in verse 19 God claims to speak openly for all to hear?

8. Why will idolaters ultimately be disgraced (v. 16)? Why will believers in Christ be freed from all shame (v. 17)?

9. What do verses 18-25 teach us about missions? How does verse 22 stand as a key verse in the chapter?

10. Compare verse 23 with Philippians 2:10-11. What is the significance of the fact that Paul applies this verse to Jesus Christ?

"Gods" You Must Carry versus a God Who Carries You

ISAIAH 46

I will be the same until your old age, and I will bear you up when you turn gray. I have made you, and I will carry you; I will bear and rescue you. (Isa 46:4)

Main Idea: Idols are crushing burdens that sinners carry, to their own destruction, but the living God carries his children from their birth to their old age, even to their glorious salvation.

I. **The "Gods" of Babylon Are a Crushing Burden, Crushed in the End (46:1-2).**
    A. Bel and Nebo are crushing burdens, unable to save.
    B. Bel and Nebo will go into captivity.

II. **The Incomparable God Carries His People from Birth to Old Age (46:3-5).**
    A. God has carried Israel from birth to old age.
    B. Who then is like God? Certainly no idol!

III. **The Idols Cannot Move, Neither Can They Save (46:6-7).**
    A. Hiring a goldsmith to make a god
    B. A motionless god cannot save.

IV. **Remember the God Who Plans and Orchestrates History (46:8-10).**
    A. God calls Israel to remember and repent.
    B. God declares the end from the beginning.
    C. God's purpose will stand to the last detail.

V. **God's Plan Is to Bring Salvation Near to Those Far Away (46:11-13).**
    A. God summons a "bird of prey" (Cyrus) to achieve his plan.
    B. God's plan is to bring salvation near to those far away.
    C. God's ultimate aim is his glory in Zion.

The "Gods" of Babylon Are a Crushing Burden, Crushed in the End

ISAIAH 46:1-2

God directly contrasts "gods" that must be carried with the true God, who carries his people. This chapter compares motionless gods made from silver and gold to a powerful God who plans all of human history and then orchestrates his plan to the minutest detail. The direct application to Israel, and indeed to all who trust in the Lord, is to understand how idols will always be a burden that leads to destruction and how the true Lord is a living God who daily carries his people through every experience of their lives.

In Isaiah 46 the Lord grants Isaiah the prophetic eye to see the history of the Babylonian Empire through to its demise before the first of its days had begun. In Isaiah's time people believed there was a strong connection between the gods of a nation and that nation's military success. If one nation conquered another, their "gods" (idols) were carried off in triumphant procession by the conquerors, a clear indication of the weakness of those gods (36:18-20). In this prophecy God ridicules the idols of Bel and Nebo long before the military conquests of the Babylonians vaulted Bel and Nebo to the head of the pantheon in the estimation of the people of the ancient Near East. Bel was the chief god of the Babylonians, often called Marduk. Nebo was Bel's son (Pfeiffer, *Old Testament History*, 344–45). (We see them reflected in the names **Nebu**chadnezzar, **Bel**shazzar, and **Bel**teshazzar in the book of Daniel.)

The chapter opens with Bel and Nebo depicted as terrible burdens carried by beasts who are weary of bearing them. The image is one of a triumphal procession in which the conquerors carry off the vanquished Bel and Nebo. Impotent, mute, motionless, and lifeless, they have been shown to be unable to save their people. As a result, they go off into captivity. More than a century before Nebuchadnezzar built an empire to the glory of Bel and Nebo, Isaiah the prophet predicted the total humiliation of Bel and Nebo through the conquest of Babylon. The story will be completed in the next chapter, Isaiah 47.

The Incomparable God Carries His People from Birth to Old Age
ISAIAH 46:3-5

By direct contrast to Bel and Nebo, however, the living God carries his people. He is not some heavy idol that is a crushing burden to his people that must be put on an oxcart and the team of oxen lashed to pull the weight. The God of Israel has carried his people from their mothers' wombs, and he will continue to carry his people until their dying day. Even strong Christians underestimate how actively God is sustaining them every moment, how it is that "in him we live and move and have our being" (Acts 17:28). So it was for Israel—from the day God called Abram from Ur of the Chaldees and from the day he delivered Jacob's countless descendants from Pharaoh at the Red Sea. Even when the exile would come, there would be a remnant of Israel, those whom God had chosen to allow to live after all his judgments. God continued to carry that nation. And he pledged to continue to carry them through all their trials.

To what idol, then, can we compare such a God (v. 5)? No man-made statue of gold or silver or wood can be compared with almighty God. There is nothing on earth—in the seas, in the air, or in the heavens—that is remotely like this infinite God. Again and again the Lord is making this same claim, saying that he is the incomparable God (Isa 40:18,25; 44:7).

The Idols Cannot Move, Neither Can They Save
ISAIAH 46:6-7

Here we have a vignette, a tragic little drama of a wealthy man who comes into the workshop of an idol maker. He weighs out the amounts of silver and gold that he wants the craftsman to use to make him his idol. When the idol is ready, he immediately bows down and worships it! He didn't worship the raw silver and gold in his bag, but now that the craftsman has shaped it, he thinks it is worthy of his worship!

He takes the idol into his house, perhaps grunting with some of his servants and maybe the craftsman as well. They set up the idol in the shrine he has made for it. Wherever he sets it, there it will stay. Isaac

Newton would later teach the human race, "Objects in motion tend to stay in motion, and objects at rest tend to stay at rest" (Berlinski, *Newton's Gift*, 98). This is true of this gold and silver *object*: it will not move until something moves it. Yet despite its motionless performance, the idolater cannot stop crying out to it to save him. When Cyrus the Great comes at the head of his Medo-Persian army, the idols of Bel and Nebo will do nothing to save those who trusted in them.

Remember the God Who Plans and Orchestrates History
ISAIAH 46:8-10

Based on this repeated exposure of the folly of idolatry, Isaiah calls to his readers to remember the God who alone *can* save, the living God. He calls on them to remember the lessons of God's mighty activity in the past—certainly the Red Sea crossing but also his deliverance of Noah in the ark and his mighty works through godly men like Joshua, Gideon, Samuel, David, and others. God calls on the "transgressors," the rebels who will read these words, to turn from their idolatries in heartbroken repentance and be "brave" in their faith.

God again points to the ability he alone has to ordain the future, predict the future, and then orchestrate human history to bring about everything he has planned, even down to the smallest detail. What idol has ever done anything like that? God makes a powerful statement for the whole world to hear: "My plan will take place, and I will do all my will" (v. 10). The word *will* in verse 10 is frequently translated "pleasure." It is the same word as in Psalm 115:3: "Our God is in heaven and does *whatever he pleases*" (emphasis added). God delights in his plan, even though it involves great suffering and destruction, because in the end it will bring about an indescribably glorious world. So God has woven in his eternal mind a magnificent tapestry of redemptive history, with multicolored threads of agony and celebration in wise proportion. The whole tapestry delights him, and he will most certainly bring about each detail in his good time.

God's Plan Is to Bring Salvation Near to Those Far Away
ISAIAH 46:11-13

In verses 11-13 God touches again on the immediate detail that he has in mind: the coming of Cyrus the Great to destroy the Babylonian Empire and crush the idols of Bel and Nebo. But he also expands beyond this to encompass his final end: the glorious salvation of his chosen people. The coming of Cyrus is not God's final end. His ultimate purpose is a host of redeemed from every nation on earth standing pure and holy in the new heaven and new earth.

So he states again emphatically that he will call a "bird of prey" from the east (Cyrus), whose swift conquest of that part of the world could be likened to a peregrine falcon swooping like a blur down on its hapless quarry. Cyrus will allow the remnant of Israel to return to rebuild the city of Jerusalem and reestablish the sacrificial system at a rebuilt temple. But this merely sets the stage for the real drama: the substitutionary death and life-giving resurrection of Jesus Christ, the Son of God.

So in verses 12-13 God calls on hard-hearted rebels who are far from righteousness to listen to the gospel message. This could be idolatrous Judahites, vanquished Babylonians, or any sinner in any generation to the ends of the earth. He calls on rebellious sinners to the only activity that can save them: "Listen to me!" Sinners are justified by faith alone, and faith comes from hearing the message about Christ (see Rom 10:17). So comes the good news: "I am bringing my justice near." Justification is that activity by which a sovereign God makes the unrighteous to be perfectly righteous in his sight. The good news of the gospel is that God is bringing his righteousness near you, you who are naturally far away from justice. He does this by the proclamation of the gospel:

> The message is near you, in your mouth and in your heart. This is the message of faith that we proclaim: if you confess with your mouth, "Jesus is Lord," and believe in your heart that God raised him from the dead, you will be saved. One believes with the heart, resulting in righteousness, and one confesses with the mouth, resulting in salvation. (Rom 10:8-10)

In Isaiah 46:13 God promises to bring his justice near, a salvation that will not delay. The immediate fulfillment of Cyrus's conquest of Babylon is just a step on the way; the final destination is the salvation Christ brings.

Applications

We cannot excuse ourselves. Though we may not go to a goldsmith with a bag of gold and ask him to melt it into a golden statue that we worship, our covetousness and materialism are every bit as idolatrous as that (Col 3:5). Anything we put ultimate value on other than Christ is a "functional savior" and an idol. This chapter reveals that idols are burdens that we carry around, burdens that will crush us someday if we do not cast them off. God has systematically exposed and destroyed all his rivals in every generation. No one worships Bel and Nebo right now, nor Baal, nor Molech, nor Asherah, nor Chemosh. That should warn us that someday our generation's idols will also be exposed and crushed by judgment. Best to throw them off now in repentance. Ask God to search your heart and expose your idols. Don't assume glibly that you have none.

Instead, delight in a God who carries you. Ponder deeply and richly how God has sustained you since he knit you together in your mother's womb. One of the most popular Christian poems of our generation is titled "Footprints in the Sand" (authorship disputed, claimed by Stevenson, Powers, Carty, and Webb). It depicts a dream in which a person saw the course of his life in a set of two footprints side by side on the sand. As various scenes from the person's life flashed across the sky, the person noticed that every time there was an extreme trial or some sorrow or burden, there was only one set of footprints. The person was deeply troubled by this and brought a charge to the Lord, reminding the Lord that he promised never to abandon him, yet when he was needed the most, he was absent. The Lord replied that when there was only one set of footprints, the Lord was in fact carrying the person in his arms. The poem is quite touching, of course. But according to Isaiah 46, it doesn't go far enough. To be faithful to the doctrine of this chapter, there should only ever be one set of footprints! There is not a single moment in our lives that the Lord does not carry us. He sustains our existence and gives us everything we need for life and godliness at every moment of our lives.

Reflect and Discuss

1. Bel and Nebo were Babylon's gods. How does this chapter show what a burden these idols were to those who had to carry them from place to place?

2. Modern-day idols include money, material possessions, career ambitions, sex, pleasure, entertainment, addictive drugs, and spectator sports. How are these idols a terrible burden for those who live for them?

3. How does the defeat of Babylon in history expose the impotence of their gods?

4. How is it vital for all modern-day idolaters to ponder the final end of all idols on judgment day?

5. In this chapter, how is the living God contrasted with these burdensome idols?

6. God says he is the one who made us and carries us from the day of our birth to the day of our death. How is this a surpassing comfort to us?

7. How does God declare his sovereign foreknowledge and control over events in this chapter? How is this a great encouragement and strength for us in our age?

8. In this chapter God challenges rebels to remember and submit to him. How should such a challenge humble us?

9. How should this chapter cause us to search our hearts to expose our own idols?

10. How should it cause us to grow in our trust in Christ, our Savior, who died and rose again and who always lives to intercede for us (Heb 7:25)?

Wicked Babylon's Fall from Its Lofty Throne

ISAIAH 47

Go down and sit in the dust, Virgin Daughter Babylon. Sit on the ground without a throne, Daughter Chaldea! For you will no longer be called pampered and spoiled. (Isa 47:1)

Main Idea: Babylon is portrayed as a pampered and wicked sorceress queen whom God will throw from her lofty throne to vindicate his chosen people.

I. **God Commands Humiliated Babylon to Vacate Her Throne (47:1-4).**
   A. God commands pampered Daughter Babylon to sit in the dust.
   B. Babylon is stripped and humiliated.
   C. Israel is avenged by God her Redeemer.

II. **God Takes Vengeance on Babylon for Israel's Sake (47:5-6).**
   A. God's purpose is to punish Israel within measure.
   B. This is God's vengeance for Babylon's cruelty to Israel.

III. **Babylon's Arrogant Security Comes to a Shocking End (47:7-11).**
   A. Babylon's arrogance: "No one sees me" and "No one is like me."
   B. Sudden devastation comes: widowhood and loss of children.

IV. **Babylon's Occult Powers Fail to Save Her (47:12-15).**
   A. Babylon's occult powers are stubble in the inferno.
   B. Babylon cannot save herself.

God Commands Humiliated Babylon to Vacate Her Throne
ISAIAH 47:1-4

There is a theological symmetry between the judgment on Babylon's gods (Bel and Nebo) in Isaiah 46 and the fall of Babylon itself in Isaiah 47. Time and again in these chapters the true and living God warns idolaters that their false gods cannot save them but will actually end up destroying them. The Isaiah 46–47 couplet is more powerful evidence to support this warning God is giving to every generation to the ends of the earth. For as we have already seen several times, "Babylon" in the Bible is more than merely an ancient city that rose from the fertile Mesopotamian plain alongside the Euphrates River. It was certainly that, and the prophecy of Isaiah 47 has as its immediate fulfillment the conquest of Babylon by Cyrus the Great in 539 BC. But the term "Babylon" reemerges in 1 Peter 5:13, where Peter writes, "She who is in Babylon, chosen together with you, sends you greetings." Since Peter was in Rome at the time of his death, it is likely that the term "Babylon" there refers to Rome, the seat of the most powerful empire on earth. In the book of Revelation, "Babylon the Great" is prophesied against repeatedly as the great city that made the nations drunk with the wine of her fornications (Rev 14:8) and that will fall under the final wrath of God. And Revelation 17–18 especially portrays Babylon as a wicked woman, a temptress, echoing the feminine imagery and the actual verbiage of Isaiah 47. In Revelation 18:7-8 "Babylon the Great" speaks words that paraphrase Isaiah 47:7-9.

Thus "Babylon" has a symbolic meaning of the world's system under satanic domination. More specifically, it seems that in every era of world history, the "Spirit of Babylon" settles down under Satan's dark wisdom to refer to whatever realm is dominating the earth militarily and/or economically. So the prediction of the fall of Babylon in Isaiah 47 is ultimately timeless, relevant to every generation of human history.

As the Lord speaks this oracle of doom to Babylon through the prophet Isaiah, he begins by commanding the "Virgin Daughter Babylon" to vacate her throne and sit down in the dust, utterly degraded and humiliated. The "Virgin Daughter" language refers to Babylon's pristine status as never having been conquered, being protected in a walled citadel that seems inviolable. She is pampered by her status as "mistress of kingdoms" (v. 5), needing to do no labor, living in luxury off the fat of her conquests on the backs of the peoples she has enslaved. But now this spoiled daughter, haughty and arrogant, is cast down with violence from her throne (vv. 1-2). She must do the labor of a common slave: grinding flour. She will be stripped bare and have to wade through streams. Her nakedness will be exposed, to her everlasting shame (vv. 2-3). This degrading demotion is the direct judgment of a Holy God acting in vengeance (v. 3) for the sake of his chosen people.

So verse 4 serves as a transition between verses 1-3 describing the judgment of Babylon and verses 5-7 describing why the judgment will come. God is Israel's Redeemer, and he will take vengeance on Babylon for the sake of his people because Babylon laid a crushing yoke on their necks, showing them no mercy (v. 6). This is the ultimate reason for this judgment on Babylon: God's desire to redeem his people from sin and restore them to himself, free from the defilements of Babylon. It is fascinating that God calls himself the Lord of "Armies" (Hb *tsebaoth*), a word that also describes "stars," by which he may have intended to call to mind the worship of the stars by the Babylonian stargazers (v. 13). Those are the very stars that God created and calls out by name (Isa 40:26); they are his servants to do his bidding, and they do not communicate his secret counsels to wicked pagan priests in Babylon.

God Takes Vengeance on Babylon for Israel's Sake
ISAIAH 47:5-6

This chapter is an oracle of vengeance on a wicked world for how it has treated God's chosen people. The mystery of divine sovereignty and human responsibility is never far from our minds as we take in the vast complexity of the book of Isaiah. God willed that Babylon conquer Judah and Jerusalem because he was angry with his people for their sins (v. 6). He gave Judah over to the control of the Babylonians, carefully measuring out the level of the suffering of his people. But the Babylonians committed two sins while serving this eternal purpose of God: first, like the Assyrians in Isaiah 10:5, although they did what God wanted them to do, they did it from wicked motives, not for the glory of God but for their own glory in building a kingdom; second, they went beyond the measured punishment of his people by treating them with excessive cruelty, laying even on the elderly a heavy yoke of oppression (v. 6; Dan 4:27).

In the book of Revelation an angel pours out a bowl and turns the waters of earth to blood because the wicked on earth shed the blood of God's people (Rev 16:3-7). So in Isaiah 47, the central motivation of God for judging Babylon is the harsh treatment they showed the exiled chosen people of God.

Babylon's Arrogant Security Comes to a Shocking End
ISAIAH 47:7-11

This section depicts the arrogant security that characterizes Babylon: "You said, 'I will be the queen forever.' You did not take these things to heart or think about their outcome" (v. 7). This arrogant security characterizes all the unregenerate wicked on earth. They push out of their thoughts the nagging conscience that tells them there will be a day of judgment someday. They arrogantly presume that things will go on like this forever. Babylon assured herself that she would never be a widow or suffer the loss of children (vv. 8-9). But both of these will come on her suddenly, in an instant. These two calamities represent the worst things that can happen to a woman in that society, for a husband and children represent economic security and hope for a comfortable future. "Widowhood" comes on Babylon when her young men (soldiers) fall in battle against the Medes and Persians. And "loss of children" follows literally, when the Babylonian population is slaughtered subsequently.

Verses 9-11 reveal that some of Babylon's security comes from her confidence in occultic powers—sorceries and potent spells. She came to two false conclusions: "No one sees me" and "I am, and there is no one else" (vv. 8,10). Both of these thoughts clearly forget almighty God, who sees everything, who alone can say, "I am, and there is none like me" (see Exod 3:14; Deut 32:39). How tragic it is when wicked people go into secret chambers and do wicked things, thinking there is no God who will judge them for their sins (Ps 14:1)!

Babylon's Occult Powers Fail to Save Her
ISAIAH 47:12-15

The Chaldeans were known for their astrology, their stargazing and interpretation of omens and dreams. All of this was an effort to discern the future so that forewarned would be forearmed. Beyond that, these Babylonian sorcerers sought demonic powers by which they could defeat human enemies. So occult power was a mainstay of Babylonian confidence: supernatural knowledge coupled with supernatural power. But verses 12-15 make plain that they will be shocked at the devastation that will come on them because their secret powers will not reveal the future accurately. God has again and again made plain that idols cannot foretell the future; only he can (Isa 41:23). And Proverbs 21:30 says,

"No wisdom, no understanding, and no counsel will prevail against the LORD." When God threatens coming wrath, the only wise counsel is to run *to* the Lord and plead for his mercy. Nothing else will succeed. So God ironically taunts them to try their dark powers one last time. These efforts will fail; their reputed power will only be stubble for the fire of God's wrath.

Applications

As we read this terrifying chapter, we are immediately led to consider the symbolic significance of Babylon in the Bible. Babylon represents the evil world system that, under Satan's secret power, dominates the face of the earth. Babylon represents "the lust of the flesh, the lust of the eyes, and the pride in one's possessions" (1 John 2:16). The geographical/national base of Babylon has migrated as one empire has given way to the next. But we who are in exile from heaven live in Babylon. In the next chapter we will be warned to "leave Babylon, flee from the Chaldeans" (Isa 48:20), which Paul picks up on (2 Cor 6:17), as does the angelic warning in Revelation 18:4. But we cannot be warned enough of the deadly dangers of this sorceress queen, of her luxuries, of her occult allurements, and of her future judgments by God. We must keep ourselves from being polluted by her many charms and defiled by her wicked and dark idolatries. We must be acutely aware that God sees what is done in secret and will most certainly bring to judgment every wicked act and idolatrous heart.

As always, this points us to the cross of Jesus Christ. Verse 4 celebrates that the Lord of Armies is the Redeemer of Israel, which he accomplishes ultimately by the shed blood of Jesus Christ. Israel is no better than Babylon; tempted again and again by Satan's dark allurements, we too are as defiled as the Babylonians. We should repent and flee to the cross for the cleansing the blood of Christ alone can give. Beyond this, we have a sacred duty to do precisely what Isaiah is doing in this chapter: warning Babylon of her impending judgment by God. We have the clear gospel of Jesus Christ to proclaim in this present version of Babylon all over the world. It is the only hope for the world, and it is our responsibility to warn the inhabitants of Babylon to flee the wrath to come.

We should be keenly aware of the growth of occult practices where we live. More and more movies, books, and songs celebrate dark forces of the occult: witchcraft, demons, omens, supernatural divination, communication with the dead—these have become much more visible in our culture over the past decade and more. Beware, for this is the very thing Isaiah 47 exposes; it will lead to Babylon's destruction.

Finally, we should see the zeal God has to avenge his people. In a wicked and turbulent world that hates Christ and attacks Christians, God will finally avenge his people and save them from their enemies. As we hear of the persecuted church in Muslim and totalitarian countries, and as we cry for justice while our brothers and sisters die, we should remember that God's zeal to avenge his people is vastly greater than we can imagine.

Reflect and Discuss

1. Who is talking to whom throughout this chapter? Note that the word *you* or *your* is used forty-six times in this chapter, including nine times in verse 12.
2. What is the symbolic significance of "Babylon" in the Bible? (See pp. 90–91 of this commentary for a brief overview.)
3. How is Babylon like a spoiled, pampered princess living in luxury? What is going to happen to her, according to verses 1-3?
4. How is God identified in verse 4? How does verse 4 connect with verse 6 to show us God's zeal for his own people as they suffer in Babylon?
5. How should verse 6 make Christians fear sin and God's righteous discipline on the church?
6. How does verse 7 show the arrogant confidence that sinners tend to have that judgment day will never come and that everything will go on just as it always has? How do we Christians have a responsibility to warn people that such a confidence is spiritually deadly?
7. What is the danger of luxury according to Isaiah 47? How is 1 Timothy 6:17-18 a healthy remedy to the dangers of luxury for Christians?
8. How do you see the growth of occultism in our culture these days? What is the danger of this to Christians?
9. How should this chapter strengthen our resolve to be holy in the "Babylon" in which we live?
10. How should this chapter strengthen our zeal for missions?

Why Does God Put Up with Us? For His Glory and Our Benefit

ISAIAH 48

I will delay my anger for the sake of my name, and I will restrain myself for your benefit and for my praise, so that you will not be destroyed. . . . I will act for my own sake, indeed, my own, for how can I be defiled? I will not give my glory to another. (Isa 48:9,11)

Main Idea: For his glory and our benefit, God delays his anger and refuses to destroy his people despite their sins.

I. **The Sovereign God Predicts and Works History to Win His Stubborn People (48:1-8).**
    A. God has predicted the future and brought it to pass (48:1-3).
    B. God does this to win his stubborn people (48:4-8).
II. **The Patient God Refines His People for His Glory and Our Benefit (48:9-11).**
    A. God puts up with his people for his own sake (48:9).
    B. God refines his people for their benefit (48:9-10).
    C. God's ultimate purpose in their salvation is his own glory (48:11).
III. **The Eternal God Will Bring Cyrus to Achieve His Purpose (48:12-16).**
    A. God is the "I Am" (48:12-13).
    B. God alone foretold Cyrus and will bring him to succeed (48:14-16).
IV. **The Loving God Will Send Another to Redeem His People (48:16-22).**
    A. The mysterious "sent one" speaks (48:16).
    B. If only God's people had obeyed his word (48:17-19)!
    C. God the Redeemer covers his people's transgressions (48:17,20-22).

The Sovereign God Predicts and Works
History to Win His Stubborn People
ISAIAH 48:1-8

Several years ago I was attending a large conference, and a popular pastor was there speaking about the mandate Christ has given the church to evangelize the lost. He shouted dramatically, "Is there anything in the universe worth more than a human soul? If you can think of anything, I challenge you to step to the microphone right now and tell us what it is!" At that moment, I thought of an answer: the glory of God! God's glory is worth more than the salvation of every human soul. I think if I had stepped up to the microphone and said that, the pastor might have said, "Oh yes, of course *that*! But *other than that* . . ."

How easy it is for us to get so swept along in the fervor for winning the lost that we forget that God esteems his own glory as far greater than all the worth of every human being who has ever lived. But the joy of the gospel is that the themes of God's glory and human salvation end up harmonizing beautifully. God is most glorified in his universe by his salvation of a vast multitude of sinners through the gospel of Jesus Christ. The concept that God saves sinners primarily for his own name's sake is taught plainly in this chapter.

God calls on his people to hear him and addresses his people as the "house of Jacob—those who are called by the name Israel and have descended from Judah" (v. 1). The problem is, they are in no way living up to the covenant heritage these names signify. They swear by the name of the Lord but not in truth or righteousness. They call themselves members of the holy city (Jerusalem), and they supposedly lean on the God of Israel, but it is all a hypocritical sham.

In this section of the chapter God plainly exposes the astounding stubbornness of his people: he says their forehead is like bronze, the sinews of their necks are bands of iron (v. 4). They heard God speak again and again through the prophets but did not understand and refused to obey. The ears of their hearts were closed and they were treacherous, rebels from birth (v. 8).

To win such a people, God has done some astounding things through his prophets. He has done what no idol could do, neither what any man could conceive: he has foretold events in past history and brought them to pass (v. 3). These refer to the many prophecies that were fulfilled in Israel's history, including the multiplication of Abraham's seed, their enslavement in Egypt, and the awesome way that God brought them out of Egypt and established them in the promised land (Gen 15). God did such things specifically to win the hearts of his people away from idols (v. 5).

But not only had God done this for centuries in the past; he was even now continuing to do this before their very eyes. In verses 6-7 he refers to the present pattern of prophecies Isaiah was continuing to give them concerning Cyrus the Great's destruction of Babylon and the rebuilding of Jerusalem (Isa 44–45). But even more importantly, he will predict the sufferings of the servant of the Lord, Jesus Christ, beginning in the very next chapter, Isaiah 49, and even more clearly in some chapters that follow (Isa 52–53).

The Patient God Refines His People for His Glory and Our Benefit
ISAIAH 48:9-11

God then explains to his stubborn people why he puts up with us so patiently. God is uppermost in his own affections and ultimately does everything in the universe "to the praise of his glory" (Eph 1:14). It is so easy for us in our pride to think that God has put human salvation at the highest level of importance in all creation. But Isaiah 48:9-11 makes plain that God does it for his own glory. This is such a strong message that God speaks it twice in verse 11: "I will act for my own sake, indeed, my own."

God says it is for his own sake that he delays his anger against his people; he is patient with them and doesn't instantly sweep them away. God has by grace left his people a remnant in every generation. So also God is measured, patient, and careful with the church of Jesus Christ, not instantly lashing out against us when we sin but giving us time to repent (Rev 2:21). Peter tells us that God's patience is to bring about salvation (2 Pet 3:15). This passage tells us that God does it so that his glorious name won't be defamed among the nations (cf. Ezek 36:22).

Instead of destroying Israel for her idolatry, God willed to refine her in the furnace of affliction. The immediate reference must be the exile to Babylon, and the analogy is the purification of silver, in which the fiery heat brings to the surface the dross that can be skimmed off. However, God says the refinement of his people in the exile was *not* like that, for such a refining is effective in the case of silver, but the Jews would return from exile still wicked in their hearts. Only Christ's final work of sovereign grace on our hearts in glorification will end forever the corruption that characterizes us to the depths of our beings.

God displays in these vital verses the central concept that our eternal benefit and his ultimate glory are perfectly harmonized in the gospel. In verse 9 the CSB includes the phrase "for your benefit" (Hb *lak*) before the words "and for my praise," which beautifully completes the balance between God's concern for his glory and for the good of his people.

In verse 11 God emphasizes his jealousy for his own glory, saying with eternal finality that he will not share his glory with any created being. This is strong evidence for the doctrine of the Trinity and for the deity of Christ in that Jesus prays in John 17:5, "Now, Father, glorify me in your presence with that glory I had with you before the world existed." If Jesus were not fully God in the mystery of the Trinity, such a prayer would be blasphemous.

The Eternal God Will Bring Cyrus to Achieve His Purpose
ISAIAH 48:12-16

God reminds his people of his utter uniqueness—this is exactly why he cannot share his glory with another (v. 11). He is the "I am," the actual true and living God, the only one who exists. He was God at the beginning of all things, and he will be the same God at the end of all things. He established the earth with his own right hand and spread out the heavens; he summons them, and they all stand up at his call. This is the actively ruling King who brings Cyrus, whom he *loves*, to achieve his purposes. God has announced this publicly, not in some mysterious occult riddle that only an inner circle of enlightened priests could decipher (v. 16a).

The Loving God Will Send Another to Redeem His People
ISAIAH 48:16-22

At this point, we hear the mysterious insertion of another voice interrupting the prophecy: "And now, the Lord God has sent me and his Spirit" (v. 16b). This may be the voice of the Suffering Servant who will be introduced plainly in the next chapter. The affliction of the exiles will not bring about the final salvation of Israel, but the work of the Suffering Servant, the Redeemer, will.

Thus in verse 17 the Lord identifies himself again as Israel's "Redeemer," who will work to redeem Israel from the bondage that sin has caused. This sin is made plain by the fact that God had spoken a clear word of righteousness by his law. If Israel had obeyed God's commands perfectly, a Redeemer would have been unnecessary. Instead, Israel's peace would have been like a river, and his righteousness would have been like the waves of the ocean. Israel's life would have been one of rich blessing—numberless descendants and a name that would never be cut off (vv. 18-19). But Israel had been unwilling (Matt 23:37). So they need the Redeemer whom he will send.

Verses 20-21 speak of the immediate work of Cyrus and the ultimate work of the servant, Jesus, in the familiar terms of the exodus. When Cyrus has finished his work in destroying Babylon, the exiles will leave Babylon with joy and singing to rebuild Jerusalem and the temple. But they will just be setting the stage for the Redeemer, Jesus Christ, to come and work the true exodus by his death and resurrection. And when the gospel of Christ comes by faith into the hearts of God's exiled people in every nation on earth, they will "leave Babylon" and declare with shouts of joy that God has redeemed his people. God calls on his holy people to come out of Babylon so that we will not share in her plagues or judgments (Rev 18:4).

But those who refuse this gospel and who continue to live in wicked rebellion against God will know no peace (v. 22).

Applications

It is so essential for us to understand God's zeal for his own glory and to see our salvation as a part of that. We should ask God to work a similar zeal in our own hearts so that we stop putting human worth above that of God's glory.

Second, we should realize how stubbornly rebellious we Christians are and how resistant to follow God's beautiful laws (vv. 4,8,18-19). We are no better than they were, and we need God to do a continual work in our hearts by his Word, his Spirit, and his Redeemer, Jesus Christ. The more we submit to his perfect law by his Spirit, the more our peace will be like a river and our righteousness like the waves of the sea. But the more we behave wickedly, the less we will experience the peace of God.

Finally, we Christians should rejoice at our redemption from captivity in the "Babylon" of sin. We should declare with shouts of joy to the ends of the earth in missionary effort that, in Christ, God has redeemed his people!

Reflect and Discuss

1. How does this chapter reveal God's patience with his people?

2. How does this chapter reveal the stubbornness of God's people, not merely the Judahites of Isaiah's day but Christians in our own day?

3. In what ways did God refine stubborn Israel in the Bible? How does he refine his people in our day?

4. What is the significance of God's repeated statements in this chapter, "For my own sake, indeed, for my own, I do this" (vv. 9,11), when it comes to God's refining of stubborn Israel? How does this relate to our own salvation?

5. How do God's predictions of the future serve his purpose in redeeming stubborn Israel? How does his bringing of Cyrus the Great fit into his plan?

6. How does God appeal in this chapter to his people in every generation to listen to his word and heed it? How would such an obedient life lead to our peace being like a river (v. 18)?

7. How does the final verse (22) explain much of the trouble in our modern-day world?

8. How is verse 22 completely answered by Christ's redeeming work on the cross, as well as by Romans 5:1: "Therefore, since we have been declared righteous by faith, we have peace with God through our Lord Jesus Christ"?

9. Why should we as sinners seek God's refining today, though it means suffering for us?

10. How can we use the message of this chapter—God's sovereign power in controlling history to achieve his salvation plan—to preach the gospel to our unsaved relatives, neighbors, coworkers, and acquaintances?

Christ Unveiled as Restorer of Israel and Light for the Nations

ISAIAH 49

[The Lord] says, "It is not enough for you to be my servant raising up the tribes of Jacob and restoring the protected ones of Israel. I will also make you a light for the nations, to be my salvation to the ends of the earth." (Isa 49:6)

Main Idea: It is insufficient for the servant of the Lord (Jesus Christ) merely to restore the exiles of Israel; besides that and against all obstacles, he will extend God's salvation to the ends of the earth.

I. **Christ Unveiled as God's Salvation to the Ends of the Earth (49:1-7)**
    A. The servant of the Lord calls to the nations (49:1).
    B. The servant of the Lord is concealed and prepared (49:2).
    C. The servant of the Lord is called "Israel" (49:3).
    D. The servant of the Lord is apparently discouraged (49:4).
    E. The servant of the Lord is prepared to restore Israel (49:5).
    F. The servant's mission extends to the ends of the earth (49:6-7).

II. **God's Day of Salvation for the Exiles (49:8-13)**
    A. God's day of salvation (49:8)
    B. The joyful restoration of the exiles from the distant lands (49:8-13)

III. **Despite All Appearances, the Exiles Will Return (49:14-21).**
    A. The Lord's sworn oath: I will never forget Zion (49:14-18).
    B. Despite all appearances, the exiles will return (49:17-21).

IV. **The Gentiles Will Aid the Redemption of Israel or Be Destroyed (49:22-26).**
    A. God calls on Gentiles to honor and help his people (49:22-23).
    B. The vicious captors are plundered and slaughtered (49:24-26).

Christ Unveiled as God's Salvation to the Ends of the Earth
ISAIAH 49:1-7

This is one of the greatest missionary chapters in the Bible, for it takes us into the secret counsels of the triune God for the extension of the glory of Christ to the ends of the earth. Here we are privy to an immeasurably deep conversation between the Father and the Son concerning Jesus's glorious mission on earth. Here God the Father tells the Son that it is insufficient glory for him to be merely the Savior of the Jews. God did not send his only begotten Son into the world to save Israel alone. But God has commanded Jesus Christ to be also the light for the Gentiles, that he may bring his salvation to the ends of the earth. So, at present, the glory of Jesus Christ is great—he sits at the right hand of God the Father. But there are as yet many elect peoples from unreached nations who have not heard of his fame or seen his glory, and that is intolerable. God wills that Jesus be a light for people from every nation on the face of the earth. God wills far greater glory than Christ presently has.

The chapter opens with the servant of the Lord calling to the "coasts and islands" and "distant peoples" to listen to his words (v. 1). This servant of the Lord is none other than Jesus, for verses 1-7 speak clearly of an individual. This individual is called "Israel" in verse 3 (which we will explain in a moment), and this might lead the reader to think Isaiah is writing of Israel. But verses 5-6 make plain that this servant of the Lord was sent in part to gather "Israel" back to God, so these verses read most sensibly as referring to a single individual. Given that Simeon called the baby Jesus "a light for revelation to the Gentiles" (Luke 2:32) and the book of Acts twice quotes this passage and applies it to Jesus (Acts 13:47; 26:23), Christians do well to understand Isaiah 49:1-7 as speaking of Jesus Christ, the servant of the Lord. And Jesus has a message for "the ends of the earth" (v. 6).

The text tells us that the Lord called the servant by name before he was born. God the Father had chosen Jesus from before the foundation of the world to die for the sins of his people (1 Pet 1:19-20) and told Joseph (Matt 1:21) and Mary (Luke 1:31) that his name would be Jesus because he would save his people from their sins. God prepared the mouth of Jesus to be a honed sword and a sharpened arrow, not to slaughter his enemies but to pierce the hardened hearts of his elect with the words of the gospel. Jesus grew up before his heavenly Father, concealed from the eyes of the world, protected in the shadow of God's hand. Twice in Isaiah 49:2 the text says God "hid" him until he was ready to unleash him on Israel. And his words would mean life to all who heard them with faith.

God also called his servant of the Lord by the name of "Israel," as we mentioned above (v. 3). This has led some people to think the "Suffering Servant" of Isaiah 49–53 is Israel. But we already refuted that notion by the clearly different use of the word *Israel* in verses 5-6. The best way to understand Jesus being called "Israel" in verse 3 is to see him as the perfect fulfillment of all that Israel was meant to be. God called his people in Egypt "Israel" and his "firstborn son" (Exod 4:22). God chose Israel to be a priest nation (Exod 19:5-6) by which the promise to Abraham would be fulfilled: "all the peoples on earth will be blessed through you" (Gen 12:3). But because of Israel's sin, they failed in that mission. Jesus would perfectly embody all that Israel was meant to be as God's "firstborn Son." This is made clear in that the prophecy of Hosea 11:1, "out of Egypt I called my son," is applied to Jesus (Matt 2:15).

Isaiah 49:4 speaks surprisingly of the apparent discouragement of the servant. He laments that he has spent his strength to no apparent purpose. The hiddenness of the work of God is paramount here, for the kingdom of God is often an apparent failure. Missionaries labor for years seeing almost no fruit. Pastors labor for years and wonder if their many sermons have accomplished anything at all. Parents labor for years only to see their children wander into rebellion. The apparent failure of the kingdom of God is nowhere more stunning than when it comes to the life and death of Jesus Christ. Jesus lived the only perfect life that has ever been lived; he preached the only perfect sermons that have ever been preached; he did a river of signs and wonders in number and in magnitude that boggles the mind; he poured himself out day after day for the Jewish people. Yet they despised and rejected him (Isa 53:3) and formally condemned him to death (Mark 14:64). When he was arrested, even his own apostles deserted him and fled (Matt 26:56); his best friend denied knowing him (Matt 26:69-75). As he was dying on the cross, all that remained of his ministry was a single apostle (John), his own mother, and a few friends of the family. It would have been easy for him to look at that meager outcome and say the words of Isaiah 49:4: "I have labored in vain." But as he died, he entrusted himself to

God and said in effect, "Into your hands, I commit my ministry. Make something of this tiny grain of wheat that is falling into the ground and dying." Verse 4 concludes with the hopeful words, "yet my vindication is with the LORD, and my reward is with my God." God the Father took the death of Christ and used it to atone for the sins of a countless multitude from every nation on earth.

So verses 5-7 address the glory of Christ in bringing the salvation of God to the ends of the earth. Jesus was sent to bring back Jacob to God so that Israel might be gathered to him. But the Father has declared for all time that that alone is not weighty enough (literally, "too light a thing"). The Hebrew word for "glory" means something massive; so it is insufficiently glorious for Jesus to be merely Savior for Israel. God has ordained that Jesus also be a light for the Gentile nations so that he may be the salvation of the ends of the earth (v. 6). So God will see to it that the one who was despised and abhorred by his own people (the Jews), called the "servant of kings," would be in the end so honored that kings see him and rise out of their thrones to pay him homage, bowing down to worship him (52:15).

God's Day of Salvation for the Exiles
ISAIAH 49:8-13

This gospel of Jesus Christ is advancing even now by the Holy Spirit's power. Quoting verse 8, the apostle Paul says, "At an acceptable time I listened to you, and in the day of salvation I helped you. See, now is the acceptable time; now is the day of salvation" (2 Cor 6:2). This is the era of God's grace, extending to the nations by the proclamation of the gospel of Christ. As sinners hear that gospel, they are moved by faith to call on the name of the Lord, crying aloud to Jesus for salvation from their sins. But Isaiah 49:8 is addressed to the servant, not the sinner! God is promising to hear *Jesus* in this "time of favor" and "day of salvation." So Jesus is our Mediator (1 Tim 2:5), and as we cry to him, he in turn will intercede for us to God, and God will hear his beloved Son and save us.

This "day of salvation" was pictured in history by God's restoration of the exiles from Babylon back to the promised land. Jesus was made by God to be a "covenant for the people" (v. 8) with the result that "spiritual exiles" will return and again possess the desolate inheritances of the promised land. Christ will speak a sovereign word to the prisoners (exiles) and lead them from darkness to their inheritance. These exiles will come from far away, from the north and west, even from the "land of Sinim" (some scholars believe this might have been China; cf. Young, *Isaiah Chs. 40–66*, 294). The regathering of physical exiles to the promised land was a picture of the spread of the gospel to the ends of the earth and of the spiritual pilgrimage that all disciples make in following Jesus from sin to heaven (Matt 7:13-14).

This "day of salvation" and the resulting pilgrimage of former exiles (both physical and spiritual) is worthy of exultant praise and worship by the heavens and the earth, set free at last from decay (v. 13; Rom 8:19).

Despite All Appearances, the Exiles Will Return
ISAIAH 49:14-21

We have already seen how the Suffering Servant could look around from the cross and see little evidence of the greatness of the kingdom of God; so also Zion (the City of God—Jerusalem) could look at her own rubble-filled and vacant streets during the exile to Babylon and say, "The Lord has abandoned me!" (v. 14). This is the way it is with the spiritual advance of Christ's kingdom, with cities of teeming millions and only a handful of known Christians in each one meeting in secret. How could there ever really be a multitude greater than anyone could count from every nation on earth (Rev 7:9)? So if Zion only looks at the outward circumstances of a desolate condition during the exile to Babylon, she may well conclude that God has forgotten her.

But God swears by himself—"'As I live'—this is the Lord's declaration" (v. 18)—that a mother is more likely to forget her nursing child (v. 15) than that God will forget his covenant promise to Abraham. God also took a solemn oath when he made that promise (Gen 15:17), implying by the movement of the fire pot through the pieces of the sacrifice, "May I cease to exist if I fail to keep my promise to you." God has inscribed his people on the palms of his hands, and he never forgets the walls of Jerusalem (v. 16). Despite all outward appearances, the exiles will return and the earthly Zion (Jerusalem) will be populated, so populated, in fact, that she will become too small for all her people (vv. 19-20). So also the heavenly Zion will look on all her children and wonder where they came from (v. 21; see Zech 8:5).

The Gentiles Will Aid the Redemption
of Israel or Be Destroyed
ISAIAH 49:22-26

The chapter ends with both a promise and a warning to the Gentile nations on earth. God will lift up his hand to the nations and raise his banner, commanding the Gentiles (both rulers and people) to assist him in gathering his scattered people and returning them to Zion. The very ones who are journeying in pilgrimage to Zion will lift up and carry others along with them, so also here in verse 22 Gentiles will carry the sons and daughters of Zion from exile home to the promised land. Literally, Cyrus the Great and all the Persian sub-rulers and people are called on to aid the resettlement of Jerusalem by any means possible. In the same way, Gentile converts to Christ are called on to be involved in evangelizing unreached people groups, giving special focus to the lost among the Jews. Believing monarchs will aid in the spread of the gospel (v. 23).

Conversely, some Gentiles will use their positions of power to resist the streaming of exiles back to Zion. Verses 24-26 speak of tyrants who hold the exiles captive and have to be crushed in order to let the children of God go free. So either the Gentiles will aid the streaming of the exiles back to Zion (in which case they will be blessed), or they will resist it and be destroyed by an avenging God.

Applications

The driving force for missions is written in this chapter, namely, that Christ's present glory is too small. "It is too light a thing" for Jesus to be worshiped at his present level; he is deprived of his glory when there is any unreached people group or any elect person who has not yet come to faith in Christ. A yearning that Christ receive all the glory he is due from all the people he has chosen should drive us in missions day after day. God the Father has ordained that Christ be a light for the Gentiles, bringing God's salvation to the ends of the earth. The apostles Paul and Barnabas took this statement (made from the Father to the Son) as their personal marching orders in Acts 13:47: "For this is what the Lord has commanded us [plural]: 'I have made you [singular] a light for the Gentiles to bring salvation to the end of the earth.'" The Greek is singular—Jesus is the only light for the Gentiles. But because we are his body and he is our head, his commission from the Father moves us to action to make it come true.

Along with this, we should feel fully the weight of Christ's apparent discouragement in verse 4 that gets resolved in that same verse by trusting in God's final plan. The kingdom of God will always appear underwhelming and somewhat disappointing in this present age compared to the grandeur of the King and the perfection of the promises he has made to us. So pastors, missionaries, evangelists, parents, and Christian laborers of all types will have to battle discouragement constantly when the results are far less than we feel they should be. Adoniram Judson was so depressed in Burma that he dug his own grave and waited for God to kill him (Anderson, *To the Golden Shore*, 378). Martin Luther was so discouraged at the poor response to his preaching in Wittenberg that he gave up preaching for more than nine months in 1530 (Meuser, *Luther*, 27–34). The kingdom of God seems so unimpressive compared to current events and mighty world empires. But don't be deceived. When we are finally in the heavenly Zion, we will be amazed at the stunning multitude of the redeemed there.

Finally, we should proclaim to the lost around us that today is the day of salvation, as Paul quotes in 2 Corinthians 6:2. We should be urgent in evangelism and not allow the unrepentant to comfort themselves that there's "always tomorrow." No, *now* is the season of God's grace, *today* is the day of salvation.

Reflect and Discuss

1. How does this chapter present the glories of Jesus Christ?
2. What is the significance of Jesus's words being like a "sharp sword"? How would you relate it to Hebrews 4:12, which says the word of the Lord is like a "double-edged sword"?
3. How do you understand Jesus's apparent discouragement in verse 4: "I have labored in vain, I have spent my strength for nothing and futility"? How does the end of the verse resolve this and show that what really matters is the final glory the Father had planned, not how it appears in the middle of the unfolding plan?
4. How could Christian workers feel tempted to be discouraged at the paltry level of their fruit after so much sacrificial labor? How could verse 4 help them also to resolve their discouragement and continue to labor for the hidden advance of the kingdom of God?

5. What does verse 5 teach us about Jesus's role among the chosen people?

6. How is verse 6 a foundational verse for missions? How is it "not enough" for Jesus merely to be the Savior of Israel? How is Jesus also the "light of the Gentiles"?

7. How does verse 7 help us understand the final glories of Christ, though he is presently despised?

8. What does verse 8 teach us about urgency in light of the gospel? How does Paul apply this verse in 2 Corinthians 6:2?

9. How does the physical restoration of the Jewish exiles from Babylon back to the promised land also give us a picture of the advance of the gospel to the ends of the earth?

10. How do verses 15-16 personally encourage you about Christ's changeless love for you?

Christ Listened to His Father to Save Those Who Listen to Him

ISAIAH 50

The Lord God has opened my ear, and I was not rebellious; I did not turn back. (Isa 50:5)

Main Idea: Christ listened perfectly to his Father and obeyed completely, even though it meant suffering; as a result, he will save all who turn from self and listen to him.

I. **A Nation Who Refused to Listen Is Sent into Exile (50:1-3).**
    A. Israel is not divorced, only sent away for sin (50:1).
    B. Israel refused to listen to the sovereign God (50:2).
    C. God is still omnipotent and able to save (50:2-3).

II. **A Servant Who Perfectly Listened Is Sent as Savior (50:4-9).**
    A. The servant speaks of his perfect obedience (50:4).
    B. The servant speaks of his humble submission to abuse (50:5-6).
    C. The servant speaks of his vindication by God (50:7-9).

III. **A Key Question: Will You Listen to the Servant or to Yourself (50:10-11)?**
    A. All who have ears to hear the servant will lean on God (50:10).
    B. All who try to walk by their own light will be tormented (50:11).

A Nation Who Refused to Listen Is Sent into Exile
ISAIAH 50:1-3

The unifying theme of this brief chapter is listening to God. Jesus Christ called on his hearers to consider carefully how they listen to God's Word (Luke 8:18) and often finished his teachings with the words, "Let anyone who has ears to hear listen" (e.g., Luke 8:8). This chapter begins with God speaking to Judah, explaining the reasons for the exile—what they were and what they weren't—and it all came down to their failure to listen to God when he called. Next comes a remarkable section of prophecy revealing the heart of the ministry of the servant of the Lord, Jesus Christ. The essence was his perfect commitment to listen to his Father and to obey even to the point of death. Along with that was Jesus's perfect teachings and the sweet sustenance his words gave to the weary. The chapter ends with a fork in the road: Will you listen to the servant, or will you listen to your own wisdom? The ends of those divergent roads couldn't be more infinitely separated—heaven for those who trust in the servant's words and hell for those who don't.

The first section of this chapter (vv. 1-3) is God's direct address to Judah. God was preparing his people more than a century in advance for what he was going to do in response to their idolatries. His desire was to strengthen their faith at precisely the time they needed it the most. For when they were languishing in Babylon, they would be most tempted to believe that God had cast them off entirely, "divorced" them, and would have nothing more to do with them (v. 1). Isaiah had just used the image of Jerusalem as a bride who was bereaved and exiled, who later is lavishly blessed with abundant children (49:18). He will develop it beautifully in chapter 62, in which God rejoices over Zion as a bridegroom over his bride (v. 5). The exile would call all that into question, and they may have felt that God had divorced Israel for her spiritual adultery. But God never divorced Israel, and he was not through with that nation. Neither can they suppose that God sold his children into slavery to satisfy creditors (Matt 18:25).

No, the reason for the exile was plain: Israel was sent far away because of her iniquities (Isa 50:1). When God came to them to demand their loving obedience, they refused to listen (v. 2). And no, the exile did not happen because God had somehow lost his power. Not at all! They could never have been captured "unless their Rock had sold them" (Deut 32:30). God's hand is not too weak to redeem them, neither does he lack power to rescue them (v. 2). God is every bit as powerful now as he was the day he led them through the Red Sea as on dry land. This is the same God who created the heavens and can do anything he wants to the stars—including turning them black. So he can do whatever he wants on earth (v. 3). Israel was sent away because they stubbornly refused to listen.

A Servant Who Perfectly Listened Is Sent as Savior
ISAIAH 50:4-9

The Suffering Servant would be entirely different. By his perfect obedience, the rebels who had been sinfully refusing to listen to God would be saved. These words must refer to Christ, for only Jesus gave himself so fully and so meekly to those who were so viciously abusing him, knowing that God would vindicate him. No one has ever so humbled himself and made himself nothing as did Jesus, even to the point of his death on the cross (Phil 2:9-11). Jesus fulfilled this prophecy.

Throughout Isaiah 50:4-9, the servant (Christ) is speaking in the first person, talking about himself. He begins by revealing the source of his astonishing teaching ministry, saying that the Lord God has given him the tongue of an instructed person and that the effect of the Father's words is the sustaining of the weary. The servant goes beyond this to speak even of the practical side of how this comes about: every morning the Father would waken the Son and pour words of instruction into his ready ear. The New Testament gives ample evidence of how this was worked out in Jesus's life. Mark 1:35 tells us of Jesus's habit of getting up very early in the morning and going to a deserted place where he would pray. Part of that time involved the Father telling the Son specifically what works he would be doing and words he would be speaking that day. In John 7:16 Jesus said plainly, "My teaching isn't mine but is from the one who sent me." And in direct fulfillment of Isaiah 50, his words were amazingly comforting to brokenhearted sinners. For example, he said to a paralyzed man who had faith, "Have courage, son, your sins are forgiven" (Matt 9:2). His call to all those suffering under sin's crushing yoke was alluring: "Come to me, all of you who are weary and burdened, and I will give you rest" (Matt 11:28). Isaiah 50:4-5 tells us that the Father taught him what to say and how to say it (see John 12:49).

The text also tells us that the servant was not rebellious to anything the Father told him to do, no matter how costly. He willingly offered his back to his tormenters, his beard to those who would pluck it out, his face to those who would spit on it (v. 6). This astonishing humility was that of the "Lamb of God" who would be led to the slaughter. In all of this degradation, Jesus was not ashamed; no, his glory was to die in submission to his Father's wise plan. His vindication would come through centuries of exaltation by the Father as the Holy Spirit applied his blood to the elect from every nation.

Paul paraphrases verses 7-9 in Romans 8:33-34. It is exhilarating for us Christians to realize that our vindication from Satan's accusation and from condemnation (Rom 8:1) has been bought by the blood of the submissive Savior predicted in Isaiah 50. No one will be able to bring a charge against God's elect because Jesus obeyed on their behalf!

A Key Question: Will You Listen to the Servant or to Yourself?
ISAIAH 50:10-11

The chapter ends by asking a question of all who are walking in the darkness of sin. Will you fear the Lord, listen to Christ, and walk humbly through faith in his light? Or will you reject Christ, light your own torch for guidance, and seek to live according to your own wisdom? The first group will be saved; the second will lie down in eternal torment.

Applications

For Christians, we must first recognize our own tendency to wander from God by refusing to obey his Word. Second, we must stand in awe of the astonishing humility and obedience of the Suffering Servant, Jesus Christ. We must feel the weight of the abuse he endured and with humble tears acknowledge that it is our sins that produced his sufferings. Third, we must consider his daily pattern of listening to his Father and seek to imitate it by having daily quiet times in the Bible and constant prayer. We must awaken our ears every day to listen to his words of instruction then seek to live out that wisdom, to bless others with the words he gives us to sustain other weary sinners. For non-Christians, here is a warning: If you refuse to trust in Christ, you are effectively making your own torch to light your way. The end of that way is eternal torment. Flee to Christ by faith!

Reflect and Discuss

1. What does this chapter reveal about the importance of listening to God when he speaks?
2. How did Israel fail to listen to God? How do we?
3. How does this chapter predict the humility of Jesus in always seeking to listen to his Father?

4. How are Jesus's early morning quiet times predicted here? How could we follow Jesus's example in verses 4-9?

5. How did Jesus's humble obedience lead to terrible suffering and death, even to death on the cross? How does verse 6 predict some of those sufferings?

6. How could greater levels of obedience by us lead similarly to greater levels of suffering?

7. What is the significance of the words of triumphant vindication in verses 7-9? How was Jesus vindicated by the Father?

8. How does Christ's resurrection victory guarantee our vindication from all accusation (compare vv. 7-9 with Rom 8:33-34)?

9. To whom does verse 10 appeal? How can Christians hear verse 10 and put it into practice?

10. What is the terrifying warning given in verse 11? How do verses 10-11 capture the wisdom of Proverbs 3:5-6?

Look to the Past to Learn How Bright Is the Future

ISAIAH 51

I am the LORD your God who stirs up the sea so that its waves roar—his name is the LORD of Armies. (Isa 51:15)

Main Idea: God's saving actions in the past are the key to our hope for the future.

I. **Listen to Me! The God of Abraham Will Again Create Righteousness from Nothing (51:1-6).**
  A. Seeking righteousness? Look to Abraham and Sarah (51:1-2).
  B. Zion will be transformed from desert to paradise (51:3).
  C. God's salvation will outlast this universe (51:4-6).
II. **Listen to Me! The God of the Exodus Will Again Make a Way for His People (51:7-11).**
  A. God's salvation will outlast human taunts (51:7-8).
  B. Awake, O Lord! Do again what you did before (51:9-10)!
  C. The ransomed will sing eternally (51:11).
III. **How Dare You Fear Man More Than Me? Through You I Will Establish Eternity (51:12-16)!**
  A. How dare you fear man more than the Lord the Creator (51:12-13)!
  B. The oppressor will die; the prisoners will be freed (51:13-14).
  C. The Lord who rules the sea will use you to establish eternity (51:15-16).
IV. **Wake Up! The Time Has Come for Your Tormenters to Fall (51:17-23).**
  A. The cup of God's wrath made you fall (51:17-20).
  B. Those days are over (51:21-22)!
  C. It is time for your tormenters to drink it (51:23).

Listen to Me! The God of Abraham Will Again Create Righteousness from Nothing
ISAIAH 51:1-6

In this chapter God speaks energetically to his chosen people throughout redemptive history—first to the Jews in exile then to all his people thereafter. In the original context God prophetically leaps ahead a century and a half, addressing his remnant as if he were looking backward at the events of the Babylonian exile. God wants them to listen to him! He desires to feed their faith by his words. He calls to those who "pursue righteousness, . . . who seek the Lord." The godly remnant in every generation groans under adverse circumstances: then as exiles in Babylon before the restoration, now as Christians suffering under the whip of the world, the flesh, and the devil. God calls on his discouraged remnant to look to what he has done in the past. It was the Lord who worked a miracle baby for Abraham and Sarah (vv. 1-2) then multiplied the Hebrews in Egypt into a mighty nation. The God who did this in the past can do it again in the future. So, exiled Israel, look to the rock from which you were cut—Abraham—and know that God can do it again. You may be few in number and weak, but God will multiply you again and settle you again in Jerusalem. So also Christians will be greatly outnumbered in whatever country they live—perhaps in Iran or in China, or even in the supposedly "Christian" West—but God is going to gather a multitude of true believers greater than anyone can count from every nation on earth (Rev 7:9).

When the exiles read these words in Babylon, Jerusalem was a pile of rubble and it seemed their national hopes were dashed. But the same God who originally created the garden of Eden would again make Zion and the promised land like a plush paradise, and he would fill it with people who would rejoice and worship the Lord their Savior (v. 3). In the meantime, God calls on his people to look to him and trust in his word. The sovereign Lord will establish his justice for the nations, even to the distant coastlands (vv. 4-5). These words go beyond merely the restoration of the Jews to the promised land under Cyrus the Great but find fulfillment in the gathering of the elect from the distant islands of the earth into the kingdom of Christ by the spread of the gospel. The ultimate end of these words is staggering: the present heavens and earth will be destroyed completely, just as Jerusalem would be. The destruction of Jerusalem was a mere dress rehearsal for the fiery cataclysm that will come on the entire universe at the end of the age (v. 6;

2 Pet 3:10,12). Jesus said, "Heaven and earth will pass away, but my words will never pass away" (Matt 24:35). The suffering remnant in every generation should realize that the Word of God is more permanent than the ground beneath their feet! God will establish a righteous salvation for his elect through his Son, Jesus Christ, and they will live forever in a perfect world that will replace this present one.

Listen to Me! The God of the Exodus Will Again Make a Way for His People
ISAIAH 51:7-11

God calls again, "Listen to me!" The same God who achieved the awesome Red Sea crossing by hacking Rahab (the mythological monster of the deep sea; Motyer, *Prophecy of Isaiah*, 408–10) to pieces, who dried up the waters of the great deep and made the seabed into a road for his redeemed (vv. 9-10), will be able to gather the ransomed of the Lord from the ends of the earth to return to Zion filled with joy, overflowing with worship to God their Savior. Again, the key to hope for the future is faith in the God of the past. Only by hope in God's promises can they withstand their Babylonian tormenters who mock the exiles: "Sing us one of the songs of Zion" (Ps 137:3). God predicts the day that those mockers will be devoured as a worm devours wool (Isa 51:8). They will pass away, but God's righteousness will endure forever, the foundation of the joy of his saved people. The slaughter of "Rahab" at the Red Sea is a prophetic picture of Christ's destruction of the Dragon, Satan, by means of Jesus's death and resurrection (Heb 2:14).

How Dare You Fear Man More Than Me? Through You I Will Establish Eternity!
ISAIAH 51:12-16

In this section the Lord speaks quite passionately about the grievous sin of fearing man more than fearing him: "I—I am the one who comforts you" (v. 12). How dare we fear man more than we fear him? Man is mortal—he dies, withering like the grass of the field (v. 12). How dare we live in constant dread every day of the fury of the oppressor, forgetting that it is the Lord who created the universe (v. 13)! God reminds his people also that he rules every single day over the events on earth. Not only did he create heaven and earth, but he also stirs up the sea so that its waves roar (v. 15). This is the God who will set the prisoner free, delivering him from the Pit (v. 14).

The eternal God designed these words to give comfort not only to the Jews in exile but also to every generation of his chosen people. How do we know this? Again, because the words of verse 16 soar far above the mere restoration of a straggling remnant of Jews to the rubble-filled streets of Jerusalem. Verse 16 has some interpretive challenges. Because the servant of the Lord speaks in similar language in Isaiah 49:2, some believe God is speaking to Christ here as well. But the audience is referred to in the second person masculine singular in verse 12 ("Who are *you* . . .") and all the way through verse 13; and Zion is addressed directly at the end of verse 16 in second person masculine singular as well. So it is probably best to think of this as God addressing each one of his elect people in verse 16: "I have put my words in your mouth, and covered you in the shadow of my hand, in order to plant the heavens, to found the earth, and to say to Zion, 'You are my people.'" In other words, by the sovereign word of God he will establish a new heaven and new earth as an eternal home for Zion, his redeemed people. So stop fearing mortal man—God will accomplish his eternal purposes!

Wake Up! The Time Has Come for Your Tormenters to Fall
ISAIAH 51:17-23

God reminds his people that Jerusalem was destroyed and the people sent into exile specifically as an act of judgment by their holy God. He gave them a cup of fury, and they drank that cup to its bitterest dregs: destruction, famine, and sword inflicted on his people. Their children fell like antelopes caught in a hunter's net. This great tragedy was no accident but rather God's righteous judgment. But now that time is over. God has removed the cup of staggering from the hand of his people and will now give it to their tormenters instead. And when they drink from it, they will fall. These were the vicious people who made God's people lie down in the mud so they could walk on their backs. The tormentors' time of torment will come back on them.

Applications

The lessons of this chapter are profound, and they minister to every generation of God's people. The basic concept is powerful: We must listen to the Word of the Lord and feed our hearts on his past achievements as recorded in Scripture so that we may be filled with a powerful hope, no matter how bleak the circumstances. We must look back with faith at what God has already done, so we can look ahead with hope at what he has said he will do. For Christians in the twenty-first century, this chapter can enable us to face mockers and persecutors who scoff at our faith and say, "Where is this 'coming' Christ said would happen?" (see 2 Pet 3:4). The same God who created the universe out of nothing and the Jewish nation out of nothing will fulfill his eternal plan.

Second, we should learn to fear God and obey him more than we fear human beings, no matter how threatening or powerful they may appear. It is a great sin to fear man more than God, who strongly challenges that sin in this chapter. We must repent of all the ways we show fear of man. This is especially true in the matter of evangelism and missions. God says in this chapter that he will set prisoners free and that he has put his words in our mouth and covered us in the shadow of his hand. These words find a beautiful application in stirring us up to courage in evangelism. Satan's prisoners must be set free by the gospel of Jesus Christ.

Finally, we should fully embrace the future this chapter clearly unfolds: for the present universe, total destruction; for the believers, a new heaven and new earth in which they will worship God eternally in joy; for the wicked tormenters, a cup of wrath. These themes should strongly color the way we live every day—pursuing righteousness in the fear of the Lord and seeking to deliver the prisoners held by chains of sin. The future should empower the present as much as the past does.

Reflect and Discuss

1. How does this chapter call on us to look back to God's actions in the past to gain hope for the future? How is this foundational to the relevance of the Bible to our lives today?

2. How are God's actions in the past with Abraham and at the Red Sea crossing able to give us hope now, despite the fact that they will never be repeated again? How does the immutability of God help us answer this question?

3. How would the fact that God raised up descendants from old Abraham and barren Sarah give specific encouragement to the Jews in exile (v. 2)?

4. God uses sharp commands in this chapter, like "Listen" (vv. 1,7) and "Look" (v. 6). Why does he speak so decisively to his people? Why do we need this kind of strong speech?

5. How does verse 6 predict the end of the present heaven and earth? How does this point forward to the new heavens and new earth in 2 Peter 3:10,12?

6. How does this chapter give encouragement to Christians who are persecuted daily by tormenters who reject their message?

7. How does fear of man act as a powerful hindrance to the spread of the gospel (vv. 12-16)? How is fear of man vigorously rebuked in this chapter by the God who makes and calms powerful storms?

8. How can we learn to fear God more than we fear man?

9. How does God speak of the future of Israel's tormenters? How does that word give encouragement to Christian missionaries and evangelists today? How can we learn to see them in light of eternity and in light of God's power to convert vicious oppressors like Saul of Tarsus (Acts 9)?

10. As you read Isaiah 51, what timeless principle unites God's suffering people in both the old-covenant and the new-covenant eras?

Awake, Zion, and Celebrate: Your God Reigns

ISAIAH 52:1-12

How beautiful on the mountains are the feet of the herald, who proclaims peace, who brings news of good things, who proclaims salvation, who says to Zion, "Your God reigns!" (Isa 52:7)

Main Idea: Zion is commanded to awake, throw off defiled garments, and celebrate the glory of God's sovereign reign.

I. **God Exalts Zion from the Dust of Exile (52:1-6).**
   A. Zion is awakened and clothed with holy garments (52:1).
   B. Zion arises from bondage and sits enthroned (52:2).
   C. Zion is redeemed to know the Lord (52:3-6).
II. **Beautiful Feet Bring Joyful News: "Your God Reigns!" (52:7-12).**
   A. The feet of messengers are beautiful (52:7).
   B. The good news is peace, goodness, and salvation because God reigns (52:7).
   C. The news produces shouts of joy (52:8-9).
   D. The salvation displays God's power (52:10).
   E. Therefore, depart in holiness and journey safely to Zion (52:11-12).

God Exalts Zion from the Dust of Exile

ISAIAH 52:1-6

In Isaiah 52 we see the amazing grace of God toward Zion, the Holy City where God puts his name and in which God dwells in active fellowship with his people. Jerusalem was that city, but it had become polluted by sin such that it had become like a prostitute (1:21) and was trampled by the feet of defiled invaders (52:1). Isaiah 52 calls on this defiled harlot to rise up out of the filth and become radiantly glorious.

Once again, the context is the end of the exile to Babylon, for in verse 2 God addresses "captive Daughter Zion." Now the filth of shame brought on by idolatry is finally to be washed away. The spiritual sloth of Zion is over, and she is commanded twice, "Wake up!" (v. 1). God is promising to work in the heart of his remnant and transform them from the inside out. They will awaken from their sinful sleep and find power in the Lord. They are to rise up from the filth and put on radiant garments of holiness. Jerusalem is to be the holy city, set apart unto the Lord, a place into which the unclean will never again enter. Formerly sitting in squalor, Zion will now sit on a throne of glory.

The price of Zion's redemption is the topic of verses 3-6. Zion was sold for nothing, so her captors have no lasting claim on her. God is thus able to redeem her out of slavery without the payment of gold or silver. The degradation of the chosen people of God has brought his name blasphemy all day long (v. 5), and so out of zeal for his own holy name God will redeem them from exile. And when he does redeem them, his people will know his name and give him praise (v. 6).

We should read these verses in light of the redeeming work of Christ. First Peter 1:18-19 says powerfully,

> *For you know that you were redeemed from your empty way of life inherited from your fathers, not with perishable things like silver or gold, but with the precious blood of Christ, like that of an unblemished and spotless lamb.*

No silver or gold could ever have ransomed us from slavery to sin but only the blood of Christ. And like Assyria and Babylon, Satan's kingdom had no lasting claim on the children of God, so the ransom was not paid to him but to the righteous claims of God's law.

Beautiful Feet Bring Joyful News: "Your God Reigns!"
ISAIAH 52:7-12

Next we see a herald running to Zion to proclaim the joyful news: "Peace! Salvation! Your God reigns!" The image of watchmen on the walls of Zion waiting for this news is powerful, for the literal walls of Jerusalem would be piles of rubble at that point. But the hearts of all exiled Jews were longing for the day when the Lord would return to Zion and rebuild Jerusalem. In this chapter that day has come at last! The news is carried by a herald, and it is so welcome even his feet would be seen to be beautiful by those eager to hear his news. The message is a triple one: (1) "Peace!" God is at peace with his people; the time of Jerusalem's warfare has ended (see Isa 40:2 KJV)! (2) "Salvation!" Zion's sins have been paid for and she will not be condemned! (3) "Your God reigns!" The glory for all this goes to God alone! The message results in overwhelming joy on the part of the "watchmen" who were waiting for this very day, whether literally in the ruins of Jerusalem or living in exile with hearts longing for Jerusalem to be restored. Every eye will see the Lord's return to Jerusalem, and all nations will hear of the greatness of Zion's God. Before all nations, he has bared his holy arm; Babylon is crushed by the power of God.

This section ends with a breathless and tripled command: "Leave, leave, go out from there!" The command refers to God's chosen people leaving Babylon and returning home to Jerusalem. As you leave Babylon, touch nothing filthy, for God yearns to cleanse you from the defilement of that city. The text mentions the carrying of the Lord's vessels, a clear reference to the sacred articles that would have been taken from the temple to Babylon by King Nebuchadnezzar (Dan 1:2) and later defiled by Belshazzar's idolatrous feast the night Babylon fell (Dan 5). Cyrus the Great would specifically bring them out and entrust them to Ezra and the Jews for the return trip to Jerusalem (Ezra 1:7). But the people would not have to leave Babylon in haste as if they were running for their lives, for the new emperor would freely and officially release them, and God himself would be their rear guard (Ezra 8:21-23).

The final verses in Isaiah 52, 13-15, so clearly belong with Isaiah 53 that I will deal with them in the next chapter. But suffice it to say at this point that the work of the Suffering Servant described in Isaiah 52:13-15 is the very payment that procures the redemption of Zion spoken of in verse 2.

Applications

The immediate application of this chapter is not as significant as its timeless application. Yes, this chapter speaks eloquently about the redemption of Zion (Jerusalem) and the restoration of a remnant of Jews under Ezra to rebuild Jerusalem after the fall of Babylon. But the ideas of Isaiah 52 soar vastly above that significant detail of redemptive history. "Zion" is an idea too big for the history of the literal city of Jerusalem to capture entirely. Paul spoke of a "Jerusalem above" (Gal 4:26) that is the spiritual mother of all the elect, both Jews and Gentiles. So the call for "Zion" to wake up and put off her slumber, to rouse up and sit in glorious clothing on a holy throne, must ultimately be seen in the redemption of all God's chosen people, Jew and Gentile, from their sin and worldliness in this earthly "Babylon" in which we all live. It is a call upward to the true and final "new Jerusalem" that is the consummation of all redemptive history, in which God will openly live with his holy people. The new Jerusalem will be a place where the spiritually uncircumcised and unclean (v. 1) will never enter (Rev 21:27) and where we will celebrate eternally the peace and salvation of our sovereign God.

So the spread of the gospel of Jesus Christ among all the nations of the earth by evangelists and missionaries is seen by the apostle Paul in Romans 10:15 as a direct fulfillment of verse 7. It is not spiritualizing Isaiah 52 to speak primarily of the work of missions in calling elect people from every tribe, language, and nation to faith in Christ. This is precisely how the eternal Zion will be populated. And Paul also quotes Isaiah 52 in 2 Corinthians 6:17: "Therefore, come out from among them and be separate, says the Lord; do not touch any unclean thing, and I will welcome you." There he is commanding Gentile converts to Christ living in Corinth to come out from virtual Babylon spiritually by living pure and holy lives, free from the defilements of the non-Christians we live with every day. Ultimately, then, Isaiah 52 is a timeless call to all of God's people (1) to be powerfully active in missions (Rom 10:13-15) and (2) to be free from defilements of lust and worldliness (2 Cor 6:17).

Reflect and Discuss

1. How does this chapter predict the joy of the restoration of the Jews from exile in Babylon?

2. How does this chapter also predict the spread of the gospel of Jesus Christ to the ends of the earth (Rom 10:13-15 compared with Isa 52:7)? And how does it address the need for Christians to be holy as we live our earthly lives (2 Cor 6:17 compared with Isa 52:11)?

3. What does "Zion" mean? Is it the same as Jerusalem? How does Hebrews 12:22 point us to a "heavenly Zion"?

4. What is the significance of the call "Wake up, wake up!" in verse 1? How does Zion need to wake up? How do we?

5. What is the significance of the fact that Zion was redeemed without silver or gold? How does 1 Peter 1:18-19 fulfill that image by pointing to the blood of Christ?

6. What is the threefold good news the herald brings (vv. 7-10)? How are these verses also fulfilled in evangelism and missions?

7. How does Isaiah 52:10 point to the spread of the gospel to all nations?

8. How is both the restoration of the remnant of Jews to the promised land and the spread of the gospel to unreached people groups a display of the sovereign power of God—"Your God reigns!"?

9. How does Ezra 1:7 fulfill Isaiah 52:11, and Ezra 8:21-23 fulfill Isaiah 52:12?

10. How would you connect the clear prophecy of Jesus Christ in verses 13-15 with the message of Isaiah 52:1-12?

Jesus, Our Suffering Servant

ISAIAH 52:13–53:12

He was pierced because of our rebellion, crushed because of our iniquities; punishment for our peace was on him, and we are healed by his wounds. (Isa 53:5)

Main Idea: Jesus Christ is presented as our Suffering Servant whose substitutionary death and victorious resurrection are predicted seven centuries in advance.

I. **Christ Repulsive but Redemptive then Exalted (52:13-15)**
   A. The exaltation of God's servant (52:13)
   B. The degradation of God's servant (52:14)
   C. The sprinkling of the nations (53:15)

II. **Christ the "Arm of the Lord" but Human and Despised (53:1-3)**
   A. The "arm of the Lord" necessarily revealed (53:1)
   B. The humanity of Christ (53:2)
   C. Christ despised and rejected (53:3)

III. **Christ Rejected but Our Atoning Substitute (53:4-6)**
   A. Christ bearing our diseases (53:4)
   B. Substitutionary atonement stated four times (53:5)
   C. "Pierced!" (53:5)
   D. Constant straying, one substitute (53:6)

IV. **Christ Innocent but Willing to Be Slaughtered (53:7-9)**
   A. Christ willingly slaughtered (53:7)
   B. Christ dead (53:8)
   C. Christ buried in a rich man's tomb (53:9)
   D. Christ innocent (53:9)

V. **Christ Crushed So We Could Be Justified (53:10-12)**
   A. The Father's pleasure in crushing his Son (53:10)
   B. The Son's success: children for God (53:10-11)
   C. Christ's spoil: the elect (53:12)

Introduction

Isaiah 53 Is about Jesus and Only Jesus

Jesus Christ, and only Jesus Christ, is the fulfillment of Isaiah's prophecy. Unlike many other important Old Testament prophecies, there is no immediate fulfillment in Israel before its long-term fulfillment in Jesus. For example, God's promise to raise up a "Son of David" from David's own body to reign in his place (2 Sam 7:12) had an immediate fulfillment in the lineage of kings that followed, but its ultimate fulfillment was in Jesus Christ. However, any effort must fail that seeks to find in the national life of Israel or in some other personage from history a fulfillment of the amazing words of Isaiah 53. For the central message of this prophecy is of substitutionary atonement, the death of an innocent substitute for the sins of his people. Isaiah could never see in the nation of Israel an *innocent substitute* for the sins of the world. Chapter after chapter of Isaiah has specifically denounced the nation's wickedness. Furthermore, one verse forever closes out the "Israel is the Suffering Servant" interpretation, and that is Isaiah 53:8: "He was struck because of *my people's* rebellion" (emphasis added). Who is "my people" to Isaiah the prophet if not Judah and Israel? And who is the "he" struck for the rebellion of Isaiah's people? Finally, this matter was settled for us in Acts 8. The Ethiopian eunuch was reading Isaiah 53:7-8 and queried the evangelist Philip, "I ask you, who is the prophet saying this about—himself or someone else?" The very next verse settles forever the question for Christians: "Philip proceeded to tell him the good news *about Jesus,* beginning with *that Scripture*" (Acts 8:34-35; emphasis added). Isaiah 53 is "about Jesus" and no one else.

Isaiah 53 Is a Miracle

In 1947 a Bedouin shepherd boy named Muhammad climbed into a cave near Jericho and discovered the greatest archaeological find of the twentieth century: the Dead Sea scrolls. The largest of them was the Isaiah scroll; carbon-14 dating sets its age at least as old as 230 BC—"*before* Christ," that is. Actually, the prophecy itself was originally made seven centuries before Jesus was born. And that makes Isaiah 53 a miracle!

Why do I say that? C. S. Lewis defines a miracle as "an interference with Nature by a supernatural power" (*Miracles*, 5). Lewis specifically discusses prophetic predictions as miracles because they defy the natural order of time. Repeatedly in Isaiah 44–45 we see God's power to predict the future, especially in the case of Cyrus. But the substitutionary death and resurrection of Jesus Christ are the greatest events in redemptive history and of infinitely greater significance than anything Cyrus did. God's ability to predict the future comes to its pinnacle in Isaiah 53, and its clear prediction of the purpose and details of Jesus's death, burial, and resurrection shine like a miraculous beacon to us sinners.

The Central Message: Substitutionary Atonement

As already noted, the central message of Isaiah 53 is substitutionary atonement. This was the central message of the whole animal sacrificial system, that the blood of a substitute can remove the death penalty for sin. Penal substitution depends on God's power to transfer guilt to an innocent substitute, symbolized in Leviticus 16:21 when Aaron puts his hands on the head of the animal in order to "put [Israel's sins] on the goat's head." Though this transfer of guilt is mysterious, God claims the right to do it, and without it we have no hope.

No passage in the Bible is so pervaded with substitution language as this one. It is especially clear in Isaiah 53:4-6. Here is proclaimed to the whole world for all time the way by which a holy God can justify rebellious sinners and still be just. A partner to this central theme is the reception of this justification by faith alone, as the apostle Paul made plain by quoting verse 1 in Romans 10:16, "Lord, who has *believed* our message?" (emphasis added) followed immediately with the assertion, "Faith comes from what is heard, and what is heard comes through the message about Christ" (v. 17). Earlier, in Romans 3:28, Paul asserted plainly that sinners are justified by faith in Christ apart from works of the law. This is the gospel, the only hope we sinners have of salvation before a holy God.

Christ Repulsive but Redemptive then Exalted
ISAIAH 52:13-15

First, it is reasonable to include the last three verses of Isaiah 52 with the comments on Isaiah 53. John Calvin called the chapter division a "dismemberment" (*Commentaries*, 111), and I concur. The same Suffering Servant is the focus of all fifteen of these verses.

The section begins with the words, "See, my servant." This is the fourth of the "Suffering Servant" passages (see 42:1-4; 49:1-7; 50:4-9). The other passages portrayed a gentle Savior who would build a worldwide kingdom (including Gentiles) but who would overcome great difficulties in doing it. Here in this chapter we learn why the servant had to suffer: because of the sins of his people. So the word *see* (Hb *hinneh*) shows the dramatic unveiling of Christ. And we are told immediately that the servant of the Lord, Jesus Christ, will "be successful" and will be "raised and lifted up and greatly exalted." The passage begins where Christ ends—in glorious exaltation, having triumphed in his mission to save sinners. The first assertion, that Christ will be successful, has the connotation of an outcome that occurs as a result of wise, skillful actions. The next three verbs build to a climax of the exaltation Christ deserves for his obedience. Because Christ died, he deserves the highest place (Phil 2:9).

Isaiah immediately turns from the exaltation to the abject humiliation that Christ would have to endure to save sinners from the wrath of God. Christ's appearance would be so disfigured that onlookers would wonder if he was even human (v. 14). This refers to the repulsive effects of scourging and crucifixion on the human body, how Jesus's bones would be out of joint and how his body would be covered with blood.

Verse 15 gives us the outcome of his suffering: the "sprinkling" of many nations. Leviticus uses this verb to speak of the application of atoning blood to cleanse sinners from their impurity (Lev 16:14-15). This technical term predicts the blood atonement by Jesus Christ for the elect from every nation, as Revelation 5:9 sings to Jesus in heavenly praise: "You are worthy . . . because you were slaughtered, and you purchased people for God *by your blood* from every tribe and language and people and nation" (emphasis added). This "sprinkling" of the nations occurs by the verbal proclamation of the gospel all over the earth, including to kings, who are amazed and speechless at the message about Christ (v. 15). Envoys will travel over the surface of the globe and tell all nations a saving message they've never heard before, and they will "see" it (by faith) and understand it. Thus are they "sprinkled" and forgiven.

Christ the "Arm of the Lord" but Human and Despised
ISAIAH 53:1-3

Now Isaiah immediately turns to the content of this message itself and the need for all hearers to combine it with faith. He asks, "Who has *believed* what we have heard? And to whom has the arm of the LORD been *revealed*?" (emphasis added). The "arm of the LORD" represents his awesome power, yet in this context it speaks of the infinitely mysterious *frailty* of the incarnate Son of God, whose seeming weakness in death was the most powerful thing that has ever occurred in human history. And if the Spirit does not *reveal* Isaiah 53 to a hearer, that person will never *believe* this message.

Verses 2-3 trace out, in effect, the biography of Jesus Christ in the wonder of his incarnation. The humanity of Christ is established in unmistakable terms, for he *grew up* before God (Luke 2:52), starting small and weak like a young plant. He was also a "root out of dry ground," an allusion to the shoot that would grow from the stump of Jesse (Isa 11:1). Jesus would be born in a time when being a "Son of David" (like Joseph, Matt 1:20) meant almost nothing because the Romans dominated the Jews. Jesus's appearance was completely unimpressive; he looked like any normal Jewish man. The glory of Jesus (John 1:14) was visible only to believers, who saw it in his sinless life, his compassionate demeanor, his powerful miracles, and his matchless words. Actually, Jesus's ordinary appearance as a man was the essence of the stumbling block he presented to the Jews: "We are stoning you . . . for blasphemy, because you—being a *man*—make yourself God" (John 10:33; emphasis added).

So Jesus was "despised and rejected" (v. 3) by his own people (John 1:11) and by the Gentiles. The word *despised* means to be grossly underestimated, and never has it been truer than when applied to Jesus Christ. His own people legally condemned him when he was on trial before Annas and again before Pilate. So also today, Jesus is the most despised and rejected man in history.

Christ Rejected but Our Atoning Substitute
ISAIAH 53:4-6

Jesus was also called "a man of suffering" (v. 3), deeply acquainted with every misery of the human race. Day after day he would stand and heal a river of suffering people one at a time (Matt 4:24; 12:15; etc.). Like a hiker who sees a friend bitten by a rattlesnake and who immediately sucks the poison out of his leg with his own mouth, so Jesus "bore our sicknesses" (v. 4). Jesus physically healed every disease he encountered, but that was also a picture of the deeper spiritual healing Jesus came to do. For we were "dead in [our] trespasses and sins in which [we] previously lived" (Eph 2:1), and Christ has borne our sicknesses and carried our pains. The word *bore* gives us the picture of a mighty Samson, who picked up the gates of Gaza and carried them to the top of a mountain (Judg 16:1-3). Jesus is mightier than Samson, carrying our sins up Golgotha.

So Jesus's central mission was not to perform temporary healings for people who would later die anyway. Many preachers have misread Isaiah 53:4-5 and concluded that Christ's atonement guarantees physical healing in this present age if we have faith to believe it. Rather, Christ's mission was to die on the cross as a substitute for the sins of his people, winning eternal life in a future world where disease and death will be abolished forever. Jesus's death would be misunderstood by onlookers, who would assume that he was dying for his blasphemy. "But he was pierced because of our rebellion, crushed because of our iniquities; punishment for our peace was on him, and we are healed by his wounds" (v. 5). Four great assertions of substitution in one amazing verse! "He" and "we" are continually in view: our sins, his suffering. The transfer of guilt—this is the essence of substitutionary atonement, and without it, we have no salvation. Note our condition: steeped in rebellion and iniquities, deserving a death penalty, at war with God, needing deep healing. All of our shortcomings were transferred to Christ at the cross. And note the specific word *pierced* in verse 5. This is a word whose force cannot be evaded, for three times in prophecy the idea of the piercing of Christ is asserted (Ps 22:16; Zech 12:10). Jesus's punishment wins us peace with God (Rom 5:1). And the wounding of Christ heals us perfectly and eternally from all the damage sin has done. This healing comes in stages: justification then sanctification then glorification. Only in our future resurrection and our life in the new heaven and new earth will our healing be complete.

Verse 6 captures in picturesque language our continual sheeplike wandering in sin; the essence of it is a determined pursuit of "our own way" in everything we do. Christ paid the penalty for that wandering.

Christ Innocent but Willing to Be Slaughtered
ISAIAH 53:7-9

The words *oppressed and afflicted* (v. 7) speak of Christ being overpowered like the Hebrews were when the Egyptians enslaved them ruthlessly. So we see this in Jesus being beaten to a bloody pulp, spat on, mocked with the crown of thorns and purple robe, led through the public streets of Jerusalem, screamed at by the crowd, stripped, and nailed, lifted up, crucified, in agony. "Oppressed and afflicted" describes the single greatest display of human injustice in all history. Yet amazingly, it is also the greatest display of God's justice in all history:

> *God presented [Christ] as an atoning sacrifice . . . to demonstrate*
> *his righteousness at the present time, so that he would be righteous*
> *and declare righteous the one who has faith in Jesus.* (Rom 3:25-26;
> emphasis added)

In other words: God would rather slaughter his own beloved Son than allow guilty sinners like us into heaven unatoned for! There has never been a greater display of God's justice in all history, nor of humanity's injustice.

Yet in all of this human injustice, Jesus did not open his mouth; he remained silent and accepted the punishment because, as our substitute, he was acting as if he were truly guilty. Were we judged, we could not answer God once in a thousand times (Job 9:3). So Jesus's silence and his meekly following his captors to his own execution (though he could have destroyed them all in an instant) speaks powerfully of his *willingly* laying down his life for us all. Unlike a dumb animal that has no idea what is about to happen, Jesus made a conscious decision to die for us, and thus his work was declared "one man's obedience," that of a new Adam, by which the disobedience of the former Adam was overwhelmed (Rom 5:19).

Isaiah 53:8-9 also asserts that this Suffering Servant would actually die for the sins of his people. He was "cut off from the land of the living" and "assigned a grave with the wicked." From the garden of Eden, God established that the "wages of sin is death" (Rom 6:23), and only by dying could our substitute pay the just penalty for our sins. Verse 9 also asserts that Jesus would die an innocent man. Peter cited this verse to proclaim Jesus's sinlessness: "He did not commit sin, and no deceit was found in his mouth" (1 Pet 2:22). If Jesus had not been sinless, suffering in our place would not have accomplished anything. Finally, verse 9 also predicts Jesus's burial in the tomb of a rich man, fulfilled when Joseph of Arimathea buried him with royal treatment in his own new tomb (John 19:38-41). These details cannot be explained away, and they completely preclude the "Israel is the Suffering Servant" interpretation.

Christ Crushed So We Could Be Justified
ISAIAH 53:10-12

In verse 10 we come on the deepest and most mysterious aspect of the substitutionary atonement of Jesus—the Father's *pleasure* in the crushing of his Son and making him suffer. This is an infinitely sublime concept, for any human father who delighted in crushing his own son would be accounted as the vilest monster. But Scripture teaches us that the love God the Father has for his only begotten Son is so fierce and powerful that the blazing of the sun cannot touch it for intensity. The best explanation of this is Jesus's own attitude toward the cross in Hebrews 12:2: "For the joy that lay before him, he endured the cross, despising the shame." The delight of the Father in Isaiah 53:10 is the same as the joy of the Son in Hebrews 12:2—not the cross itself but the glory it would win for God and the salvation it would work for a multitude greater than anyone could count from every nation on earth (Rev 7:9). The actual torture of Jesus was an agony beyond measure for the Father, as he showed by darkening the skies eerily and by shaking the ground when his Son died. This was immeasurable pain, followed by infinite pleasure and joy.

And the results of this agony are clear: "seed," children for Abraham and for God. This is "the LORD's pleasure [that] will be accomplished" (v. 10). I picture the Father having composed a magnificent violin concerto with every note penned by his sovereign will then handing it to his skillful Son who played it to perfection, filling the world with a music so sublime we will be melting to its melody for all eternity. And despite all the anguish of his soul (v. 11), Jesus would see the final success of God's plan and be deeply satisfied with what he achieved. For by his death Jesus has justified the ungodly (v. 11; Rom 4:5). In Isaiah 53:12 the link between Jesus's atoning death and his constant intercession is made clear—those Jesus died for he also prays for. The image of Jesus at the right hand of God interceding for us (Rom 8:34) is comforting to us who still battle constantly against the world, the flesh, and the devil.

The section ends where it began, exalting Jesus Christ. God assigns to Jesus the elect from the whole earth as the "spoil" he has plundered from his enemy. And those saved souls will spend eternity bowing their knees before Jesus Christ, to the glory of God the Father.

Applications

This chapter builds faith in those who hear it all over the earth, if God wills to reveal Jesus Christ by the Holy Spirit. The fact that it speaks so plainly of Christ's substitutionary death seven centuries before Christ is evidence of the supernatural origin not only of the book of Isaiah but, indeed, of the whole Bible. So this has evangelistic and apologetic power; we should quote its details to lost people. We should also build our own faith in Jesus daily by pondering Isaiah 53:5-6. This will humble us and also exalt us.

We should find eternal security in these few verses as well, for God made a plan for our salvation before the foundation of the world and predicted it clearly through Isaiah. Jesus achieved it two thousand years ago. And Jesus is at the right hand of God, interceding for us until we are at last with him in heaven.

We should use this chapter as grounds for personal and corporate worship. Hymn writers should continue to do what they've been doing for twenty centuries—using the ideas from these fifteen verses to write new hymns of praise to God.

Finally, we should seek by the Spirit to imitate Christ's full obedience to the Father, for though we will not be called on to die a substitutionary death for anyone, yet our service in taking the gospel to the ends of the earth will require a similar taking up of our cross daily and following Jesus.

Reflect and Discuss

1. How would you define a "miracle," and how does this chapter meet that definition?
2. How could meditating more on Isaiah 53 help strengthen your faith in Christ? How could it help enrich your worship life?
3. Isaiah 52:13 speaks of Christ being "raised and lifted up and greatly exalted." How does that relate to Philippians 2:9?
4. In what way was Christ disfigured beyond a normal human being? How does this verse (v. 14) make the agony of the cross even more vivid?
5. How does verse 15 speak of worldwide missions in Jesus's name?
6. In what way is it true that the Father must reveal Christ as the "arm of the LORD" or people will never see it?
7. How does Isaiah 53:2-3 give us a brief biography of Jesus Christ? How was Jesus like a "root out of dry ground"?
8. How are verses 4-6 crystal clear about substitutionary atonement—Christ dying in our place? How is this the center of the gospel?
9. Why is it vital to see Christ's willingness to die in our place (v. 7) and his innocence (v. 9)? Why are both of these vital for our salvation?
10. How do you understand the mystery of the Father's pleasure in crushing his Son (v. 10)? How does Hebrews 12:2 perhaps help us understand it better?

God's Grace in Christ Makes Zion Glorious

ISAIAH 54

"Rejoice, childless one, who did not give birth; burst into song and shout, you who have not been in labor! For the children of the desolate one will be more than the children of the married woman," says the LORD. (Isa 54:1)

Main Idea: Zion is pictured as both a woman (formerly barren, now fruitful) and a city (formerly destroyed, now rebuilt). These are ultimately pictures of the new Jerusalem, the bride of Christ, in eternal glory.

I. Zion, a Formerly Barren Woman, Is Now Supernaturally Fruitful (54:1-5).
   A. Rejoice! You will no longer be barren.
   B. Get ready for many children.
   C. Your time of disgrace is over forever.

II. Zion, a Formerly Rejected Wife, Is Now Restored in Covenant Love (54:5-10).
   A. The many names of God
   B. Israel a rejected wife: because of idolatry
   C. God tenderly restores the sinful wife.

III. Zion, a Formerly Destroyed City, Will Be Beautiful and Secure (54:11-17).
   A. Zion's past afflictions
   B. Zion's future glory
   C. Zion's future security

Introduction: "Expect Great Things from God; Attempt Great Things for God!"

On Wednesday, May 30, 1792, at Friar Lane Baptist Chapel, Nottingham, England, a leatherworker named William Carey preached one of the most influential sermons in history. The text was Isaiah 54:2-3: "Enlarge the site of your tent. . . . For you will spread out to the right and to the left, and your descendants will dispossess nations and inhabit desolate cities." Carey argued that this text refers to spreading the gospel of Christ to the ends of the earth. His so-called deathless sermon had two exhortations: (1) expect great things from God; (2) attempt great things for God (Walker, *William Carey*, 78–80). This slogan helped launch the modern missionary movement.

Now, we might well wonder how in the world Carey came to the conclusion that Isaiah 54:2-3 was talking about the growth of the church through missions. It is an Old Testament prophecy in language that any Jew would have recognized as referring to Zion, i.e., Jerusalem, the city of God on earth, the Jewish nation's capital city. What right did William Carey have to think Isaiah 54 was talking about missions?

To answer that, we go to Galatians 4, where the apostle Paul gives us the interpretive key to Isaiah 54. Paul was writing to Gentile converts to Christ who were being led astray into a false gospel mixing Jewish legalism with faith in Christ. Paul pleaded with them to return to the true gospel of justification by faith in Christ apart from works of the law. He proved that Abraham, the father of the Jewish nation, was justified by hearing a promise and believing it, just as they had been. He also made plain that Gentile Christians were truly sons and daughters of Abraham by faith. In Galatians 4:22-28 Paul turns to a spiritual allegory to teach them that the true sons of Abraham are born again by the power of the Holy Spirit, not by biology or by circumcision. He speaks of two women, the slave woman and the free woman. The slave woman (Hagar) bears children in the ordinary way, and they are slaves. They represent Jews who do not trust in Christ and who try to earn their salvation by works of the law. He says that Hagar represents the present (physical) city of Jerusalem because she is in bondage along with her children. "But the Jerusalem above is free, and she is our mother" (Gal 4:26). There, Paul uses a strange, mixed metaphor: *a city that is a mother*. He then quotes Isaiah 54:1: "For it is written: 'Rejoice, childless woman . . . for the children of the desolate woman will be many, more numerous than those of the woman who has a husband'" (Gal 4:27). In other words, Gentiles who believe in Christ have been supernaturally born again and are children of the mother city "Jerusalem above," the heavenly Zion (Heb 12:22).

So although there is an immediate fulfillment of Isaiah 54 in the restoration of the physical city of Jerusalem by the exiles streaming back from Babylon (and to ignore that theme makes certain aspects of Isaiah 54 unintelligible), yet to stop there is to miss the power of what Paul sees in Isaiah 54 as recorded in Galatians 4. Paul, in reaching for Isaiah 54:1

to support this point, is giving us permission to see the spread of the gospel of Jesus Christ to the ends of the earth in Isaiah's joyful command to Zion to enlarge her tent and get ready for lots of children. William Carey was spot-on in his sermon! Every person born anew by the Spirit enlarges the heavenly Zion. The final population will be a multitude no one can number from every nation on earth (Rev 7:9).

Zion, a Formerly Barren Woman, Is Now Supernaturally Fruitful
ISAIAH 54:1-5

Actually, the word *Zion* does not appear in this chapter, but it is reasonable to see overwhelming thematic similarity between these verses and Isaiah 52, in which Zion is mentioned four times. In Isaiah 54:1-5 the Lord gives Zion a series of vigorous commands, staccato in rhythm, and all have to do with the overwhelming joy Zion should have at the sovereign God blessing her: Rejoice! Burst into song! Shout! Enlarge your tent! Do not be afraid! Don't be humiliated!

Here Zion is pictured as a formerly barren woman who is about to give birth to more children than she can count. God is saying Israel had been spiritually barren, not spreading the knowledge of the true God to all nations. His judgment fell on Israel for her idolatry, and she was exiled. But now God is going to work an overwhelming reversal in Zion's fortunes, and she who was once barren will be bearing a vast number of children. For Zion to be told to "enlarge the site of your tent . . . do not hold back," is to say, "You are about to have a family so huge it will stagger your imagination!"

Of course, the return of the exiles from Babylon to rebuild the rubble-filled city of Jerusalem was an immediate fulfillment. But it is insufficient. Only forty-two thousand Jews returned with Ezra. And though the resumption of Israel's history in the promised land was significant, it was merely the setting of the stage for the real drama to come: the atoning death and glorious resurrection of Jesus Christ as predicted in Isaiah 53. So the outpouring of the Spirit on the church in Jerusalem on the day of Pentecost unleashed the forces that would result in the fulfillment of Isaiah 54:2-3. Missionaries have been taking that gospel to the most distant reaches of the earth, and the church of Jesus Christ numbers now in the hundreds of millions.

Zion, a Formerly Rejected Wife, Is Now Restored in Covenant Love

ISAIAH 54:5-10

The second image of this chapter is of a formerly rejected wife, now restored to her husband in covenant love. God's complex relationship to Israel is reflected in the many names God gives himself: (1) Husband, (2) Maker, (3) Lord of Armies, (4) the Holy One of Israel, (5) Redeemer, (6) the God of the whole earth. Each of these names reveals a certain aspect of God's love relationship with Israel in the old covenant and with the church in the new covenant. No one image captures all aspects. But the predominant theme in verses 5-10 is of a formerly enraged husband who now tenderly calls his sinful wife back into his arms.

The prophet Hosea was tasked with marrying a prostitute and living out in his own marriage what God felt like when Israel strayed into idolatry. God's jealousy was kindled, and "in a surge of anger" he "deserted" and hid his face from his bride (vv. 7-8). But now, that "brief moment" (seventy years—a blink of an eye in God's time) has passed. God the husband was tenderly bringing her back, forgiving her, restoring her in covenant love, like the day the rainbow proved to Noah that God's wrath had been spent (vv. 9-10).

So Israel's restoration after the exile lines up with these words. But how can these words relate to Gentile converts to Christ? Well, in a way Israel in the promised land represented all nations, similar to the way Adam represented all individuals in the garden of Eden. So all nations should feel ashamed of Israel's idolatries and betrayal of her Maker/ Husband, for we were no different. We were all lusting after idols (Rom 1:25), and so Israel's spiritual adulteries are ours, her shame is ours, and so is her redemption.

Zion, a Formerly Destroyed City, Will Be Beautiful and Secure

ISAIAH 54:11-17

The final image in this chapter is of a formerly devastated city now spectacularly rebuilt, with a beauty that far exceeds its former glory. Jerusalem was storm-tossed (v. 11) by her Gentile invaders and destroyers, left as a smoldering pile of rubble. But in the sovereign plan of God, this troubled city will be rebuilt, with foundations set in lapis lazuli, battlements of rubies, gates of sparkling stones, and all her walls of precious stones (v. 12). These are the very images seen in Revelation 21 of the new Jerusalem that will descend gloriously from heaven, ready for her wedding day—a beautiful bride, a glorious city, the same vision in Isaiah 54.

This radiant city will be filled with the children verses 2-3 mentioned (v. 13), and they will all be taught by the Lord and will know him intimately (Jer 31:34). They will be stunningly prosperous, perfectly secure, established in the righteousness of Christ (Isa 54:14). The city will never again be terrified by invasion or siege, for all her enemies will be destroyed (v. 15). The new Jerusalem's perfect security is the church's final destination, when the gates of the walls will always stand open, for there is no threat at all. But the implication of triumph over an enemy who might assault, an enemy who might forge a weapon against Zion, speaks also to the present church age, when the "church militant" advances to win the lost, overcoming the attacks of the world, the flesh, and the devil. God is well aware of the skill of Zion's enemies, for there is no skill, no power, no weapon that God did not first conceive (v. 16). So God knows their limitations as well. No accusation will succeed, for all will be answered by the imputed righteousness of Christ. As Paul writes, "Who can bring an accusation against God's elect? God is the one who justifies. Who is the one who condemns?" (Rom 8:33-34).

Applications

The best two applications we can take from this chapter come from William Carey: (1) expect great things from God; (2) attempt great things for God. This chapter is indeed about the spread of the gospel to the ends of the earth, beginning from Jerusalem (Luke 24:47). For us to live our lives indifferent about missions, ignorant of what God is doing among the unreached peoples of the earth, excited instead about sports or hobbies or food or careers, is to open ourselves up to great shame on judgment day. We should live daily expectant of God doing great things to redeem his elect from every tribe, language, people, and nation. Second, we should attempt bold things for the spread of the gospel. For immature Christians who have been living the secular dream in the pampered West, it begins with great repentance at former indifference and sinful indulgence. It moves on from there to whatever God may call you to attempt for his glory in missions. It might be to reach out in your own city to some marginalized urban poor or to find an unreached people group that has settled in your city and begin to befriend them. Attempt great things for God in terms of intelligent prayer and sacrificial giving to missions. And if you are feeling pulled to go overseas, whether short or long term, do not quench the Spirit! Attempt something you never thought you would do—get on a plane and go to some uncomfortable place and see how God might choose to use you.

Reflect and Discuss

1. William Carey based his "deathless sermon" on this text, in which he urged hearers to dive into missions: "Expect great things from God; attempt great things for God." How do you see missions in verses 1-3? How does Carey's slogan challenge you to be more involved in missions?

2. The apostle Paul used this chapter in Galatians 4:22-28. Read that section again. What is the "Jerusalem that is above" in that passage? What is the Jerusalem that is below? How does this give us an insight into Isaiah 54?

3. How does Isaiah 54 address the actual historical setting of the city of Jerusalem at the time of the exile to Babylon? What does the fact that God ordained the rebuilding of Jerusalem despite the amazing obstacles teach you about God?

4. Verses 2-3 imply a huge number of "children" being born to "mother Zion" (Rev 7:9). How should this encourage us to risk great things for the spread of the gospel?

5. God speaks of a brief "surge of anger" toward Israel in Isaiah 54:7-8. What does this teach you about God's anger toward his children? How does it relate to God's discipline of us when we sin (Heb 12)?

6. Verses 9-10 liken this period of the restoration of Israel after the exile to the time after the flood. What is the similarity?

7. Verses 11-12 are quite similar to Revelation 21:10-14. Talk about that similarity. Talk about the future glory and beauty of the new Jerusalem.

8. How does Isaiah 54:13-14 speak of our "education" in the new covenant and our future knowledge of God in heaven? How do these verses relate to Hebrews 8:11?

9. How do verses 15-17 speak of the future peace and security we will experience in heaven? How could these verses comfort the persecuted church in the Muslim world?

10. How does Isaiah 54 build up your faith in God's awesome and sovereign plan? How could it help you go through trials well? How could it motivate you to serve him better?

All Are Invited to an Eternal Feast

ISAIAH 55

Come, everyone who is thirsty, come to the water; and you without
silver, come, buy, and eat! Come, buy wine and milk without silver
and without cost! (Isa 55:1)

Main Idea: God calls on poor, thirsty, hungry souls to a rich, free banquet—salvation in Christ!

I. **God's Invitation: Come to the Feast (55:1-5)!**
    A. Who is invited? Thirsty, dissatisfied beggars
    B. What is the fare? Water, milk, wine, choicest foods
    C. What is the cost? Free!
II. **God's Command: Seek Me Now (55:6-9)!**
    A. Seek the Lord while he may be found.
    B. Forsake your wickedness.
    C. God's lavish forgiveness soars above us.
III. **God's Provision: His Word Is Powerfully Effective (55:10-13).**
    A. God's word is like the rain: powerfully effective.
    B. God's messengers go out with joy.
    C. The future world will be free from the curse.

God's Invitation: Come to the Feast!

ISAIAH 55:1-5

In 1845 Hans Christian Andersen wrote a short story called "The Little
Match Girl" in which a poor, young girl ventures out into the city
streets on a cold New Year's Eve to sell matches. She suffers badly from
the cold but is terrified to go home without selling any matches because
her father will beat her. As she makes her way through the cold, dark
streets, she looks in the windows of wealthy homes and sees feasts of suc-
culent delicacies, but no one notices her and invites her in. She finds
a nook and starts to light her matches one by one to cheer and warm
herself. In the dancing light of the matches, she imagines sitting at a
rich banquet herself and enjoying the food and warmth. The story ends
tragically as she dies out in the cold.

I have often thought of the gospel invitation to come to Christ in the light of that sad story. The Scripture pictures us sinners as on the outside of the kingdom, needing to enter in order to be saved. Inside the kingdom there is a lavish feast of blessing. Outside there is nothing but darkness, misery, and suffering. Jesus told a parable of a king who desired to throw a lavish wedding banquet for his son, and he sent messengers to invite people to come, but everyone who was invited refused to come (Matt 22:1-14). In many ways this story is more tragic than "The Little Match Girl," for the blindness that causes us to refuse such an amazing invitation is the root issue of our plight before a holy God. In Isaiah 55 God is extending an urgent invitation to sinners all over the world to come to Christ and feast. The only question for each of us is, Will we enter while there's time?

The chapter begins with an invitation to a feast offered to thirsty beggars who have no money (v. 1). It is also offered to people who do have resources but are foolishly squandering them on things that do not ultimately satisfy (v. 2). This royal feast offers first the beverages then the "choicest of foods." The three beverages focused on are water, wine, and milk. These three represent different aspects of what Christ yearns to do for our souls.

Christ offers **water** to souls dying of thirst. Water represents life, for without it we die. Jesus promised the thirsty person, "The water I will give him will become a well of water springing up in him for eternal life" (John 4:14). Secondly, he is offering **milk**, which represents nourishment, like an infant gets from his mother. Peter commands Christians, "Like newborn infants, desire the pure milk of the word, so that you may grow up into your salvation" (1 Pet 2:2). Finally, Christ offers **wine**, which has the power to give joyful celebration. Jesus changed the water into wine at the wedding in Cana to enable them to celebrate freely. All people need not only bread and water merely to exist but something that enables them to sing and dance and leap for joy. In Ephesians 5:18 we are warned not to get drunk on wine but to be filled with the Spirit.

So Christ reasons with us, begging us to stop wasting our lives on things that will never satisfy. He pleads with us to come in out of the cold and have a seat at his banqueting table, and he will satisfy our hearts with water, milk, wine, and the choicest of foods. And the price is astonishing: zero for us but infinite for him, for Jesus paid his blood for this feast. So we are to "buy" it without money, meaning to commit to it by faith, knowing that God himself is the one who gave us that faith.

Verses 3-5 identify the basis of this rich invitation: the covenant blessings God promised to David. The "Son of David" who will rule eternally on David's throne (2 Sam 7) is Jesus Christ, and in his name nations who have never heard of the God of Abraham will come running to Christ and find a place prepared for them at God's feast.

God's Command: Seek Me Now!
ISAIAH 55:6-9

Having invited the poor sinners of the world to sit at his banquet, in verses 6-9 he sharpens the sense of urgency that they do so immediately. Verse 6 commands sinners to "seek the LORD while he may be found" and to "call to him while he is near." To call on Christ for forgiveness is essential to our salvation, for "everyone who calls on the name of the Lord will be saved" (Rom 10:13). But the real issue here is urgency: sinners must seek the Lord and call on his name "while he may be found." This is a clear warning that the opportunity to come in from the cold and sit in God's warm banqueting hall will not last forever. "Now is the day of salvation" (2 Cor 6:2). God will not always stand extending his hand of gracious invitation to sinners to enter his feast. There will come an end—either at the sinner's death or at the second coming of Christ—and then it will be too late.

To accept this gracious invitation to the feast, the sinner must "abandon his way and . . . his thoughts" (Isa 55:7). The mind of the flesh is death, hostile to God (Rom 8:6). In order for a spiritual beggar to come in from the cold, he must repent, forsaking his wicked thoughts and corrupt lifestyle. And if we do, God will have compassion on us and will "freely forgive" (Isa 55:7). In verse 8 God asserts that his thoughts are not our thoughts, neither are his ways our ways. Actually, God says, "as heaven is higher than earth, so my ways are higher than your ways, and my thoughts than your thoughts" (v. 9). What an amazing assertion! I read once of an Argentinian chess grandmaster named Miguel Najdorf who in 1947 played forty-five games simultaneously *while blindfolded* (Hearst and Knott, *Blindfold Chess*, 25)! That was the most amazing mental achievement that I've ever heard of by a human being. But today God actively controls the events of the daily lives of seven billion people on earth, skillfully orchestrating their free decisions into his eternal plan. God's mind is as far above ours as the stars are above the surface of the earth.

Verse 8 begins with the word *For*, making a connection with verse 7, and there are two ways to look at that connection: (1) We should forsake our wicked ways and thoughts (v. 7a), *for* God's ways and thoughts are not evil like ours but are holy and exalted; or (2) God's lavish forgiveness (v. 7b) is so astonishing that it soars above ours as far as heaven is above the earth. God is really, really good at forgiveness; we generally are not. Either way, we come away in awe at how lofty God is and how gracious to invite sinners like us to sit at his banqueting table!

God's Provision: His Word Is Powerfully Effective
ISAIAH 55:10-13

The final section highlights the power of God's word—his instruction, promises, and warnings—to produce the transformation needed for sinners like us. Again, verse 10 starts with the word *For*, meaning God is continuing his train of thought. The lavish pardon and the invitation to his feast he offers are communicated to us in his word. He compares his word to the "rain and the snow" that fall from heaven and do not return to it without watering the earth, making its plants sprout. In the same way, God sends forth his word by the power of the Holy Spirit. It makes a circular trip like the cycle of precipitation: "For from him and through him and [back] to him are all things" (Rom 11:36). And God is asserting that it will never return to him having accomplished nothing but will most certainly achieve what he sent it to do.

Because this is always true, we must realize that God is either showing mercy by the sending of his word or he is hardening sinners by that same word (Rom 9:18). That is the only way to see that God's word *never* returns to him without results but *always* achieves the purpose for which he sent it. As the invitation to come to God's banquet is published far and wide in this world, it is obvious that most people reject it (as the parable of the Wedding Feast of Matt 22 asserts). God wills to harden some by the invitation to sit at his table, and he also wills to show mercy to his elect. To some people, evangelists are the fragrance of Christ; to others they are the stench of death (2 Cor 2:15-16).

So Isaiah 55:12 may be speaking of the experience of missionaries and evangelists sent out to summon people to Christ's banqueting table. They will go out with joy, and the Holy Spirit will peacefully guide them. But the ultimate end of the gospel is the joy of the redeemed in the new heaven and new earth. The language of verse 13 is of the complete removal of

Adam's curse: "Instead of the thornbush, a cypress will come up." The curse on the earth will be gone forever, and those who feast in the kingdom of heaven will look on a perfected earth and will glorify God.

Applications

This chapter completes an amazing run of chapters in Isaiah. Isaiah 53 spoke so clearly of the substitutionary work of Jesus Christ for us sinners, Isaiah 54 proclaimed the need for Zion to expand because of the vast numbers of Gentiles who would enter, and Isaiah 55 calls sinners from every nation on earth to forsake sin while there's still time and find a feast of grace and forgiveness in the kingdom of Christ.

So evangelists and missionaries should make full use of this chapter to call sinners to repentance and faith in Christ. Pastors should appeal to their congregations to feast on Christ and to stop glutting themselves on materialism, which does not satisfy. We should press on to an ever-greater seeking of Christ in daily quiet times, to "seek the LORD while he may be found" (Isa 55:6) early in the morning as Christ sought his Father while it was still dark (Mark 1:35). This chapter can also be used to convict and warn the "almost persuaded" person who is presuming on a future time when they will come to Christ. They may die before that day ever comes.

This chapter also should urge us to seek life, nourishment, and joy (water, milk, and wine) in the Word of God. Just as the plants need the rain, so our growing souls need God's Word.

Finally, this chapter should cause us to be more diligent in evangelism, going out with joy and being peacefully guided (v. 12) to invite lost people into the banqueting hall in Christ.

Reflect and Discuss

1. How does this chapter cause you to thank God for his mercy to you in Christ?
2. How do the invitations of verses 1-3 (a series of strong commands from God) help us to focus our hearts "on things above, not on earthly things" (Col 3:1-2)?
3. What are the differences between water, milk, and wine? How is Christ the fulfillment of each of these in our souls?
4. Why is it vital for us to realize that we must receive the feast "without silver and without cost"? How is it helpful to realize that, while the feast costs us nothing, it cost Christ everything?

5. How is Christ the fulfillment of the covenant God made with David in 2 Samuel 7, to which Isaiah 55:3-5 refers? How does that covenant relate to the feast of verses 1-3?

6. What does it mean to "seek the LORD *while he may be found*"? How does it relate to 2 Corinthians 6:2?

7. Why is it imperative for sinners who want to sit at God's banqueting table to forsake their evil ways and wicked thoughts?

8. What does God mean when he says, "As heaven is higher than earth, so are my ways higher than your ways, and my thoughts than your thoughts" (v. 9)? How does that relate to our wicked ways and thoughts (v. 7a)? How does it relate to God's abundant forgiveness (v. 7b)? How is God infinitely better at forgiveness than we are?

9. How does God's word never fail to achieve what he sent it to do (vv. 10-11)? If most people who are invited to God's feast reject it, how can it be true that God's word never fails to achieve the purpose for which he sent it? How do Romans 9:18 and Matthew 22:14 help to answer this?

10. How does Isaiah 55:12-13 relate to missions in this present age? How does it also give us a foretaste of what it will be like to explore the perfect beauty of the new earth God will create?

The Wheat and the Weeds: Holy Living in a Mixed-up World

ISAIAH 56–57

For the High and Exalted One, who lives forever, whose name is holy, says this: "I live in a high and holy place, and with the oppressed and lowly of spirit, to revive the spirit of the lowly and revive the heart of the oppressed." (Isa 57:15)

Main Idea: The people of the world are mixed like wheat with weeds; the humble "wheat" will be gathered to live with God eternally; the idolatrous "weeds" will be blown away.

I.   **The Wheat: Humble Outcasts Welcomed (56:1-8)**
   A.   Living in light of God's coming righteousness (56:1-2)
   B.   Humble outcasts welcomed to God's house (56:3-8)

II. **The Weeds: Self-Indulgent Leaders Devoured (56:9-12)**
   A.   Invitation to beasts to devour (56:9)
   B.   Israel's self-indulgent leaders (56:10-12)

III. **The Wheat: Righteous People Rescued by Death (57:1-2)**
   A.   The death of the righteous misunderstood (57:1)
   B.   The righteous rescued from evil by death (57:1-2)

IV. **The Weeds: Idolatrous People Exposed and Blown Away (57:3-13a)**
   A.   Mockers summoned for judgment (57:3-4)
   B.   Idolatrous worship exposed (57:5-13a)
   C.   Idolatrous worshipers blown away (57:11-13a)

V.   **The Wheat: God Dwelling with Humbled and Healed Sinners (57:13b-19)**
   A.   The humble welcomed to dwell with God (57:13b-15)
   B.   Contrite sinners healed by God's judgment (57:16-19)

VI. **The Weeds: God Condemning the Wicked to Endless Restlessness (57:20-21)**
   A.   The wicked endlessly restless (57:20)
   B.   The wicked condemned to no peace with God (57:21)

We who delight in Christ's banquet of grace (Isa 55) must share daily life with people whose "god is their stomach" and whose tastes are entirely earthly. Jesus told the parable of the wheat and the weeds to capture the mixed nature of life in this world (Matt 13:24-30). The wheat and weeds live life in close proximity together, but in the end they will be eternally separated: the wheat gathered into the barn (heaven) and the weeds thrown into a blazing furnace (hell).

Isaiah 56–57 describes in a back-and-forth rhythm the two classes of people—the wheat and the weeds—in powerfully vivid terms. The great challenge is to set these words in Isaiah's context. Isaiah is looking ahead with prophetic vision to a day when eunuchs and aliens, excluded from the temple in the old covenant, will be welcomed in the assembly and God's house will be a house of prayer for all nations. But he also speaks clearly about the great wickedness of Israel's watchmen living self-indulgent lives of feasting and about Judah as sons of a sorceress who pursue idolatrous worship practices adopted from Canaanite religions. These things happened much more clearly before the exile, during the days of Manasseh, and were the very practices that led to the exile. So Isaiah looks immediately to his own day and right after but also to the centuries beyond, in the days of the church, when Gentile outcasts will now be welcomed. The strongest contrast is between the lowly of spirit whom God welcomes into his high and holy dwelling place (57:15-19) and the restless wicked who will never know that peace (57:20-21).

The Wheat: Humble Outcasts Welcomed
ISAIAH 56:1-8

This section gives an amazing foretaste of the day when Christ would destroy the "dividing wall of hostility" by abolishing the "law consisting of commands and expressed in regulations" that separated Jews from Gentiles (Eph 2:14-15). The new covenant would create new people who "preserve justice and do what is right" (Isa 56:1). Declared holy though justification, they would live holy lives by the power of the Holy Spirit. Isaiah describes this in old-covenant terms—keeping the Sabbath, offering sacrifices (vv. 6-7)—but these are types and shadows of the reality that is Christ (Col 2:17). In point of fact, eunuchs in particular were permanently excluded from entering the Lord's assembly (Deut 23:1). So how could they be welcomed in here? The text says that a eunuch who is converted and who holds fast to his covenant through faith (vv. 3-4) should never say the Lord would exclude him from his people or, "I am a dried-up tree." Actually, the Lord promises here to give such a humble outcast who comes to him in faith a place within the walls of his sanctuary and an everlasting name that will never be cut off. It is impossible for us to hear these words without thinking of the new covenant in Christ, in which any who call on the name of Jesus will become "living stones" who are fitted together to be a spiritual house where holy sacrifices are offered to the Lord (1 Pet 2:5) and in which Jewish and Gentile Christians will be built together to become a dwelling where God lives by his Spirit (Eph 2:22). God promises to bring to his holy mountain the eunuchs and foreigners who convert to the Lord, who love his name and serve him (Isa 56:6-7). Jesus quotes verse 7 in Mark 11:17, showing that the temple was always meant to have a worldwide focus, a yearning for the nations to come to faith in the one true God. But only in Christ has that shadow become a reality. In verse 8 God promises to gather in dispersed people beyond merely the remnant of Israel, a promise reiterated in John 11:52 in which John says Jesus would die for non-Jewish elect "to unite the scattered children of God."

The Weeds: Self-Indulgent Leaders Devoured
ISAIAH 56:9-12

The final verses in the chapter expose the wickedness of "Israel's watchmen," the leaders of the nation. They are blind, ignorant, mute, and lazy rather than watchful, wise, and diligent. They are fiercely devoted to their food (v. 11), reminiscent of those of whom Paul says, "Their god is their stomach" (Phil 3:19). They are drunkards who can't wait for the next bacchanal and who assume that this corrupt way of life will go on forever (v. 12). But it won't. A different kind of feast occurs, when wild animals come and devour these self-indulgent watchmen (v. 9).

Setting these verses in prophetic context is not easy to do because the focus in Isaiah 40–55 has been postexilic, and there is no example of this kind of corruption among postexilic leaders like Ezra and Nehemiah. Therefore, it is better to see this as Isaiah's condemnation of the wicked leaders and false prophets that led up to the Babylonian exile, including Manasseh (Ezek 34:1-6; Zech 11:16-17). However, the lessons can be applied more broadly because this kind of self-indulgent leader is common in every era.

The Wheat: Righteous People Rescued by Death
ISAIAH 57:1-2

The focus moves back to the godly in 57:1-2. It may be that these godly people are those who die because the watchmen failed to protect them. But Isaiah gives an amazing and timeless word of comfort to those who mourn the death of the righteous in every generation. Because of Christ's victory over the grave, death is no longer something that holds terror, but rather delight. People may misunderstand the death of the righteous, thinking that God has done them wrong by abandoning them to the same fate as the wicked who die. But nothing could be further from the truth. Psalm 116:15 assures us, "The death of his faithful ones is valuable in the LORD's sight." So none of the righteous ever die "accidentally." Rather, God has acted to take the righteous from the presence of evil. They are swept up into heaven and never suffer again. Therefore no one should grieve the death of the righteous as if there were no hope (1 Thess 4:13).

The Weeds: Idolatrous People Exposed and Blown Away
ISAIAH 57:3-13A

The next eleven verses swing back to summon, expose, and condemn the wicked idolaters who worship in the Canaanite fashion. These are called "witch's sons, offspring of an adulterer and a prostitute" (v. 3). They mock the godly and live rebellious lives (v. 4) as they worship in the pagan pattern, burning with lust under trees, slaughtering children, pouring out drink offerings, and making grain offerings to the deities (vv. 5-6). The language is overtly sexual (vv. 7-8), reflecting both the sexual acts performed in these pagan rituals and the spiritual adultery the chosen nation of Israel was committing against her Husband, the Lord.

The mention of the king and envoys in verse 9 may hark back to Hezekiah's faithless overtures toward Egypt (Isa 30:1-7) in order to warn future kings not to act that way. The Lord is determined to expose fear of man and failure to fear him (51:12-13). God will give their idols a chance to "rescue" them, which they will not do because they are chaff that the wind will blow away (57:13). God's tendency to hide and to be silent leads people to question his existence and fail to fear him as they should (v. 11). It is so in our day as well: people cannot see God, and they connect dots in life that "prove" there is no God, so they do not fear him, love him, or trust him. Again, these verses seem to be dealing with preexilic sins during Manasseh's reign (2 Kgs 21:6), which would lead to the exile in Babylon.

The Wheat: God Dwelling with Humbled and Healed Sinners
ISAIAH 57:13B-19

Suddenly, the text turns back again to the righteous, promising that they will inherit the land and possess God's holy mountain. God will build up the highway and remove every obstacle for his people to reach him, to dwell with him (v. 14).

Isaiah 57:15 is one of the greatest verses in the book; it describes God's person and dwelling place, as well as those with whom God desires to dwell. God is revealed as the "High and Exalted One, who lives forever, whose name is holy." What awesome words! They reveal God's supremacy above all creation, the infinite gap that separates him from the whole universe. He is eternally alive, and his kingdom will go on forever. How could any sinner ever live in the presence of such a holy God? But because of the atoning work of Jesus Christ on the cross, God is willing to live with oppressed sinners who are lowly of spirit. God promises to revive the spirit of the lowly and the heart of the oppressed who will come to him in repentance and faith.

Verses 16–19 assert that these people so exalted as to live in the presence of this holy God are nothing more than sinners saved by grace. They deserved to be accused for sin, and their sins made God angry with them (v. 16). They were sinfully greedy, stubborn in pursuing the sinful desires of their hearts (v. 17). But God, because of the greatness of his grace and mercy, was willing to heal them of their ways, though he saw every evil thing they did (v. 18). The result of this astonishing healing grace was the creation (out of nothing, as in Gen 1:1) of praise on the lips of these repentant sinners (v. 19). God gives "peace, peace" (perfect peace) to those both "far or near" (Jews or Gentiles who trust in Christ) (Eph 2:17).

The Weeds: God Condemning the
Wicked to Endless Restlessness
ISAIAH 57:20-21

But tragically, the wicked will never know this peace. The New Testament speaks of a status of peace with God through justification by faith in

Christ (Rom 5:1) and an experience of peacefulness that comes by trusting in Christ Jesus no matter what the circumstances (Phil 4:6-7). The
wicked have neither. They are at war with God, and their hearts are
constantly restless, churning up "mire and muck" through their filthy
lusts and dirty deeds. "'There is no peace for the wicked,' says my God"
(v. 21). This condemnation from God is in direct contrast with verses
15-19, referring not merely to earthly restlessness but to the eternity
of wrath that follows such a life. The wicked in their restless roaming
are exactly like their father, the devil, who is frequently portrayed in
Scripture as roaming restlessly over the surface of the earth (Job 1:7;
2:2; see also the demons in Matt 12:43).

Applications

Christians should expect to live their daily lives in a mixed world, surrounded constantly by those who are refusing to sit at the banquet table
of Isaiah 55. But we should also celebrate the amazing grace of God
in the new covenant, welcoming by faith in Christ aliens and strangers, eunuchs and the uncircumcised, who would have been excluded in
the old covenant. The promise made to the eunuchs in 56:5 is sweet to
childless couples who are active in evangelism and missions. Even if they
can't have physical children, they can lead others to Christ and gain "a
memorial and a name better than sons and daughters."

The exposure and condemnation of lazy, self-indulgent leaders is
a timeless warning for every generation. Each of us struggles with the
fleshly desire to live for food and drink, for earthly pleasures. Leaders
have both greater responsibilities and greater temptations in these
areas. Elders of local churches should read such descriptions of corrupt
leaders and pray that God would protect them from these same kinds
of sins.

Isaiah 57:1-2 is a vital reminder that the godly are taken out of this
world to be spared from evil and by dying enter into peace in Christ.
This will help especially those who grieve over Christians who die young.

Isaiah's exposure of the Canaanitish idolatry in Isaiah 57:3-13 reso-
nates with us who live in an increasingly pagan Western world.

We should memorize Isaiah 57:15 and realize that we cannot have
too high a view of God's exalted holiness or too amazed a reaction that
such a God would dwell with sinners like us.

Finally, Isaiah 57:20-21 accurately diagnoses the reason for the constant strife in the world, both at the personal and the international levels.

Nations usually go to war against nations because their godless leaders are restless, seeking consolation in the possessions of their neighbors.

Reflect and Discuss

1. How does the parable of the Wheat and the Weeds (Matt 13:24-30,36-43) help explain the back-and-forth rhythm of these two chapters from the righteous to the wicked?
2. How does Isaiah 56:1-2 connect with 1 John 3:1-3, which teaches that our future perfection in Christ should make us zealous to be pure and holy now?
3. How does Isaiah 56:3-5 give a foretaste of the new covenant in Christ, when old-covenant barriers are completely removed (Eph 2:11-22)?
4. How does Isaiah 56:6-8 serve as a great motivation for missions?
5. How do you see the same traits of wicked leaders described in verses 10-12 in present government and church leaders?
6. How could the knowledge that righteous people die to be spared from evil, to enter into peace in death, give a special comfort to those who grieve over loved ones who have died in the Lord, especially those who die young?
7. How do you see a growth of paganism in your country today?
8. How does God's apparent silence tempt people to think there is no God (Isa 57:11)?
9. What does verse 15 teach you about God and about heaven?
10. What do verses 20-21 teach you about the root cause for the misery, strife, and warfare in the world today? How are the wicked like Satan in his restlessness?

Hypocritical Religiosity versus Genuine Love for God and Neighbor

ISAIAH 58

Isn't this the fast I choose: To break the chains of wickedness, to untie the ropes of the yoke, to set the oppressed free, and to tear off every yoke? (Isa 58:6)

Main Idea: God exposes hypocritical fasting, calling his people to a genuine fast of loving the poor and delighting in him.

I. **Exposing Hypocrisy and Oppression (58:1-5)**
   A. Hypocrisy of Jacob exposed (58:1)
   B. A nation that seemed to seek God (58:2)
   C. Fasting while sinning (58:3-5)
II. **The True Fast: Mercy Ministry (58:6-12)**
   A. The true fast: denying self to serve others (58:6)
   B. Breaking the chains of oppression (58:6)
   C. Feeding the hungry, housing the homeless (58:7)
   D. The true sacrifice: spend yourself, not merely your money (58:10).
   E. The lavish rewards of serving the needy (58:8-12)
III. **The True Sabbath: Holy Delight (58:13-14)**
   A. The self-denial of the true Sabbath (58:13)
   B. The delight of the Sabbath: God himself (58:13-14)

Exposing Hypocrisy and Oppression
ISAIAH 58:1-5

Jesus summarized all the laws of God in two: love the Lord your God with all your heart, with all your soul, and with all your mind, and love your neighbor as yourself (Matt 22:37,39). A magnificent harmony exists between these two. They are not independent but fit together beautifully. Love is a heart issue, having to do with the magnetic attractions of the heart. Hypocrisy is the enemy of love, both toward God and toward neighbor.

As he did in Isaiah 1:10-20, the prophet exposes the hypocrisy of a people riding a machine of religion while living corrupt lives that crushed the poor and needy. Christians today face the same charge: outward observance of church attendance and Bible studies with little genuine sacrifice for the poor and needy. Religion that does not result in care for the poor, the widow, and the orphan is defiled in God's sight (Jas 1:27). So God calls his prophet to raise his voice like a trumpet to declare to his people their sins. They were a people who sought God day after day and showed "delight" in knowing his ways, but the grammar of Isaiah 58:2 implies it was all a façade.

It gets even clearer in verse 3, when this people's arrogance toward God comes oozing to the surface. They arrogantly demand to know why God has not responded to their fasting and prayer. How did they know that God had not seen or noticed? Probably they were expecting some earthly blessing: a bumper crop, a military victory, a flow of gold into the royal coffers. They were purely mercenary in their religion. But even worse, they were blind to their own wickedness. On the day of their fasts they dealt wickedly with one another and with their workers. Their self-denial made them irritable; their fasts always ended in contention, even in brawls (v. 4). And they oppressed their workers with extra labor and harsh commands (v. 3). God tells them plainly that such "fasts" would never result in their voices being heard "on high" (v. 4).

The True Fast: Mercy Ministry
ISAIAH 58:6-12

God graciously teaches his sinful people what kind of religion he will honor (v. 6). This passage is one of the most important in the Bible for understanding mercy ministry: how vital it is to God, what it entails, how it must come from a heart of love for God and neighbor, how costly it must be, and how richly God will reward it. What God demands is more soul-searching than we can imagine: "Offer *yourself* to the hungry, and satisfy the afflicted one" (v. 10; emphasis added). The Hebrew behind this demand implies a long-term, deep-heart commitment to the poor and needy. NIV says, "If you spend yourselves in behalf of" the poor and needy. It's not enough to give bread or money occasionally in a cold-hearted manner. You are to give yourself first, and then you are ready to give materially. Jesus "spent himself" on behalf of his people who were infinitely poor and needy. To "spend yourself" means to allow your heart to be knit with the afflictions of others. Fasting is a symbolic affliction, a voluntary refraining from food, which you can choose to end anytime you want. But the hungry have no choice and cannot stop the involuntary fasting they are doing through their poverty.

So God calls on his people in every generation to learn how to have their souls afflicted with the sufferings of others. The Lord said, "You always have the poor with you" (Matt 26:11; see Deut 15:11). He calls on us to break the chains of wickedness and untie the ropes of the yoke of oppression (Isa 58:6). This involves seeking out societal injustice wherever it is and using powerful means to end it: *break* the chains, *tear off* the yoke! He calls on us to share our bread with the hungry and our homes with the homeless. Because the poor man is human, he is my own flesh and blood (v. 7). I must not turn away. I must spend myself on him.

God promises lavish blessings on any who by faith in him and out of love for others live this kind of life. He promises that our "light will appear like the dawn" (v. 8), and our "light will shine in the darkness, and [our] night will be like noonday" (v. 10). This is glory language: we will shine with the glory of God in this present age, and our deeds will shine with glory for all eternity. We will live a protected life of joy and peace, with our prayers regularly answered from on high. As soon as we call on him, the Lord will answer, "Here I am," as though he were our servant, and not we his (v. 9). The rebuilding of ancient ruins is a clear allusion to the rebuilding of Jerusalem by the exiles, but it is also a metaphor for the building of a work for the glory of God that will last eternally—even the building of the heavenly temple of God with living stones rescued from the wreckage of Satan's devastation (Matt 16:18; 1 Pet 2:5).

The True Sabbath: Holy Delight
ISAIAH 58:13-14

The final section of this chapter addresses the Sabbath observance, a vital part of the religion of the old covenant. The Sabbath has its origin in the pattern God established at creation: In six days he made heaven and earth, and on the seventh day he rested from all his labors. The Sabbath observance was a shadow of our heavenly rest in Christ. Through Isaiah, God was commanding God's people to obey the law of Moses, to "remember to dedicate the Sabbath day." God commands them not to desecrate his "holy day" by doing whatever they wanted, going their own ways, speaking idle words, and seeking their own pleasure in worldly pursuits

(v. 13). So verses 6-12 define a holy fast but verses 13-14 a holy feast. The essence of this feast was spiritual delight, finding supernatural pleasure in God himself. God says it plainly: "Delight in the LORD" (v. 14).

The tendency of Israel was either to disregard the day altogether (Num 15:32; Ezek 20:13) or to become enslaved to minutiae of man-made regulations that made the day a terrible burden (Mark 3:2-3). But God's good intentions for the Sabbath are nowhere clearer in all of Scripture than in these two verses. In heaven we will come into our inheritance, which will be a full and perfect experience of God himself—delighting in his radiant glory. Once a week, God commands his people to set aside their earthly labors and feast on him by faith. In the old covenant Israel was to do this on the seventh day, looking back to creation (Exod 20:11). In the new covenant Christians do this on the first day, in commemoration of Christ's resurrection and looking forward to the resurrection of their own bodies and of the world itself. Isaiah 58:13-14 contains timeless words, teaching us to turn away from worldly labors and entertainments and to dedicate ourselves more fully to God, finding delight in him by the Word and the Spirit. It must not degenerate into legalism (Col 2:16), and it must be done with a sense that in Christ we have already come into our Sabbath rest (Heb 4:1-9). But if Christians will follow these words, setting the first day aside as sacred, determining to turn away from selfish pursuits and delighting in the Lord, he will "make [us] ride over the heights of the land" and enjoy what we inherited from Jacob: salvation in Christ.

Applications

This chapter speaks plainly to Christians about three vital issues: religious hypocrisy, mercy ministry, and the Sabbath rest. The third of these we have just addressed plainly. I would just add that it is wise for Christians to learn how they can clear out Sundays as days of spiritual focus. In our entertainment-crazed age, filled with Sunday sports and endless electronic recreations, the need to fast in order to feast may never have been greater in the history of the church. Ask the Lord to show you how to rearrange your priorities and schedule to "call the Sabbath a delight."

Concerning religious hypocrisy, Christians need to realize that God looks beyond the "machinery of fasting" to see the heart behind it. And if our "fasting" actually makes us carnal, irritable, argumentative, and even violent, not to mention unjust to paid workers (vv. 3-4), it's time to repent from our religion. By contrast, both Isaiah and James (Jas 1:27) command us to a religion that makes us love God with all our hearts and love our neighbors sacrificially. The demands of the poor and needy on the consciences of Christians are relentless, and Isaiah 58:6-12 sharpens their cries to an urgent level. The central challenge for us is not merely to give money to charities but to offer ourselves (v. 10) on behalf of the poor and needy.

Reflect and Discuss

1. How does Isaiah 58 challenge Christians toward a fulfillment of the two great commandments of loving God and loving people wholeheartedly?
2. How could fasting help you in your walk with God?
3. How do verses 1-4 help fasting to be a genuine expression of piety?
4. God reveals his desire that his people make consistent sacrifices to alleviate the suffering of others. What are some specific ways that you can begin to change your life to obey the pattern of verses 6-12?
5. Verse 6 commands us to break chains and ropes of wickedness that oppress people. What does this mean? How is such a ministry costly and dangerous?
6. Verse 7 gets very specific about feeding the hungry and housing the homeless. What kind of challenges are involved in this that require Christian wisdom in addition to sacrificial love?
7. How do the promises attached to sacrificial love for the poor (vv. 8,10) motivate you?
8. Verse 10 carries with it the greatest single sacrifice a person could ever make for the poor—"offer yourself." What is the difference between giving money to the poor and spending yourself for the poor?
9. How do you observe the Christian Sabbath? As with any command given in Scripture, there are opposite dangers of legalism and license when it comes to Sundays. How can we make Sunday a more focused day of "delight in the Lord" without becoming legalistic?
10. What would be some of the benefits for Christians cheerfully abstaining from worldly recreations on Sundays so they can set their hearts on Christ and on things above (Col 3:1-4)?

The Lord Intervenes to Save Depraved Sinners

ISAIAH 59

The LORD saw that there was no justice, . . . so his own arm brought salvation, and his own righteousness supported him. (Isa 59:15-16)

Main Idea: The Lord looks on our wickedness and works his own salvation and vengeance on earth.

I.   **Accusation by the Lord: You Are Radically Depraved (59:1-8)!**
  A.   There's nothing wrong with God's arm or ear (59:1-2).
  B.   Your radical depravity is exposed (59:3-8).
  C.   You cover your wickedness with wispy cobwebs (59:6).

II. **Confession by the Humble: We Acknowledge Our Wickedness (59:9-15a).**
  A.   From "you" to "we": confession flows from the humble.
  B.   Our condition is desperate (59:9-11).
  C.   We need a Savior (59:11-12).
  D.   Our sins are pervasive (59:13-15a).

III. **Intervention by the Lord: Salvation and Vengeance (59:15b-18)**
  A.   God saw that there was no man to intercede (59:15b-16).
  B.   God clothed himself with righteousness and zeal (59:17).
  C.   God worked salvation and vengeance himself (59:16-18).

IV. **The Result: Worldwide and Eternal Salvation for the Repentant (59:19-21)**
  A.   From east to west, they will fear and glory in the Lord (59:19).
  B.   The Redeemer comes to the repentant (59:20).
  C.   The promise of the Lord's covenant is the word and the Spirit forever (59:21).

Accusation by the Lord: You Are Radically Depraved!
ISAIAH 59:1-8

The depravity of the human race is unfathomable, universal, and radical. The clearest description of sin in the Bible is Romans 3:9-18, in

which the apostle Paul levels the pride of every human being on earth
with the tattoo of a mournful drum:

> *There is no one righteous, not even one.*
> *There is no one who understands;*
> *there is no one who seeks God.*
> *All have turned away;*
> *all alike have become worthless.*
> *There is no one who does what is good,*
> *not even one.* (Rom 3:10-12)

To support this terrible truth, Paul reaches for Isaiah 59. Centuries
before Paul wrote his epistle, Isaiah was the mouthpiece of almighty
God to an equally radically depraved humanity.

God begins by speaking of the gap that stands between him and the
sinful nation of Israel. The suffering Israelites cried out to God for deliverance, and they wondered why God had not answered their prayers.
God says plainly it is not because his arm has become too weak to save or
his ear too deaf to hear (v. 1). The problem lies entirely with the people:
their sins have produced a separation between them and God so that he
will not hear or act on their behalf (v. 2). God has told us that he lives
in a "high and holy place" (Isa 57:15). Holiness means perfect separation; God is infinitely above all his creatures, even if they were morally
pure, as the radiant seraphim show by hiding their face in his presence.
But God is especially separate from all evil: "Your eyes are too pure to
look on evil, and you cannot tolerate wrongdoing" (Hab 1:13). So there
is nothing wrong with his arm, nor with his ear. There is something
deeply, radically wrong with us.

Isaiah 59 begins with God accusing sinners directly: your iniquities, your sins, your blood-stained hands, your iniquity-defiled fingers,
your lying lips, your muttered injustice (vv. 2-3). The depravity exposed
in verses 3-8 is pervasive, including wicked plans and evil deeds. Their
minds are corrupt and their actions are murderous. The image of repulsive creatures—viper's eggs and spider's webs—shows how evil these
people have become.

Most striking of all is the effort wicked people make to cover themselves, to escape their guilt. Adam and Eve, realizing in their sin that
they were naked, sought to cover themselves from each other and from
God. Sinners make wispy cobwebs as a flimsy covering for themselves
(v. 6), but it will not shield them from God's holy eyes.

Confession by the Humble:
We Acknowledge Our Wickedness
ISAIAH 59:9-15A

At this point the text turns inward and humble: the prophet, speaking for the redeemed among Israel (and among the Gentiles who find salvation in Christ), makes no effort to deflect the accusation of verses 1-8, no effort to deny. Everything said about us is true, painfully and shockingly true. The text moves from "you" and "they" to "we" and "us." True salvation must always begin with honest confession and humble pleading for mercy.

Verse 9 acknowledges that justice and righteousness are far from us, a painful admission because perfect righteousness is required for heaven (Matt 5:20,48). The sea of sin in which we all swim has drowned all hope for light; we yearn for light, but all is darkness. The image of woeful sinners groping in the dark like blind men, moaning mournfully for salvation, is deeply moving and pathetic. It is also the condition of the human race apart from Christ. So in verses 11-12 the humble sinner cries out honestly about sin and yearns for a Savior.

The section probes the dimensions of the sin. It is horizontal, consistently violating the second great command to love our neighbor as ourselves, as verses 3-8 make plain. Verses 14-15 add to this, speaking of truth stumbling in the public square. But the vertical dimension is infinitely more significant: We have lied to the Lord, we have turned our backs on him and rebelled against his holy commands, sinning from our hearts, not superficially (v. 13).

This heartfelt confession is a model for the redeemed in every generation. It is obvious that every single human needs a Savior.

Intervention by the Lord: Salvation and Vengeance
ISAIAH 59:15B-18

God surveys the decadent condition of the human race with a penetrating gaze, and nothing escapes his notice. Neither does he look on such depravity without deep emotion; he was deeply offended (v. 15b). Beyond this, he was intensely aware that no man could save the sinful human race. No one was free from sin, and no one could work salvation for him; so he had to do it himself. Verse 16 says this was amazing to God! We should not imagine that this word means that God had not known how corrupt the human race was. Rather, this is anthropo-morphic language to reveal how shocking the true condition of man's depravity and utter helplessness is.

But God would not sit idly by and allow the human race to drown in its depravity; God's zeal for his own glory and for the salvation of his elect moved him to decisive action. His own arm worked salvation for himself, and his own righteousness supported him (v. 16). He clothed himself with armor for battle: righteousness for a breastplate, a helmet of salvation, garments of vengeance, and zeal as a cloak (v. 17). Clearly this is Christ alone, God's decisive intervention to save the world from its radical depravity. The clothing imagery here was fulfilled in the incarnation, as Jesus took on a human body and entered the world as God's zealous commitment both to salvation for his elect and to vindication of his justice. Christ's heart burned with a holy zeal to purify the people of God from their sins (John 2:17).

But these verses do not only mention salvation but also vengeance. Just as God chose Jesus to be his servant to work salvation for his chosen people, so God chose Jesus to be the instrument of his vengeance. Revelation 19 portrays Jesus, the Word of God, as having a sword coming from his mouth with which he will strike down the nations (vv. 15-16), and the vengeance he will inflict in the name of his holy Father will be terrible. In verses 17-18 we see him put on garments of vengeance to repay fury to his enemies for their wicked deeds, even to the distant coastlands (Isa 34:2).

The Result: Worldwide and Eternal Salvation for the Repentant
ISAIAH 59:19-21

The dual displays in Scripture of Christ's zeal for righteousness—in the past at the cross and in the future at the second coming—cause the elect in the west and in the east to fear his name and delight in his glory (v. 19). They do so by faith, for both displays cannot be seen now by the eye of flesh. Verse 19 says the movement of fear and glory will come like a rushing stream "driven by the wind of the LORD." But the "wind of the LORD" can also be translated "the Spirit of the LORD," and it is completely reasonable to see this expression as foretelling the spread of the gospel of the glory of Christ by the power of the Holy Spirit. Paul quotes verse 20 in Romans 11:26 to speak of the consummation of the age of the gospel in the mysterious salvation of the final generation of Jews just before the end of the world. Christ is the "Deliverer" who will come "from Zion" (Rom 11) or "to Zion" (Isa 59); Zion represents both the heavenly city and the Jewish nation. Jesus is a Jewish Savior, for he said to the Samaritan woman, "Salvation is from the Jews" (John 4:22). But the Jewish nation needs *him* to come to *them* in the end, to remove the hardness from their hearts and take their godlessness away from them (Rom 11:26).

So Isaiah 59:21 speaks of a marvelous covenant that the Redeemer will work for his chosen people: he will put his Spirit on them and his words in their mouths, and neither will depart from them "from now on and forever."

Applications

We should realize that the words spoken of the wicked in verses 1-15 were true of us to the very core of our being before God worked salvation for us. We should realize how impotent we were to save ourselves—and how blind and mournful and spiritually dead we were. Paradoxically, such meditations have the power to make us indescribably happy while being so deeply humbled. This humbling can enable us to be patient under trials, to not complain when things don't go our way.

Beyond this, these verses should give us an accurate diagnosis of the true spiritual condition of the lost world around us. It should enable us to see the reasons for the injustice, murder, perjury in court, and defrauding of unwary consumers. It should make us more zealous to share the gospel with the desperately lost people around us.

Reflect and Discuss

1. How does this chapter describe the total depravity of the human race in graphic terms?
2. How does this explain why it seems God doesn't answer prayers?
3. Why is it vital to meditate much on the concept of human depravity apart from Christ?
4. How should we see our own sinfulness in light of these verses? How should these verses drive us to the cross of Christ?
5. How does verse 6 particularly expose the foolishness of sinners trusting in their own righteousness on judgment day?

6. How do verses 9-10 reveal the spiritual darkness of people apart from the light of the gospel (Eph 4:17-19)?

7. Isaiah 59:15-17 shows the solitary action of almighty God in addressing human sinfulness. How do these verses point ultimately to the cross of Jesus Christ?

8. How do verses 17-18 show the solitary role of almighty God in judging sinners?

9. Paul paraphrases verse 20 in Romans 11:26, speaking of Christ's redeeming work in Israel, turning the people from their sins to faith in him. How does it read differently here? How do you explain the difference?

10. What final promise does verse 21 make to God's people?

The Glory of Zion

ISAIAH 60

Arise, shine, for your light has come, and the glory of the LORD shines over you. (Isa 60:1)

Main Idea: The stunning glory of Zion, the heavenly City of God, is revealed in words that soar beyond any earthly fulfillment in the physical city of Jerusalem.

I. **Zion Is Commanded to Arise and Be Glorious (60:1-2).**
   A. Zion commanded to arise and shine (60:1)
   B. Zion's glory a contrast to the darkness of the nations (60:2)

II. **The Nations Are Drawn to the Glory of Zion and Glorify It More (60:3-9).**
   A. The magnetic attraction of Zion's glory (60:3)
   B. Zion's sons and daughters carried home (60:4,9)
   C. God's house beautified by the diverse glories of the nations (60:5-9)

III. **Zion Is Increasingly Beautiful as the Riches of the Nations Stream In (60:10-18).**
   A. Nations and kings will rebuild Zion (60:10).
   B. God's wrath will be atoned for (60:10).
   C. Zion's gates will be eternally open: security and prosperity (60:11,17-18).
   D. All nations who refuse to serve Zion are warned (60:12).
   E. Zion will be beloved and served, no longer hated (60:13-16).

IV. **The Eternal Glory of Zion (60:19-22)**
   A. Sun and moon are replaced by the glory of God (60:19-20).
   B. The people of God are eternally righteous, to the glory of God (60:21-22).

Zion Is Commanded to Arise and Be Glorious
ISAIAH 60:1-2

In this chapter it seems that the Holy Spirit of God overwhelmed Isaiah with words of stunning radiance that flowed through his pen. These words give us an amazing foretaste of the glories of heaven. The chapter is about "Zion" again, for Zion is mentioned clearly in verse 14, and the feminine grammar of verse 1 points to Jerusalem as the bride of God. God commands Zion to arise and shine, showing that only the sovereign power of God through his word can accomplish Zion's glory. Zion was humiliated by the wrath of God and is in ruins (v. 10). But the work of God the "Savior and Redeemer" (v. 16) is clearly on display and results in an ever-increasing glory that will act with magnetic power on the darkened nations of the world. For Zion to arise and shine is nothing less than a resurrection from the dishonor and guilt of sin and death, accomplished by the sovereign power of the Spirit.

As we have seen before with chapters that speak of the redemption and glory of Zion, an immediate fulfillment is in the restoration of the exiled Jews from Babylon to Jerusalem and the rebuilding of the city and the temple under Ezra, Nehemiah, and Haggai. But the words soar so far above as to make it obvious that the Lord had something far better in mind. Isaiah employs language his people would have been familiar with concerning the rebuilding of the city and its sanctuary using building materials from the nations. Just as Solomon employed the best craftsmen in the world for felling timber (the Sidonians, 1 Kgs 5:8), so the eternal Zion will also be built with the diverse glories of the nations. So Isaiah 60 has predominantly in view the heavenly Zion of Hebrews 12:22 and the coming new Jerusalem of Revelation 21:9-25. Both are built by the spread of the gospel to every nation on earth, and the flow of their diverse worship radiantly beautifies the heavenly glory of both. The building materials of the new Jerusalem are "living stones" (1 Pet 2:5) quarried from Satan's dark kingdom (Isa 60:2, "darkness will cover the earth, and total darkness the peoples") from every culture on earth, and irradiated by the gospel for eternal glory. No chapter so clearly celebrates the rich diversity of ethnic heavenly worship as does Isaiah 60.

The Nations Are Drawn to the Glory of Zion and Glorify It More

ISAIAH 60:3-9

The magnetic draw on the elect from every nation is the existing glory of God seen in the church on earth and in the promises of God in Scripture. As missionaries bring the gospel to a new region and some of its people believe and begin loving each other, living holy, and worshiping God by the Spirit, the unconverted elect in that region will see the light of Zion's glory in their lives and in the words of Scripture, and they will come to the light of Christ. Nations will come to Zion's light and kings to the brightness of her radiance (v. 3). Zion will look up and see the streaming of the nations as more and more of the elect come to Christ. Zion's heart will tremble with joy at the success of the gospel and the stunning diversity of cultural patterns of worship that the nations will bring with them through the gates of Zion. No religion is so embracing of nonmoral diversity as is true Christianity. Islam seeks to export Arabic culture everywhere, but Christianity celebrates the amazingly diverse ways genuine converts have worshiped Christ.

So the sons and daughters of Zion will be carried on the hip to Zion (v. 4), and caravans of camels will bring the riches of the nations into the city. Marvelously, offerings are accepted from Kedar and Nebaioth the sons of Ishmael, the father of the Arab nations (Gen 25:13). Though Ishmael was the son of the slave woman (Gal 4:22-25), cast out and a model for the nonelect in Romans 9:7-9, yet some of Ishmael's descendants are included in the harvest from every people group on earth (Rev 7:9). Thus, missionaries boldly seek to reach Muslims in Arabia, knowing that though some will violently persecute, others will stunningly be saved.

Zion Is Increasingly Beautiful as the Riches of the Nations Stream In

ISAIAH 60:10-18

The glory of Zion keeps increasing as the chapter unfolds. Foreigners will take an active role in rebuilding this eternal city, and kings will humble themselves to serve her. The image of gates standing open day and night to receive the streaming of wealth from the nations far exceeds any assistance Cyrus or Artaxerxes gave to the Jews. These open gates are a picture of total security and of overwhelming prosperity, "the wealth of nations" being brought into Zion, even with their kings led in procession (v. 11). The continual success of the gospel will make Zion more and more prosperous, more and more glorious. God promises that the "glory of Lebanon" will come to beautify the place of God's sanctuary. In Solomon's day King Hiram of Tyre had his skillful woodsmen hew down the cedars of Lebanon and float them to port cities in Israel for the building of God's house (1 Kgs 5:8-10). Now God is interested in human beings—Lebanese souls, won to Christ by courageous witnesses.

In the center of this chapter, however, is a stern warning to all nations on the face of the earth concerning Zion. In verse 12 God warns that any nation that will not serve Zion will eternally perish; those nations will be annihilated. During this present age of gospel advance, many rulers and nations use their temporal power to resist the church of Jesus Christ and the spread of his gospel. But just as in Psalm 2, those kings and nations are warned that they must repent and serve the Son, lest his anger ignite in a moment and they be destroyed in their rebellion (vv. 10-12). In the final state of Zion, the new Jerusalem will have no enemies left, for all who refused to serve Christ will be in everlasting torment in the lake of fire (Rev 21:8). Thus will her gates always stand open, and the redeemed will continually bring the glory of the nations into the eternal city (Rev 21:25).

In the end Zion will be infinitely better than anything this earth has ever seen. Solomon's Jerusalem was stunningly beautiful, adorned with the best materials money could buy. He made golden shields to hang in the royal palace. But when his foolish son, Rehoboam, took his place, God raised up an Egyptian army who carried off the treasures of the city, including the golden shields. So Rehoboam made bronze ones to replace them (1 Kgs 14:25-27). But in Isaiah 60:17 the process is eternally reversed. Everything will be immeasurably improved in the new Jerusalem: gold instead of bronze, silver instead of iron, bronze instead of wood, iron instead of stones. That is to say, words can't describe how glorious the eternal city will be. The walls of the city will be named "Salvation," and her gates will be called "Praise" (v. 18).

The Eternal Glory of Zion
ISAIAH 60:19-22

The chapter ends with a foretaste of the heavenly Jerusalem not at all different from the vision the apostle John had on the island of Patmos. Revelation 21–22 concludes the Bible with a stunning depiction of the new Jerusalem, adorned like a bride for her husband, radiant with the glory of God: "The city does not need the sun or the moon to shine on it, because the glory of God illuminates it, and its lamp is the Lamb" (Rev 21:23). The same prediction is made here in Isaiah 60. In this present age the sun sets, bringing darkness; the moon wanes, depriving the earth of its gentle beams. But the glory of God will never set or wane, and the new Jerusalem will be radiant with God's glory at every moment. This is the eternal destiny of Zion, for verses 19-20 speak of the glory of the Lord as her "everlasting light," and verse 21 speaks of perfect righteousness and eternal possession of the land.

Applications

God means for his suffering people to renew their hope every single day by meditating intently on the present and coming glory of Zion. We should read Isaiah 60 and Revelation 21–22 again and again and remind ourselves of how magnificent that city is now (in the heavenly realms) and how glorious it will be (in the future new earth). Only faith can see either glory, so we must be regularly in the Word, drinking in the promises of God. As we are radiant in hope, we will be magnetically attractive to lost people who are walking in satanic darkness (v. 2) and who are without hope and without God in the world (Eph 2:12). If we shine with hope while suffering afflictions (like disease) or persecutions or deprivations, unbelievers will be strongly motivated to ask us to give a reason for the hope that is in us (1 Pet 3:15). But if we grow weak in faith through neglect of the Word, we will live much the same as they do.

We should also embrace the missionary thrust of this chapter. The wealth of the nations streaming through the gates of Zion represents the astonishing diversity of cultures worshiping Christ by faith. We should delight in that and move out for the sake of unreached people groups. We should meditate on the significance of Ishmael's sons (Kedar and Nebaoith) giving offerings acceptable to God. We should expect God to save many Arab Muslims, despite the overwhelming obstacles. And when it comes to the diverse nonmoral aspects of their worship, we should allow it to push us out of our own arrogant cultural superiority when it comes to patterns of worship. Too many local churches have "worship wars," and people assert that this or that pattern of music is the only way to worship. Isaiah 60 should cause us to be more expansive, for God delights in far more forms of worship than you or I do.

Reflect and Discuss

1. What does the presence of the strong commands "Arise, shine" tell us about the sovereign power of God in the glory of Zion?
2. How are the nations in darkness now, according to verse 2? How does it relate to Ephesians 2:1-3? How is the gospel's light the only answer to this satanic darkness?
3. This chapter is filled with the image of Gentile nations and their kings streaming into Zion's gates with amazing treasures to enrich Zion. How is this a picture of the spread of the gospel to the ends of the earth?
4. How could the specific mention of Nebaioth and Kedar, Ishamel's sons, in Isaiah 60:7 (cf. Gen 25:13) give us a great encouragement about missions to Arab Muslims?
5. In what ways do "foreigners rebuild [the] walls" of Zion now, if Zion is a heavenly city? How do kings serve Zion now (v. 10)?
6. How does the fruit of Christ's atonement for the inhabitants of Zion come across in verse 10?
7. What is the terrible warning in verse 12? How do some kings use their temporal power to hinder the church?
8. How does verse 14 show the amazing transforming power of the gospel?
9. What similarities do you see between Isaiah 60:19-22 and Revelation 21:9-25?
10. How does the radiant glory of Zion relate to our own resurrection glory, as in Matthew 13:43 and 1 Corinthians 15:43?

The Messiah Announces Good News

ISAIAH 61

The Spirit of the Lord GOD is on me, because the LORD has anointed me to bring good news to the poor. (Isa 61:1)

Main Idea: The Messiah announces the good news of his mission to bring salvation to the poor, brokenhearted captives of the earth.

I. **The Messiah and His Mission (61:1-3)**
   A. The Messiah anointed with the Spirit (61:1)
   B. The Messiah's mission to poor prisoners (61:1-3)
II. **The Transformation of the Messiah's People (61:3-9)**
   A. From weak captives to mighty trees of righteousness (61:3)
   B. Rebuilding ancient ruins (61:4)
   C. Enriched, not enslaved, by the nations (61:5-9)
III. **The Messiah's Garments of Joy, Righteousness, and Salvation (61:10-11)**
   A. The Messiah's garments (61:10)
   B. The Messiah's harvest of righteousness (61:11)

The Messiah and His Mission

ISAIAH 61:1-3

Picture one of the most dramatic moments in redemptive history (Luke 4:16-30). The Lord Jesus Christ had returned to his hometown of Nazareth. Reports about the amazing things he had already done in Capernaum had reached his neighbors, and the town was abuzz with the news. The Sabbath day came, and everyone assembled in the synagogue. Jesus stood and went forward, and the scroll of Isaiah was given to him. He unrolled it to the very place we are considering now, Isaiah 61, and read the ancient words powerfully. You could have heard a pin drop. After reading verses 1-2, he sat down and the eyes of everyone in the synagogue were fixed on him. He opened his mouth and spoke, and the world has never been the same since: "Today as you listen, this Scripture has been fulfilled." The word *fulfilled* must have hit everyone there like a thunderbolt! Isaiah had written the passage more than seven centuries before that electric moment. Now a man they had watched grow up from a little boy in that tiny locale was claiming to have fulfilled this prophecy!

In so doing, Jesus makes my task as a commentator much easier, not only for this one passage but indeed for the whole book of Isaiah. The spirit of this commentary is the proclamation of Jesus from the prophetic writing of Isaiah. Some interpreters think it poor scholarship to go directly to Jesus from the ancient text or to use the data from the Gospels as an interpretive key. But as a Christian, I think it sheer unbelief not to proclaim Christ from Isaiah 61 or to act as though Luke 4 itself were not as perfectly inspired from the Holy Spirit as was Isaiah 61. Jesus Christ of Nazareth is the fulfillment of chapter 61; faith settles that hermeneutical question for all time.

And Isaiah 61:1-3 describes powerfully both the anointing of the Messiah and his mission. In verse 1 the Messiah ("Anointed One") proclaims his anointing by the Father with the Spirit. In the Old Testament men were anointed with oil for key offices in Israel: kings (1 Sam 10:1), priests (Exod 30:30), and prophets (1 Kgs 19:16). This was symbolic of the Holy Spirit's power equipping them for their weighty tasks (David in 1 Sam 16:13). Men can anoint only with oil; God alone can anoint a man with the Holy Spirit. And no one in history was so powerfully anointed with the Holy Spirit as was Jesus Christ. This was clearly pictured by the Spirit's descent as a dove at Jesus's baptism, and Peter proclaimed it to Cornelius: "God anointed Jesus of Nazareth with the Holy Spirit and with power, and . . . he went about doing good and healing all who were under the tyranny of the devil" (Acts 10:38).

This was the fulfillment of the sevenfold mission that the Father gave to Jesus in Isaiah 61: to preach good news to the poor, to heal the brokenhearted, to proclaim liberty to the captives and freedom to the prisoners, to proclaim the year of the Lord's favor and the day of God's vengeance, to comfort those who mourn in Zion, and to give them a crown, oil, and splendid clothes in place of their ashes of degradation and captivity. The Messiah accomplishes all these things primarily by *preaching good news*. The recipients of this good news are pictured as in a desperate condition throughout this chapter: they are "poor," "brokenhearted," "captives" and "prisoners" who "mourn" and are clothed with "ashes" and "despair." They live in "ruined cities" devastated for generations (v. 4). They are disgraced by the mocking nations (v. 7). They are plundered by "robbery and injustice" (v. 8). It seems difficult to imagine how a verbally proclaimed message could achieve such a triumphant release and lavish enrichment.

But this is precisely what the gospel of Jesus Christ does. This prophecy of Isaiah would have been first seen through the lens of the Babylonian exile and the restoration of the remnant to rebuild the promised land. But Jesus took these promises to an infinitely higher level. The true captivity that Christ came to destroy was captivity to sin and to Satan (John 8:32,34). He said it was by knowing the truth that such captives were set free. Thus proclamation of the gospel sets captives free! So also Jesus's healing ministry was seen as a work of liberation from the power of Satan, the "strong man" who guards his captives fiercely (Luke 11:21-22). When Jesus healed a bent old woman, he proclaimed that Satan had bound her and he had set her free (Luke 13:16).

Thus it is clear that the mission of Jesus in proclaiming the gospel and doing astonishing miracles of healing was a direct fulfillment of Isaiah 61:1-3. Jesus came "to proclaim the year of the LORD's favor" (v. 2). This is the opening of a worldwide era of grace from almighty God, in which the debts of sin can be cancelled and prisoners can be set free to worship God in joyful liberation. As Paul said in 2 Corinthians 6:2, "See, now is the acceptable time; now is the day of salvation!"

When Jesus read this passage, however, he stopped abruptly in verse 2 after the proclamation of the year of the Lord's favor. The verse in Isaiah continued, "and the day of our God's vengeance." These words Christ did not read that day but not because he will not fulfill them. He most certainly will in his *second coming*, when he returns to earth to slay all the wicked with the sword of his Word (Rev 19:11-16). The warning about the coming wrath of the Lord is mixed right in the middle of the sweet passage from Isaiah 61:1-3, and it is right for the messengers of the gospel to warn sinners of the coming wrath so that they might flee to Christ.

The Transformation of the Messiah's People
ISAIAH 61:3-9

Here we read of the radical transformation of the poor, brokenhearted, mourning, ash-covered captives whom Jesus has come to save. In salvation, Christ has removed from us our disgrace, our ashes, and our chains; instead, he has crowned us with beauty, anointed us with the oil of joy, and clothed us with robes of perfect righteousness.

Moreover, having been given the gift of imputed righteousness by faith in Christ, we also receive the Holy Spirit, as Jesus was anointed, and we are unleashed on a world devastated by sin and Satan. We "rebuild ancient ruins," even cities that have been devastated for centuries (v. 4). Certainly the returning exiles did this physically in Jerusalem, but these words are more perfectly fulfilled spiritually by the building of the church of Jesus Christ out of the rubble of human history. People's lives are laid waste by sin, as are whole human societies all over the face of the earth. The trail of wreckage left by sin has only one chief Rebuilder: Jesus Christ. And Christ has chosen to rebuild lives and societies by his transformed people. We are the rebuilders of "ancient ruins."

So verses 4-9 picture the mission of the church, now unfolding for twenty centuries, to build the new Jerusalem living stone by living stone, quarried from Satan's dark kingdom. Certainly the church has done literal rebuilding of physical ruins: after earthquakes, after wars, after floods, the church is there to help rebuild. But the real rebuilding of ruins is done within a single human heart who genuinely repents of sin and turns to God through Christ. The rubble of personal sin is cleared away, and a "righteous tree" grows up for all to see.

Messiah's people are given a role as "the LORD's priests" (v. 6). To them has been committed the good news that Jesus first announced in Nazareth. These priests of the Lord minister the word of God to every tribe, language, people, and nation on earth. Those who repent and believe from all the Gentile nations will honor the messengers and lavishly enrich them (vv. 5-7). God's hatred of injustice will find fruition in the mission of his "priests." Where Messiah's people had once been disgraced, they will be held in honor, recognized as the Lord's blessed covenant people (v. 8).

The Messiah's Garments of Joy, Righteousness, and Salvation
ISAIAH 61:10-11

The chapter concludes with the Messiah (Jesus) speaking again of how God the Father has robed and equipped him to be Savior of the world. Verse 10 is written in the first person, as Christ declares his supreme delight in his Father. These verses also embody what his chosen people will experience in their relationship with the Father through Christ's imputed righteousness: a worldwide harvest of righteousness and praise for God.

Applications

As we read this chapter, we must begin where the chapter ends up: worship. If the Messiah's mission has redeemed us, the clearest evidence will be the desire we have to give him praise and worship.

Second, we are led to meditate on God's amazing grace to such degraded sinners as we were. We were enslaved through our own willful rebellion. The ashes of disgrace on us were well earned. We were not merely victims of sin and Satan's oppression; we were oppressors ourselves. But God, in the richness of his mercy and love toward us, has given us a crown, oil, and rich garments instead of our chains, stench, and rags.

Third, we should be energetic in the mission the Messiah has entrusted to us: to proclaim liberty to the captives all over the earth. By proclaiming and living out the truth of his Word, we will rebuild ancient cities and clear away piles of rubble. This points to the need to build healthy local churches that are obedient to the full commands of the Bible by the power of the Holy Spirit. Healthy local churches are colonies of heaven, havens of peaceful order in the midst of a war zone of sin's destruction.

Reflect and Discuss

1. How does this chapter display the magnificence of Jesus Christ as the Messiah?
2. What kind of courage do you think Jesus displayed by proclaiming he fulfilled this chapter?
3. What is the significance of the expression "year of the LORD's favor"? How does it relate to 2 Corinthians 6:2?
4. Read about the Jubilee in Leviticus 25. How does this picture the "year of the LORD's favor"?
5. How is the plight of sinners enslaved in Satan's dark kingdom pictured in the words of this chapter?
6. What lavish gifts of grace does Jesus give to sinners according to verses 1-3?
7. How do verses 4-9 picture the church's ministry in the world?
8. What does verse 8 teach us about God's holiness?
9. How is Jesus described as arrayed for his role as Savior in verse 10 (Heb 1:9)?
10. How does verse 11 picture a harvest of righteousness and praise all over the world as a result of Christ's ministry?

Christ's Passionate Zeal for the Glory of His Bride

ISAIAH 62

I will not keep silent because of Zion, and I will not keep still because of Jerusalem, until her righteousness shines like a bright light and her salvation, like a flaming torch. (Isa 62:1)

Main Idea: Christ's passionate zeal for the glory of Zion, his bride, is relentless, calling forth a corresponding zeal from his people until her radiant beauty is finally and perfectly consummated.

I. **Christ's Passionate Zeal for Zion's Glory (62:1)**
   A. Christ's relentless proclamation for Zion's sake
   B. Christ's goal: Zion's radiant salvation
II. **Zion's Glory on Display for the Nations (62:2-5)**
   A. Zion's radiant glory is seen by the nations.
   B. Zion's population is ever increasing.
   C. The Lord delights in Zion's glory.
   D. Zion's sons delight in Zion's glory.
III. **Relentless Watchmen Posted on Zion's Walls (62:6-9)**
   A. The Lord appoints and charges watchmen.
   B. The Lord swears to make Zion prosperous.
IV. **Zion's People Redeemed to Build Zion (62:10-12)**
   A. The highway of Zion's construction
   B. The promise of Zion's consummation

Christ's Passionate Zeal for Zion's Glory
ISAIAH 62:1

There is a dramatic pause, and the hearts of everyone in the sanctuary rise in anticipation. Processional music starts. The doors at the back of the church swing open, and everyone stands, turning back to look. The bride, radiant in beauty, begins her long-anticipated walk down the aisle. For the first time that day, the bridegroom sees her, and his heart swells with love and anticipation. Her physical beauty is enhanced by all the preparations she has been about since early that morning: her hair is perfect, cosmetics flawless, jewelry sparkling, dress spectacular. The bridegroom's eyes drink in her glory in a way unique to the assembled throng. Soon, she will be *his* wife, and he will love her and be joined to her in a mysterious covenant known as marriage.

Every wedding I have ever observed has followed this pattern. Ephesians 5:32 says that marriage is a profound mystery patterned after the perfect union between Christ and his bride, the church. In Revelation 21 John describes that union:

> *I also saw the holy city, the new Jerusalem, coming down out of heaven from God, prepared like a bride adorned for her husband. . . . [One of the angels said,] "Come, I will show you the bride, the wife of the Lamb." He then carried me away in the Spirit . . . and showed me the holy city, Jerusalem, coming down out of heaven from God, arrayed with God's glory. Her radiance was like a precious jewel, like a jasper stone, clear as crystal.* (vv. 2,9-11)

The glory of the church was perfected, ready for her Bridegroom, Christ Jesus, to come and take her forever. Every Christian wedding ceremony is a foretaste of this final reality.

However, there is a significant difference. In our culture the bridegroom contributes nothing to the radiant beauty of the bride on her wedding day. Tradition often dictates that he not see her at all that day until those doors swing open and she begins her processional. But the radiant glory of the bride of Christ—the church, the heavenly Zion, the new Jerusalem—is completely the work of the Bridegroom, Jesus Christ. He found her corrupted and defiled, ugly through rebellion, spiritually dead. He redeemed her by his own blood, raised her from the dead spiritually, washed her with water through the word, in order that he might present her to himself as a radiant bride, holy and blameless in his sight (Eph 1:7; 5:25-27; cf. Ezek 16:1-14). Throughout every generation of church history Christ has been patiently and passionately preparing his bride for the wedding day. Every beam of her glory on that day will be his, every sparkle of radiance, every holy aspiration and passionate desire for him he worked in her heart by his Holy Spirit. When she is finished, she will *descend from heaven*, coming down as God's perfected work. And when the new heaven and new earth finally come, they will shine with God's glory. But nothing in that new creation will be more glorious than the bride of Christ!

Isaiah 62 is a brief description of the relentless passion Jesus Christ has for the glory of Zion. Again, "Zion" in prophetic perspective is the new Jerusalem, the people of God, chosen in Christ before the foundation of the world, redeemed from every nation by the blood of Christ. In verse 1 Christ declares his passionate zeal for the final glory of his bride. Many commentators believe the speaker in this verse is Isaiah the prophet, and I respect their views (Young, *Isaiah Chs. 40–66*, 467; Ridderbos, *Isaiah*, 550). It may well be. But I was compelled by Jesus in Luke 4:21 to see the first-person speaker of Isaiah 61:1 as Christ himself, and it is powerful to see the same here. Even if the speaker were Isaiah, his zeal for Zion's glory came from the Spirit of Christ anyway.

So, in Isaiah 62:1 Christ proclaims his relentless zeal to speak his powerful word until Zion's "righteousness shines like a bright light and her salvation, like a flaming torch." Christ will not "keep silent" because his bride is not yet perfect: some elect have not yet been saved; other elect have not yet been glorified spiritually; none of the elect have received their resurrection bodies. So there is massive work still to be done on Zion until her glory is perfected.

Yet it is not only Christ who must be zealous for Zion's glory. Later in this chapter he will post watchmen on Jerusalem's walls and command them to give themselves no rest and to give God no rest until Zion is the praise of the whole earth. So the Christian reader of Isaiah 62 is drawn quickly into Jesus's zeal for his bride, the church, and challenged to be as passionate for her consummation as he is.

Zion's Glory on Display for the Nations
ISAIAH 62:2-5

A key to the building of the heavenly Zion is the present glory of the church on earth. The immediate and partial fulfillment of this chapter is, of course, the restoration of the physical city of Jerusalem by the remnant from Babylon. But the small, rubble-filled city of Nehemiah and Ezra was hardly the final consummation of the vision of Isaiah 62. Rather, we must see the ever-increasing glory of the church of Christ as the fulfillment of verses 2-5. As the church grows both numerically and in holiness, nations will see her righteousness, and kings will be forced to acknowledge her glory. The nations and their kings will see the functioning of healthy local churches and see the transformation of their own citizens from darkness to light (v. 2), and they will be attracted to her King, Jesus. Thus will the glory of the spiritual Zion (even while in construction) be attractive to the elect from every nation who have not yet been converted. Zion will be populated more and more; she will no longer be deserted and her land will not be called desolate.

Key to this process is the commitment of the sons of Zion to her final glory. The same love Christ has for his bride, so must her sons have. In a difficult mixing of metaphors, verse 5 implies that the sons of Zion must marry her and delight over her as Jesus does. What this means is that, by the power of the Spirit (Acts 1:8), the church must be committed to evangelism and discipleship, driven on by the goal of the final consummation of the bride of Christ.

Relentless Watchmen Posted on Zion's Walls
ISAIAH 62:6-9

To this end, the Lord posts watchmen on Jerusalem's walls. Their mission is one of intercession above all else: they are commanded to remind the Lord of Zion's incompleteness, of her neediness, of the work yet to be done. They are to give themselves no rest and to give him no rest until God establishes Jerusalem and makes her the praise of the whole earth (v. 7). This work of relentless intercession in the face of overwhelming opposition to the building of the church is one of the most difficult tasks ever entrusted to God's people. God tests his people by this, for the glory of the church seems so dim, the enemies of the church seem so powerful, and the work seems so immense. Furthermore, every one of us is relentlessly committed to our own pleasures. For us to learn to give ourselves no rest until Zion is perfect in glory is an extreme work that will challenge every child of God until the day we die.

Thankfully, despite these overwhelming challenges, God has sworn with his right hand and strong arm to make Zion prosperous. Using the language of covenant blessings, he speaks of never giving to her enemies the grain and wine that belong to her.

Zion's People Redeemed to Build Zion
ISAIAH 62:10-12

The final section of this amazing chapter speaks of constructing a highway from the nations to Zion. The redeemed of the Lord are urgently commanded here to "go out, go out through the city gates." The image is clearly borrowed from the experience the exiles would have in fleeing Babylon, the city of destruction. All the redeemed from every nation on earth will have essentially the same experience spiritually that the exiles would have physically: Rescued from evil "Babylon" (Satan's world), they are commanded to flee it (Rev 18:4) so that they may journey to Zion along a prepared highway and populate her. But it is a highway that the redeemed are just as urgently commanded to build as to travel on (v. 10). Thus do previous generations of faithful Christians leave behind them a smooth highway for their spiritual descendants to travel on. They raise a banner for the peoples (v. 10) by the proclamation of the salvation that the Lord alone is working among the nations (v. 11). The end result is that God's "Holy People, the LORD's Redeemed," will be overflowing in Zion, "A City Not Deserted," cared for by almighty God (v. 12).

Plainly these images speak of the great worldwide work of the church in the Great Commission, preaching the gospel of Christ crucified and resurrected, making disciples who are being taught to obey everything the Lord has commanded (Matt 28:19-20).

Applications

Christ's relentless passion for his bride's perfection dominates this chapter and challenges every generation of Christians to join him. Jesus will never stop speaking his word into the hearts of his church, "cleansing her with the washing of water by the word . . . to present the church to himself in splendor, without spot or wrinkle or anything like that, but holy and blameless" (Eph 5:26-27). The immediate application for us as members of his bride is to be holy ourselves (1 Pet 1:15). This text challenges us to love the Bridegroom with undivided love, to put away all idols and worldly affections. It also challenges us to be just as zealous for the holiness of other Christians, to be energetic in the work of the church. It calls on mature Christians to disciple younger believers, "bringing holiness to completion in the fear of God" (2 Cor 7:1). This chapter should put within us a vision for the final perfection of the bride, a yearning to see her finally glorious in heaven.

This chapter also commands leaders (especially elders: Acts 20:28) to act as watchmen on the walls of Zion, overseeing the doctrinal and practical lives of the flock. Just as watchmen are awake all night because danger may come at anytime, so elders must keep careful watch at all times. And, clearly, Isaiah 62:6-7 calls on relentless intercession for the church's final glory. This is perhaps the hardest work for any Christian, for we easily get weary in prayer.

Finally, as we've seen again and again in Isaiah, this chapter has a clear missionary thrust. We should be traveling on the highway to Zion as we are inviting others to travel with us *and* also making the highway as smooth as possible by the clear preaching of Christ and holy living in the pattern of Christ.

Reflect and Discuss

1. How does the passion of Jesus Christ for the glory of Zion, his bride, drive this whole chapter?
2. How is Christ's ministry of the word, implied in verse 1 and openly taught in Ephesians 5:26-27, essential to the perfection of his bride?
3. How should Christians also share Christ's passion for the perfection and glory of his bride? How could we live that out in our daily lives?
4. How is the church's growth in holiness attractive to the nations and their kings (vv. 2-3)?
5. How does the fact that Christ delights in the church (vv. 4-5) encourage you?
6. How do elders/pastors serve as "watchmen on your walls" in a local church (Acts 20:28-31)?
7. How do the words "There is no rest for you" and "Do not give him rest" (vv. 6-7) challenge you to pray for the church's growth worldwide?
8. How does verse 8 help us to rely on the sovereign power of God in the work of perfecting the church?
9. How do we travel on the highway to Zion (John 14:6) *and* also build up that highway so others can travel on it (v. 10)?
10. How does the courage and faithfulness of previous generations of Christians smooth the highway for those who follow (v. 10)?

God's Passionate Response to Sin Draws Forth Intercession

ISAIAH 63–64

I looked, but there was no one to help, and I was amazed that no one assisted; so my arm accomplished victory for me, and my wrath assisted me. (Isa 63:5)

Main Idea: God's passionate response to sin, both in wrath for the nations and discipline for his people, should call forth persistent and fervent prayer from God's people.

I. **The Lord's Terrifying Day of Vengeance on His Enemies (63:1-6)**
II. **Persistent Intercession and Lamentation by God's Watchman (63:7–64:12)**
   A. The intercessor recounts the Lord's history of love (63:7-9).
   B. The intercessor confesses sin (63:10).
   C. The intercessor prays based on the Lord's history (63:11-16).
   D. The intercessor laments over the Lord's disciplines (63:17-19).
   E. The intercessor pleads for God to descend (64:1-5a).
   F. The intercessor confesses sin again (64:5b-7).
   G. The intercessor pleads for God to act (64:8-12).

The Lord's Terrifying Day of Vengeance on His Enemies
ISAIAH 63:1-6

Having soared with the vision of the heavenly Zion in Isaiah 62, we now descend to the terrifying reality that the vision has not yet been realized. The earth is still filled with evil, and God's passionate response to that evil unifies these two chapters.

These verses are simply terrifying. They should cause all faith-filled readers to tremble at his word (Isa 66:2), for when the great day of God's wrath comes, who is able to stand (Rev 6:17)? We trust that Christ will rescue us from the coming wrath (1 Thess 1:10), but still the words are fearsome. Our approaching God is pictured as coming from Edom and Bozrah (Edom's capital city), and his garments are stained crimson.

He is striding vigorously, filled with energy, not depleted at all from his slaughtering. A questioner asks, "Who is this?" Who is this one so powerfully "striding in his formidable might?" The mighty figure answers, "It is I, proclaiming vindication, powerful to save." The Lord executes his wrath with awesome power but only in perfect righteousness. And he does it by *speaking*—by the word of his power. The questioner asks him, "Why are your clothes red?" (v. 2). And the answer is, "I trampled the winepress alone. . . . I trampled them in my anger and ground them underfoot in my fury; their blood spattered my garments" (v. 3).

The wrath of God against Edom and Bozrah here is symbolic. Certainly Edom (Esau) was an ancient foe of Israel, but as we saw in Isaiah 34, Edom represents all the godless nations, those in rebellion against God. In the same way, Esau is singled out in the New Testament as representative of the godless reprobate (Rom 9:13; Heb 12:16). And when the "year of the LORD's favor" comes to an end, the "day of God's vengeance" begins (Isa 61:2)—the time for God's wrath to be poured out on the godless. The second coming of Christ depicted in Revelation 19:11-16 will stand as the clear fulfillment of the blood-spattered warrior of Isaiah 63, for there Christ is depicted as wearing a robe stained in blood, slaughtering his foes with the sword coming from his mouth.

Before that day however, many dress rehearsals of judgment fall on countless godless nations who have opposed God and sought to destroy his people. All of them are mere foretastes of God's final wrath on earth. Verse 4 says God had stored up his wrath against them, not forgetting any of their wicked acts, especially those done to harm his chosen people. And when the time came, he trod the winepress *alone*. God created the universe alone (44:24), so God also works both vengeance and salvation alone (63:5). Christ's solitary redemption at the cross and his solitary slaughter of his enemies in Revelation 19 fulfill this perfectly.

Persistent Intercession and Lamentation by God's Watchman
ISAIAH 63:7–64:12

This overpowering image of the wrath of God against the godless on earth is just what many in Israel were waiting for. But the same holiness of God that motivates this destruction motivates his severe chastisements of his people's sins. And the fact that "Edom" has not yet been finally punished and that Zion is not yet fully glorified means that it is time for the "watchmen on your walls" (in this case, Isaiah the prophet) to cry out relentlessly to the Lord (Isa 62:6-7). So the rest of these two chapters flow in a marvelous rhythm of worship, confession of sin, longing for God's closeness, and pleading for God to intervene. This is how a watchman must intercede.

The Intercessor Recounts the Lord's History of Love (63:7-9)

Isaiah begins by going over the history of the Lord's mighty acts of salvation for Israel in the past. This history is vital to the intercessor's confidence that God loves his people and will not cast them off because of their sins. So Isaiah begins by speaking of the Lord's faithful love (Hb *chesed,* "covenant love") and his "praiseworthy acts" on behalf of Israel. The foundation of these many acts of kindness in history is his election of them as his children (v. 8) and his amazing compassion for them in their suffering. Verse 9 says, "In all their suffering, he suffered." Indeed, the only pain, grief, or affliction God ever suffers comes from his voluntary compassion for his people (Exod 2:24-25). God's commitment to link his heart with that of his people is the basis of any confidence Isaiah would have in interceding. God sent the "angel of his presence" to redeem them from their slavery. God spoke plainly of him in Exodus 23:20-23, saying, "Do not defy him, because he will not forgive your acts of rebellion, for *my name is in him*" (v. 21; emphasis added). This is an extraordinary assertion to make of an angel, so this angel of his presence is none other than the preincarnate Christ. Since the next verse mentions the Holy Spirit, it is fascinating to see the Trinity here in Isaiah 63, directly active in Israel's redemption from slavery in Egypt.

The Intercessor Confesses Sin (63:10)

Tragically, Israel's history was one of consistent rebellion against the grace of God. Verse 10 says that in their rebellion, they "grieved his Holy Spirit" (cf. Eph 4:30). (The fact that the Holy Spirit can be grieved is great evidence of the Spirit's personhood, for one cannot grieve an impersonal force.) Israel's rebellion against God, from the desert after the Red Sea crossing through the history under Joshua, the judges, and the kings, was deeply grievous to God. Because of Israel's rebellion, God became their enemy and fought them.

The Intercessor Prays Based on the Lord's History (63:11-16)

The Lord (or perhaps, the intercessor) remembered the days of the past. The dominating image of this section is the Red Sea crossing, the power of God in delivering his people from the Egyptians and from the sea. The crossing occurred at night, with the light of the pillar of fire the only illumination. The sea walled up to the left and to the right, a dark threatening corridor of imminent death. The people went down into the Red Sea as the dead go down into the grave. But the angel of the Lord who led them in the form of the pillar is the same Savior, Christ, who will lead all his people out of the grave into the light of resurrection. The dawn that ended that terrifying night saw God bringing them up from the sea to "make an eternal name for himself" (vv. 12,14). But the question the intercessor now presses to the unchanging God is, Where now is the God who did all these great things in the past (v. 11)? The intercessor is following God's own command in Isaiah 62:7-8 to remind God of his past actions and to give him no rest until he saves his people. The intercessor calls on God to stir up his zeal and his might, to stop restraining his yearning and compassion for his people (v. 15). Despite the fact it seems God has forgotten his people, the intercessor reminds both himself and God that he is our Father by adoption (v. 16). And though perhaps Abraham and Israel may become so disgusted with their descendants that they would refuse to recognize them, God's commitment to his sinful children is infinitely greater and will never fail (v. 16). So he calls on God, their ancient Father, to be their Redeemer.

The Intercessor Laments over the Lord's Disciplines (63:17-19)

These verses return to the theme of lamentation over Israel's sin and, even more, over God's disciplines for those sins. Verse 17 is perhaps a little surprising, for it seems like the intercessor is blaming God for Israel's straying ways and hardened hearts. But God is perfectly holy and hates wickedness more than we can possibly imagine. The intercessor knows that our hearts naturally stray from God's ways and become hardened in sin unless he intervenes with his sovereign grace. And if he fails to intervene, the straying and hardening is inevitable, though we are completely to blame for it. The whole ethos of this intercession in Isaiah 63–64 is asking God, Why do you apparently do nothing when we need you so desperately to save us from our sins and the sins of our enemies? So the intercessor pleads with God to stop his people's straying, for it is this very thing that has led to God's righteous judgments on Israel—the trampling of God's sanctuary by Israel's wicked enemies (v. 18). Isaiah the prophet, writing these words more than a century before the Babylonians would destroy the temple, gives future intercessors the words to say at that time—intercessors like Daniel, who would pray, confessing Israel's sin and pleading with God for her restoration (Dan 9). So also Christians in every generation who are lamenting our sins and God's righteous discipline should employ these concepts.

The Intercessor Pleads for God to Descend (64:1-5a)

The intercessor continues with a plea for God to "tear the heavens open and come down." He yearns for the omnipotent God to show up and make the mountains quake at his presence (v. 1). The Hebrew grammar actually reads in the past tense, as if to say, "If only you had already torn open the heavens and come down," then none of this would have happened. But though it is past in grammar, the desire is for an immediate answer and action by almighty God. Perhaps the most perplexing quandary to a Bible-believing Christian is, "Lord, if you are omnipotent and if you tenderly love your children, then why do you seemingly do so little to rescue them from their vicious enemies?" The tearing open of the heavens is an awesome description of the rending of the God-appointed barrier that exists between the physical heavens (sky and outer space) and the "third heaven" (2 Cor 12:2) where God dwells in unapproachable light. This dramatic plea is fulfilled ultimately in Jesus Christ, in both his first and second advents. At his baptism the heavens were torn open (Mark 1:10), but amazingly instead of a God of terror throwing lightning bolts to ravage the wicked of the earth, a single dove descended peacefully and landed on Jesus, the Lamb of God! God did tear the heavens open, but instead of wrath for sin, the world received a dovelike Spirit and a lamblike Savior. The heavens were torn open again when a vicious group of unbelieving Jews were stoning Stephen to death. But instead of a wrath-filled God, Stephen saw Jesus standing to receive him into heaven, and filled with his dovelike Spirit, his dying words were, "Lord, do not hold this sin against them" (Acts 7:56-60). I believe the martyr Stephen's prayer was partially answered in the conversion of Saul of Tarsus, who had abetted Stephen's execution; however, God did not hold that sin against Saul but extended grace instead.

The desire for God to rend the heavens and come down is right and good, as long as we recognize that, were it not for the blood of Jesus, we would all be the brushwood that would be ignited, we would be the water that would boil. We would be God's enemies and the nation that would tremble at God's presence (Isa 64:2). Peter explains God's seeming reluctance to "tear the heavens open and come down":

"The Lord does not delay his promise, as some understand delay, but is patient with you, not wanting any to perish but all to come to repentance" (2 Pet 3:9).

But the intercessor *should* pray, indeed he *must* pray, for God to tear open the heavens and come down in the power of his Holy Spirit to do more saving acts, "awesome works that we did not expect" (Isa 64:3). In light of the Great Commission, this is a prayer for revival, for God to transform them from seething enemies to delightful children of God. Verse 4 is a powerful reminder of the special privilege of prayer to the only living God: "From ancient times no one has heard, no one has listened to, no eye has seen any God except you who acts on behalf of the one who waits for him." This is the patient intercessor's greatest hope, which alone can spur him on in prayer. God answers the prayer of the godly who delight in his ways (v. 5a).

The Intercessor Confesses Sin Again (64:5b-7)

But the problem is, no intercessor on earth is sinless, always doing what pleases God. So the intercessor must confess his sins and the sins of his people honestly to God (v. 5b). In fact, when seen in the light of God's holy and perfect standard, it becomes clear that even our most righteous people are "unclean" and our most righteous acts are "like a polluted garment" (v. 6). All of God's people on earth "wither like a leaf, and our iniquities carry us away like the wind" (v. 6). That is why Jesus Christ, our Mediator, must ultimately be the intercessor whose prayer alone God the Father will answer. His righteous acts are alone perfect in God's sight. Then, in Jesus's name alone can we fulfill the role of intercessor. Apart from the work of the Spirit, none of us intercedes, none of us strives to take hold of God. Apart from the work of the Redeemer, God would most certainly hide his face from the most righteous intercessor we would choose from our number (v. 7). So the faithful prayer warriors among the church must intercede for God's elect with humility and total reliance on the finished work of Christ (Heb 10:20).

The Intercessor Pleads for God to Act (64:8-12)

This paragraph completes the entire section, the ministry of the intercessor on behalf of his people. The focus of the entire prayer has been, "O Lord, we, your sinful people, desperately need you to cover our sins and act on our behalf! Please, O Lord, tear open the heavens and come down to destroy our enemies, despite the fact that we deserve all the judgments you have wisely meted out to us! Please, O Lord, no longer be silent or restrain your affections for us. Act, O Lord!" So the intercessor turns again to God the Father (who has adopted us), to God the potter (who has shaped us), to act on behalf of his sinful people (v. 9).

What is fascinating about this entire intercession, beginning in 63:7 and through to this section, is how the intercessor in effect wants God to have a *selective memory*, remembering his mighty acts in the past for his people, remembering the covenant he made with Abraham, remembering the salvation he worked at the Red Sea through Moses, remembering that he has adopted them to be his children and that he formed them like a potter does the clay, but to *forget* their sins that caused all these judgments! Their cities have become a wilderness, Jerusalem a desolation. It is especially poignant that after the image of a glorious heavenly Zion in Isaiah 62, here we are told that the earthly Zion has "become a wilderness" (64:10). The beautiful temple where their fathers praised God has been burned down. Again, Isaiah as the intercessor is supernaturally empowered to drop himself more than a century and a half ahead in time into the moment in redemptive history when he could pray for the remnant to be restored to the promised land, to rebuild the rubble-filled city of Jerusalem and reestablish a holy temple where his people can again praise God. So the intercessor pleads with God to stop restraining himself, to stop being silent. Amazingly, this is the very Hebrew word used in Isaiah 62:1 in which Christ said, "For Zion's sake I will *not be silent!*" In effect, the intercessor is showing him his writing and urging him to keep his promise!

Applications

The first application of these chapters is to stand in awe and trembling at the wrath of God against his enemies. The image of a blood-soaked warrior is terrifying when we realize that we all deserve to be included in the slaughter. Furthermore, we must embrace that this is very much the purpose of the second coming of Christ, for he will come to "trample the winepress of the fierce anger of God, the Almighty" (Rev 19:15). We should never be ashamed of the clear warning of the wrath of God and the future trampling of the godless. Rather, we should plead with sinners to repent while there's time, to flee the wrath to come.

The remainder of the two chapters form the basis of a pattern of intercession in the light of the watchmen on the walls of Zion who are charged to remind God and to give themselves no rest or him no rest until he establishes Jerusalem as the praise of the whole earth.

A Christian may well take up this challenge but may say, "Lord, I don't know what to pray for." Isaiah 63:7–64:12 gives a wonderful answer to that uncertainty. Pray like this! But pray from a new-covenant perspective, based on Christ's finished work. Pray based on God's history of love toward his church, especially now in light of Christ's saving acts toward the church (63:7-9); pray with genuine and humble confession of sin, that our sins have grieved the Holy Spirit (63:10); pray based on Christ's resurrection from the dead as the fulfillment of the pattern of the Red Sea crossing (63:11-16); pray with a deep lament for our wandering ways and our hardened hearts, knowing that only in the new covenant and by the ministry of the Holy Spirit can the heart of stone be removed and the heart of flesh given (63:17-19); pray for God to tear open the heavens and come down—in gentle, saving love toward his elect now (revival!) and in wrath toward his enemies at the second coming (64:1-5a); acknowledge that even our best acts would be unclean apart from the blood of Christ and that we are pathetically weak in intercession (64:5b-7); and ask God to *move out powerfully* on behalf of his elect people, saving the unconverted and transforming the converted from often sinful to increasingly holy people (64:8-12).

Reflect and Discuss

1. Why do you think Christians are tempted to be ashamed of the potent and graphic images of God's wrath in Scripture?
2. How does "Edom" represent the godless of the world in Romans 9:13 and Hebrews 12:16? How do we see the spirit of Esau alive in our world today?
3. How should the reality of the coming righteous wrath of God motivate us in evangelism and missions? How should it motivate us to put sin to death in our own lives?
4. Jesus says that he trampled the winepress alone, that from the nations no one was with him, and there was no one to help (63:3,5). Why is this?
5. How does Isaiah 63:7–64:12 give a pattern of intercession for us to follow today?
6. Why is it vital for us to keep in mind God's amazing acts of salvation in the past, for Israel in the Old Testament (especially the exodus

and the Red Sea crossing) but even more the finished work of Jesus Christ at the cross and the empty tomb?

7. Why is genuine, heartfelt confession of sin vital in this kind of intercession for Zion (God's chosen people) now (63:10,17-19; 64:5b-7)?

8. Isaiah 64:1 asks God to tear open the heavens and come down. The image in these verses is of wrath and judgment. But the image of the torn-open heavens both at Christ's baptism (Mark 1:10) and at Stephen's martyrdom (Acts 7:56-60) is one of gentleness, grace, and mercy to a sinful world. How can we understand both aspects of God's mighty actions on earth?

9. Isaiah 64:6 says, "All our righteous acts are like a polluted garment." How do we understand this in light of our adoption as sons and daughters of God and of the cleansing blood of Christ?

10. How do 2 Peter 3:9 and 3:15 help us make sense of God's seeming inactivity when the wicked seem to prosper so much?

"Behold, Me!" and My New Creation

ISAIAH 65

For I will create a new heaven and a new earth; the past events will not be remembered or come to mind. (Isa 65:17)

Main Idea: God puts himself gloriously on display in redeeming Gentiles, judging the wicked, and creating a new heaven and new earth.

I. **"Behold, Me!" God's Saving Grace to the Gentiles (65:1)**
   A. God allowing himself to be sought: "Behold, me! Behold, me!"
   B. Sought by Gentiles who were not seeking him
II. **"Behold, My Judgments!" on Wicked Israelites (65:2-7).**
   A. God's amazing patience with rebellious Israel (65:2)
   B. Israel's repulsive, arrogant, pagan idolatry (65:2-7)
   C. The end of God's patience: "Behold, my judgments!" (65:6-7)
III. **"Behold, My Servants Singing!" While the Wicked Are Shamed (65:8-16).**
   A. God making distinctions: good grapes saved, bad ones rejected (65:8)
   B. Blessings for the remnant (65:8-10)
   C. Slaughter for those who abandon the Lord (65:11-12)
   D. Blessings and curses (65:13-16)
IV. **"Behold, My New Universe!" but First, Millennial Blessings (65:17-25)**
   A. "Behold, a new heaven and new earth!" (65:17)
   B. "Behold, a new Jerusalem!" A place of eternal delight (65:18-19)
   C. The blessings of the millennium, then of eternity (65:20-25)

"Behold, Me!" God's Saving Grace to the Gentiles
ISAIAH 65:1

Verse 1 displays the amazing grace of God, who presents himself with astonishing persistence and humility to the world's nations who do not seek him at all. The verse essentially says, "I allowed myself to be consulted, and I permitted myself to be found." In other words, God took the initiative to reveal himself and draw from the Gentiles a yearning to seek him and find him. If God does not "permit himself" to be found and consulted, we will never seek him or find him. Paul quoted this verse in Romans 10:20 to speak of God's grace displayed in the amazing harvest of Gentiles into the church of Christ. God's humble persistence in revealing himself to the Gentiles is stunning, for "Here I am, here I am" could be translated, "Behold, me! Behold, me!" (Hb *hinneni hinneni*). In the preaching of the gospel of Christ, God persistently stands in front of individuals from every nation on earth and says, "Behold, me! I am ready to save you! All you have to do is seek me, and you will certainly find me!"

"Behold, My Judgments!" on Wicked Israelites
ISAIAH 65:2-7

Paul directly contrasts the receptivity of the Gentiles with the stubbornness of the Jews by applying verse 2 to Israel in Romans 10:21: "All day long, I have held out my hands to a disobedient and defiant people." Again, we see the remarkable patience and humility of God with Israel. For generations, the Lord had stood like the father of the prodigal son with his arms outstretched, waiting for the son to stop sinning and come home to a rich welcome. But these wicked people refused (Isa 65:2). They continually sinned right in God's face, defiantly embracing pagan rituals as described in verses 3-4 and 7. Their paganism included such repulsive practices as necromancy and eating pig meat in defiance of God's holy laws. Actually, these bizarre rituals made their hearts proud, and they considered themselves too holy for those who hadn't learned their secret arts (v. 5). So they rejected God's definition of holiness, choosing instead one from paganism. Their attitudes and actions were utterly repulsive and provocative to God, like "smoke in [his] nostrils, a fire that burns all day long" (v. 5).

God reveals his judgments on this paganized nation of Israel using the same Hebrew word: "Look [Behold; Hb *hinneh*], it is written in front of me, I will not keep silent, but I will repay; I will repay them fully." God's silence and seeming inactivity were difficult for the people to bear in Isaiah 64:12; here God reveals that he will not remain silent but will bring on these wicked people the judgment they so richly deserve.

"Behold, My Servants Singing!" While the Wicked Are Shamed

ISAIAH 65:8-16

In these verses God shows his determination to make distinctions among the Israelites—between the good and the bad. In verse 8 God speaks of a whole cluster of grapes that still has some good grapes in it. He will spare the whole cluster so that he may pluck out the good grapes and enjoy the sweet juice from them. These few good grapes are the remnant chosen by grace from among the Israelites, of which Paul writes in Romans 11:5 and to which Isaiah had referred in 1:9. In Isaiah 65:8-16, these "good grapes" (cf. 5:2) are directly contrasted with the bad ones, and their fates are held up for comparison side by side.

For the remnant who seek the Lord by faith (v. 10), God promises to produce descendants who will inherit the mountains of Judah and dwell there richly blessed (v. 9). The promised land (from Sharon in the west to Achor in the east) will be fertile, a rich pastureland for their flocks to graze in and lie down in peace (v. 10). These are the blessings of faith and obedience, blessings of the old covenant in Moses. But given that the chapter begins with Gentiles seeking and finding the Lord, it is reasonable to see these as spiritual blessings for all the elect in the church age and literal blessings in the millennium and in the new earth.

But for the wicked who abandon the Lord, who forget his holy mountain and go running after pagan deities and who follow pagan practices (like ritual feasts for "Lady Luck"), God will slaughter them all with the sword (vv. 11-12). Unlike the Gentiles in verse 1, God called directly to these people, but they refused to listen.

Therefore, verses 13-16 describe the contrasting outcomes for God's servants and God's enemies. Each of these contrasts is introduced with the word *behold*, although it doesn't generally show up in English translations: "Behold, my servants will eat, but you will be hungry! Behold, my servants will drink, but you will be thirsty! Behold, my servants will rejoice, but you will be put to shame!" The ultimate end of this is the difference between heaven and hell: in heaven the redeemed will spend eternity feasting at Christ's table, drinking freely from the river of the water of life, and shouting for joy from a glad heart; in hell the damned will be tormented by thirst, weeping and gnashing their teeth, and crying out from an anguished heart (v. 14).

These sins in verses 2-5 and 11-12 are part of this present order, the world as it now is. Soon, God will change everything; then the former things will be forgotten in the light of the coming world.

"Behold, My New Universe!" but First, Millennial Blessings
ISAIAH 65:17-25

This astonishing section opens with the amazing words, "For [behold!] I will create a new heaven and a new earth." God uses the same Hebrew word for "create" that he used in Genesis 1:1; it is a work of sovereign power no less awesome than the original creation. The opening word "for" explains why the former troubles will be forgotten and hidden from sight (v. 16). The new heaven and new earth that God will create will be so glorious that the former world will shrink into insignificance. Isaiah 65:17-25 pictures a vastly improved earthly experience in terms with which his old-covenant audience would have been very familiar: the city of Jerusalem a place of great rejoicing, free from weeping (v. 19); amazing longevity (v. 20); houses built and vineyards planted, and their blessings enjoyed by those who built and planted, not by invading enemies (vv. 21-22); rich blessings on the labors of their hands (v. 23); children born into prosperity, not calamity (v. 23); and intimacy with God in prayer (v. 24). It concludes with promises of harmony even in the animal world—the wolf and the lamb feeding together, and the lion eating straw like the ox, just as was said of the world when the Messiah would come (Isa 11:6-9); even the serpent is completely humbled and eats dust for food; there will be no evil or destruction on God's holy mountain (v. 25).

All of this amazing peace and prosperity is common in the language of prophetic writing. Yet these words are among the most controversial in the book of Isaiah. The difficulty lies in trying to harmonize the images in these nine verses with other passages of Scripture, most especially the teaching about the new heaven and new earth in 2 Peter 3 and Revelation 21–22. John's vision in Revelation of the new heaven and new earth includes the death of death. But in Isaiah 65:20 we have merely the deferral of death, resulting in remarkably long life:

> In [Jerusalem], a nursing infant will no longer live only a few days,
> or an old man not live out his days. Indeed, the one who dies at a

hundred years old will be mourned as a young man, and the one who
misses a hundred years will be considered cursed.

To make matters more confusing, that verse contains two other things we would not expect in the eternal state: infants born and people being accursed. No one will suffer under a curse in heaven, and heavenly marriage and procreation are ruled out by Jesus's statement to the Sadducees in Matthew 22:30.

These problems are significant for any evangelical, no matter what their eschatological system, whether premillennial, amillennial, or post-millennial; there is just no easy way to harmonize Isaiah 65:17-20 with Revelation 21:1 and 4. Some amillennial commentators argue that "the sound of weeping and crying will no longer be heard in" Jerusalem means that whatever verse 20 is talking about, there is no more death in that glorious place (Storms, *Kingdom Come*, 166–69). They say that verse 20 is speaking in language we would understand of the complete destruction of death from the beginning of life to the end. But that seems forced to me. Isaiah 25:7-8 had no problem describing clearly the total end of death. These verses seem to be speaking of a lessening but not removal of the curse of death, resulting in remarkable longevity. Indeed, verse 22 implies this when it says, "My people's lives will be like the lifetime of a tree."

The task of explanation is easier for millennial interpreters, for this passage seems very much to describe the vast improvement of earthly life in a millennial kingdom with Christ reigning on earth, as described in Revelation 20:1-6. According to premillennial theology, the millennium comes after the second coming of Christ and has these features: (1) peace on earth among all nations; (2) material prosperity, free from famines and poverty, with rich harvests; (3) longevity restored but death still in existence; (4) creation largely delivered from its curse, with humanity living in harmony with other creatures; and (5) King Jesus and his people visibly running the kingdom, centered in Jerusalem (Boettner, *Millennium*, 290–92). It is not difficult to see that many of those wonderful aspects are culled right from Isaiah 65. I tend to lean in this direction based on this very chapter. But it is easy for me to respect evangelicals who have other ways of explaining the graphic imagery of prophetic literature while still honoring the inspiration of every word of the Bible.

Whether the Lord Jesus returns and reigns on earth in a millennial kingdom or immediately sets up the eternal state with no more death, either will be such a display of his grace and power as to make our present sufferings seem unworthy of comparison. God is wise. He will do what seems best to him!

Applications

First, the unifying word of this chapter is "Behold" (Hb *hinneh*, "Look"), as though God were standing before us in the text revealing some vital truths that we can "see" only by faith. Therefore, we must see by faith God's amazing grace in holding out his willing hands for repentant sinners through Christ. Second, we must discern and reject the weird "holiness" of bizarre spirituality that will become more and more appealing in a post-Christian world. People are essentially spiritual, and we are likely to see more and more witchcraft and wickedness. It is vital for us to define holiness as God does: conformity to his character as his Word defines. Third, we need to see ahead of time the zeal of God to separate the wheat from the weeds of the human race (Matt 3:12). Finally, we need to see the glory of God in the coming kingdom—millennial (possibly), then eternal—in which Christ will finally triumph completely over sin and death. The more we see by faith these various things, the more zealous we will be to purify ourselves from all wickedness and to spread the gospel of Christ, which is the only hope of salvation from the coming wrath.

Reflect and Discuss

1. How does God use the word *behold/look* to unveil surprising truths in this chapter that we can "see" only by faith?
2. What is the first thing God wants us to behold in verse 1? Why is a vision of God vital to salvation?
3. How does God show amazing grace and patience to sinners in verse 1? How does Paul use verse 1 in Romans 10:20?
4. How does Israel provoke God continually in Isaiah 65:2-7? How are these verses a warning to the present-day church?
5. What distinctions does God make in verses 8-16? How does this relate to Matthew 3:12?
6. What glorious things does God promise are coming in Isaiah 65:17-25?

7. How are these verses difficult to interpret, especially the combination of the expression "new heaven and new earth" (cf. Rev 21:1,4) with the presence of infants and death in verse 20?

8. How would the millennial reign of Christ on earth, in which death is greatly curtailed but not removed, glorify him?

9. How would the eternal state in which death is completely removed glorify him more?

10. How does this chapter motivate you toward personal holiness? How does it motivate you toward evangelism and missions in the name of Jesus Christ?

The Final Chapter: Eternal Worship versus Eternal Torment

ISAIAH 66

"For just as the new heavens and the new earth, which I will make, will remain before me"—this is the LORD's declaration—"so your offspring and your name will remain. All mankind will come to worship me." (Isa 66:22-23)

Main Idea: This final chapter divides the human race into two categories: true versus false worshipers. It describes plainly the heart and behavior of both, as well as their eternal destinies: heaven and hell.

I. **True Worshipers Are Delightful; False Worshipers Are Detestable (66:1-4).**
   A. True worshipers tremble before the throne and God's word (66:1-2).
   B. False worshipers make detestable sacrifices (66:3).
   C. False worshipers are judged for not heeding God's word (66:4).

II. **False Worshipers Persecute; True Worshipers Prosper (66:5-14a).**
   A. False worshipers persecute the true (66:5).
   B. False worshipers are destroyed by the Lord (66:6).
   C. True worshipers are born instantly by the Lord (66:7-9).
   D. True worshipers prosper richly in Zion (66:10-14a).

III. **False Worshipers Are Condemned; True Worshipers Are Commissioned (66:14b-21).**
   A. False worshipers are condemned to the Lord's wrath (66:14b-17).
   B. True worshipers are commissioned to bring in the nations (66:18-21).

IV. **True Worshipers Eternally Live; False Worshipers Eternally Die (66:22-24).**
   A. The new heavens and new earth endure eternally (66:22).
   B. True worshipers will live eternally (66:22-23).
   C. False worshipers will die eternally (66:24).

True Worshipers Are Delightful;
False Worshipers Are Detestable
ISAIAH 66:1-4

We come at last to the end of our journey through this astonishing book, and what a fitting conclusion it is! This most visionary of prophets has given us a most fitting end to his work—a revelation of the eternal state of both the righteous and the wicked. The book of Isaiah ends with the new heavens and new earth, and with Zion, the new Jerusalem, eternally populated by true worshipers from every nation on earth. Yet also the book ends with a clear depiction of hell, the state of eternal death in which rebellious humanity will suffer in plain view of the redeemed. It is appropriate that the theme of worship—both true and false—unifies this final chapter, for the human race was created to worship and serve almighty God in spirit and in truth; but by our sinfulness, we "exchanged the truth of God for a lie, and worshiped and served what has been created instead of the Creator, who is praised forever" (Rom 1:25). False worship (idolatry) has been front and center throughout this book, as has God's work of redeeming his elect from idolatry into true worship. So worship is a suitable unifying theme for Isaiah 66.

The chapter opens with the infinite God humbling all human efforts at building a religious container for God and calling it a temple. He asserts his immensity in clear terms: "Heaven is my throne, and earth is my footstool. Where could you possibly build a house for me?" (v. 1). God created everything in the universe; all of the building materials that any human worshipers could use to construct a temple came first from his own hand (v. 2). Solomon conceded this sentiment when dedicating his magnificent temple: "Even heaven, the highest heaven, cannot contain you, much less this temple I have built" (1 Kgs 8:27). There is no container for an infinite God. Now in saying this God is not rebuking the efforts of the Jewish people in rebuilding the temple after the exile, which he wanted done (Isa 44:28). But we must remember the revulsion God declared over the mindless religious machinery of the Jews in Isaiah 1:10-16 and 29:13.

The true worshiper is one who is "humble, submissive in spirit, and trembles at [God's] word" (66:2), and such a one attracts God's regard and honors God truly. Few verses in the Bible are as powerful as this for teaching us what God wants. A truly humble sinner captivates God's attention and delights his heart. Conversely, the false worshiper may outwardly obey the Levitical rituals, offering an ox, a lamb, a grain offering, or incense (v. 3); but to God, if they are offered by arrogant sinners, they are like killing a man, breaking a dog's neck, offering pig's blood, or praising an idol. These false worshipers (whether law-abiding Jews or utter pagans) basically make up their own religion, choosing their own ways (v. 3).

So, because they refused to tremble at God's word, because they refused to listen to his commands, because he "called and no one answered," God will bring down on them what they most dread—the terrors of his holy wrath (v. 4).

False Worshipers Persecute; True Worshipers Prosper
ISAIAH 66:5-14A

For the rest of the chapter God addresses the true worshipers, bringing them comfort and encouragement. Certainly the false worshipers are much in view, but they are always referred to in the third person, their punishment clear for his elect children to see. The false "brothers" mock and expel those who tremble at God's word (v. 5). This mockery (essentially, "Let us see your joy in the Lord now!") is exceptionally evil and brings the vengeance of God on the city and their corrupt temple (v. 6). This hatred and expulsion were immediately fulfilled by the unbelieving Jewish nation, who killed the Lord Jesus and the prophets and also persecuted the apostles (1 Thess 2:15). Jesus predicted this would occur, saying there would come a time when the Jews would drive the true worshipers of God out of their synagogues, and they would even think that in killing Christians they were offering service to God (John 16:2). The destruction of Jerusalem and its temple by the Romans in AD 70 is a direct fulfillment of Isaiah 66:6.

Yet the explosive expansion of the church of Jesus Christ by the gospel the apostles preached was likewise a direct fulfillment of Isaiah 66:7-14. These verses predict the instant birth of children of Zion—"a land [was] born in one day [and] a nation [was] delivered in an instant" (v. 8). The outpouring of the Holy Spirit on Pentecost resulted in both Jews and Gentiles from all around the Roman world coming instantly to faith in Christ. And in a stunningly short time the gospel spread like wildfire throughout Asia, Macedonia, Achaia, Greece, and even to Rome and beyond. The true worshipers delight in the building of the heavenly Jerusalem in the church age and the new Jerusalem in eternity. They will rejoice greatly in her beauty and drink deeply from her abundant streams of blessing (vv. 10-11). The wealth of nations will flow into Zion like a flood (v. 12; cf. 2:2). God's grace will carry the true worshipers into eternal habitation in the new Jerusalem, and there they will richly flourish in joy for all eternity (vv. 13-14).

False Worshipers Are Condemned; True Worshipers Are Commissioned
ISAIAH 66:14B-21

It is also clear that the enemies of the gospel will fight Christ every step of the way. So God reminds his children that he will most certainly visit his wrath on all his enemies. Verses 15-16 give a powerful depiction of God's judgment with a fiery sword, promising that the Lord will slay his enemies. Their repulsive worship habits are exposed in verse 17, those who "dedicate and purify themselves" by "eating meat from pigs, vermin, and rats." The phrase "dedicate and purify" is strongly religious, implying that these actually believe that their religion has made them pure in God's sight. Ironically, this might include "law-abiding" Jews, in their self-righteous, Christless worship (reestablishing animal sacrifice after the curtain in the temple was torn in two from top to bottom; Matt 27:51), as well as pagans, who follow satanic rituals in their bizarre religions. As a matter of fact, Paul warned the Gentile Christians of Galatia that to embrace the false gospel of the Judaizers was to go back to "weak and worthless elements" and to be "enslaved to them all over again" (Gal 4:9). That is amazing! Legalistic, Christless Judaism is as demonic as overt paganism. So even the Jews who offered oxen, lambs, and sheep in the temple after Christ had abolished animal sacrifice were seeking to "dedicate and purify" themselves by effectively washing in pig's blood and eating rat meat. God decrees in verse 17 that they are condemned to perish together.

Conversely, in verses 18-21 God reveals to his children his plan to gather true worshipers from every tribe, language, people, and nation. God promises to gather all nations and languages to come and see his glory (v. 18). He will dispatch some of his "survivors" (the remnant of the Jews chosen by grace; Rom 11:5) to the nations who had not yet heard his fame or seen his glory. A small sampling of those nations is listed in verse 19: Tarshish (distant Spain); Put and Lud (northern Africa); Tubal (north, in the Caucasus); Javan (Greece); and the Mediterranean maritime regions. The inhabitants of Put and Lud are described as archers, warlike, and terrifying, but some will be elect, ready to hear the gospel of Jesus Christ. The missionaries will proclaim God's glory in Christ to these nations, and many will begin spiritual pilgrimages to Zion ("my holy mountain," the new Jerusalem) by Christ, who is the "way, the truth, and the life" (John 14:6), the only pathway to heaven. The language is fascinating, for they will come "on horses and chariots, in litters, and on mules and camels" (Isa 66:20). People will "come" to the new Jerusalem in an amazingly wide variety of ways, but the destination is the same. And the elect from every nation are called "brothers" with the Jews who trusted in Christ (v. 20); not one of them will be missing, for "all" the brothers will come, and they will themselves become offerings to the Lord in his house. The apostle Paul's ministry was a direct fulfillment of this, for he was called to a priestly ministry among the nations so the Gentiles might themselves be an offering acceptable to the Lord, sanctified by the Holy Spirit (Rom 15:16). And even these Gentile believers can immediately serve as "priests and Levites" to the Lord, for the old order of priestly divisions is superseded.

True Worshipers Eternally Live;
False Worshipers Eternally Die
ISAIAH 66:22-24

The final paragraph depicts the new heavens and new earth as the final destination of this amazing journey of missions. That new universe will endure forever and ever. And so will its holy inhabitants, the redeemed from every nation on earth. They will worship God in spirit and truth forever. Isaiah uses one final image from the old covenant and the old order of things: "from one New Moon to another, and from one Sabbath to another" (v. 23). But Revelation 21:23 tells us that the new Jerusalem will not need the light of the sun or the moon to shine on it, for the glory of God will illuminate it.

The book of Isaiah ends with a clear view also of the fate of the rebels, those who worshiped created things and refused to repent and trust Christ. They will be burning in an eternal fire, tormented by eternal worms, a horror to all mankind. They will be in full view of the redeemed, for verse 24 tells us that the redeemed will be able to see their dead bodies as they leave the city. This verse was the basis of Jesus's powerful warning about the eternal nature of hell's torments in Mark 9:48.

The fact that the redeemed can see the "smoke of their torment [going] up forever and ever" (Rev 14:11) shows us that God will not hide their fate from his children. Actually, their torment is a clear reminder of the grace God has shown to the elect, who deserved the exact same punishment and whose sins were propitiated only by the Lamb's blood. God uses the righteous suffering of these rebels eternally to "make known the riches of his glory on objects of mercy" (Rom 9:23). Only by the grace of God in Christ did any of us escape.

Applications

The first two verses of this chapter teach us to abase ourselves in humility before the infinite God of the universe. Heaven is his throne; the earth is his footstool. There is nothing that we can offer in worship that he did not first give us. And we could never erect a container, building, or structure that could hold such a God. So we must learn to be completely humble before him, falling on our faces, trembling at his word. We must learn to have absolute reverence for the Bible, the Word of God. We should despise nominal religion, no matter how "biblical" it is. Hypocritical Christians today can deceive themselves, following the outward worship patterns of the New Testament by going through the motions every Sunday at church.

We should also embrace the clear teaching of the terrifying fate of unbelievers and idolaters in this chapter. God is patently clear in this chapter that his wrath will burn for eternity against all false worshipers who do not find the truth in Christ. We should not shrink back from the doctrine of hell as a place of eternal, conscious torment but should clearly warn lost people as Jesus did in Mark 9.

We should also rededicate ourselves to the glorious work of worldwide evangelization in Jesus's name. Isaiah 66:18-21 clearly predicts the spread of the gospel to the distant shores of this planet. Twenty centuries of fulfillment should give us a tremendous sense of confidence that God's power is fulfilling this prophecy before our very eyes. So let all Christians have a passion for missions, displayed in prayer, effort, finances, and sacrifice. Many of our best and brightest will be called on to go to terrifying, warlike people (who maybe do not fight as archers but who are powerful with the weapons of our day) and win some of them to Christ.

Finally, let us long for the day when the new heavens and new earth will shine with the glory of God in Christ! Let us thank God for the blood of the Lamb, who purified us so that we may worship his name forever! To God alone be the glory!

Reflect and Discuss

1. How do the words of verse 1 humble you when you consider God's infinite majesty and greatness?

2. Why is it vital to consider that God's hand made everything we could ever give to him as a sacrifice or from which we could ever build a temple?

3. What kind of people does God "look favorably on" in verse 2? What does it mean to tremble at his word? Why do you think God so highly esteems such a person?

4. What elements of false worship and wicked idolatry are revealed in this chapter?

5. What is the connection between verse 5 and 1 John 3:12?

6. How did the three thousand who were baptized into the church of Jesus Christ on Pentecost begin the fulfillment of a nation being born in an instant in Isaiah 66:8?

7. How does the concept of the new Jerusalem bring you comfort and joy?

8. How do verses 18-21 predict the spread of the gospel of Jesus Christ to distant nations? How do you personally desire to be involved in the work yet to be accomplished? What do you think God wants you to do about unreached people groups?

9. What do verses 22-23 teach you about the future world, the new heavens and new earth?

10. Why is it vital to embrace the biblical concept of eternal conscious torment in hell? How could that doctrine help us to worship God for his grace to us? How could it motivate us to evangelize the lost?

WORKS CITED

American Association of Port Authorities Annual Report, Port Rankings. Accessed August 29, 2016. http://aapa.files.cms-plus.com/PDFs /WORLD%20PORT%20RANKINGS%202009.pdf.

Anderson, Courtney. *To the Golden Shore: The Life of Adoniram Judson.* New York: Dolphin, 1961.

Augustine. *The City of God.* In *Nicene and Post-Nicene Fathers.* Volume 2. Edited by Philip Schaff. Peabody, MA: Hendrickson, 1995.

Berlinski, David. *Newton's Gift: How Sir Isaac Newton Unlocked the System of the World.* New York: The Free Press, 2000.

Boettner, Loraine. *The Millennium.* Philadelphia: Presbyterian and Reformed, 1957.

Bradley, Walter L. "The 'Just-So' Universe: The Fine-Tuning of Constants and Conditions in the Cosmos." Pages 151–70 in *Signs of Intelligence: Understanding Intelligent Design.* Edited by William A. Dembski and James M. Kushiner. Grand Rapids: Brazos, 2001.

Bridges, Jerry, and Bob Bevington. *The Bookends of the Christian Life.* Wheaton, IL: Crossway, 2009.

Bright, John. *A History of Israel.* 3rd edition. Philadelphia: Westminster, 1981.

Bunyan, John. *The Holy War.* In *The Works of John Bunyan, Volume 3: Allegorical, Figurative, and Symbolical.* Edited by George Offor. Carlisle, PA: Banner of Truth, 1991.

Butler, L. "Solar Probe Plus: A NASA Mission to Touch the Sun," April 18, 2015. Accessed August 29, 2016. http://solarprobe.jhuapl.edu.

Calvin, John. *Calvin's Commentaries.* Volume 8. Translated by William Pringle. Grand Rapids: Baker, 1996.

Cantor, Norman F. *Alexander the Great: Journey to the End of the Earth.* New York: Harper Collins, 2005.

Churchill, Winston. *Churchill by Himself: The Definitive Collection of Quotations*. Edited by Richard M. Langworth. New York: Public Affairs, 2008.

Dalberg-Acton, John. "Letter to Bishop Mandell Creighton, April 5, 1887." *Historical Essays and Studies*. Edited by J. N. Figgis and R. V. Laurence. London: Macmillan, 1907.

Edwards, Jonathan. "Sinners in the Hands of an Angry God." In *The Works of Jonathan Edwards*. Volume 2. Carlisle, PA: Banner of Truth, 1986.

———. *Treatise Concerning the Religious Affections*. In *The Works of Jonathan Edwards*. Volume 2. New Haven, CT: Yale University Press, 1994.

Frost, Robert. "The Road Not Taken." In *Mountain Interval*. New York: Henry Holt and Co., 1920.

Grudem, Wayne. *Systematic Theology*. Grand Rapids: Zondervan, 2000.

Hammond, N. G. L. *The Genius of Alexander the Great*. Chapel Hill: University of North Carolina Press, 1997.

Hearst, Eliot, and John Knott. *Blindfold Chess*. Jefferson, NC: McFarland and Company, 2008.

Herodotus. *Histories*. In *The Landmark Herodotus: The Histories*. Translated by Andrea L. Purvis. Edited by Robert B. Strassler. New York: Anchor, 2009.

Keller, Timothy. *Counterfeit Gods*. New York: Dutton, 2009.

Lancaster, Bruce. *The Golden Book of the American Revolution*. New York: Golden, 1958.

Lewis, C. S. *Miracles*. New York: MacMillan, 1978.

Liberman, Mark. "Sex-Linked Lexical Budgets." Accessed August 29, 2016. http://itre.cis.upenn.edu/~myl/languagelog/archives/003420.html.

Lineweaver, Charles H., and Tamara M. Davis. "Misconceptions about the Big Bang." *Scientific American* 292 (2005): 30–45.

Lowe, Keith. *Savage Continent: Europe in the Aftermath of WWII*. New York: St. Martin's, 2012.

Luther, Martin. *Saemmtliche Schriften*. Edited by J. Walch. St. Louis: Concordia Publishing House, 1881–1910.

McGinley, Phyllis. *Times Three: Selected Verse from Three Decades*. New York: Viking, 1961.

Meuser, Fred W. *Luther the Preacher*. Minneapolis: Augsburg, 1983.

Meyer, Joyce. *Healing Scriptures*. Fenton, MO: Joyce Meyer Ministries, 2008.

Motyer, J. Alec. *The Prophecy of Isaiah: An Introduction and Commentary.* Downer's Grove, IL: IVP Academic, 1993.

Okwu, Michael. "Ceremony Closes 'Ground Zero' Cleanup." CNN. com, May 30, 2002. Accessed August 29, 2016. http://edition.cnn. com/2002/US/05/30/rec.wtc.cleanup.

Oswalt, John N. *The Book of Isaiah: Chapters 1–39.* NICOT. Grand Rapids: Eerdmans, 1986.

Perlo-Freeman, Sam, Aude Fleurant, Pieter Wezeman, and Siemon Wezeman. "Trends in World Military Expenditure." SIPRI Fact Sheet, 2016. Accessed August 29, 2016. http://books.sipri.org/files /FS/SIPRIFS1604.pdf.

Pfeiffer, Charles F. *Old Testament History.* Grand Rapids: Baker, 1973.

Piper, John. *The Future of Justification: A Response to N. T. Wright.* Wheaton, IL: Crossway, 2007.

Pritchard, J. B., editor. *Ancient Near Eastern Texts.* 3rd edition. Princeton: Princeton University Press, 1969.

Ridderbos, J. *Isaiah.* Bible Student's Commentary. Grand Rapids: Zondervan, 1985.

Schaeffer, Francis A. *He Is There and He Is Not Silent.* In *The Complete Works of Francis A. Schaeffer: A Christian Worldview, Volume 1.* Westchester: Crossway, 1982.

Sebestyen, Victor. *Twelve Days: The Story of the 1956 Hungarian Revolution.* New York: Pantheon, 2006.

Sibbes, Richard. *The Bruised Reed and the Smoking Flax.* In *The Works of Richard Sibbes.* Volume 1. Carlisle, PA: Banner of Truth, 1979.

Storms, Sam. *Kingdom Come: The Amillennial Alternative.* Ross-Shire, Scotland: Mentor, 2013.

Thomas, D. W., editor. *Documents of Old Testament Times.* London: Nelson, 1958.

Thomas, I. D. E. *A Puritan Golden Treasury.* Carlisle, PA: Banner of Truth, 1997.

Tozer, A. W. *The Knowledge of the Holy.* San Francisco: Harper Collins, 1978.

Walker, F. Deauville. *William Carey: Father of Modern Missions.* Chicago: Moody, 1980.

Watts, John D. W. *Isaiah 34–66.* Word Bible Commentary 25. Waco, TX: Word, 1987.

"World Urbanization Prospects." Accessed August 29, 2016. https://esa .un.org/unpd/wup/Publications/Files/WUP2014-Highlights.pdf.

Wright, N. T. *What Saint Paul Really Said: Was Saul of Tarsus the Real Founder of Christianity?* Grand Rapids: Eerdmans, 1997.

Yeung, Peter. "Refugee Crisis: Record 65 Million People Forced to Flee Homes, UN Says." Independent.com, June 20, 2016. Accessed August 29, 2016. http://www.independent.co.uk/news/world /europe/refugee-crisis-migrants-world-day-un-a7090986.html.

Young, Edward J. *The Book of Isaiah, Volume 2: Chapters 19–39.* Grand Rapids: Eerdmans, 1997.

———. *The Book of Isaiah, Volume 3: Chapters 40–66.* Grand Rapids: Eerdmans, 1997.

SCRIPTURE INDEX

399